Colleen Dewhurst

Her Autobiography

Written with and Completed by

Tom Viola

A LISA DREW BOOK

SCRIBNER

A LISA DREW BOOK / SCRIBNER
1230 Avenue of the Americas
New York, NY 10020

SCRIBNER and design are trademarks of
Simon & Schuster Inc.
A LISA DREW BOOK is a trademark of
Simon & Schuster Inc.

Designed by Brooke Zimmer
Set in Ehrhardt
Manufactured in the United States of America

1   3   5   7   9   10   8   6   4   2

Library of Congress Cataloging-in-Publication Data
Dewhurst, Colleen.
Colleen Dewhurst : her autobiography / written with and
completed by Tom Viola.
p.   cm.
"A Lisa Drew Book."
Includes index.
1. Dewhurst, Colleen. 2. Actors—United States—Biography.
I. Viola, Tom. II. Title.
PN2287.D462A3   1997
792'.028'092—dc21
[B]   97-5803
CIP

ISBN 0-684-80701-7

CONTENTS

EDITOR'S NOTE

"Do you play bridge?"

I first met Colleen backstage after a performance of *More Stately Mansions*, when she was interviewed by my brother Mike, a *Milwaukee Journal* critic whom she particularly liked. Her dressing room was loaded with gifts, and I must have raised my eyebrows at the profusion of Tiffany boxes. "I've just married George again," she said by way of explanation. Colleen had a way of beginning conversations in the middle with her friends and, apparently, total strangers. "Tell me, my dear," she said, "if it doesn't work out, do I have to return them?" This was my introduction to one of the most remarkable people I have ever known.

Several years later, a friend of mine at another publishing company told me that that house had a memoir by Colleen Dewhurst under contract but unfortunately was closing its trade book division. If I was interested, I was advised to contact her agent, which I immediately did. This was in 1976 and resulted in a three-hour meeting with Colleen about the book, or so it was intended, but it was impossible to keep her focused. As we parted, I raised the subject again. "Do you play bridge?" she asked. "Vaguely," I answered, which was enough to secure our author-editor relationship. Soon we embarked on something of a quid pro quo situation where I would periodically visit that splendid island of love and lunacy called the Farm, trading off bridge games in the evening for work on the book during the afternoons.

Thirteen or fourteen years into this process, I began to feel guilty about how much I was enjoying this nonproductive relationship, which had resulted in about one hundred rough pages, and attempted to apply some pressure by saying our company lawyers were going to demand the advance back if we couldn't come up with more material. Although I will admit now there were no such lawyers, she was sufficiently alarmed to introduce into the mix her assistant at Actors' Equity, Tom Viola, who proved to be a godsend. They made real progress, and by the summer of 1991, approximately the first half of what follows was written by Colleen and Tom, and she had done extensive taping of material that would fit later in the book. Then, tragically, on August 22 she died.

In the following months her sons Alex Scott and Campbell Scott, her partner of thirteen years, Ken Marsolais, Tom and I talked about whether to finish the book. In spite of our grief, or perhaps in part because of it, we decided to go ahead. Tom came up with the brilliant idea of interviewing various of Colleen's friends, associates, and fellow actors, to fill the gaps. In ways we never expected, it made the book even richer because while Colleen's devotion to her family and profession, her strong principles and her great wit came through clearly in her own words, her extreme generosity, abhorrence of intolerance, and selfless endeavors for various causes are not qualities she could comfortably reveal about herself. The result is a truly three-dimensional portrait, and what began as a memoir has become a memorial. Thanks to film and videotape, some of her greatest performances will never be lost. And now, thanks to the help of so many of her friends, her own voice will never be stilled.

The publication of this book marks the end of a twenty-one-year odyssey. My deepest gratitude goes to my fellow travelers—Alex, Campbell, Ken, and most especially, Tom Viola—for making it possible.

Lisa Drew, 1997

PREFACE

"Is ten chapters a book?"

In January of 1990, I began to work with Colleen Dewhurst on her autobiography. At the time, she was into the second year of her second term as president of Actors' Equity Association. I had been her assistant for the previous two years. About a month before, on a day in December, Colleen had seemed particularly agitated when she came into the office at Equity. She said nothing as she strode past my desk, which sat in the small office outside her own. I could hear her shuffling papers and rifling through the drawers in her desk.

"Damn it," she muttered. I figured she was looking for a match. She was often looking for a match. "Tom, would you come in?" she finally said. I did. Once inside, she motioned for me to sit down in the high-backed wicker chair across from her. She was already smoking a cigarette. So it wasn't a match. All bets were off.

Pushing her auburn hair over the top of her head, as she often did to focus herself at the start of a conversation, she looked up and gently shoved a short stack of dog-eared typewritten pages that I had never seen before across the desk to me, like a croupier sliding thousand-dollar chips.

"Would you read this? I've got to finish my book. I thought maybe you could help me." There was a pause. Not one that indicated that she didn't know what to say as much as she wasn't sure *how* to say it. "It was due twelve years ago." Oh. Twelve years? *Twelve?* I had no idea what she was talking about. But Colleen often jumped into a conversation as if in the middle of a sentence and two courses into dinner. I had learned that if I listened long enough, feigning immediate and complete comprehension while trying to keep my eyes from glazing over, I would eventually get what she was saying without letting on that, for the moment, I was completely lost. She looked back at me, glanced down at this pile of paper between us, and laughed. I'm not sure whether it was the look on my face giving away my confusion or the notion of being twelve years late for anything. Even for Colleen, whose concept of time and punctuality was, at best, lyrical, a lapse of twelve years must have set a personal record.

"I haven't looked at this in about ten years," she said, blowing cigarette smoke over the mystery manuscript sitting between us. "But I'm told they won't wait any longer." *They,* she went on to explain, were her publisher's lawyers and *they* wanted something on paper—other than her signature. So with that, Colleen added "collaborator" to my job description and we set to work on her book, eventually abandoning the ten-year-old pages completely and starting from scratch: chapter one, page one.

For the next year and a half, on weekends and holidays, I would go to "the Farm," Colleen's home about an hour by train outside of New York City, to work with her on what became the *new* manuscript. Initially we were both confused about how to proceed and could be easily distracted from the job at hand. Watching television, playing "dictionary" and charades with the rest of her family, talking about "things at Equity," building fires in the fireplace, preparing meals and eating—any activity was enough to keep us from working on "the book." When a few such weekends had passed and we still hadn't written a word, I suggested that perhaps we didn't really need to work together right away.

"You don't like coming up to the Farm?" she asked.

"Yes, of course I do. But Colleen," I finally said, summoning up all my nerve, "we're not getting anything done."

"I see," she said. "And you feel we should?"

"Well, yes." There was a long pause. "How about if you just sit down with a tape recorder and talk about a certain subject that we'll choose in advance." This way, I figured, I could work from the tapes at home or in the office, spend some weekends at home, and still bring my first draft up to the Farm for us to revise together. She reluctantly agreed.

The following Thursday, when Colleen came into the office, she reached into her purse and handed me two cassette tapes as if she were turning over incriminating evidence. "I nearly bored myself to death," she said. That night as I played them back, I heard that wonderful voice—a voice that could fill a theater and still reach into an individual soul—become fainter and fainter until finally her mumbling fell silent, leaving only the muffled sound of the television playing in another room of the house.

"I stopped listening when you fell asleep," I told her the next day.

"Good idea," she said.

We didn't mention the book again for a week. Neither Colleen nor I knew exactly what to do, but clearly we needed to figure out how to begin if anything was going to get done. In slight desperation and suppressing a good deal of aggravation, Colleen suggested that I come up to the Farm, interview her in person and work from this new set of tapes. "If I have someone to talk to it won't be so damn dull," she said. "I can't believe I ever signed that . . . effing contract."

Our first session, the following weekend, went on for a few hours and stopped only with her amused accusation that I was "stifling yawns." Later, during dinner, when someone asked how we were doing, she said, "*I'm* doing fine but I think we nearly lost Viola." On Monday, I found a woman eager to transcribe anything spoken by "Miss Dewhurst" for a modest fee. On Friday, she came to the Equity office and a little less enthusiastically handed over pages of margin-to-margin lowercase type made up of phrases and half-sentences connected by an ellipsis (. . .) or the phrase "can't understand over the laughter." She also informed me that she thought we needed to renegotiate her fee. "Miss Dewhurst," she wearily said, "is the only person I know who speaks at length without benefit of syntax or punctuation." She was right. The tapes were basically uneditable. Worse, Colleen didn't have much interest in reworking them. We'd have better luck dancing to Colleen's stream of consciousness than transcribing it.

Despite the failure of our attempts at transcripts, Colleen and I would still schedule "work sessions on the book." Coming to the Farm was never a problem. The problem was moving from the couch in front of the television set to sitting at a desk in front of the word processor. "Do I have to?" she'd say. "How much do we have to do? Is ten chapters a book?" (The old discarded manuscript had ten very rough chapters.)

"No, Colleen. Ten chapters is a long proposal. You skipped that step and jumped right to getting an advance."

"Well, that was good."

"Yes, but now we need ten chapters and then at least ten more."

"Oh, for Christ's sake."

After a few more fitful and equally unsuccessful attempts, we did, quite by accident, settle on a working procedure. It was a very simple one that should have been obvious from the start.

We had been sitting in the family room watching *Jeopardy*, talking back to Boris, the parrot, who passed the time sitting on top of his cage spitting sunflower shells at the TV. We were both getting fairly annoyed with Boris, who, between potshots, insisted on talking over Alex Trebeck. But the last straw was drawing a blank on the category—"Broadway, for five hundred dollars."

"These two have tied to win more Tony Awards as Best Actress in a Musical than anyone else," Alex read from the game board.

"Who are Mary Martin and Ethel Merman!" Colleen said confidently, ahead of the three contestants.

"Who are Angela Lansbury and Gwen Verdon?" a bespectacled young man offered on the screen.

"Correct!" Alex replied.

Colleen snapped off the television in disgust. "What do I know about musicals?" Then, as if to share what she did know, she began telling a story about the actor Jimmy Coco. This, I thought as I listened, would be perfect for the book. "Colleen," I said out loud, "why don't you come into the living room and tell me that story again and I'll just type as you talk."

"Do we have to? Now?"

"Sure. Maybe it's a chapter."

"Oh, God," she moaned, lifting one German shepherd off her leg and another from her lap before pulling herself off the comfortably beaten-up couch.

Three hours later, we actually had a first draft of what follows as the "Introduction." From that day forward, we worked in the living room without benefit of tape. Live. I sat at the word processor, set up on a makeshift wooden table in front of a window with a view of the backyard and woods so that we could keep an eye on the dogs. Colleen would sit to my right in a large over-stuffed chair. Next to her chair was a card table that held the printer, assorted pages from the old manuscript, her current Diet Pepsi, empty Diet Pepsi cans, an ashtray (always full) and, if we were lucky, a lighter that worked.

Colleen would talk, reminisce, and muse. I would type, ask questions, and try to keep her on track, forcing myself to recall all I knew about syntax and punctuation while simultaneously translating into sentences the insights and anecdotes that were purely Colleen's. I would then edit this material, late, when most everyone had gone to bed after nightly charades, making notes of follow-up questions to clarify or reorganize what Colleen had spoken of hours before. The next day the process—talk, type, edit—would begin again.

Gradually, over the next sixteen months, a lot of work got done, and about three-quarters of what was then called *Why Am I Laughing?* written in Colleen's unmistakable voice, made it to paper. In between hours at the word processor, we read and napped in opposite ends of the house, always to meet in the family room for meals and to watch *Jeopardy*. In the evenings, various family members, houseguests, and visitors would gather in the living room for "dictionary," arguments, and charades. (How such a brilliant and celebrated actress could not clearly pantomime *book, movie, song,* and *sounds like* continues to baffle me.) We watched the seasons change and we celebrated holidays. Occasionally I went to meetings or the movies with other members of the household.

I didn't notice right away when Colleen began to tire more easily. But once I did, asking her to look back on her life became both a gift and a burden and, without either of us saying so to the other, a way for us not to project into the uncertain future.

The last time we sat down at the word processor together was in April 1991. We had long before stopped working through the book in exact chronological order, a tacit acknowledgment that perhaps we might not have time to complete this project. That weekend, we finished what we called the "*Murphy Brown* section." We talked about pulling the "Equity section" together next from some old notes she had made, and she closed for the day by telling me a virtually unprintable but hilarious story that she made me promise never to repeat. She seemed so tickled that I found this story so funny that she repeated the punch line twice, breaking herself up the second time, her laughter shaking down into a cough. I don't know if Colleen expected this to be the last work session. I didn't.

"I think that's pretty good," Colleen said, over a slow puff of smoke as I read back to her what she had discussed about working with Candice Bergen, a woman she clearly admired, on a show she certainly enjoyed.

"Are you going to do another episode this season?" I asked, more in an effort to hold on to the future than to try to schedule it.

"Who knows?" she said. "I'd love to." But on August 22, 1991, the future came. Colleen died, surprising many and breaking the hearts of us all. Any talk of "the book" was put aside. Our incomplete manuscript and Colleen's old original chapters and notes we had scribbled together were placed in a cardboard box and slipped under my desk at work.

More than three years passed. There were occasional conversations involving myself; Alex and Campbell Scott, Colleen's sons; Ken Marsolais; Lisa Drew (Colleen's incredibly patient and loving editor) and, of course, the lawyers about what might be done with a two-thirds-complete autobiography. "I don't know," Alex, Campbell, and Ken replied.

"Maybe it can be completed," Lisa offered.

How the hell would we do that? I thought. *It's an autobiography.*

"Somebody will do something or somebody owes us a check," the lawyers reportedly stated.

"We'll figure it out," we all said together.

More time went by and the prospect of doing extensive research and writing from an impersonal, objective point of view in order to finish what had been Colleen's very personal, subjective account of her life excited none of us. Hence nothing got done. But after talking with Elizabeth Wilson, a dear friend of Colleen's, and listening to her relate stories of her life with Colleen, I thought, *Why not let those who knew Colleen finish the book for her? This might keep Colleen's personal account of herself from turning into yet another standard "and then she did" biography.* Thus began my process of interviewing more than fifty of Colleen's colleagues, friends, and family, many of whose voices join Colleen's in the following pages.

As was inevitable in working with Colleen—and as I was often told by others—we laughed a lot, cried a bit, and confided much about each other that had nothing to do with the project at hand. Today that's what I remember most—the experience of watching and listening, as a remarkable and gentle woman reluctantly sifted through her life. As was made clear to me over the ensuing interviews, in opening her heart so generously, Colleen showed many others the way to their own. And by having the courage to throw herself into the middle of life, she moved mine and others lucky enough to walk with her on to a more adventurous path.

I don't know how it goes for others who work together on a book such as this, but often after sharing certain personal stories, Colleen would grin and say, "But we can't use that." Sorry. Most often the reason was not that she was afraid of revealing something painful or embarrassing about herself, but that she felt a particular story about her was actually even more revelatory of whoever shared the experience with her. "That's theirs to tell," she would say. "Not mine." Invariably after one of those most potent memories, she would look up and add, almost as a dare, and clearly to get us off the subject of her, "And what about you?" So I'd tell a story. One of my own. One *not* for my book, as if there was to be one. But one that when combined with hers brought us a more appreciative understanding of each other.

The same thing happened in many of the interviews. Many people were very forthcoming, each speaking candidly for the tape. But occasionally, after the recorder had stopped, conversation would continue as intensely personal thoughts were revealed; thoughts about Colleen that had been on people's minds since her death nearly five years earlier. Some of these made it into these pages and some, as Colleen would say, "were not for the book." And I make no apologies for that. Even in these days of obsessive personal disclosure, there are some memories and experiences that come from too tender a place in the heart to be revealed to strangers. But in the swap of shared experience, both with Colleen and with those who still hold her so dear, I learned much about trust, which must preclude any exchange of genuine friendship and love. And no one understood the love that bonds a friendship better than Colleen Dewhurst.

What follows is Colleen's story, most of it told by her. If she had lived long enough to complete this manuscript, undoubtedly she would have read this book, page by page and cover to cover for audiocassettes so that you would not only hear her thoughts but have that voice recount these memories for you. But, as anyone who knew her will attest, there would have been no keeping her to the text. So imagine the cover of the audio: COLLEEN DEWHURST: AN AUTOBIOGRAPHY—AS AD-LIBBED BY THE AUTHOR.

In those sections not told in Colleen's voice, others recall days of success and disaster, years of shared pleasure and passion and, of course, always the laughter. Many of these names will be as recognizable as Colleen's, others will not. But each tells a tale that completes a story that Colleen could not. Most things don't get done as you planned them. And Colleen's remark "That's theirs to tell" takes on a whole different meaning now than when she first made it. Maybe she knew, long before I did, how we would tell her story.

So now the lawyers are happy. But, much more important, I sincerely hope that Colleen is. I'm glad and grateful that she waited twelve years to begin this project in earnest. And—like so, so many others—I wish there had been at least twelve more years for us all to laugh about it after she finally got around to scribbling "The end."

T.V., 1997

Colleen Dewhurst

INTRODUCTION

"Write the fucking book!!!"

It's a beautiful day. I'd rather be outside right now lying in the sun, lady of all I survey, on land that was originally a farm over two hundred years ago. There are trees I can see from the window here that are easily that age. Instead, I sit writing in this old farmhouse—Flood Farm—that after twenty-five years we still seem to be in the middle of restoring.

Over ten years ago, I had an idea that brings me to this very moment. This particular thought was of stuccoing some of the walls and the ceilings in the house which, at the time, seemed rather ordinary and inconsequential. As I look up at the ceiling today, sitting here in the living room, there are three large and ugly gray puttied areas. Two are where the stucco has since fallen down. The third is from a leak in my shower, immediately above, that has managed to continue over the years to seep slowly into the ceiling.

So, you may ask, what does any of this have to do with today? Simple. This idea of home repair and how to pay for it, plus the hard fact that I had (and still have) a mortgage, led me, at the suggestion of a friend, to meet with an editor of a certain publishing house. I had confided to this friend, at that time, that I was having money problems. She suggested that I write a book. I told her, quite honestly, that that was the last and farthest thing from my mind, stuccoed ceilings or not. Not to worry, she said, going on to inform me that if a publisher was interested in someone writing a book, they paid what is called an "advance." Money. Before you ever actually write a word. That news immediately moved me into action. And two days later, I found myself sitting across a desk with my friend's agent and an editor who wanted to know what kind of book I had in mind.

I explained to this editor that I would not write about anything personal and would not discuss either my marriages or my children, nor would I speak about people whom I loathed. In other words, I was not interested in writing a "tell-all" book. I mentioned nothing of home improvements. He stared at me for a minute, as if unsure of what he had just heard. I could tell that I may have possibly ruined my chances of ever seeing an advance or stuccoing my ceilings.

"Miss Dewhurst," he said, "could you tell me then what you do plan to write about?"

"I think I should write about the theater," I responded.

He did not seem terribly impressed or excited by that reply, and the meeting came to a quick end. Nevertheless, a week later I did receive a call from him informing me that, yes, his publisher would be interested in publishing a book that I would write and, best of all, yes, I would receive an advance.

I must now admit that, to me, this seemed to be the perfect ending of a wonderfully successful transaction.

Years passed, and in that time I did not write a thing, my newly stuccoed ceilings caved in again, and my original publishing company went out of business. I refuse to believe this was in any way my fault. But when that occurred, I was contacted, out of the blue, by another editor. This one was a woman— Lisa Drew, by name—whose brother was a theater critic I had known quite well in Milwaukee, Wisconsin. Lisa worked for a very reputable publisher and told me that her company would be interested in picking up the rights to my unwritten book.

It was just about that moment when I realized that the advance given to me years ago had not been a gift. In fact, it was more like a home-improvement *loan*, repayment of which would be my delivering a publishable manuscript. Failure to do so, I was graciously informed, would turn what I had mistakenly thought to be a gift into a debt. Ms. Drew managed to make all of this quite clear to me, and somewhere along the way, I became acutely aware that this book you are about to read *had* to be written.

One day, about a year later and after I had closed in the Broadway production of *You Can't Take It with You*, I was walking east on West Fiftieth Street. As I approached the corner of Sixth Avenue, I heard my name called out.

"Colleen!" I turned to see Jimmy Coco bounding across the avenue toward me.

"I'm rich!" he yelled, waving his arms and jumping up and down as he ran between cars. "I'm rich!"

Once he crossed the street, I began running toward him. We met and embraced. Needless to say, not just a few people had stopped dead in their tracks to observe this scene as Jimmy had always been particularly recognizable and unavoidable, especially if he was running—and screaming.

"You've got to write that fucking book!" he said. "Honey," he continued, "I travel all over the country. Speak on every damn talk show and sign my book on how to lose weight. All I have to do is try not to gain weight and that money just keeps rolling in."

I was, by now, aware of the crowd we were drawing. Jimmy was either unaware or just didn't give a damn. And as I recall, the only comments I could interject were things like, "You're kidding" and "That's terrific." As we broke apart to go wherever each of us was rushing to that afternoon, Jimmy just kept yelling to me, "Write that book, honey! Write it!"

We hurtled away from each other in opposite directions, and I kept thinking that we must have looked like someone's nightmare version of those two lovers running toward each other across green fields and into each other's arms.

Write the damn book! I kept hearing.

I walked away as quickly as I could, looking at the pavement and hoping that everyone was not still frozen in place. But Jimmy's words kept playing over and over again in my head: *I'm rich, baby! I'm rich!! Write the fucking book!*

My editor, Lisa Drew, had not given up and made me constantly aware that someday she was going to "get this book." Through the years, every time I opened in a play, I received a telegram on opening night from Lisa which said: BEST WISHES. THIS MIGHT BE A CHAPTER.

But I was still having very little success actually sitting down and writing. Finally Lisa asked to see what I had done, to read some words on paper, anything that would assure her I was working, which, I will now confess, I was not. However, since our first conversation, I had discovered that Lisa is quite a good bridge player. I knew that the inevitable could no longer be avoided, and I reluctantly made a date for her to come to the Farm for the weekend. She would be able to read all day, and in the evening we would play bridge. Of course, I had the cards. What I lacked was a manuscript.

For the next two weeks, I locked myself in the living room whenever I had an extra minute and spoke into a tape recorder on some particular subject and bored myself to tears. As the day of Lisa's visit arrived, I entered a mild hysteria when I realized that all these tapes had to be transcribed. I, of course, had never learned to type. So the entire household began to scour the area looking for people who did.

The first typist we found was my son Alex's first love, Lisa Ticknor, who shut herself in the studio with my tapes and began typing. The rest of us continued to pore through the local want ads looking for anyone with even the most basic secretarial skills. We found two others who were given the remaining tapes and informed that they were to deliver their completed pages by eleven o'clock the following night. *I* may have dilly-dallied for years, but *they* were not to dawdle.

Lisa arrived as planned, and we had a lovely dinner. No one mentioned the book. We then proceeded to the bridge table and began to play. And still, no one mentioned the book.

As we played in the den, Lisa Ticknor would fly past every thirty minutes or so, dashing up the stairs to my bedroom. Whenever he could, Ken (and you'll find out who he is later) would get up from the game and disappear up the stairs into the bedroom where he attempted to arrange stacks of pages into sequence and some proper chapter-like form before coming back to the table to play his hand.

At the end of the game, I excused myself and calmly went upstairs, retrieving what seemed to me to be a rather sufficient manuscript. Granted, I hadn't read it. But it certainly looked substantial. I brought it down, like an offering, and handed it to Lisa, who quickly retired with it to her room.

The following morning, several of us were grouped in the kitchen nervously awaiting Lisa's first appearance. Looking back, I was caught between hoping that it was OK enough to shut her up for a while or that she would just hate it outright and be honest enough to say that I was out of the ball game. Lisa entered quietly. We all pretended to be busy with breakfast, nonchalantly toasting bagels and sipping our coffee.

"I like it," she said, looking around the room. "But who the hell is your typist?"

We all broke up and then told her the truth of what had been going on the night before as various figures had flown past her and up the stairs.

Lisa came back about a month later, bringing the edited manuscript with her. We sat for hours in the living room as she went over each chapter, telling me what she liked as well as what she did not like. That evening, as before, Ken, Lisa, and I sat down with a local friend of ours, who had agreed to make a fourth, to play bridge. We had barely started playing when the intercom frantically buzzed. Ken jumped up to answer. It was Leon (more on him later), whose elderly father had arrived from England just three weeks before, certain that if he did not visit his son here in the States, his son would never make it back to England before the old man's death. His premonition nearly proved to be true, as he suffered a heart attack upon landing at Kennedy Airport. After spending his first three weeks in America in a hospital, Leon's father was finally released and brought to the Farm with great joy and concern. Now it seemed Leon's father was having another seizure. The three of us sat silently waiting. Ken finally came back to tell us that everything would be fine. Leon was calm. His father was comfortable and resting.

We had been playing for another hour or so when we were interrupted by the sound of glass breaking from somewhere in the studio across the driveway. No one moved. The intercom buzzed again. This time, I picked it up. It was Nana (more on her later also), telling me that there now appeared to be a slight disagreement between Alex and his girlfriend (the typist). Ken and I calmly excused ourselves and left the room, going outdoors where we could hear a shouting match between the two, part of which, with our appearance on the scene, now became directed at us.

Fifteen long minutes later, when we felt the screaming had quieted down, Ken and I returned to the house. The two women were sitting quietly, just as we left them, unmoved, with their cards still in their hands. No one spoke or acknowledged the commotion or the broken glass. But as I sat back down at the table, I realized that all the windows facing the driveway were wide open. There was no way Lisa and our guest could not have heard the entire ruckus—every word. But it was also obvious that, not knowing each other well and having very little in common except partnerless bridge, they had not spoken a word to each other since we left, despite the cursing and shrieking they had just overheard. Smiling, we continued to play once more.

We were still playing at midnight when the kitchen door slammed and a friend of ours, who was then managing director of a prominent theater company, suddenly appeared unannounced in the room. We were quite startled but nevertheless introduced him to our guests. Barely acknowledging the introductions, the director distractedly pulled a chair up to the table and sat despondently with his head in his hands.

"They're trying to take my theater away from me," he moaned. Once more the two ladies sat quietly as Ken and I and the director had a lengthy and heated discussion as to how and why that could not be possible; if it was, who was responsible; if it happened, what could be done. At one point well into this discussion I asked where his wife was.

"She's asleep in the car in the driveway," he replied, before jumping right back into the conversation with Ken. Once again, there was no response from our guests, as if it was perfectly normal not only for us to leave them holding the cards but for him to leave his wife asleep in the car in the driveway for the duration of the discussion of his professional crisis. After about thirty minutes, the three of us—Ken, the director, and I—embraced, and he left, presumably with his wife still unconscious in the front seat.

The game continued for another half an hour as if this had been a purely social evening (now morning) of bridge, chest pains, shattered glass, screaming, and treachery. I have no idea which of us won.

When I came downstairs the next morning, Lisa was already packed and ready to take the next train into the city. I tried to persuade her to stay longer, but she informed me that she always did her laundry on Sunday. I tried again to convince her to stay. Again she declined. It was then that I realized she was indeed the perfect editor for me, as I could be dissuaded from anything on the spur of the moment and, clearly, this woman could not.

We all said our good-byes. As Lisa got to the door she turned and looked back at me.

"Colleen," she said. "I'm getting this book. Because if I don't get the book, I write the weekend."

1

"Young ladies do not turn red and sweat!"

I was an only child. I have practically no memory of the first four or five years of my life except that the boundaries of that life were defined by my parents and dominated primarily by my mother. The only other figures I remember during that period were of doctors and of nurses, who were nuns, bending over me, again and again, in an operating room.

I was born in Montreal, Canada, and, from the time that I was very young, about two years old, I had some sort of illness of which, again, I have no clear memory or understanding. I can only recall being taken to various hospitals on what seems to have been every Saturday morning. All I ever learned from my mother about this time of my life was that at some point, the doctors said there was nothing they could do about whatever was wrong.

My first clear memory, at about four or five, is of entering a house somewhere in Sherbrooke, Canada, and looking at my mother, while a man who was sitting with her on the couch explained that he always read from the Bible before he operated. My next memory is of lying on a kitchen table and listening to this same man inform my mother that, as he had no nurse, she would have to assist in the operation.

I had no idea what was about to happen, but I remember looking up at her as she stood above me and prepared to put what I now know was an ether cone over my face in order to render me unconscious and obliterate any memory I might have had of what was to follow. What matters now is that since then I have come to understand how desperate for help my mother must have been to entrust her only child to some quack physician, reading from the Bible and operating with a knife in the kitchen. For her to assist in this madness must have been a horrifying experience. My mother and I never returned to that house nor to any other operating table.

For the next few years, I wore a white handkerchief around my throat and was always being given some sort of medication, which I hated. As a very young child, I spent a great deal of time in my bed surrounded by electric heating pads and, as I was very skinny, being told constantly to eat.

One day, my mother came abruptly into my room.

"Come into the bathroom," she said, motioning for me to get out of bed. I went in and sat on the edge of the bathtub as she opened the medicine chest above the sink. Handful by handful, she grabbed the brown medicine bottles that lined the shelves and dumped them and their contents into the wastebasket.

I sat there watching in silence, listening to the glass bottles shatter against each other. After the medicine chest was emptied, she leaned over to me, still sitting on the tub, and gently removed the white handkerchief from around my neck.

"My dearest Biddy," she said, calling me the name by which she most often addressed me when I was a child, "you will never have to take any of those again. It's over."

I felt such joy in that moment. I think, because children do believe in miracles, that it seemed only natural to me that my mother could make this happen. I realize now that I never doubted that she could. It was only ever a question of *when*. With the brown bottles of bitter medicines and the white handkerchief gone, all that remained was the scar on my throat—a mark that has nearly vanished over the years—and, to this day, the constant demand from those who love me to eat.

I don't have much appetite for food. As a child, I had always eaten in the kitchen with the maid an hour before my parents would sit down to eat in the dining room. Every Sunday I was allowed to eat with my parents at the big table. I have always believed that the reason I speak so fast today is that as a child, I always had so much to say, after a week of eating alone, that on Sunday I would try to get it all out before my father would finally have to tell me, "Enough." Bedtime was different. Every night, Monday through Sunday, when I went to bed, my mother would sit with me for fifteen minutes to a half an hour and listen as I would tell her everything that had happened to me that day. I never sensed with her the need to rush that I felt with my father at Sunday dinner. My mother and I continued to share this time, every night, until the day I left home.

When we moved to the States from Canada, the first place we settled in was Boston, Massachusetts. There, Mother, Dad, and I lived in a two-bedroom apartment on the fifth floor of an old stone building that had a long wooden veranda on the back of each floor, from which the women hung their laundry and yelled back and forth to each other all day.

The building sat on a well-traveled street. Since I wasn't in school at the time, whenever my mother sent me out of the house, I would sit out front on the stoop for hours. Being an only child and ill for such a long time, I had never played with other children. I had no idea of what I was supposed to do or how

I was to behave with anyone other than my parents. I was desperate for some-one to talk to. So I would sit on that stoop all afternoon, waiting for some grown-up to come along. As they approached, I would run up to them on the sidewalk, take them by the arm and say that I was putting them "in jail." This meant they were now bound to come and sit with me for a while. I can't imag-ine what these people must have made of this—and, obviously, I was turned down quite a bit. But, surprisingly enough, now and then, some kind man or woman would come up on the porch and sit beside me for a few moments. I have no memory of what we would talk about except that after a few minutes of conversation, I would "release" the person and, content for the moment, go back inside to my mother, or sit quietly looking down the street, waiting for another prisoner.

I liked the evenings best when the three of us, Mother, Dad, and I, would sit around the huge, ugly mahogany radio listening to *Mirt and Marge, Sun-bonnet Sue, Tom Mix,* and *Buck Rogers.* My best friend at this time was a cat named Tiger. Although I had a very strict bedtime, I was allowed to take Tiger to bed with me and usually did.

My father was a first-class fire-engine chaser. It could be two or three o'clock in the morning and if we were awakened by the sound of sirens and the sight of lights flashing down the street, my father would jump up out of bed and throw on his clothes. From my room, I could hear my mother say, "Fred, this is ridiculous." But there was no stopping him. He was up and out the door, only to return a few hours later.

My mother was a heavy cigarette smoker. I can still remember hearing her tell my dad at night that he had to go down to the drugstore and get her a pack of cigarettes. If it was too late and the store was closed, he was to pound on the door until the owner came down from upstairs and opened shop just for him. From my room, I would hear them arguing about this until finally I would hear the door slam as he left. And each time, I would listen for him until he came back silently with the pack of cigarettes.

During the day, my mother read constantly, one book after another. My father read only the newspaper and the occasional sports magazine. Dad had been quite a well-known athlete in Canada, where he had played football with the Ottawa Roughriders. He was also instrumental in bringing amateur ice hockey there and had organized exhibition games across the border in such American cities as Buffalo and Syracuse.

My mother had been considered quite a beauty as a young woman in Ottawa. As a girl, she loved ice skating and had studied piano. There was a time when it was thought that she might become a concert pianist. This she did not do. But what enabled her in later years always to take care of us was that she was excellent at typing and shorthand, skills no doubt enhanced by her profi-ciency at the keyboard.

My mother had been previously engaged to another young man when my father, who had seen her at the ice rink, began to appear with members of his football team at any restaurant or club where he knew he would see her. Finally, in spite of her engagement and after forcing some sort of introduction, he began to take her out.

My mother's mother was furious, and whenever my father brought my mother home, my grandmother would turn out all the lights in the house except for one in the entryway that she would flick on and off until he left. But my father's persistence paid off. Ultimately, my mother broke her engagement, ran away and married my father. Much later, I learned that my mother had always disliked her mother—my grandmother—intensely. I think some of her motivation to marry my father was not so much a credit to his persistence as it was a clear act of defiance.

As a child, I never knew that my mother felt this way about her own mother because, once we moved to the States, we continued to visit my grandparents in Ottawa, two or three times a year—usually once or twice in the summer and then at Harvesttime (the Canadian Thanksgiving) or Christmas. We would arrive in Ottawa and my parents would leave me with my grandparents so that they might travel through the area for a week or so to visit old friends.

Mother adored her father and I, too, came to love my grandfather. His name was Thomas. He was a handsome man, very tall, with thick, white hair. But what I remember most about him was that he was gentle and kind. When we arrived, he would immediately take my mother into their tiny backyard and show her the flowers and vegetables that he was growing. They would sit quietly until my grandmother followed them out of the house and brought my mother back inside, leaving my grandfather and me free to go to the park across the street. Granddad and I would walk over hand in hand. There we would spend the afternoon talking as he pushed me on the swings or put me on one end of the seesaw, moving it slowly up and down from the opposite end. He would stay with me for hours and never seemed bored.

My grandmother was a great talker. She'd begin by telling me or my mother or whoever would listen how ill she was feeling, how difficult life was, and continue with the latest gossip about the neighbors and our relatives. Every day, it seemed to me, my grandmother would be on the phone, early in the morning, discussing with various old friends and aunts spread all over Ottawa—with great pleasure and in great detail—the latest on whoever she knew was in the hospital and likely to die. She was consumed by this constant talk of illness and dying. My grandmother finally reached a stage where she would manage to be admitted to the hospital herself at least once a year and spend a week or two moaning and crying, although there was not a thing wrong with her.

Years before, my grandfather had had a very large and successful farm "up the Gatineau." There my mother was born and lived until she was ten. My grandmother, who I gather considered herself to be quite a beauty, was never happy there and felt that she belonged in the city. Eventually, after years of hearing her complain, my grandfather sold the farm and they moved to Ottawa. There he invested his money from the sale of the farm in various real estate ventures that were not particularly successful. My grandfather had been a great farmer. A businessman he was not. But they made do. Years went by and my granddad finally ended up as a night watchman for the Canadian Pacific Railroad. I never heard my grandfather complain of his life in the city. But I do remember that whenever my mother would arrive, there would be such joy in his face as if, at last, he could share his small garden with someone who loved it as much as he did.

We moved from Boston to Dorchester, Massachusetts, when I was six. There I entered school for the first time. We lived in a very clannish Irish neighborhood. I was painfully shy and still never had a real friend my age. As soon as I could walk, I had been taught by my mother to curtsy whenever I was introduced to an adult. I didn't know how to behave with other children. When I entered the first grade, I was brought in and introduced to the teacher as the new girl in the neighborhood. Naturally, I did as my mother had told me and curtsied, to the astonishment of the teacher and the great amusement of my classmates. For the next few weeks I was constantly harassed as I walked home from school, and on occasion I was beaten up.

There were two sisters, about my age, who lived next to me in Dorchester. I had tried in my own awkward way to become friends with them but to no avail. After coming home from school one day, I went outside to take a drink of water from the spigot on the side of the house. These two little girls saw me, ran across the yard, and jammed my head into the spigot, cutting my lip and chipping my front tooth. When I turned around to face them, they pushed me down and ran back across the yard and up onto their porch. Bleeding, I ran into the house and started to cry when I saw my mother.

"What happened, Biddy?" she asked. Just then my father came in the front door from work and listened to the story I was telling her.

"All right," he said, as he watched her put a cold cloth on my swollen lip. "That's the end of this. Biddy," he continued, taking the cloth from my lip, "I'm going to teach you how to fight."

"I don't think that's the thing to do," my mother said, following us into the dining room.

"I'm not teaching her how to start a fight," he protested. "I'm teaching her how to protect herself so this will not happen again."

For the next half hour, my father proceeded to show me how to "put up your dukes," "jab with your left," and hit.

"When you see the opening," he said, gently jabbing at me with his left, "throw your right." So there we were, sparring around the dining room, left-

left-left-right, left-left-left-right, as my mother stood watching in the archway, silent and skeptical.

The very next day, on my return from school, these same two little girls who bloodied my lip stood out front with three boys from the neighborhood, playing with a rope as a lasso. I knew when I saw them that I was in trouble, since I had to pass by them to get to my house. As I came up they stood in a line and blocked the sidewalk. The boys pushed me back and forth as the girls put the lasso over my head and down around my waist. They began to swing me in a circle. For the first time, I was very cool. I didn't cry. I wasn't afraid. Instead, I quietly clenched my fist as they spun me across the cement. As I came around again, I did just as Dad had taught me and hit one of the girls with my right fist as hard as I could. I connected with her nose. She immediately spurted blood and screamed like a ninny. The others dropped the rope and ran. The spinning stopped. I shook myself loose as she stood there bleeding and crying.

I was exuberant. I skipped up the steps of the porch with a feeling I had never had before. As I entered the house my mother was coming toward the door, having heard the screaming from outside. I told her what had happened, grinning from ear to ear. Before I could finish, the phone rang.

"I see. I see," my mother said, listening to a voice that even I could hear on the other end. She continued to listen in silence for a bit longer.

"Let me tell you," she finally said, looking over to me, "I couldn't be a bit happier," and hung up. "They think you have broken her nose," she said, turning back to me.

I didn't say a word. When my dad came home, I immediately told him what had happened. He was very proud. From then on, I loved to fight and, although I never started it, when necessary, I was quite good at it. I became known in the neighborhood as a very rough and tough little girl and not the kid who was odd enough to curtsy to the teacher.

As I got a little older, I would go to the park across the street from my grandparents' home, on occasion without my grandfather, to stand on the edge of the field and watch the neighborhood boys play baseball. Whenever a ball was hit foul I would run after it and throw it back into the game for them. I was entering my tomboy stage and, even then, had a very good arm. After a few throws, they would finally yell to me, asking if I wanted to play. I would shout, "Yes!" and run over to join whichever team was short a player.

But I was very shy and continued to stand on the edge of the field waiting to be invited to play. I never took it for granted that the boys would really want me to play, even though I knew I was good and could throw and bat as well as the best of them. Eventually, they stopped asking me if I wanted to play, and one team would simply choose me outright. I was thrilled. I loved those days and those games.

My grandmother soon began to try to correct the various unladylike things she claimed I learned from my father. When I came back across the street from the ball field, she would grab me as I came in the door and exclaim how dirty I was. She would march me upstairs where there would be an ice-cold bath awaiting.

"Young ladies," she explained as we climbed the stairs, "do not turn red and sweat!" This was only the first item in what was to become her ongoing and extensive "young ladies do not" litany.

"Young ladies do not play games with boys," she continued, scrubbing my head and hands. "They don't go barefoot. They don't laugh loudly and, my dear, they most definitely do not whistle." And on and on for what seemed to me an eternity. Oddly enough, she never forbade me outright to play baseball during my visits. By then, my mother's secretarial skills were an additional source of income for my grandmother, so she dared not go against her. As this was the case, baseball and perhaps even the occasional bit of whistling, loud laughter, and bare feet would be fine.

My whole grade-school experience is like a kaleidoscope to me. I managed to attend five different schools from first through sixth grades as my family moved from town to town and state to state.

After Dorchester, we moved to Auburndale, Massachusetts, where we lived on Commonwealth Avenue in the upper part of a nice house next to a beautiful church. I loved it there because I found a best friend, Peggy Ansley, and fell in love with a redheaded boy named Leonard. Nevertheless, I was the definitive tomboy. I wore high-cut boots and sent away for a Buck Rogers helmet and glasses. My crowning glory was the day my mother let me tuck a tiny knife into the top of those high-cut boots. I built forts in the snow in the backyard into which I could crawl and dream. I was still one of the best fighters in school. That year, I was given my first bicycle for my birthday. It was red with big balloon tires. I loved that bike more than any car I've ever owned.

I was in the third grade in Auburndale. The school was in one of those friendly old stone buildings with cutout flowers pasted on the windows. One blustery, cloudy day after school had let out, I ran outside to meet my friend Peggy to walk home. Before we left, I ran back inside to get my jacket, which I had forgotten. I ran past the empty first- and second-grade rooms. As I started past the door to my classroom, where my jacket was still hanging on the far wall, I glanced in and saw my third-grade teacher with her head on the desk. Her arms were folded underneath her face and she was sobbing. Lowering my head, I tiptoed by her and picked up my jacket. I stood there for a minute listening to her. But she did not lift her head. I ran back through the cloakroom and down the stairs. I found Peggy, and we started walking home. I did not tell her what I had seen or heard, but the memory of that moment has never left me.

That afternoon had been our school's official spring celebration in which every class did something for the May Day and Easter holidays all rolled into one. For weeks, each class had been working on a presentation and that morning, all of our parents had come to school and watched as each class came out dancing, singing, or doing a skit. Our teacher had decided that we would do the maypole dance. We had not been very good at it through the rehearsals, as she had wanted it to be quite intricate. I remember us all in the yard—boys and girls together—with long, clothesline-like strings tied to the top of a pole. She tried and tried with little success to get us to wind the strings down the pole as we skipped merrily in a circle.

That morning, we came to school with all the girls in their prettiest dresses and the boys in dark trousers and white shirts. The maypole was now hung with red, white, and blue crepe-paper ribbons. When it was our turn, we each took our place holding a ribbon. Our teacher put the record on the Victrola, and we began the maypole dance. The wind took some of the ribbons out of our hands at once. For those who managed to hang on, of which I was one, the crepe just billowed up and tangled as we started skipping around the pole. It was utter confusion. We kept bumping into each other and, before long, we were giggling and simply running around out of order. I fear I was one of the worst offenders, first running in one direction and then the other. We began to laugh harder and harder until finally the boys just began to pull the crepe paper off the pole and throw it about, which I thoroughly enjoyed. All of our parents were very good about it all. They laughed with us and gave us a very nice applause. As I think about it, I don't think I could do a maypole dance today.

I don't remember class after that, but I know I shall always remember the sound and sight of my teacher sobbing. I don't know why I remember that scene, but whenever I think of it, I have the same experience. My stomach and throat tighten, and I can still feel tears come to my own eyes. I suspect she was a teacher I did not like very much, but it doesn't matter. Perhaps this was the first time that I mentally photographed and understood an adult in pain. Not only had I observed the person in this painful, private moment, but I had some understanding that I had somehow contributed to it.

I REMEMBER a dark night, my mother and father driving home with me supposedly asleep in the backseat. It was the first time I ever heard the word *divorce*. They spoke very quietly, in order not to wake me. It was my mother who wanted the divorce. I didn't know what the word meant, but I was struck with a fear like none I had ever had before. I knew it was something terrible.

Months later, I lay in bed and learned through the wall that my father had lost his job. He had been working as a buyer for the Great Atlantic and Pacific Tea Company. My mother, at this time, held the job of secretary to the president of the same company. She continued to hold this job and support us. This was the beginning of a long period of lying in bed at night and hearing my father break down, with my mother's voice quietly encouraging him that things would be all right, until she would finally get him to sleep. That word—*divorce*—that she had spoken in the car that night she did not repeat after he lost his job.

I didn't understand then why we had to move to West Newton from Auburndale, which I loved. But obviously, when my father was fired, we couldn't afford to live where we were. I remember nothing about where we lived in West Newton, except that we moved into a few rooms of a large house that wasn't ours. I hated it. The family who owned this house had a little girl about my age and a younger boy. This little girl and a friend of hers played doctor all the time with her little brother. They didn't like me. I hated them, and I hated playing doctor.

I do remember that there was a large park near this house and I came to love a certain tree that grew there. Soon my whole life was about climbing trees. I sat in them for hours. As soon as school was out, I was there in the park and up into the tree. I missed Peggy. Oh, how I missed her. I had no best girl-friend anymore. I had nobody who wanted to build forts with me or wear Tom Mix's magic ring.

My father was finally offered a job in New York City with the W. T. Grant company. We packed up everything once more and left West Newton, moving to a very nice apartment on Bronxville Avenue, close to Sarah Lawrence College. Our apartment building stood with a number of other buildings on a great big concrete courtyard. I loved to roller-skate, and to this day I can remember how good the concrete was for that. There seemed to be miles of it.

On summer nights, all the kids would pour out of those buildings after dinner and into the courtyard. We would play hide-and-seek until the shadows grew so long that our parents would come out and call to us as we heard other voices calling to us, "allie, allie in free, allie, allie in free." What wonderful places we had there in which to hide. We were the scourge of the landlords, running through the basements of different apartment houses, down corridors to hide in storage closets. From these dark and hidden places, each of us tried to make it back to home base before we could be spotted. Better yet, with just a little slower start than you might normally make, you could maybe let Frank, Larry, or Allen see what basement you had run into and just which boiler you were hiding behind.

One day, my mother informed me that she was sending me to a dance teacher who lived in an apartment up the avenue. I was terribly embarrassed. I didn't understand why I had to go to a dance teacher. Nobody I knew went to a dance teacher. But my mother, in her infinite wisdom, realized I had reached my gangly, awkward stage. My mother, however, never used negatives—"This is wrong with you," "Why can't you . . ." Instead, she simply stated what she thought to be the obvious.

"You will take dance lessons." Simple. To the point.

So I went, with shuffling feet, to a large apartment building a few blocks away and entered a large ballroom on the first floor. There, each week, was a very Spanish-looking lady, who had her hair pulled back in a bun and wore long earrings. She was about five feet tall and I was already five feet seven inches. Dropping the needle on the phonograph, she would turn, stride toward me, grasp me around the waist, and push me around the room. My body was as tense as a board. The only thing that helped me was that I could stare right over her head at the walls and out the window. It seemed horrible to me at the time. But no amount of pleading or foot-stamping would change my mother's mind about these lessons, so I kept going, but never told anyone what I was doing. I continued to disappear from my friends for one hour a week, a wasted hour, as far as I was concerned, as it meant no baseball, no roller skating, nothing. Just this strange lady and I, whirling around the floor, never speaking. I think I was worst at the tango. Years later, however, I became rather grateful for those lessons from that woman, whoever she was, because as an adult I love to dance.

When I was in the sixth grade, there was a boy in my class named Bill Gurnsey. Bill had red hair and played the violin. He was very quiet. I can't say that I ever saw him hang out with anybody, and he certainly wasn't with our crowd. One day, I came home and my mother said that Mrs. Gurnsey had called.

"Bill has invited you to see a movie with him at Radio City," she said. "I told Mrs. Gurnsey that this was all right with me, if it was all right with you."

"But I hardly know Bill Gurnsey," I replied. I was very embarrassed.

The next day, Bill stopped me in the hallway at school. His face was as red as his hair.

"Would you really like to go to the movies Saturday afternoon?" he asked. I stammered and scrambled around before finally saying simply, "Sure."

After our first "date," Bill stopped me four or five times in the hallway at school and asked me to the movies at Radio City. I always accepted. Each time, on Saturday, his mother and aunt would drive us into New York, where we would see a Shirley Temple film or a Freddy Bartholomew movie, like *Captains Courageous.* Bill's mother and aunt would always tactfully sit four rows behind us. We would sit in front, shoulder to shoulder, and watch the film. Afterward, we would all go to Schrafft's for a soda. From there we would drive, for what seemed an interminable time, back home. The mother and aunt would talk while Bill and I sat in the backseat of the car in silence. If a question, such as "How did you like the movie?" was asked of me directly, I answered in a word.

As a child, I was always tense around grown-ups. I never learned how to talk to them. I suppose that was because there were always just the three of us in my family, and we moved so many times. Once in a while my mother would give a dinner for some business acquaintance of my father's, but there were few times when they had friends over. Consequently, I never really had to learn to deal with adults who weren't relatives or teachers. It was always an agony for me to talk to my friends' parents for any length of time, and I couldn't wait to get away from them.

Before I entered seventh grade, my family moved again, this time to Crestwood, but it wasn't the wrench that the other moves had been, because all the kids who reached seventh grade in Crestwood also went to Roosevelt Junior High School. One night, at about six or six-thirty, shortly after we had moved in, we heard boys outside the house yelling, "Colleen, Colleen, oh Coll-*leeeen.*" My parents and I sat there, in our English Tudor row house, listening. After this hooting had occurred three or four times, my father finally got up and started for the door.

"Oh, Daddy," I pleaded, "don't go out there. Don't embarrass me."

"I don't care," he said. "Nobody is going to stand out there on the street like that and call your name."

He threw open the door and shouted, "If anyone wants to see my daughter, come to the door. Otherwise, I want all of you to get out. *Now!*" The boys scattered, except for one who was short, blond and tough-looking, and came up the front stone stairs toward my father.

"What's your name?" my father asked.

"Billy Bender," came the reply.

"Come in," my dad said. And this boy, whom I had never seen before, entered.

"This is my daughter, Colleen," my father said by way of introduction, "and this is her mother, Mrs. Dewhurst." My mother sat quietly as my father continued this line of questioning. I just sat and stared at him. Billy answered all of the questions my dad asked him, and after about fifteen minutes, my father escorted him back to the door and he left.

We both went to Roosevelt. I liked Billy Bender for a long time, even though he did not have a good reputation. I had reached the stage where I realized that you had to be careful of your reputation. One girl whispered to me that Billy had actually taken a bath with a girl. I never asked him about this; I was dying to, but had no idea how. Nobody could have been sweeter or nicer than Billy, but all I ever thought of when I was with him was that he had taken that forbidden bath.

For me, the seventh and eighth grades were very happy and frightening times. I guess those years were my rites of passage. I began to go to school dances and parties in my friends' homes. In spite of assurances that these get-togethers would be well chaperoned by the parents, these evenings always led to "spin the bottle," "post office," and perhaps the most dangerous game of all, "flashlight," in which couples sat in a dark room and nestled together while one boy walked around with a flashlight. If this boy's light hit a couple that was kissing, he then sat down with that girl, and the other boy was now stuck with the flashlight. This game usually came to an end when the lights in the room were turned on by somebody's mother.

There were also dates for movies, during which we both sat tensely. The boy was wondering if he should try to put his arm around me, and I was wondering what to do if he did. School dances were wonderful because I got to wear long dresses. In the seventh grade, Billy Bender and I won a contest at one of these dances doing the "big apple." Billy and I loved to dance and we had worked out all kinds of fancy dips and spins between us. He'd throw me into the air. I loved it. We could out-jitterbug anyone. I'm sure this wasn't what my mother or the Spanish lady—who had tangoed me across the room—had in mind, but I sure knew how to follow Billy.

Dances and dating and "spin the bottle" was 50 percent of me; the other 50 percent was captain of the seventh-grade girls' baseball team. I was the pitcher and a good hitter. That year, our team had won the championship. We were now to play the eighth-grade championship team that was captained by a girl named Joan Melber, who was a terrific athlete and a good friend. In the final inning of this game, we were behind by one run. I came up to bat with two outs and one runner on base. I hit a ball to center field that we all knew was a home run and would win the game. Much as kids do today, we always put the girls who couldn't catch in the outfield. Joan's team was no exception. Everyone watched the ball, including me. I was by now on my way to second base as this poor girl stared up into the sun and moved tentatively back and forth, trying to figure out where the ball would fall. To everyone's astonishment and to my horror, the ball just happened to land in her outstretched glove and stay there. The game was over. I still have the seventh/eighth-grade Annual in which the headline reads: MELBER'S TEAM BEATS DEWHURST. It even mentions in the article the stunned astonishment on the face of the girl who caught the ball, as she had never done so before.

Years later, Joan Melber, who was by then Joan Warburg, caught up with me again when I was playing in *Children of Darkness* at the Circle in the Square in New York City's Greenwich Village. Since we last had seen each other on that ball field, Joan had married and now had four lovely children. The same energy with which she had played softball as a girl was now focused on adult concerns. She was active in the arts, serving on the boards of numerous foundations and not-for-profit organizations, and was very involved in national and local politics. We renewed a friendship that continues to this day. I enjoy seeing Joan for our occasional dinners because we can start right off telling truths and old stories that we wouldn't share with anyone else. Her children and mine have often commented that they would love to have a tape attached to the underside of one of these tables in order to hear what the "two old ladies" have to say.

JOAN MELBER WARBURG

Colleen and I go way back—to 1937, when she was in the seventh grade and I was in eighth at Roosevelt Junior High School in Yonkers, New York. This was the beginning of a beautiful and lasting friendship that I will always cherish. We were both involved in sports—baseball, soccer and basketball—and often on the way home from school, several of us played touch football in my yard. Much to her friends' dismay, Colleen moved to Wisconsin after the eighth grade.

In looking over our junior high school publication, *Panorama,* I see that Colleen was voted "cutest" in the seventh grade and "wittiest" the next year, in the eighth grade. There is also a headline: DEWHURST TEAM WINS KICKBALL TOURNAMENT. During the baseball season of 1938, *Panorama* reported "the way we backed up when Dewhurst comes to bat." She was also quoted as saying, "It is known that I can be serious at reasonable times." Wasn't this prophetic? Even then, in seventh and eighth grades, Colleen had a husky voice (so it was not, as some think, all due to smoking) and that wonderful hearty laugh and beautiful smile that everyone remembers.

On her infrequent trips back East during our teen years, she always looked me up. But we did eventually lose track of each other. It wasn't until 1958 that we caught up with each other again. My mother told me that she had read that Colleen was performing in the Village [Greenwich] in a play called *Children of Darkness.* Without getting in touch with her in advance, we went to see her in the show. I sent her a note backstage after the show. Seeing her after the performance was a wonderful and joyous reunion.

That was the first time that I had seen Colleen on a stage. It was a wonderful experience, but the truth is if she had changed her name, like so many actors did then, I'm not sure we would have ever known it was her. After that night, we once again made an effort to stay in touch. Colleen was living with George [C. Scott] then and whenever I would try to call her, after a little time had gone by, George would have changed their phone number. They lived on Fifty-seventh Street for a while, and then down in the Village before moving out of town to the Farm in South Salem, New York, north of New York City.

I first heard Colleen referred to as "mother earth" by my late husband, James Warburg. He and I always greatly enjoyed our evenings with Colleen in New York after a performance. Conversations often went far into the night and ended many times with scrambled eggs before any of us retired. After they moved from the city, we also spent many wonderful afternoons at their pool with Colleen, George, Alex, and Campbell, as well as memorable parties with innumerable guests at the Farm. My husband died in 1969. And at that time, there was nothing quite like an old friend, particularly such a warm, caring, and fun person as Colleen. Our visits became frequent dinners with just the two of us that always lasted for hours. We closed many a restaurant in Bedford and Pound Ridge. During these dinners, we caught up on each other's lives and innermost secrets. We rarely discussed show business, although inevitably someone would recognize Colleen and ask for an autograph, or the bartender would send over a round of drinks. But she was nonchalant about it and always very gracious. We would spend hours in very intimate talk about our lives. Colleen was always keenly interested in other people, but at the same time, she could tell long, long stories, many of which were classic.

I guess the two I recall immediately were the story of her son Alex's first wedding—the telling of which went on nearly as long as the event and ended, I think, with everyone getting thrown out of the hotel. The other was the tale of her receiving a phone call at the Farm from the producer of *Plaza Suite*, starring George Scott and Maureen Stapleton, while it was trying out in Boston before opening on Broadway. "For God's sake," the producer begged her, "will you come up here and sober these two up?" I guess they had missed two or three performances. So Colleen went up and somehow saved the day— the story of which was at least as funny as the show.

Colleen led a very different life from most of my friends, and as we grew older we developed a very special relationship. I used to kid her and say, "I'm the squarest person you know, Colleen . . . and I'm not all that square." I just adored her. She was my oldest friend.

ొ ొ ొ

In addition to my love of baseball, I was also playing tackle football with the local boys in the fields behind the house. One day when I came back from playing, looking like a wreck and covered with dirt, my mother casually walked past me and said, "Darling, don't you think it's time to stop playing tackle and start playing tag football?"

"Why?" I asked, looking up at her.

"Oh, no particular reason," she said, after staring at me for a minute. "I just feel that it is very rough." I'm sure that having caught a glimpse of me running up the field with three or four boys in quick pursuit had begun to make her tense. It could not have been more than a month later that she called upstairs and asked if I needed anything at the drugstore.

"Could you get me some Tangee lipstick?" I nervously asked, coming to the top of the stairs.

She looked up at me for a minute and I thought she was going to say no. Instead, she smiled and said, "Yes, I'll pick that up for you." I'm sure she drove to the drugstore thinking, *Tackle football must be just about over.*

After having attended numerous parties at my friends' homes, I asked my mother if I could give one. She said yes, and after we had sent out the invitations, we began to discuss what we would have to eat and what games we would play. When talking about one or two games that we played at the other parties, I mentioned "spin the bottle."

"Absolutely not," she said. Once my mother made such a statement, there was no way back. At age thirteen, I wasn't old enough to realize this yet. I cried. I pleaded. I said I would be embarrassed in front of all my friends if we didn't play at least one kissing game. My mother knew that I had played "spin the bottle" and "post office" at other parties (I don't think she had any idea about "flashlight"), but that did not, in any way, influence her. "*We* are giving this party," she said, "and we don't have to give the same party as everyone else. I assure you that you will have a wonderful time."

For the next week, leading up to the party, I continued to rant and rave, and she continued to calmly describe to me what the evening would be.

"Those are kids' games!" I remember screaming at her.

"And that's exactly what we're giving," was her reply, "a party for kids."

No matter how I tried to change it, the evening arrived as my mother planned. I remember my friends coming to the door, the girls in pretty dresses and the boys in suits and ties. From the beginning, my mother was always in evidence but not obtrusive. She was fun and got on with all my friends. Nevertheless, I was certain the evening would be a disaster, but as she moved us from game to game, such as "roll the potato" and the "three-legged race"—all games that in a way put girls and boys together, bumping into each other or tied to each other in some fashion—all of us, in spite of ourselves, were having a good time.

There were fun prizes she had purchased for every game and she managed to see that everyone received something. At the end of the evening, as parents or older brothers arrived to take the kids home, she gave everyone pins, and the last prize went to the one who burst the most balloons that had been taped around the house.

When everyone had gone, I went upstairs and took my bath. When I was in bed, my mother came into my room.

"It was a wonderful party," I told her.

"Did you have a good time?"

"Yes, I did." She smiled and asked me about a certain boy in the group. I could feel myself turn red. She laughed but, as she did for years, she could always tell, in any group of boys, the one I was interested in.

I realize now that the most incredible thing she did was that when we had discussed the kissing games she never, in saying "no" to me, implied in any way that she thought that there was anything dirty or wrong about me having played those games in other houses. She knew that I did because I had told her so. It was simply that in her home, she would give a different party.

2

"You are not to drive anyone's car."

During those years of my early childhood, my parents and I took the traditional two-week family vacation every summer. It was always the same story. The morning we were to leave, my father would complain about how slow we were. He always drove, my mother beside him. I would be in the backseat. Our final stop, every summer, was Ottawa, Canada.

The first week of these vacations, my father always rented a cottage for us in Vermont or New Hampshire, along the Saint Lawrence River. My dad was a great driver and thought of nothing but how fast he could make it to our destination. Only a gas station was an acceptable stop, and at each one, I was confronted with the same question: "Do you have to use the ladies' room?" My answer was always the same: "No." Then I would wait until we had driven another five or ten miles and announce that I had "to go." My father would drive on for another two miles before speaking to me from the front seat. "Didn't I ask you back there? Now there's no place to stop." My mother would finally interrupt.

"Fred," she'd say, "there's no reason to get upset. Just pull up here on the side of the road."

I would tramp through the grass and weeds five to ten feet, and race back out to the car in record time. I realize now that I saw more of nature during those quick visits to the woods than any other time, particularly once when I spotted a porcupine who had two babies with her. The four of us remained perfectly still. "There's a porcupine back here with two babies," I called out to the car.

I heard my mother get out of the car and slowly come toward me in the woods.

"Don't move, Biddy," she said quietly. When she got to where she could see the four of us—me and the porcupine family—she said, "Darling, move as fast as you can toward me and away from the porcupine." I had heard all the tales of how they could shoot their quills at you. But I hadn't thought of that then. They just seemed kind of cute.

I sat in the backseat during these trips and tried to amuse myself, counting cows and reading the Burma Shave signs. I also developed a strange attachment to anything that I had with me in the backseat—candy bar and chewing gum wrappers, magazines, everything. In those days, no one was concerned, as we are today, about throwing things out the window of the car and onto the highway.

"Biddy, what is all that scrunched up in the corner? Just throw it out." It made me feel sad to think about throwing out all that I had collected during our hours on the road. But I knew I couldn't explain to her that somehow they had become like my friends in the backseat. It almost seemed cruel. Rather than try to explain, I'd let these stray pieces of paper fly out the window and disappear behind us down the road. Perhaps these kinds of attachments happen when you're an only child.

I loved when we arrived at our rented cottage. It was a different one every year, but they always seemed basically the same. Our cabin would be on a lake in the middle of pine forests. Usually the porch was screened in. When we first opened the door, we were hit with the musty smell of the lake and the rain. My mother and I would quickly open all the windows, while telling each other how wonderful this cabin was because it was so much bigger or better than last year's.

While we were doing this, my father would immediately begin to wash and wax the car. Mother would go for a walk. Left on my own, I'd take off my shoes and go to the water, waiting and praying for her to come back quickly and say it would be all right to go swimming.

Whenever our cottage was along the Canadian side of the Saint Lawrence, I never had to plead with my mother to go swimming. The water was deep and dangerous, but no matter what hour we arrived, she would go directly into her room, put on a bathing suit and robe, and emerge carrying a white bathing cap.

"Are you ready, Biddy?" she'd call.

"I'm ready."

Down at the water, I was always stunned when she would drop her robe because I rarely saw my mother except fully dressed. She'd then put the cap on and dive headfirst into the water. Thinking back, I realize this was one time when I could see my mother as she must have always been when she was young. She never swam with me. Instead, she would swim way out toward the middle. From the shallow water, I could see her diving in and coming up. I'd swim toward her, and once I caught up with her, we'd paddle around each other and laugh, just, I think, from the joy of being in the water.

I don't remember ever actually talking with Mother while treading water together, as people often do. It seemed out of place. But thinking back on those moments, it seemed she had a freedom from her body, from her husband, and even from me that was not to be violated. In those moments in the water, she seemed to possess a joy that she never had anywhere else.

On our return to the States, my dad would refuse to stop for anything until we arrived back home. Mother would always stay awake with him, driving through the night. Often they would sing. Half asleep in the backseat, I would hear "Shine on Harvest Moon," "Me and My Shadow," and "Just a Gigolo," and I would feel safe. How could I feel safer?

My father lost his job again in the spring of my eighth-grade year. I could hear them from my room at night. My mother's voice was always quiet and comforting. I could hear my father crying and in despair. In the weeks that followed, she would again be typing his résumés, going over the applications, and returning phone calls. But it was soon to be the end of the three of us.

As weeks passed without my father finding a job, it became evident that all was not well between my parents. In the summer between eighth and ninth grades, we moved to Milwaukee, where my father finally found a job. Nevertheless, the end of my freshman year of high school, my mother did what she had always wanted to do since before I was born: She left my father.

My father's absence did not change my gypsy-like schooling. I spent my first two years of high school in Whitefish Bay, Wisconsin, and then went to Shorewood High for my junior year. Shorewood was, of course, the sworn enemy of Whitefish Bay High School. At the end of my junior year, my mother found an apartment she really liked in Riverside. So I went to Riverside High School, which was, as you might expect, the sworn enemy of Shorewood. This was absolute agony. Each time I entered the scene, all the girls had their cliques and groups of friends already set since grade school.

Nevertheless, I was very happy at Whitefish Bay when, as a freshman, Jack, the senior-class president, asked me to the junior prom which helped, in some way, to raise my status from new girl to being part of the "in" crowd.

The night of the prom, I wore a dress that my mother had picked out which, of course, was different from all the other girls' dresses. Mine was very simple, sheath-like with swirls of deep purple over a beige background. Everyone else was dressed in outfits that made them look like bridesmaids at a wedding. I was very happy, however, because the colors of my dress did guarantee me an orchid corsage.

When we arrived I found out, to my surprise, that as Jack's date, I was to be part of the "Prom Court." The Junior Prom Queen and her court, of which I was now a member, were escorted to the top of a staircase at the entrance to the school. There we stood, waiting at the top of the staircase with our dates waiting for us below. What I didn't know at the time was that our dates had been asked to pick out a song for the band to play as each of us came down the stairs. We'd be met by our escorts, who would then dance us onto the floor.

I was second-to-last to descend, just before the Prom Queen. I listened as the girls before me entered. Their gentlemen had picked such tunes as "Lovely to Look At" or "Oh, What a Beautiful Baby" to be played with their entrance. As I was given the signal to start down the staircase, the band struck up something I didn't quite recognize. It took me four or five steps to realize that for my entrance Jack had chosen "Charming Scatterbrain." The parents were seated along the balcony, behind a netting, and had applauded each couple as they whirled onto the floor. Jack and I spun out amid gales of laughter.

The dean of women at Whitefish Bay High School had taken a strong and immediate dislike to me. This situation came to a head in my sophomore year when I was with a group of close friends in the ladies' room. Four of them were smoking. I was not. Suddenly, a teacher entered the room. The girls quickly dumped their cigarettes in the johns, and we ran past her into the hall. An hour later, I was called into the dean's office. She told me that this teacher had reported that there were five girls smoking in the ladies' room—but that she had only recognized one of the smokers. Me. She asked me if I was smoking. I told her truthfully that I was not. She then asked me to name the four girls I was with.

"I can't do that," I answered.

"Let me inform you," the dean went on, "that you will stay one extra hour in my office after school for the next four days. One hour for each girl. However," she added, "I will remove an hour for each name that you can bring yourself to remember."

She then called my mother.

When I got home, Mother told me that she had an appointment the next day to speak with the dean about what had occurred.

"Were you smoking?" she asked.

"No, I was not," I replied.

The next day after school, I went to the dean's office and sat for an hour, which I did again for the next three afternoons. When I got home at the end of the first day, my mother had already been to see the dean.

"Could the teacher who reported you have recognized the other girls?" she asked.

"At least two of them," I replied.

"I am not fond of this dean," my mother said very coolly. "And I believe that if you say you were not smoking, you were not smoking."

She continued, saying that, in their meeting, the dean had commented on the way I dressed. That visibly disturbed me.

"You dress very well, honey," Mother said. "Your clothes are simply different from what the other girls pick to wear."

She went on to tell me that she ended the conversation with the dean by telling her that she was very proud of her daughter and that she would not ask me to report the names of the other girls. She felt the dean may have had a problem with me because I was loud, but that I obviously also had a sense of morality that she could not understand.

"You would do me a great courtesy," my mother said in leaving that office, "by not passing your idea of what is right on to Colleen."

I was received very coolly by the dean when I went in for my second day of detention. What upset me the most was that, on each day, the four girls who had been smoking and with whom I'd run past the teacher, stuck their heads into the office where I was sitting out the hour and waved. But never did any of them volunteer to take her own hour.

This incident at school was quickly followed by two other scrapes, each a little worse than the one before.

One evening that winter, a small group of us, including two of the girls who had been involved in the girls'-room incident, were walking home during a snowstorm, kidding around and throwing snowballs at each other. The streets of Whitefish Bay at that time were lined with lovely colonial-looking streetlights. Before long, we began to throw snowballs at them. From my years on the ball field, I had a much better arm than the rest of the crowd. Each time we'd hit one, we'd all run laughing for about a block and begin again. I don't remember exactly how many streetlights we managed to break, but, as I recall, I led with the greatest number of hits. Finally we reached the corner, where we all split and went to our own homes. About an hour later, one of my friends called to warn me that the police had come by her house to question her about the broken streetlights, and that they were trying to find out who was involved.

Our doorbell rang about an hour later. My mother opened the door and discovered the police. After they had spoken alone for a minute or two, she called me into the living room. The officer explained to me that he had spoken to my friends—and he named each one of the girls that I had been with—and that they had all agreed that I had broken all the streetlights. (So much for having a good arm.) Even my mother, who was sitting there in silence, realized that, while this could be true, all of us had taken part. Nevertheless, this incident ended with my mother having to pay the city for all the broken lamps.

Probably the reason I remember both these incidents so well is that in each case, I was involved with close friends who, for reasons that I don't understand to this day, would not take even partial responsibility. What I am also aware of now is that my mother, in both incidents, never suggested that I act in any way other than as I did.

Two or three weeks later, I had said good-bye to my mother at the trolley stop in Whitefish Bay before she went to Milwaukee to do some shopping. The last thing she said to me as she got on the trolley was, "You are not to drive anyone's car." Since I confided everything, I had told her that for the last year I had been trying to get my boyfriends to teach me to drive. "No, no," I replied. "I won't try to drive."

On my way back, I stopped by a girlfriend's home and we started back to my house. As we walked, a car pulled up beside us. There were two boys we knew in the front seat. The driver was a boy named Hans, whose father owned a bakery. He was driving with a learner's permit. His friend was a senior who had a driver's license. They asked if we wanted a ride to my house.

"Only if I can drive," I replied without a moment's hesitation. Hans moved over as I climbed into the driver's seat. His friend moved into the backseat with Edith. We drove a block or two before I made a right turn and lost control of the car, running over the sidewalk and into the yard of a house, hitting a tree.

I remember Edith in the backseat crying, "Oh, Dewy, you've really done it now!"

Perhaps I should mention here that this was Hans' father's brand-new car.

No one was hurt, although I did have a little trouble with my ankle as I tried to get out of the car. I kept apologizing to Hans, who only wanted me and Edith to leave so that he could report that an accident had occurred while a licensed driver was at the wheel. Edith and I went to our separate houses. When my mother came home, I was lying in the den. As she opened the front door I called out, "I was driving someone's car and I hit a tree."

My mother walked past me without speaking. Ten minutes later, she reentered.

"Have you been hurt?" she asked.

"I think something is wrong with my ankle," I answered, and told her what had happened. She immediately went to the phone and called Hans' father. About half an hour later, the doorbell rang and my mother escorted a police officer into the den where I still lay on the couch. He questioned me about what had happened, and I told him the entire story.

As my mother showed him out, she thanked him for coming.

"I think something is wrong with her ankle," he said.

"I'm aware of that," Mother replied.

I was out of school for about a week with a bad ankle. When I returned, I was met by the wiseguys with the greeting, "Look who's here. 'Crash' Dewhurst is back." And I lived with that name until I moved again at the end of the year.

My father had been gone for over a year when my mother and I moved to Shorewood, one town south of Whitefish Bay and a little closer to downtown Milwaukee. I hated having to move. I had already changed schools so many times and now, after having established myself—for better or worse—at Whitefish, I was to begin my junior year at rival Shorewood High. Nevertheless, I continued to contact my friends at Whitefish and always sat with Whitefish whenever the two schools played each other in football or basketball.

I remember that year as only one long blur of feeling out of place and like an outsider. Nevertheless, years later when I was shooting *And Baby Makes Six* in San Francisco, I was approached by a gentleman and his wife who said that they were very excited to meet me as they were planning the thirtieth reunion of what would have been my class of Shorewood High School, and had been trying to reach me. It seems there are now two "celebrities" from that class of Shorewood High—myself and Supreme Court Chief Justice William Rehnquist. I do not recall young Billy, and am sure that he does not remember young Colleen.

At the end of my junior year at Shorewood, my mother and I moved to 1742 Prospect Avenue, which managed to transfer me to Riverside High School for my senior year. Riverside High played both Whitefish Bay and Shorewood. Although this left me rather unsure of just where I should sit at basketball and football games, I made many good friends at Riverside.

My rather disjointed high-school career left me one English credit short for graduation. I had taken every possible English class offered by Riverside, with one exception. So in my final semester I took, for the first time anywhere, speech. All my old shyness took hold of me with the prospect of having to speak before a class. I was still a terrible blusher. And although I was always a class clown and rather loud, I could not speak alone in front of people. I was certain I would hate it. For the final exam, each of us was required to present a monologue before the class. For some reason I cannot remember, I chose a speech from *Dulcy*, which had been played on the stage by Billie Burke. Perfect casting. After my presentation and to my astonishment, the speech teacher entered me as "Dulcy" in a statewide competition, which I did not win or even come close to winning. The entire event is a blur of horror. Nevertheless, this same teacher went on to cast me as Olivia in the school production of Shakespeare's *Twelfth Night*. The only thing I can remember about it is that I did have them falling in the aisles when Olivia counts the ways of her beauty and is supposed to lift her veil. Unfortunately, my veil got hooked on something and could not be lifted. I tried with increasing frustration to rip this veil up and off, as I continued to itemize my beauty. But I was never able to get the veil past my chin. The audience broke up and would not stop laughing until I finally left the stage. This one moment is all I can remember from what, I guess, must be acknowledged as the first time I ever appeared in a play. And as far as I was concerned, at that time, it would be the last.

3

"What it means, Colleen, is that you've just been kicked out of school."

My mother sacrificed a great deal to see that I could go to college, although I was not fully conscious of it at the time. It was not so much that she felt it was important for me to receive an education, but that I come to realize, as she had, that life was about learning. Therefore, it was not important to her what curriculum I studied in college or where I studied it. I understand now that what mattered to her was my taking the next step to finding out more about myself and what it was I wished to reach for and do as an adult. So sometime in my senior year of high school, and about the time I began to think seriously about going to college, Mother asked me what I wanted to do with my life.

"I want to be an aviatrix," I replied without hesitation. This was during a period when I was reading a great deal about Amelia Earhart and Anne Morrow Lindbergh and, with the outset of World War II, of women such as Jacqueline Cochran, who were flying the large transport planes full of supplies from the United States into England.

"That's very interesting," Mother replied with her usual aplomb. "But I would strongly suggest that you go to at least two years of college first. If, after that, this is still your goal, we will look into what you must do to become an aviatrix." Simple.

During my senior year at Riverside High and during the time I considered myself to be the next Amelia Earhart, I had been selected—and to this day I cannot understand why—to compete for an English scholarship at Lawrence College in Appleton, Wisconsin. I didn't care about the exams, but everything about being on a college campus unchaperoned appealed to me, and if it meant competing for a scholarship to do so, I thought, *Why not?*

I arrived at Lawrence on the weekend of the tests with a boy named Tom, also from Riverside, who had a very good friend at Lawrence who was a member of a fraternity. Our first night on campus, Tom asked me if I would like to go with him to a fraternity party. I was delighted. The rest of the evening proved to be the realization of all I wished college life to be. You could enter this party only by sliding down a coal chute into the basement of the fraternity house. Tom and I danced for the entire evening and, before the night was over, our song had become "Moonlight Cocktail." I was thrilled, and suddenly my mother's idea that I go to college made good sense. The air transports would have to wait. I continued to see Tom for a while upon our return to Riverside High and, although neither of us ultimately received the English scholarship, I was so impressed by the frat party that I decided to apply to Lawrence for regular admission.

Years later, when I was trying out the play *An Almost Perfect Person* in Arlington, Illinois, the producer, Wally Perner, told me that there was a gentleman waiting outside to see me, who said that he had gone to school with me at Riverside. When he came toward me, I knew immediately that it was Tom. He told me that just prior to reading of my arrival in town he had heard "Moonlight Cocktail" over the radio, and hearing it had given him the courage to come over to the theater to see me. Over the next few weeks that I was in town with the play, we had a lot of laughs—the best of which was the evening we spent singing our infamous rendition of "Moonlight Cocktail"—"a couple of jiggers of moonlight and there you are"—over dinner.

In spite of my frat-house debut and without any hope of an English scholarship, I was accepted at Lawrence College for regular admission in the spring. After graduation from Riverside High, I spent the summer months getting ready to leave for Lawrence. During that time, girls from a number of different sororities on campus came by to look me over subtly in order to get an idea if I was acceptable for their particular sorority. Lawrence had a somewhat "high-toned" reputation, and it was very important for a girl to be accepted into the "right" sorority if she hoped to have an active social, as well as academic, life.

I came home about ten days before I was to leave for Lawrence, to find my mother in her usual chair in the living room, waiting for me. She asked me to sit down.

"I'm very sorry to tell you that about an hour ago I received a call from your father," she said very quietly and directly. "He says that he is unable to come up with his half of your tuition for Lawrence."

I sat across from her, dumbfounded. I couldn't consider the ramification of what was being said to me and, for once, had absolutely no reply.

"I'm so sorry, Biddy," she whispered, still using the name she had called me as a child. "I know this is a terrible blow to you. But there is no way that I can think of for me to make up your father's half."

I didn't speak. I couldn't believe that now, after looking forward to it for months and after all the preparation, I wouldn't be going to Lawrence. I realize now that up until that moment, I had always believed that anything was possible for my mother. She could do anything she set her mind to. I had even told myself that if my father did not come through, of course, she could get me to Lawrence on her own. But now she had just said she could not. We sat without speaking for what seemed like an eternity.

"I know how you looked forward to this," she finally said, breaking the silence. "But," she added, "while I was waiting for you, I decided to call Milwaukee Downer College to see if it was still possible for you to apply for admission there." I looked up at her for the first time since she broke the news.

That afternoon, Mother and I took the bus to Milwaukee Downer, where she had already made an appointment for me with the dean of women. The two of us entered the campus offices and, together, filled out the various forms and spoke with the director of admissions, who asked me what my overall high-school average had been.

"Oh, about eighty-five percent," I replied rather unenthusiastically. Milwaukee Downer was for "young ladies" and, for me, at that time, a definite step down. For if there was one place I did not wish to be it was at an all-girls' college. We left, and first thing the next morning, I received notice by phone that I had been admitted to Milwaukee Downer College for Women. But there was very little time for me to brood about what had happened. School began in two weeks.

On my first day, when I arrived at Milwaukee Downer, I noticed that there was a huge bulletin board near the entrance to campus. It listed, by class, the "honor roll" and the "probation list" for all to read. I guess they weren't fooling around here. Under "Freshman—Probation" was only one name: Colleen Dewhurst. It was a mystery to me how a freshman could enter school and on the first day, without having been to a class, already be on probation. But somehow, perhaps because I had registered so late, or due to my "unenthusiastic" 85 percent, I had managed it. Whichever, someone saw me coming.

I learned very quickly that at Milwaukee Downer, if you were on probation, you were not able to take part in any after-school activities, including sports. This was just the motivation I needed for the next three months to study as hard as I could, and in January, I moved from probation to the honor roll. And for the next two years, depending on my after-school schedule, I seesawed back and forth between the honor roll and probation, as needed, working just enough to ensure that I could continue to play baseball and field hockey.

Each year, Downer presented a spring show in which the four classes presented a skit in competition for a prize that was determined by vote of the entire faculty. I took it upon myself to write a skit for the freshman class about the twelve months of the year, casting twelve of my classmates as the months, one each for January through December. I decided, like most first-time writers, that I would best direct my work and, unlike most first-time writers, I did. After a few rehearsals, I realized that one of the months had been miscast. So, upon the suggestion of the other eleven months, I stepped in, since, after all, I had written the lines. My script was shameless and, I'm certain, truly dreadful. I played upon the heartstrings of the audience at this all-girls' college in the worst way, insisting that as it was wartime, Miss July would sing a rousing and patriotic rendition of "Yankee Doodle Dandy" while bringing Miss December to tears with a sickening romantic poem about missing our servicemen across the ocean, particularly on snowy evenings. In spite of my script and our initial setbacks in casting, we won first prize—the first time the freshman class had ever done so.

Flush with success, I went home that night and informed my mother that I had changed my mind. I no longer wanted to be an aviatrix; I wanted to be an actress. No matter that I had never before shown any interest at all in performing or in even attending the theater. One show, one award, and I was certain that I was destined for the stage.

I've never forgotten my mother's response to this ebullient news.

"I'll have to see you do something," she said calmly. "I love excellence in the arts and I don't mind what is terrible. But what I fear the most is mediocrity. It fools and misleads too many people."

As I was not a member of the drama club, I didn't know what I could possibly do or show her. I remembered, however, that a friend of mine, Sue Esser, was directing some scenes about the wonders of science for presentation at chapel. I went to Sue and begged her to let me play the part of the mother who comes to plead with Dr. Pasteur to give the rabies shot to her son. Sue was completely confused as she, too, had never known me to display any interest in the theater or the drama club. But I cajoled and pleaded with her until she agreed to give me the part.

Once I was cast, however, I found it too embarrassing to rehearse. As I recall, I had to enter the stage and beg the student playing Dr. Pasteur in a crepe beard to save my son's life, finally flinging myself at his feet. Somehow, I learned my lines and blocking. The night of performance, my mother appeared at chapel. From that point I must have been in an absolute state of terror, as I can remember very little of the show or, for that matter, the entire evening.

The next morning, Mother told me that she had seen an ad in a magazine for the American Academy of Dramatic Arts. As neither of us knew anything about schools for actors or where you began—and the Academy had, as they still do today, listed an illustrious group of graduates in their ad—Mother called and made an appointment. An audition was arranged for the coming September that, if I was accepted, would have me entering the Academy in what would have been my junior year at Milwaukee Downer.

Very soon after my declaration, Mother surprised me with tickets for two

plays in Chicago: a Saturday matinee and an evening performance. I was to
have the treat of going down with her to see the plays and staying overnight in
the Drake Hotel. We took the train to Chicago on Saturday morning and went
to the matinee of a three-person hit comedy, the title of which I cannot for the
life of me remember. We had dinner and then went to an unknown play trying
out in Chicago called *The Glass Menagerie* by a then-unknown playwright,
Tennessee Williams, and starring Laurette Taylor. I remember the two of us
sitting in the theater, going outside at intermission, and returning to our seats
without saying a word. When we went back to the hotel, we still said very little about what we had seen. But the next morning, on the train going back to
Milwaukee, there was no way to shut me up. I wanted to reexamine and relive
what I had seen all over again. Never had I been able to enter other people's
lives and a home that I didn't know and be so moved. I had no idea then that
not only was I seeing the work of one of the great American playwrights, but
also one of the final performances of one of the great creative artists of the
American theater, Laurette Taylor. I only knew that I could not forget what I
had seen on that stage. I understand now that I had experienced what every
playwright, director, and actor wants an audience to experience. I lived and
breathed with those characters. I had shared emotionally a complete lifetime
with them all. A lifetime that would now always be a part of mine.

ONCE HAVING settled that acting was what I wished to do with my life, I did
not bother, throughout my sophomore year, to put much time into my studies.
I came home one day in June, after school had recessed for the summer, to
Mother telling me that she had something to read to me. By this time, I knew
that whenever my mother asked me to sit down because she wished to speak—
or worse, to read to me—that I was in dangerous territory. She held in her
hand a letter from Lucia R. Briggs, president of Milwaukee Downer. Miss
Briggs wrote that she understood that my mother was sending me to New York
in the fall to study at the American Academy of Dramatic Arts. Enclosed with
Miss Briggs' letter were my marks for the last semester. I had managed to
receive an *A* in creative writing, a *C* and two *D*'s in subjects I can't remember,
and an *F* in chemistry. Miss Briggs went on in her note to say what my IQ
was—which in those days was never revealed and which my mother did not
repeat—as proof that I had not worked up to my potential at all. This, she
wrote, was further proven by the fact that I appeared on the honor roll whenever it suited me—usually in the spring and fall, as those semesters were field
hockey and baseball seasons. Going on, she was of the opinion that I thought
that life was a great joke and consequently spent most of my time laughing my
way through it. She signed off by saying that it was now her suggestion that I
go to work for a year, learn how much an education costs, and how far you
could go with just two years of a liberal arts degree. Her last line was brief and

to the point: "With the knowledge that Colleen is leaving Milwaukee Downer for the American Academy at some time in the future, she is, at this time, officially asked to leave as of now. Sincerely, Lucia R. Briggs."

"What does that mean?" I asked my mother.

"What it means, Colleen, is that you've just been kicked out of school," was her equally brief reply.

MANY YEARS LATER, I received another letter, this time from Lawrence University, which, by that time, had merged with Milwaukee Downer. This letter informed me that I was to be awarded a doctorate in the arts. So I dragged my two sons, who were then about seven and eight, out to Appleton, Wisconsin, to see their mother receive an honorary degree from an institution at which she had only attended one fraternity party. I could only hope that somewhere, somehow, my mother was aware of it all.

I arrived at Lawrence the day before the graduation ceremonies. There I attended a reception for the honorees, where one of my former classmates told me that I had been submitted by the Milwaukee Downer alumni for this honorary doctorate. She went on to say—with cocktail in hand and staring straight into my eyes—that the alumni committee had received a "yes," but a month later had been told by the president's secretary that they couldn't understand why they were having difficulty "finding Miss Dewhurst's records."

"But," she concluded, "we had no further contact with the president's office, and now here you are."

The next day, I donned cap and gown and marched with the graduates and other honored guests to the stadium to receive our degrees. I listened as several men and women, from all over the world, were given doctorates in medicine, science, and literature. Each had a long and impressive list of academic credits and accomplishments. When I rose to receive my diploma, the president made very strong eye contact with me in a way that he had not made with the others, before beginning to read the following:

"Miss Colleen Dewhurst attended Milwaukee Downer College for . . . some time," he read, making no further mention of my academic background and moving immediately to various plays that I had done. I can only assume that my real academic records were never found (or perhaps they were) and that somewhere Lucia R. Briggs was spinning in her grave.

Since that time, I have received seven doctorates, each of which means a great deal to me, but none can ever have the same meaning as this, the first, presented to me by the one school that many years before I had hoped would be my alma mater.

IT TOOK A MOMENT, but as the reality of Miss Briggs' dismissal finally sank in, I could only respond with my own dismissal of her suggestion. "Funny old

Lucia Briggs, what a character," I said over my shoulder, as I got up to get a Coke from the refrigerator.

"Maybe funny old Lucia Briggs," my mother replied, raising her voice just enough to ensure that I could hear her in the next room, "but we are going to do exactly what she suggests." I stood frozen in my tracks at the refrigerator—and not from the cold. "You will get a job," Mother continued, "and work for a year. I will call the Academy and say that we wish your entry there to be a year from this coming fall."

For the next hour, I cajoled, screamed, and pleaded—but to no avail. I knew that it was pointless to continue, because once my mother had determined any course of action there was no turning back.

That summer, per Miss Briggs' suggestion, I got a job in a department store selling sports clothes. After I'd been there for a week, I returned home one night at six o'clock.

"How was your day?" Mother asked.

"Fine."

"Did you sell much?" she continued.

"Oh, not much," I replied. "A sweater here and a jacket there."

"Was it a long day, honey?"

"Yeah, but it was OK."

Mother then handed me a box of my favorite candy as a gift for my first week at work.

"I was so proud of you going out and getting a job and not complaining once you'd gotten adjusted to the idea that you had to work," she said. "So I took the bus and went downtown today, thinking I could take you to lunch on your lunch hour."

I stared at her as she continued.

"When I arrived, they told me that you had not arrived Thursday morning, nor had you arrived this morning. You had not been fired, they said. You simply hadn't appeared."

She paused.

"Where have you been going for the last two days?"

"To the public library," I said. "I was going to go to work, but when the bus came to my stop I just couldn't get off. I went another five stops to the library, got off and went in there. I've read a lot of strange and interesting things since then. I was going to tell you," I continued, "but I just couldn't."

There was a long pause. Then she started to laugh. And I laughed and it was over. There was no further discussion of my returning to my job selling sportswear. But it was not over in terms of my getting another job.

I could not bear the idea of working in Milwaukee while my friends continued at Milwaukee Downer. I didn't know what to do. So I called Christine Pacelli, a friend of mine who lived in Gary, Indiana. I asked Chrissy if I could come down and share an apartment with her while I looked for a job, and after hearing my sad tale of woe she agreed, making me probably one of the few people in the world who ever escaped *to* Gary, Indiana.

When I arrived in Gary and started looking for work, I discovered, much to my dismay, that "funny old Lucia" was quite right. Two years of liberal arts and first string on the field hockey team didn't qualify me for much. I didn't know how to type; I had never bothered taking it in school because I didn't want to be trapped in a typist's job. I couldn't take shorthand, and I couldn't run a switchboard. I had no practical skills.

But it was wartime and everyone was talking about how much money girls could make working in defense plants. *OK*, I thought to myself, *that'll show them both* (meaning Lucia and my mother). *I'll be a welder.*

So I had my first interview with a gentleman in a defense plant. He was very interested and all was going well until we got to "place of birth—Montreal, Canada." I was carrying an alien registration card which every noncitizen was required to get during wartime. He explained to me, quite courteously, that it was against the law to hire an alien in a defense plant. I was furious, both to be called an alien and not to be able to "show them," and left the office in a huff.

"We're good enough to fight with but not to work with," I said, as I got up to go. The interviewer just shrugged his shoulders, unimpressed.

I finally got a job running an elevator in the Model Building, which had only six floors. After I had been there about two weeks, my mother came down from Milwaukee to visit Chrissy and me and to see how my job was going. I can remember opening the door and Mother getting on that elevator. She was a very beautiful and distinguished-looking woman. She stepped on as a crowd pressed in behind her, and began to call out their floors. We went up to the sixth floor, dropping off people along the way before proceeding back to the first floor, picking up people on the way down. When everyone had gotten off on the first floor and the car was empty, my mother starting laughing very hard.

I was quite annoyed and said, rather sharply, "What is so funny?"

"Darling," she said, "you have not managed to hit one floor all the way up or down." As people began to get on the elevator, she broke up all over again as she stepped off.

Fine, I thought. *That'll do it. She'll have me out of here by tomorrow.*

"I'll see you this evening for dinner," I heard her say as the elevator filled with people. "I'm very, very proud of you, my dear." And as the door shut, I knew that I was going to stay right where I was, up and down, up and down, six flights of floors, eight hours a day for the foreseeable future.

About two weeks later, I had a toothache that caused the right side of my face to swell out horribly. The Model Building was filled with dentists, and one of them, a Dr. Schmidt, got on to go up to the sixth floor as he had every day since I'd been there. This time, however, he spoke to me.

"What is the matter with your mouth?"

"I have a toothache," I answered.

"Why don't you come in and let me take a look at it."

"Do you give gas?" I asked, not realizing quite what I had said.

"No," he replied, "I do not. But let me take a look at it anyway."

When I was through at five o'clock, I went to Dr. Schmidt's office, where he tried to talk me into taking a shot of novocaine and having the bad tooth extracted right there. I had been afraid of dentists since I was a child and told him, no, I couldn't do that. So he gave me the name of another dentist. I went to see him the next morning, and he extracted the tooth with gas.

When Dr. Schmidt came into the elevator that afternoon, he asked me if I would come up to see him after work, which I did.

"What are you doing running an elevator?" he said as soon as I walked in.

"I'm working to earn money to go to school."

"I need a receptionist," he said. "I've been working without one for a month."

"I don't type or take shorthand," I replied, but he assured me those skills wouldn't be necessary.

"The main thing," he continued, "is that you sterilize the instruments each morning, make appointments, and get the money from the patients before they leave the office."

That didn't sound too difficult, but I explained that I could never assist him at the chair—not having any idea that, in fact, people went to school to do just that—and that the door would have to be closed anytime he was drilling, as I couldn't bear the sound.

Even with my few qualifications and many reservations, I was hired. By the time I arrived the next morning, Dr. Schmidt had already spoken to the building manager, and I rode the elevator, driven by someone else, to begin work as a dental assistant. Today, this strikes me as the most bizarre job I have ever had. I had no problem making appointments or sterilizing the instruments. I did have a problem, however, getting payment from the patients. If I said, in my best voice, "That'll be five dollars, Mrs. Whoozy," and Mrs. Whoozy said she didn't have it but would pay the following week, I always responded, "Oh. Of course, sure. That's fine," feeling as if I owed an apology for having asked.

Dr. Schmidt was willing to overlook this slight problem, as he was forever on the make, and billing was not always his highest priority. But, in his way, he was very good to me and we never had to enter into a really serious tussle in this office that was barely big enough for both of us and his patients.

When spring came, I began to call Dr. Schmidt about once a week to explain in a hoarse whisper that I was not feeling well and would not be able to come in that day. I would then don my bathing suit and run to the dunes behind the house where Chris and I lived on Lake Michigan. I loved living on the lake. It was like being at home. One day as I was lying there sunning, a shadow came over my face. I opened my eyes to see Dr. Schmidt looking down at me.

"I'll be waiting in the car to drive you to the office," he said. I never skipped work for swimming again.

THERE WAS A small bar and restaurant about a block from our house. It was very cozy. Chris and I would go there occasionally for dinner or just to have a drink in the evening. Everyone in the place knew one another by sight, and we'd nod and say hello. One night while we were there I was introduced to a handsome young man named Bob, who had been discharged from the army. He was very attractive and fun to be with, and over a short period of time, we fell in love. It was wonderful for me, in the isolation of Gary, Indiana, and my job, to meet someone with whom I enjoyed spending so much time. His family lived nearby in Miller and they were all, particularly his father, wonderful and warm to me.

After about three months, Bob told me that he wanted to get married, even though he knew that I would be going to school in New York in September. He never objected to my going away to school but he wanted us to be married before I left. I had told my mother about Bob and when she came from Milwaukee to meet him, she stayed in the one decent hotel there. I knew at once that we were in trouble when Bob arrived in the hotel dining room without wearing a jacket or tie.

Although Bob was eligible to go to school under the GI Bill, he did not wish to do so. He was also not a man given to social chitchat, and I can only presume that my mother was a very forbidding figure to him. Dinner was relatively uneventful. After Bob left, Mother said that she liked him, but found it appalling that he would not take advantage of the opportunity he had to go to college. She was also afraid that, since he was not interested in school, he would keep me from continuing to study and doing what I really wanted to do with my life. But, all these reservations aside, the one thing she did not want was marriage before I left for New York.

Nevertheless, we were engaged.

I think Mother knew that once I reached New York and began school, everything would naturally fall into place, including a separation from Bob. My mother had always said that she would never interfere with two choices: first, what I wished to do with my life and second, with whom I wished to spend it. I believe that she kept that promise and never made a false move in either of those areas with this one exception. From conversations with Dr. Schmidt and Christine, Mother began to think that Bob and I were becoming closer than we should and that there was the chance that we would marry before I left for school.

Soon after Mother returned to Milwaukee, I received a telegram at work from her that said: "I want you to return home at once and not wait until the end of summer. If you choose to marry Bob at this time, I will not help in sending you to school in New York. Love, Mother."

I was furious and very angry with Dr. Schmidt and Chris when I realized that they had been in contact with my mother, passing along information about the nature of my relationship with Bob. Naturally, I felt that everyone was against me and treating me as a child. I called Bob. We drove around for hours, talking. I will never forget his goodness and understanding of the situation that night. He had been pressing me for months to marry him before I left and I had refused. Obviously, I instinctively knew that if our relationship would not hold while we were separated, no wedding vows could make it last.

But that evening, in the car, I announced, "I'll marry you. I'll marry you now." We spent the entire night like that—Bob explaining that he did not want to marry me while I was angry, and me becoming more and more incensed. He knew how much I loved my mother. But he had never been able to talk with her or even begin to have any kind of relationship with her. Mother was always courteous and pleasant, but it was obvious that for her, their relationship would go no further.

The next day, I told Dr. Schmidt that I had had it with all of them and that I was going to marry Bob as soon as possible. Obviously, this too was passed on to my mother. At about midnight, I called home and said that Bob and I were on our way to Milwaukee. Mother never asked anything. She simply said, "I'll be waiting for you."

When we arrived, Mother stood at the open door to her apartment, with a cup of tea in her hand, watching Bob and me coming down the long hallway toward her. As we got closer, I could see that the cup was shaking ever so slightly.

"Am I greeting the happy bride and groom?" she asked.

"No, Mother, you are not," I replied icily.

With that she turned and walked back into the apartment. Bob and I followed her inside. Mother sat in her winged high-backed chair, elbow on the arm, her free hand lightly grasping the armrest. She was wearing her green bathrobe but was otherwise completely girdled and hosed underneath. Her white hair was swept up, reminiscent of the Gibson era. There was no doubt that she was once again in command. But for the first time since he had met her, Bob was not intimidated.

"I want to reassure you that your daughter is still a virgin," Bob said before my mother could speak. In those days, such a thing held great importance and supposedly answered any further questions. But I never will forget the expression that passed my mother's face for just a second. In that one moment I realized that fact held absolutely no importance for her.

Mother laughed and said, "Well, Bob, I see you can talk."

"I know that I am not your choice as a husband for Colleen," he said, undaunted, "because you think it will interfere with her going to New York and pursuing a career." Although I continued to be the topic of their conversation, neither of them even looked at me. As I sat there quietly, it struck me that suddenly they were becoming allies. I would go to New York wearing the engagement ring. And, as I listened to them discussing the mechanics of my leaving, I was drained of all feeling for anything or anyone. I felt as if the two of them were reaching a decision about something that would greatly affect me without my participation at all. And this was exactly what was decided. I would go to New York, already engaged.

The next day, Bob and I returned to Gary. I packed my clothes and moved back to my mother's in Milwaukee. And two weeks later, I was on a plane to New York—wearing Bob's ring.

4

"The Prom King"

When I first came to New York to go to the American Academy of Dramatic Arts, it was located in Carnegie Hall. I had flown in with my mother from Milwaukee the year before to audition, during which I was to present a dramatic and comedic piece to one man who would decide, upon the basis of those five minutes, whether or not I was to be accepted.

I walked into a medium-size office, where a tall, rather dramatic-looking man sat behind his desk. He may have been fifty-five, but to me he seemed eighty. I stood in the middle of the room in front of him with absolutely no idea of what actors did to audition. I didn't know that you went to the library and prepared a piece from plays that you read and studied. I had not done any plays. I just knew that I wanted to be an actress. This seemed quite logical to me and to my mother, who probably just wanted me out of town.

I was scared to death as I proceeded into my dramatic piece which (I cannot to this day believe) I had written myself. I played a woman saying good-bye to her lover. As he goes out the door, she is casually laughing. Closing the door, she leans against it and proceeds to realize, very dramatically, that each and every piece of furniture is laughing at her. I had written dialogue with each chair. Finally, after exhausting herself talking to the furniture, she ends up in a heap on the floor, sobbing uncontrollably. The premise was that this was a woman who laughed her way through every experience, never facing that she was in any way affected by the great loss she had just suffered.

I was all of nineteen when I wrote and performed this material. What I should mention is that at that age, I had never had a lover. I was just a virgin who dated a great deal. But I certainly thought it would be wonderful to have a lover; instead, I just read a lot. Whatever I knew of those emotions came from books, although the talking to the furniture I invented myself.

I then did my comedy piece, of which I have no memory.

From this audition, I was accepted by the American Academy and felt quite pleased with myself. I discovered later that everyone who auditioned had been accepted. It didn't matter. I was still pleased. The program lasted two years. After the first year, I was invited to return for the second year of study. When I first arrived in New York, I stayed at the Barbizon, a residence for women at Sixty-third Street and Lexington Avenue. My mother had tried to get me into the Three Arts Club, then in the West Fifties, which had been made famous in the play *Stage Door,* but it was so well known that there was now a long waiting list. I'm sure that she felt the Barbizon would be the next-best thing, as no men were allowed above the first floor.

In those first few months at the Academy, Bob and I wrote back and forth. But before long, I wasn't writing as much, and soon, not at all. I handled all of it very badly and immaturely. I finally wrote him a "Dear John" letter in which I truthfully said that I realized that there was such a gap between us in terms of interests that I could not see any way to resolve it. I loved New York City and acting and knew that I would stay there forever.

Soon after, I met James Vickery. Jim and I had been in the same scene-study class. I thought he was one of the handsomest men I had ever seen. I maneuvered working on a scene with him that had to be rehearsed outside of class. Things proceeded very quickly and four or five months later, in June, Jim and I decided to marry. It was odd, but the day before I was to marry Jim, I received a lovely letter from Bob in which he told me that he knew now, once he had calmed down, that I was right. I loved his "P.S." which said: "Tell your mother that if she did nothing else for me I am going to college. That should make her happy."

Years after having received Bob's letter—when I was doing my one-woman show *And Sarah Laughed* in Naples, Florida, I received a note from Bob's sister, who lived in the area and who had always been very kind to me. It said that she and her husband were coming to the theater that evening, and went on to say how excited they all were to see me. She also told me that Bob, who now lived farther north with his wife and family, would be coming with them. I was delighted by the warmth of the letter, but at the same time was extremely nervous. I hadn't seen Bob since I left Milwaukee to go to New York and hadn't heard from him since reading his note the day before my marriage to Jim.

A very close friend of mine, Betty Chamberlain, who was in the class behind me at Riverside High School, was also in Naples at that time for a small reunion of some girls from that class. I told her that Bob would be there, and she seemed as excited as I was nervous. Before going to the theater that night, I called Bob's sister to tell her that I would love it if they would come backstage after the show.

I recognized Bob at once and came out to a very warm and loving welcome from them all. I was sorry that I was not staying another day so that I could visit with them. But I was particularly moved that Bob's father, who had been so kind to me, was still alive. As soon as I saw Bob, I had to admit that he looked wonderful. We shook hands in greeting as I was introduced to people I didn't know and made polite small talk. Bob and I just chatted for a second.

"How is your mother?" he asked.

"She died," I replied, "quite a while ago."

"I'm sorry," he said, and I felt that he truly was. Afterward, when I went back to see the group at the reunion, Betty let me know that she had also managed to get a good look at Bob.

"Hmmmm. . . ," she whispered to me as I sat down with the others, "still very attractive, dear."

BETTY CHAMBERLAIN

Colleen came to Milwaukee in her senior year of high school, and that's when I met her. For some reason, that very powerful mother of hers was always moving them from place to place. Mrs. Dewhurst was really a piece of work, devoted to her religion and to Colleen, but rather rigid in her beliefs. Once when I spent the night at Colleen's, we had been smoking in her bedroom when her mother, who detested our smoking cigarettes, knocked on the door. We hurriedly put them out, pitching the butts out the window and trying to get fresh air into the room. Mrs. Dewhurst knocked again. This time we opened the door. "What did you do?" she said, looking us both up and down. "Swallow them?" That was a typical Mrs. Dewhurst comment. I don't mean to be totally negative about Colleen's mother because she had quite a wonderful daughter, so she must have been doing something right.

Colleen was like the original hippie in high school. She cared not at all about what she wore, and that was when the rest of us thought it very important always to be in a pleated skirt and sweater. Her mother, of course, was perfectly attired and groomed beautifully, which was quite a contrast to her daughter. Colleen didn't give a damn, and she got away with it beautifully. Even then, as a very young woman, she had a very real presence. She had that booming voice, and I can remember wanting to hide as she laughed loudly on the bus or in the movies. She was very uninhibited.

Then we went on to Milwaukee Downer College together. After a short period of time, she left there and went to the American Academy in New York. The president of Milwaukee Downer thought it would be a swell idea if she left to go there. Nevertheless, Colleen had many, many friends in Milwaukee who cared about her and with whom she kept in touch over a period of years.

We both had been at Milwaukee Downer on V-J Day, when World War II ended with victory over Japan. So a bunch of us decided that we would go into the city, rent a hotel room and celebrate. Everybody was happy, screaming and yelling, and we thought this was just such fun and so sophisticated of us to be there. All of a sudden, Colleen got up. "I'm bored with Milwaukee," she said.

Right then, she got up and went by herself to get on a train to Chicago. She was certain it was going to be more fun there. My jaw dropped. I thought it was so adventuresome to be where I was. Not Colleen. She was just getting started. When she arrived back on campus days later, she never told us what she did. And at that time, it was probably just as well and certainly a portent of the distances her life would take her from the rest of us.

I remember Colleen came back to Milwaukee early in her career and was playing in stock somewhere. A few of us attended one of the performances but didn't go backstage because we were so intimidated. I don't think until her death did she ever stop talking about how disappointed she was that we hadn't come back. Over the years, she was very loyal to her friends here and had a memory of us all that was so specific. It was very touching.

A few more years went by, but at some point I went to visit her in New York. This was around the time when she was first living with George [C. Scott]. I recall she asked me if I thought it was an inappropriate thing for her to bear a child before marrying George. It was a very intense question and I'm sure that whatever I said had no bearing on what she did. But she did want to talk about it.

More time goes by and Colleen is in Lake Forest, Illinois, doing what was to be the first production of her successful revival of *A Moon for the Misbegotten*. She called and wanted to know if a few of us wanted to come down to see it. Well, we had a wonderful time and I invited her up to a cottage we had not far away, on Lake Michigan. She drove up by herself and spent a few of her days off there. Those days really gave us an opportunity to catch up.

The next time I heard from Colleen was when she was back in the Chicago area doing *An Almost Perfect Person* at the Arlington Park Theatre. This time, not only did she come up to the cabin, but she brought that whole crazy cast with her. Oh, God, I don't know who they all were, but I can still see George Hearn getting out of the car with some woman named Tasha, who arrived at our cabin in the middle of winter in the woods on Lake Michigan in a fox coat and high heels. It was quite a day, and we all had a very good time.

๏๏ ๏๏ ๏๏

My mother was not much happier about my marrying Jim than she had been about the prospect of my becoming engaged to Bob. But once the date was set, she made arrangements to come to New York some time before the wedding to meet Jim. On her arrival, Mother called my apartment and asked that Jim and I meet her for dinner in the lobby of her hotel, the Barclay. I thought it would be best to meet her before Jim arrived. So I asked him to arrive about half an hour after I did.

I felt a horrifying déjà vu as Mother and I were seated in this well-appointed dining room and, just moments later, I saw Jim being escorted by the maître d' to our table. He wasn't wearing a tie. My heart sank. But Mother did not fight with me about Jim. I think that by this time, she felt I was determined and ready to get married, so we might as well all get it over with.

Arrangements were made. Jim and I were to be married in the Church of the Ascension on East Twenty-ninth Street, better known as "The Little Church Around the Corner" and "The Actors' Church," because it was the first church at the turn of the century that welcomed actors. It is a beautiful church. It didn't matter to my mother in what denomination of Protestant church I was to be married, as long as she could make two changes in the ceremony to coincide with her own private religious beliefs. One, "till death shall ye part" was to be struck and replaced with "as long as ye both shall live"; two, "love, honor and obey" was simplified to read "love and honor." The minister, Father Ray, had no problem with these changes. For once, everything seemed to be going smoothly.

Then the week before the wedding, Father Ray fell and broke his leg. Another minister was brought in. This minister was not pleased with any changes in text but agreed to abide by what Father Ray had already approved. The next day, this new minister called my mother in Milwaukee to say that he was sorry to inform her that he would be unable to perform any ceremony until I was baptized, which, he added, he could do in the back of the church in a very few minutes just before the actual wedding ceremony. Mother told him that as far as she was concerned I had already been baptized in a "baptism of the spirit" and that she did not believe in nor would she permit another academic baptism simply to appease his wishes.

It became frighteningly clear that there was no way Jim and I were going to get through this ceremony in a simple or orthodox manner. The more we tried to conform to everyone's wishes, the more complicated it all became. When the minister realized that my mother would not yield and submit me to his baptism, he flatly refused to perform the wedding. Unyielding and undaunted, Mother assured me there was nothing to worry about. She had contacted yet another church across the street from "The Little Church Around the Corner" and determined that I could be married there without benefit of prior baptism in the vestibule. I could only assume that she also planned to put someone in front of the church stated on the wedding invitation and have that person point across the street to the church where the wedding would actually take place.

When she arrived in New York, two days later, she came directly to my room in the Barbizon Hotel and told me that Father Ray, who had broken his leg, had called the day before and apologized for all the trouble being caused by the second minister about my baptism. Father Ray had contacted yet a third minister, who had agreed to marry me in "The Little Church Around the Corner" without a last-minute baptism. Mother immediately canceled her alternative plan with the alternative church across the street. By this time, neither of us cared one way or the other. I'd have been happy to be wed by a John the Baptist lookalike midstream of the Hudson River. We just wanted the whole day to be over and done with.

As we sat together on my bed in that cell-like room in the Barbizon overlooking East Sixty-third Street, Mother explained that she had written to Jim's parents weeks before to tell them "how delighted I am to be Jim's mother-in-law," and that she looked forward to meeting them in New York. She said, however, that she found it strange not to have received any reply from them and had sent another letter with the wedding invitation, reiterating that she looked forward to meeting them. "I received this," she said, handing me a piece of paper torn from a calendar tablet. On it was written: "The Vickerys will not be there." We sat in silence. I stared ahead, not thinking about what was in my hand but focusing, for some reason, on the sounds of the traffic in the street below us.

"What can I tell you?" I finally said, turning to her. "The Vickerys are not happy about this wedding."

"Is their objection to you?" Mother asked rather sternly.

"I think they feel it is all too grand," I replied, looking down at my feet. "And they have never really liked me. I always read when Jim takes me with him to visit them."

Our eyes met and we broke into helpless, somewhat hysterical laughter.

"We will not tell Jim about this note," my mother said, crushing it in her hand and replacing it in her purse. "I will simply say that I heard from his parents and that they were unable to attend." Thankfully, Jim's sister Ruby and some aunts and uncles would be in attendance, representing the Vickery family.

The morning of the wedding began with Mother and me fighting about my hair. My favorite series of pictures of the wedding are of my mother and me climbing out of the limousine in front of the church, Mother looking quite beautiful in something very lavender and chiffony and me coming up behind her still trying to adjust my veil and hair. The next shot is on the path in front of the vestibule. This time, I'm leading the way, still fiddling with the veil. Mother is following a few feet behind, waving her finger, obviously telling me that my hair was a disaster.

Once inside the church, I was accosted by Jim's best man, who informed me that minister number two, whom we had thankfully not heard from in weeks, had attacked the groom the minute he entered to tell him that he was obviously going to be damned for marrying a woman whose mother would not allow her to be baptized. Jim had no idea what he was talking about. At that point, the best man told me, minister number three, the one found by Father Ray, entered and politely but firmly asked number two to leave. Minister three came in and spoke to me very warmly and sweetly. Looking back on this now, I think what I found most interesting was that no one ever mentioned that *I* would be damned. Only Jim would suffer the pains of hell, for touching the untouchable.

Although my father had been invited to the wedding and was present, I walked down the aisle unescorted. And it was my mother who answered "I do" from her seat in the pew directly behind me when the minister asked, "Who giveth this woman?" Our vows were exchanged without a hitch, complete with Mother's deletions. Minister number three had obviously worked himself into such a rage over what had gone on before that he delivered the ceremony in a wonderfully reverberating voice, as if determined that this would indeed be— despite all the drama that preceded it—one of the great and true marriages. What no one—including myself—expected was the recessional. There, before God and all assembled, Jim and I exited the church to the strains of "My Wild Irish Rose" played upon the pipe organ.

The reception at a restaurant on Park Avenue was fine—boring and sedate. Within a few hours, Jim and I were driven by my father to Carmel, New York, where we had reserved a room at an inn. For months before we married, Jim and I kept looking at ads in the *New York Times* for honeymoon cottages on various lakes. I, in my blissful ignorance, thought that we would go upstate somewhere and spend a wonderful month, swimming and loving and lying about. I soon realized there would be no money for that. Instead, Jim and I took this room in Carmel for a week. I can remember the three of us—Dad, Jim and I—having dinner on the road in a rather unattractive diner. After dinner, my father left, leaving Jim and me to travel the rest of the way to Carmel alone. As we waved good-bye, it was one of the few times that I waved good-bye to my father and wished he'd have stayed.

We were at the inn for four or five days before, in what was to be the pattern for the next thirteen years, I called my mother to say that we had no money and what were we to do? She wired us money for train tickets to Milwaukee, so we went there and stayed for the rest of the week. From there, we rented a cottage on a small, beautiful lake about thirty miles outside the city, near West Bend, Wisconsin. We were dead broke and my mother let us know in no uncertain terms that she would not be supporting us while we were in town. I immediately got a job at West Bend Aluminum while Jim was hired by a harvesting plant to take the kernels off of corn on the cob. I lasted but two weeks at the aluminum plant before the fumes made me so sick that I simply could not return. Worse, I remember standing at my post, lowering trays of aluminum parts into a vat of chemicals, when I spotted a group being shown through the plant, as if on a tour. I recognized two of the group as a friend of my mother's and her daughter, with whom I had gone to Milwaukee Downer. I quickly ducked into the ladies' room and stayed there for an hour, smoking, which was against regulations. Here I was, I thought, supposed to be off on a romantic honeymoon and instead, I'm stuck standing over some vat of boiling poisons.

During the thirteen years that we spent together, I realized that Jim Vickery was one of those men who had been lost from the day he was born. He seemed to have it all. He was extraordinarily handsome. Mother used to refer to him as the "Prom King." He had a lovely sense of humor and was a talented actor, but he could never, never shake the insecurity that his family had always made him feel about himself.

From this, he became a man who was constantly threatened by what I call "they." "They" didn't want him to succeed; "they" didn't like him or his work; "they" would never give him a job. For all the years I knew him, Jim was unable to experience even a moment of simple joy. There was always a cloud around him, always the expectancy of failure, never of success. Naturally, it affected everything he did, anything he touched. Like each of us, he attracted what he expected and his life became a series of ongoing little agonies.

I learned of Jim's death some years ago when I received a letter from his lawyers informing me that I had been listed as the recipient of his union insurance. It was obvious to all concerned, including his present wife, myself, the lawyers and the union, that this was merely an oversight, the result of something that had been signed decades before and never changed. I told the lawyers that, as this was an error, I would write a letter to the union explaining that I did not wish to be the beneficiary. Instead, the claim should be turned over to his wife, who was also an actress and a lovely woman who had cared for him for years and with whom he had found a home.

I thought that this would be the end of it. Instead, I received another call from the lawyers saying that the union could not turn it over to anyone but me. If I refused to accept it, the entire sum would revert to his family. It was truly amazing to me that after all the years, so many years, I could still carry the hurt and anger that came with reading "the Vickerys will not be there." The feelings consumed me again.

"No," I said. "That family gets nothing. They deserve nothing for what they did to him. If I have to, I'll simply accept it and turn it over to his wife." Which is exactly what was done. I am stunned that I can still feel, even as I write this, the unforgiving rage I have for what a parent can do to a child, and specifically in this case, what Jim's parents did to him.

5

"It's just that with you, something always happens that isn't expected."

Of all the teachers I had during my two years at the American Academy, the one who made my time there most worthwhile and left a lasting impression even to this day was Charles Jehlinger, the longtime director of the school. Mr. Jehlinger was in his eighties when I entered the Academy, and no longer taught class. He was rarely seen by the students and, for this reason, was greatly feared because his criticism was known to be very biting and brutally accurate.

In two years, I met Mr. Jehlinger only once. I had been rehearsing my second-year exam, playing Mariella in a scene from *The Shining Hour,* which was to be presented for agents and producers on the stage of Broadway's Belasco Theatre. I had been very fortunate to be assigned this particular role. I was equally unfortunate in that the director was a woman named Rita Romilly, a woman with whom most of the students at the Academy had worked. I had only heard about her and knew that she had her disciples and her favorites. To some she was known as "the best" and to others as "the bitch." It became rapidly evident to me, during rehearsals, which was which.

Miss Romilly took an instant dislike to me. From the start, it was a horrendous rehearsal. Anything I did was not only criticized but led into long harangues by Miss Romilly about how Mr. Jehlinger was "a god" with the implication being that she was his Saint Peter. I felt like Judas.

When something like this occurs in a creative atmosphere, you finally cannot act. I was in such despair, a friend suggested that I ask for an audience with Mr. Jehlinger. My first response was that I could not do it. But I was so desperate, I finally went to his office and begged his secretary for an appointment. The secretary's attitude was very cold, but she finally said she would see what could be done.

The next day, halfway through rehearsal, Mr. Jehlinger entered the room. He stood behind Miss Romilly, who was facing the stage. We froze in our tracks. Miss Romilly turned and, seeing Mr. Jehlinger, asked him to sit down.

"I would prefer to stand," he said.

She turned back to the stage and asked for the scene to begin again. Before my entrance, halfway through, Mr. Jehlinger stopped various actors and spoke to them very briefly. Finally, I entered. I had not spoken one word when he stopped the scene and asked me very quietly if I knew where I was coming from and what I expected to accomplish when I entered the room. I was a nervous wreck but went back and reentered. Mr. Jehlinger never spoke again and left before the scene was completed. That evening, I received a note that I was to meet with Mr. Jehlinger the following day at eleven o'clock. I spent a sleepless night.

I arrived the next morning and was ushered immediately into his office. Mr. Jehlinger was standing with his back to the door, waiting for me. The door shut behind me. He turned and indicated with a slight upward turn of his hand that I should be seated.

"Why do you wish to see me?" he said.

"I'm not doing well in rehearsal," I replied, "because I think Miss Romilly feels I cannot do the part."

"Miss Dewhurst," he answered after looking at me for a minute, "it is not important whether you get on or not with your director. This is where you are. In a play being directed by Miss Romilly. Can you do this part?"

I stared at him, completely numb, before finding the wherewithal to finally reply, "Yes, sir, I can."

"That's all you need to know." He went to the office door and opened it. My audience was over. I was being dismissed. As I started for the door, this eighty-year-old man, who was no more than five feet four inches, slapped me on the back. I turned to him stricken with fear. To my surprise, Mr. Jehlinger was smiling.

"Be dangerous, girl," he said. "Something interesting might happen."

In spite of Miss Romilly, I am grateful to the Academy for introducing me to two directors, Edward Goodman and John Richards. Mr. Goodman was famous for having directed Katharine Cornell. As students, we all found him to be quite theatrical, looking like "Mr. Esky," the dandy on the cover of the old *Esquire* magazine. He wore hats like John Barrymore, had a large handlebar mustache, and carried a very fancy walking stick, the head of which was a flask. I had met no one like him back home. To us all, he most resembled our fantasy of someone "in the theater." John Richards was from Tennessee. He was kind and enthusiastic and, although less outwardly eccentric than Mr. Goodman, like Edward, lived for the theater. John was terribly funny and I loved his classes because he told story after story in a wonderful southern accent that made even his most mundane remark seem somehow fantastic.

After graduation, John spoke to me about joining a group he was forming to work in summer stock at a theater in Gatlinburg, Tennessee, a small resort town in the Smoky Mountains. John had been raised nearby in Knoxville, where his sister still lived in the family home. I was terribly excited. I had a job, my first job, and I would be paid for working professionally with my friends— other graduates of the Academy. What could be better?

And so, after the spring term, we went from classrooms and rehearsal halls in midtown Manhattan to a small theater in Tennessee. That summer, we all lived together in a large and very beautiful lodge that John had taken for us and, after less than ten days of rehearsal, opened in the town's community house with *Personal Appearance*, a play best known as the basis for one of Mae West's films, about a Hollywood star who is driven to California by her chauffeur. En route, the car breaks down in a small town. There, the star (whom I was to play) is given a room in the garage mechanic's home, and to pass the time, proceeds to seduce the young man and wreak havoc upon his family.

Our dressing rooms were in a building next to the community house and consisted of one large sheet hung between the two communal areas where the actors and actresses were to change. There I learned to dress and undress very quickly without revealing much of anything. This ability has stood me in good stead through the years when someone in some distant town apologizes for the lack of privacy.

Opening night in Gatlinburg arrived. We were all terribly excited. The Knoxville critic came and, as I recall, he was very good to us, so much so that John made an agreement with two wealthy brothers from nearby Miller, Tennessee, that every week we would play one performance in Miller on the night we were "dark" in Gatlinburg.

By the time we had done *Personal Appearance* for five performances in Gatlinburg, we were quite sure of our success in Miller. The brothers, who were very old friends of John's and equally enamored of the theater and a good stiff drink now and again, were very kind and very excited to have a group from New York City playing their town at their invitation. So the curtain went up in Miller on *Personal Appearance* to a full house in the high-school auditorium. It didn't take long for me to realize that every funny line I had in Gatlinburg was met in Miller with stony silence. When John came back after the first act, I said that I thought the audience didn't like the show very much.

"Now, honey," he replied, "you must realize you're in the Bible Belt. They'll warm up as we go along."

What a difference a few miles and scripture can make! They never did warm up. Nevertheless, at the end of the play, about twenty of the local ladies appeared backstage graciously offering cider and cakes for the cast. In what I can only assume was a subtle response to the "morals" of my character, I was not offered any of these desserts. I was distraught. Meanwhile, John and the two brothers kept reassuring me how wonderful I'd been, before looking around the room and breaking into gales of laughter. Somehow, I didn't feel any better.

The following week, a review of *Personal Appearance* appeared in Miller's local gazette. It seemed the reviewer was very impressed with everyone in the cast but failed to mention me, the star. "Colleen Dewhurst," she finally wrote in the last paragraph, "looked the part," before devoting the last sentences of the review to Alix Gordon, a local friend of John's who did him the favor of playing my maid. Alix had one line in the play, which she spoke as she entered, carrying my bags for my first entrance. She made quite an impression in Miller, however, as the review closed with, "We hope in the future to see more of Miss Gordon in leading roles." I don't know what became of Miller's own Miss Gordon, but this was the first review of *my* career. I was devastated. John's reaction to all this, still laughing, was that I was so wonderful in the part that they truly believed I was the character, a trashy Hollywood home wrecker. Nothing could comfort me, and as I played the last performances of *Personal Appearance* back in Gatlinburg, all I kept thinking of was how I had been branded a floozy and a flop in Miller.

I was next to play the housekeeper, a small role, in *Night Must Fall.* As we left for Miller in the station wagon, the whole company assured me that this small role, played in unattractive age makeup, would probably be my break-through. It wasn't. Those same ladies came back and once again ignored me. No cake. No cider. Nothing. After playing three other character roles in a row, to about the same success, I was cast as one of two wisecracking, sophisticated, drinking ladies in *Penny Wise.* This, we figured, would be the nail in my pro-fessional coffin. That Friday, the company could hardly contain itself as they waited for the silence with which the audience would greet my first entrance. They were not disappointed.

By that time, however, I was no longer upset. I had become quite fed up with Miller, the ladies and the lack of after-show refreshment. Halfway through the play, I had been directed to march across stage to make myself another drink. I poured the whiskey, went for the seltzer, and having pushed down the nozzle, could not release it. As the soda continued to splash into the glass, I desperately tried to manually stop it any way I could, but it quickly overflowed out of the glass, squirting all over the front of my dress and the bar.

"Oh, shit!" I said without thinking, and slapped the top of the bottle. It stopped squirting. There was a moment's pause before the house roared with laughter for what seemed five minutes. Every line I spoke from that point was received with gales of laughter and applause. That night backstage, I could have any cake I wanted. With those two words, uttered quite unintentionally in the heart of the Bible Belt, I had become the darling of Miller, Tennessee.

As in almost every stock company, each actor would have one week off. Mine came about the sixth or seventh week of performance and, after nearly two months of rehearsing one show during the day and playing another at night, I was really looking forward to the free time. As luck would have it, the Sunday before my vacation, John "fell off the wagon." I spent my vacation week as his companion/nurse. One of my duties for John that week was to pick up the cash receipts for each evening at the theater and return to place them in John's awaiting and rather unsteady hands.

After this quick transaction, John and I would sit alone together on the balcony of the lodge, which hung over a steep cliff and did not have much of a railing. One impulsive move or unsteady step would have sent John, or anyone nursing his third or fourth cocktail, headlong into the valley. It was incredibly beautiful at night on that balcony, however, as you could look out over the Smoky Mountains for miles, and that particular week the moon was coming full. Each night on that balcony John would greet me with the same remark.

"Honey," he would say, "I'm higher than a Georgia pine," before regaling me with stories about Thomas Wolfe, who had written *You Can't Go Home Again* and *Look Homeward, Angel,* and had lived a part of his life in that area of Tennessee.

In the valley below the balcony lived a wonderful woman and old friend of John's, Miss Smart, whom we all loved. She owned a small inn and lived alone. Local people knew very little about her. She kept to herself but loved to sit and talk with those of us from John's theater company. When we weren't working, some of us would go down and visit with her at the inn for hours. One night, as we sat on the balcony in the moonlight, John started talking about Thomas Wolfe again. Many of the characters in *You Can't Go Home Again,* he said, were real people from the area. He went on to pick different characters and show how their names in Wolfe's work were actually synonyms for real names, none of which I knew.

"Think about the names," he said, after going on about people who meant nothing to me, "and think about the people you've met." We sat in silence for a few more minutes as I tried to come up with some remark that might make sense to John. "I'm certain that Miss Pert in *You Can't Go Home Again* is our own Miss Smart," he whispered as if not wishing to be overheard. Miss Pert was the character with whom Wolfe's autobiographical character is involved before he leaves for New York.

"But Colleen," he added, staring into the moonlit valley and turning his half-empty glass around in his hand, so that the only sound was that of the wind and the dull clinking of the ice knocking together, "you must never bring up Thomas Wolfe to Miss Smart or tell her that I have told you this. We have never talked about Wolfe in any terms but as some distant figure and as an author we both admire. I have never heard of her mentioning him in any way to anyone else."

As it got later and the moon shone brighter and the wind continued to whistle through the tall pines, John would reach the stage where he began conversing with his dead mother. "Honey," he said suddenly out of nowhere, "she's here. She's with us right now."

"Who's here?" I asked.

"My mother," he replied.

When he would reach this stage over the next few nights, John would proceed to talk to her about his sister and various members of the family.

"Can't you feel her?" he would turn to me and say.

"Yes," I replied, not at all sure I could but certain, for John's sake, I should.

"My mother loves you," he said.

"Thank you" seemed the only appropriate response.

By the end of the week, I had gotten used to the fact that any time after ten-thirty or so, this third person, Mother, would arrive. During those times, I learned a great deal about John and his past. One night, John suddenly turned to me and said, "You know, honey, you're very easy to get along with and good in a company. You don't cause trouble, but you are a catalyst." I barely knew what the word *catalyst* meant.

"What do you mean?"

"Well," he continued slowly, "it's as if when you enter a group, even if you barely know anything about it, everything that has been just below the surface comes up. Not because of anything you've done but, for some reason, just by your being there. I don't know why that is, but it's true. It isn't always a bad situation," he continued. "It just is that, with you, something always happens that isn't expected."

I often think of that conversation to this day. Once in a great while, as I sit in the middle of what seems to be a volcano erupting around me, I think of what was said that night. I have no idea whether this was John's opinion or Mother's, but whoever I was talking to wasn't wrong.

On April 2, 1974, Colleen was presented with the American Academy Alumni Award of Achievement at the 1974 graduation ceremonies of her alma mater, the American Academy of Dramatic Arts. The graduation ceremony, which took place at the Morosco Theatre, was a long affair that ended with just enough time for the theater to be cleaned and the stage set for that evening's performance of A Moon for the Misbegotten, *starring Colleen Dewhurst. These were her remarks:*

> *Thank you. I wish I could smoke.*
>
> *I have come here completely unprepared because I could not even visualize myself trying to give a speech. Actors are only comfortable with scripts. I heard an analyzation once that said the reason actors act is because for three hours every night, they know exactly what is going to happen to them. And what I feel now is that I don't know what's going to happen next.*
>
> *I want to thank everybody who's come. I have wonderful friends; it is especially a surprise to see two great ladies of the theater here, Maureen*

Stapleton and Elizabeth Wilson, who I'm sure cannot believe, under any circumstances, that I could be giving a speech.

Well, so far so good. But it's all right because if I get myself in terrible trouble, Jason Robards and Charles Durning, over there, have promised to streak.

I'm just looking at you all. I don't think I would want to be sitting there again where you are for one million dollars. Nor would I for one million dollars change or give up one second of the twenty-seven years I've gone through since my own graduation. Every second in some way accounts for my being able to be up here today speaking to you.

Jason, maybe we should just do the third act.

I can't believe I'm going to give any kind of advice . . . but I will say that if this is what you want, let nothing stand in the way. You can't give it time. This is it. This is where you're going. It's important to understand that in every life there are rejections, by husband, by lover, by Father, by Mommy, by the job, the usual things, once, twice, three times. But you must realize that as an actor, you will face rejection every day and it will feel quite personal. But you must try never to allow yourself to become bitter.

It seems to me that this is one of the tragedies that I've seen written on many faces. You can't talk about the establishment. You can't talk about the one who got the break, the one who didn't, and how "they" didn't let you. Bitterness will destroy not only you, but also the talent that you have to offer.

There will be agony days and hate days. Use them. I'm frightened every time I'm out of work, whether it's for four months, five months or a year. I think, Well that's it, I can't do it. *But when I'm working again, I find out that during that year or six months when I thought I wasn't using myself as an actress, in fact, I was learning because I was living. And when I hit that next script or next stage, without knowing it, I have kept growing as an artist.*

Now I've become terribly serious and I've depressed myself.

I must mention the name of a gentleman, who I can't believe is here, who taught me at the American Academy and gave me my first job in Gatlinburg, Tennessee: Mr. John Richards, the first one who ever paid me. I remember doing a play down there at which there were several drunks in the front row. I thought what I had to do on that stage was going to be emblazoned across the sky, but they couldn't have been less interested. Oh, they found me terribly funny, especially when I sobbed a lot. But this was not the reception I had hoped for. After the curtain call, I remember running offstage because I was going to punch them in the mouth. John, over there, grabbed me and gave me some of the simplest and best advice I've ever received: "Suit of armor, darling," he said. "Suit of armor."

I have this feeling I should be drawing to some super conclusion, but I can't think of a thing. For what it's worth, I got married to someone at the American Academy. But, as I say, the important thing is to live.

I want to tell you how really thrilled and honored I am to be asked here today. I did not realize that I was to give an address. Nevertheless, my wish and my hope for you would be that you experience the joy that I have had, as well as the agony. But most of all, the love. I wish it all to all of you.

6

"Is that you, O daughter mine?"

My first professional jobs were in summer stock, in small, medium and large companies that presented ten plays in ten weeks from June until Labor Day. In those days, every spring, much as the swallows returning to Capistrano or salmon swimming to spawn upstream, stock producers from the Midwest would come to New York to cast from the hundreds of actors who would count on these few months of employment as their only work in the theater that year.

At that time, the core of each summer stock company was made up of a stage manager and six resident actors: a leading man and woman, a character man and woman, and an ingenue and juvenile. If there were two or three plays that required a larger cast, individual actors would be "jobbed in" from New York for a week of rehearsal and a week of performance. In some cases, five or six of the summer plays would be "star vehicles," featuring a familiar actor or actress who would come in, rehearse with the resident company, play for a week, and move on to repeat this performance in the same play at another theater with a new company of resident actors. This is summer stock by the book, the G-rated, MGM/Judy Garland/Mickey Rooney version of putting on a show in the barn.

Fresh out of the American Academy and just back from working in Tennessee, I was eager to begin working professionally in stock. To be hired for the best stock jobs, you had to be a member of Actors' Equity, the professional actors' union. To become an Equity member, you had to be hired for an Equity job, but in order to audition for an Equity job, you needed to be an Equity member. You may begin to see the dilemma here. Which came first, the chicken or the egg?—the Equity job or the Equity card? How could I join the union if I couldn't get an Equity job and how could I get an Equity job if I couldn't get into an Equity audition? Without an Equity card, I knew I was never going to have a career in the theater. I was determined to get that card. I cared more about getting my Equity card than where I slept or if I ate.

At the American Academy, there was a group of us who, over the course of two years, came to know one another very well. In this group was a young man from Manasquan, New Jersey, who was considered to be a "perfect juvenile"—that is to say, he was youthful, blond and attractive. He had an idea that we could create our own summer stock company in his seaside hometown by simply posting bond (which his mother could provide) with the union and signing professional contracts, then the six of us would immediately receive our Equity cards. That we would also build the sets, collect the furniture, make the costumes, manage the box office and put on ten shows didn't seem unusual or unprofessional to us, although it might have seemed so to Equity. Since none of us ever complained to the union about working conditions or salary, and since we were a small, practically nonexistent theater operating far from the beaten path, our actions were never questioned. We were just very excited, the six of us, to be on the beach in New Jersey, playing leading roles in wonderful plays all summer, and coming home after Labor Day as Equity members.

I have been embarrassed enough about this incident never to have revealed it before now to any of the current Equity staff or council with whom I have worked and served for the last six years as president. But yes, this is the way Equity's president entered the union. Times were different then. I was desperate. If, however, this gives anyone reading this book ideas, forget it. You couldn't get away with it today, and remember: I'm the president and I'm watching.

The following summer, I auditioned and was hired as leading woman by a new, legitimate Equity company, the Shapleigh Playhouse, in Shapleigh, Maine, whose home was also in the proverbial barn. I was very excited to have the opportunity to be working in my first professional company of Equity actors. I felt I had arrived.

I had been told in New York that in Maine I would be living in a cottage on a lovely lake. Upon arrival, I was taken aback to find that indeed I was in a cottage, not quite on the lake, in which there was one large room, a quarter of which had been curtained off. Behind this curtain were four bunk beds which I was to share with three other women—two apprentices and the ingenue. In the larger part of the room was a cot, where our leading man slept, and there was also what appeared to be one very large tin bathtub. On the small porch surrounding two sides of the cottage was an outhouse. There was no running water. Upon investigating the bunk beds, I discovered there were no sheets, only a wool blanket, to which I knew I was allergic. As I remember this now, the most interesting part of it all is that although I was appalled, I stayed.

The theater itself was really quite lovely, with the box office and lobby located in the lower part of the barn and the theater-in-the-round situated above. The ceiling was very high, with beams left untouched from the original structure. It did not take long to discover that the audience, which was sitting nearly on top of the actors on all sides, had to duck occasionally as one of the bats from this wonderfully preserved structure swooped down to take part in the drama onstage. Complaints were regularly made to the management and we were regularly informed that the bat problem would be taken care of.

Clint Anderson played the lead in that summer's production of *I Remember Mama*. One night, in a very tense scene he had with me, I suddenly became aware that the audience was addressing me personally, out loud, in fear. Unbeknownst to me, a bat had swooped down to the stage and, as the audience watched in horror, proceeded to disappear in the folds of my long period skirt. As I moved, my dress swishing about the stage, they knew the bat was there moving with me. Fortunately, I did not. Like the audience, Mr. Anderson had also seen the bat and kept moving closer to me, in a way that had never been rehearsed. I couldn't understand what he was doing, particularly when he abruptly reached out and shook my skirt. To my amazement, and then to my horror, I saw this dazed bat drop to the floor at my feet and, shaking his wings, dart back up into the rafters. Needless to say, I finished the scene as quickly as possible and ran for the dressing rooms, unsure that I ever wanted to stand under those beams again.

In this same play, I had to make pancakes in a very old-fashioned kitchen in which I stood on one side of the table on the edge of the stage and mixed the ingredients, with the front row of the audience sitting on the other side of the table not eight inches away. This was a dangerous situation for three reasons: First, I was bound to be nervous on opening night; second, cooking is not one of my accomplishments either on- or offstage; and third, according to the script, I never stopped talking from the moment I was to start making the pancakes.

I had no more than started when I became conscious of little whispers just on the opposite side of the table. Finally one woman who obviously could not stand it any longer exclaimed, "Too much flour!" My whole body went rigid, losing my place in the script. By the time I composed myself enough to remember my lines, I was completely lost as to how to continue to make those pancakes. As I started pouring milk into the bowl, the same lady again said, in a whisper heard across stage, "There's too much flour!"

"Hush!" said the woman sitting next to her. "It doesn't matter."

"But it's wrong," replied her friend, causing the entire audience to scream with laughter.

I was now simply beyond caring. I thrust my hands into the pasty mix and threw the batter into the pan. I have always complimented myself on the fact that though it flew through my mind to take that pancake and thrust it into the lady's face, I controlled myself, finished the scene and exited to great applause.

I never knew who it was, but as Mr. Anderson was the most experienced actor in our company and the most mature, I have always suspected that he was responsible for the sudden, unannounced appearance of an Equity representative. This woman had been asked to look at the theater and carefully inspect our living quarters, not so "near the lake." She asked to be taken to the cottage, and on entering it, asked what the tin bathtub was for. We explained that on certain days we would draw water from the lake, heat it and, depending on whose turn it was, either bathe or make ourselves scarce so Mr. Anderson could do the same.

"Where is the bathroom?" she asked.

We simply walked to the porch and opened the door to the outhouse.

"Where do you sleep?" she asked.

We explained our sleeping arrangements: leading man on the cot, the four of us behind the curtain.

"No sheets?" she said as she turned down one of the blankets.

By that point and due to the added confidence we now felt with the appearance of an Equity official, the three of us said that we were willing to continue working only if certain circumstances were changed. But strangely enough— in spite of the tub, the toilet and the sleeping arrangements—the most important issue was the bed linens, and thanks to Equity's quick intervention, that night we had sheets.

We were in our eighth week, my week off, when it became clear that our producer was not in a good financial position. Clint came to me to say that the producer was going to have to close the theater.

"The important thing now," he said, "is that we hold on to all monies received at the box office if we hope to have our transportation home paid. It's a union rule. If we don't grab the money first, you can bet it won't be handed to us."

As I had the week off, I was designated to stand at the box office and, as soon as the play began, take the cash box. I was not to be intimidated by the cashier or anyone else who might attempt to remove it. Clint was in the play but said that he would come downstairs at his first exit to give me moral support.

That night, I went to the theater and stood by the cashier. When the last ticket was sold, I asked her to hand me the receipts. She handed me the box without an argument. At just that moment, a police car with two of the local town police appeared, who announced that they were closing the theater and asked to be given any money that had been collected that evening. I explained that I was to hold the money in order to ensure that the actors' transportation back to New York could be paid. We argued back and forth for a few minutes before the sheriff reached out and took my arm with one hand and with the other tried to grab the cash box from me. Just then, thank God, I heard Clint exclaim, "Take your hands off of her." The sheriff dropped his hands as Clint proceeded to explain the union rules. With the cash box under his arm, he then went back up the stairs to make his next entrance onto the stage.

In that last week at the Shapleigh Playhouse, I received a call from James

Noble, an actor who was then playing at the Kennebunkport Playhouse, in nearby Kennebunkport, Maine. I had first met Jim that summer when driving over once or twice to see their productions. Jim said he heard that we were closing, and informed me that Kennebunkport's last play, *Guest in the House,* had two leading women in the cast. Edwina Middlebrook was Kennebunkport's resident leading lady, as I was at Shapleigh. She and Jim had played opposite each other at Kennebunkport for a number of years. They would be jobbing in Marian Seldes for the second leading-woman's role. Something occurred at the last moment that forced Edwina to return to New York, making her unavailable for the production. Jim had very kindly suggested that the producer, Bob Courier, job me in to replace Edwina, as I was unexpectedly free and just thirty minutes away.

Kennebunkport was a well-established and respected theater. I was very happy to hear of the job, but as Mr. Courier had not yet seen me, I was unsure whether I was receiving a real offer or not. Jim assured me that I was to be hired, and handed the phone to Bob Courier.

"Hello," Courier rasped into the phone.

"Hello," I replied. There was no response.

"Say something to her," I could hear Jim say in the background.

After what seemed minutes, Jim came back on the phone.

"Everything's fine," he said. "You're hired."

"Are you sure?" I asked. "Mr. Courier didn't really say anything."

"Never mind. Just come over. I'll be looking for you."

The next day, I was driven over to the Kennebunkport Playhouse. Jim met me and was very kind. I went into rehearsal the following day with Jim and Marian Seldes. I had yet to see Mr. Courier. We rehearsed all week and I was conscious during that time that someone, who I thought must be Mr. Courier, was hovering about the edges of the rehearsal room and wandering outside the playhouse. I finally asked Jim when he thought I would actually meet the elusive Mr. Courier. There must be some kind of oversight, I thought, as I had yet to sign a contract.

Two days before we opened, Jim handed me a contract that I signed. Marian and Jim were very supportive, and Jim kept trying to explain to me that Mr. Courier was basically very shy and probably could not think how to go about introducing himself at this late date. *Guest in the House* opened to a good reception. At the final performance that week, I told Jim that I had not yet received my check and that I would not go on until I received it. Jim understood my feelings and stormed out to the front of the house. Minutes later, he returned with a check that was incorrect. He went out again and this time returned with a check made out in the correct amount and told me that Mr. Courier wanted to sign me on as his leading lady for the following summer. I was dumbfounded. I still had yet to meet this man. I figured his continued absence had meant that he was displeased with my work and sorry that I was on his stage. During all of this, Jim was very quiet, very relaxed. He understood, as I would come to understand, that this was simply normal behavior for Bob Courier.

I was, however, ecstatic with his offer. Not only did I have a job for the following summer, but I would be working in one of the best summer stock theaters of that time and, wonder of wonders, close to the ocean. I could not have been happier. I worked at Kennebunkport for the next four summers and did eventually meet Bob Courier. By the second summer, I also came to love Bob, and soon replaced Jim as the "old hand" who tried to explain Mr. Courier's eccentric ways to the new actors in the company.

These summer seasons are now jumbled together in my mind, but certain productions and incidents will remain forever engraved. One year, Mr. Courier had fired the ingenue during the dress rehearsal of the summer's opening production. The second week's play, *Beauty and the Beast,* was to go into rehearsal the next day with this same ingenue playing the "beauty." In the middle of the night, Bob informed me that I was now to play the role. I was shellshocked. First of all, no one should ever attempt to do *Beauty and the Beast* in summer stock. Secondly, the "beast" was being played by Ernie Parmentier, a slender, good-looking young man who stood about five feet six inches and had been hired that summer as the company's resident juvenile. I, as the "beauty," stood at five feet eight inches and looked as if I could kill him. Even his lion mask did not help to dispel the threat I posed to Ernie's beast.

Mitch Erickson, who is still a dear friend and one of the great stage managers in the New York theater, was cast as my father. During rehearsals, Mitch, Ernie and I quickly realized that this was to be the fiasco of the season, which, for some reason and at the most inopportune times, would send us into hysterical laughter, somehow forgetting that the fiasco was us.

Beauty and the Beast went from bad to worse, culminating in my first appearance at the dress rehearsal. I was costumed in some cute ruffled dress with a big bow in the back. My hair was in little corkscrew curls—also with a big bow in the back. As I emerged from my dressing room in this costume I heard Mitch and Ernie break into gales of laughter, which they barely contained through the entire day.

Mitch and I had a scene in the forest which I can still remember.

"Daddy, Daddy," I spoke in fear and trembling, "we must catch a train and get out of this forest and away from the Beast."

"Daughter," Mitch would reply, "there are no trains, there are no planes, there is no way to get out of this forest."

While working on this book, I met Mitch in the elevator at Equity, told him I was writing about Kennebunkport and wanted to be sure that I remembered *Beauty and the Beast* correctly. Without missing a beat, Mitch replied across the crowded elevator, "Daughter, there are no trains, there are no planes, there is no way to get out of this forest."

The doors opened and Mitch nearly fell out of the elevator doubled up with laughter. "Call me," he said as the doors shut, "I remember it all."

So do I. In dress rehearsal, when we were with each other in the forest for the first time, Mitch, with his hair grayed and lines drawn in all over his face, and I, all curled, frilled and trembling, could barely look at each other. By the time Mitch finally got to the aforementioned line, we realized that the forest we could not escape was this damnable play. In the eight performances we did, Mitch and I were never able to get through that scene without breaking up. By the last performance, we had to play it with our backs to the audience and never looking at each other.

Another summer, I don't remember which, was made up primarily of plays in which stars were to be jobbed in. By this time, Bob and I were very good friends. I trusted him and felt that he was one of the first people who respected my work (in spite of *Beauty and the Beast*).

That summer, I was living in the main building, a very beautiful old New England farmhouse to which was attached an extension with four or five small bedrooms. Charles Coburn came in that summer to play Grandpa in *You Can't Take It with You*. I was to play Grand Duchess Olga Katrina, never guessing that thirty years later, I would repeat this role on Broadway. Coburn was delightful in the role and memorable to the female members of the cast, as he was a dedicated "fanny pincher." We all enjoyed him but loved him the most when we discovered that when he was invited to one of the posh parties given by one of the local ladies, Mr. Coburn would continue to pursue his favorite pastime and pinch the bottoms of the very dignified and the very rich.

Jeffrey Lynn came in to do *Captain Carvallo*, a play about an army officer who leads an invasion into a small country and ends up being lodged in the home of a woman, whom I was to play, with whom he falls in love. At the end of the play, my character sends him away saying, in a very dramatic speech, that she does not love him. Mr. Lynn was a very charming and nice man, who had made a name for himself in movies. After the first reading of the play, I was taken aside by Bob Courier, who explained to me that Mr. Lynn felt that he would be playing *Captain Carvallo* with the ending reversed. He was the star. He would take the speech of the woman and leave *her*. I couldn't believe my ears and simply stood in amazement.

"That doesn't make sense," I said. "The play's not that good to begin with, and my only interesting scene is the last one."

They suggested that I see if Mr. Lynn would like to go swimming that afternoon. Perhaps that would lead into a discussion in which I could subtly point out my feelings about his proposed change. So I asked Mr. Lynn if he wanted to go down that afternoon for a swim. He did, so during a break in rehearsal, we left for Kennebunk Beach.

Even in the middle of summer, the Atlantic Ocean off the coast of Maine is very cold. As this was not my first summer at Kennebunkport, however, I was accustomed to it. Not thinking that Mr. Lynn might not be prepared for the shock, as soon as we got to the beach, I threw down my towel and ran into the water, waving for him to follow. He waved back and ran into the surf, letting out a yelp as his feet first hit the water and becoming absolutely motionless by the time the water reached above his waist. He did not move for minutes. He then slowly turned around and gingerly made his way back to shore, picked up his towel and left. I didn't know what to think. Mr. Lynn never mentioned the beach again, although Bob did tell me that he had told him that he had had a "very nice time."

Nevertheless, Jeffrey and I did become very good friends, and I thought right up to the dress rehearsal that I could change his mind about reversing the ending of the play. But he would not be moved. He was adamant. A play that the audience did not find too interesting to begin with had, by the last curtain, become a complete enigma to them. This was my first awakening as to what a star can demand and the dangers of a too-cold surf.

Summer stock is a place where, for many reasons, people often go completely crazy. Kennebunkport was no exception. When I moved into the main house, I began to have strange little visits from Mr. Courier. The first was just before the first day of rehearsal for *Beauty and the Beast,* when there was a knock at my door at two o'clock in the morning. I got up and opened the door. There Bob stood holding a silver tray with one small watercress sandwich, a linen napkin, and a cup of tea. I quickly scrambled back into bed. Bob placed the tray on my lap and pulled up a chair and explained, without any acknowledgment that there might be something strange to this visit, that as there was no ingenue coming up from New York, I would be playing Beauty.

Bob Courier was a very handsome man, tall and rugged-looking with curly black hair. At that hour of the morning, I felt I was looking at Heathcliff out of *Wuthering Heights,* a man with the same peculiar look of isolation and darkness. This was the first of a number of early-morning visits from Bob during which tea and a sandwich would be served to me in bed on a tray. There was nothing menacing or awkward about these visits. Looking back, it was rather like a Gothic novel, brother and sister living in their family home, the last of a strange family and isolated from the world, but about whom the townsfolk whisper. Whatever news Bob brought with the tray would be quickly told. Although I was never hungry, I always felt compelled to eat the sandwich and drink the tea that he brought, like a well-trained child. While I ate, we would talk. We didn't gossip about the company or laugh about the day. It is the only time I can actually remember Bob wanting to talk personally about his feelings and about life. Once I finished eating, Bob would take the tray and leave in as quiet and orderly a fashion as he had entered. We never spoke of the conversations we had, nor did I ever speak of them for years to anyone in the company except Mitch.

The next time Bob arrived at the door, it was again with the silver tray, little sandwich, linen napkin and bad news. This time he told me that Hurd Hatfield, who was to arrive in two days to do *Dark of the Moon,* had decided to bring his own leading lady to play the role in which I had been cast. It was a part I had looked forward to playing, and I was heartbroken. Bob, once again in his own sweet way that he kept hidden under this bear-like exterior, was telling me something that he knew would hurt me and that he knew he could not change.

The final one of these late-night visits was after the first reading of *The Heiress,* in which I was playing Catherine, opposite the star, John Carradine, who had come in to play my father, Dr. Sloper. There was no one within our resident cast truly right to play the role of Morris, Catherine's suitor (a part that had been played to perfection by Montgomery Clift in the film version). An actor from Portland had been recently hired into the resident company. He was a very pleasant actor, but just didn't have the edge that the character needed. Carl Benson, our resident leading man, had the edge, but looked more at home in boots and a flannel shirt than in silk shirts and a period tie.

Bob finally decided to cast Carl, in spite of his not being exactly right, knowing that, despite his look, he could act the role. With the arrival of John Carradine, rehearsals began and the cast had its first reading. At about three o'clock the following morning, I heard the knock of doom at my door. By this time, I knew who and what to expect. I opened the door and ran back into bed. This time, Bob set on my lap a tray with a single serving of tomato soup in a beautiful bowl and two very neatly cut pieces of buttered toast.

"Mr. Carradine has spoken to me about Carl," he said sitting on a chair next to the bed. "He thinks he is too powerful and lacks the classical look the role must have."

During the read-through, Mr. Carradine had observed Al, the actor from Portland who had been assigned a small part in the play, and afterward told Bob that he wanted Al to play Morris. This to me seemed the final blow. I had survived *Beauty and the Beast* and waited eight long weeks to play Catherine, a role that demanded all of my attention and opposite an actor I admired. What I felt this early summer morning was not simply disappointment but rage and despair for I knew, particularly after the experience with Jeffrey Lynn in *Captain Carvallo,* that I could not win this battle with Mr. Carradine. He was the star.

The next day, Carl and Al, both having been informed of the change, entered rehearsal. Carl behaved like a gentleman and, I must say, Al for all his supposed good fortune, seemed a bit dismayed. Rehearsal, with the books in our hands, was dismal. It became clear that Mr. Carradine was both the star of the show and our director. Mr. Carradine would literally take me by the shoulders and place me in the position he wished me to be onstage, which, more often than not in my most important scenes, was facing upstage with my back to the audience.

At the lunch break, our director, who had been sitting quietly in the darkened theater observing all of this, took me aside to say that my anger was very evident. "If you continue like this," he added, "not only will you be playing the entire evening with your back to the house, but you will be dreadful in the role, as you and Carradine have no rapport. You had better find some way to relate to Mr. Carradine or you will ruin the play."

I was furious (for I knew he was right) and walked toward a small balcony outside the barn to have a cigarette. As I entered I saw that Mr. Carradine was also standing there, looking out over the fields. Mad as I was, I could not just turn around and leave. I lit up and stood silently beside him, staring out at the same scene. Minutes passed in silence.

"I loved your recording of the Rupert Brooke poems," I finally said without looking at him.

There was another long silence.

"Really," he replied. "Which one did you like the best?" he asked, implying that he didn't quite believe that I had heard the recording.

"'Breathless, we flung us on the windy hill, and laughed who had such proud and timeless things to say,'" I quoted, staring straight ahead.

Before I could go on, Mr. Carradine picked up from my line and recited the entire poem, never looking away from the field. Just as he finished, we were called back into rehearsal. During this entire exchange we had never looked at each other. We both stamped out our cigarettes, walked off the balcony back into the barn, picked up our scripts and proceeded to work from where we had left off. We took our previous positions, I once again downstage, back to the audience, delivering my lines upstage to John. I hadn't spoken two sentences before John abruptly cut me off and spoke to the director, who was still sitting like a ghost in the darkened theater.

"Why is she standing down there during this scene?" he asked, as if the poor director had just placed me there an hour before. "Colleen," he said, turning back to me gallantly, "come here." He took me, once again by the shoulders, and pushed me upstage so that as I spoke to him the audience's focus would be on me.

"Now," he said, "let us begin this scene again."

The rest of that afternoon was very convivial and creative, as John and I began to move around the stage in a natural and intuitive way. Late that night, once again, over a sandwich and tea, Bob told me that Mr. Carradine wished to have Carl Benson return to the role of Morris, and I began to have some hope.

Opening night of *The Heiress* went very well, except for two things. First, the critic from the Portland paper had gone to the Ogunquit Playhouse for an opening there and had made arrangements to see *The Heiress* on our second night. The second, at that time, was a bit more serious, but also at that time, made the first seem like a blessing of sorts.

That night, at our opening performance, when the actress playing Aunt Penniman came to the famous scene in which Morris comes to elope with Catherine, we exchanged possibly four lines of a five-minute scene before Aunt Penniman stopped speaking completely. Suddenly, a scene that was supposed to be about Aunt Penniman assuring Catherine that her lover will arrive became a monologue for me, in which I repeatedly assured myself that nothing was wrong, Morris was just a little late. Still nothing from Penniman. I continued talking, responding to my own reassurance that all was indeed not well, all the while running back and forth from the window to where Penniman stood frozen in silence like a statue in the middle of the drawing room. Gratefully, the scene finally ended and we both exited offstage.

"Oh, Colleen, I am so sorry," Penniman whispered behind the set in the dark. "I couldn't turn the page."

"What are you talking about?" I said in rather stunned amazement.

"You know, when you study, you learn your lines and when you reach the bottom of the page, you turn it so that in your mind you can see your next line at the top of the next page. Well, I just couldn't turn the page," she said.

God knows I had gone up on my lines once or twice that summer, and still do. I can, however, always manage to remember the theme of the scene. Not Penniman. She couldn't turn the page, and until she could, nothing was going to happen. That night she couldn't and it didn't. I realized then the importance of that much-hated word *motivation*. Whatever her method (or lack thereof), I must say that, thankfully, Aunt Penniman never got stuck at the bottom of the page again.

That summer, at the opening night of each new play, the cast and crew would have a party, hosted by whoever in the resident company was playing the leading role. I had posted a sign on the bulletin board, inviting the cast to the usual "bring your own" gathering. I have no memory of that party but assume it went as they usually did, until all hours. Nevertheless, I got up the next morning and went to the first rehearsal for the next week's production.

At five o'clock that afternoon, I went back to my room and napped for a bit before walking over to the theater about an hour before that night's curtain for *The Heiress*. When you entered the stage door of that barn theater, the dressing rooms were to your left—about nine cubicles lined in a row against the back wall. To your right was the stage. I greeted the crew, all of whom seemed to be unusually quiet, and entered my small dressing area, which was just next to Mr. Carradine's on the right. I hadn't been there two minutes before the stage manager entered without knocking and in sign language asked me to come outside. We walked clear to the opposite end of the theater, away from the dressing rooms, where I was informed that Mr. Carradine had arrived about a half an hour before and appeared to be drunk. It was impressed upon me that we were not talking about being a bit tipsy. We were talking drunk. Very drunk.

"OK," I said. "Now what?"

No one knew. Coffee had been made and refused. Everyone seemed just to be waiting. For what, I didn't know. I went back to my cubicle and closed the door.

"Is that you, O daughter mine?" I heard in stentorian tones from next door.

"Yes, John," I replied.

"Come and talk to me."

I entered his dressing area and stood next to where he was sitting in front of his mirror.

"Did you have a good time at your party last night?" he asked.

"It was OK."

"I was terribly hurt that I had not been invited to be a part of the celebration," he said, his chin resting in his left hand.

"Well," I hesitantly replied, "you were staying at the Colony Hotel away from us all and we just figured that you would be, well, with your own people there. I had put the notice on the board inviting everyone, which I thought included you."

"My dear," he said, looking at me hazily in the mirror, "I am now only a star in summer stock and nowhere else on the American stage. That, for me, is all past. I am alone. My wife has left me, having fouled our nest."

This speech continued for another ten minutes. I soon realized, from the rustlings outside, that the rest of the cast and crew could hear these proceedings and were waiting for some kind of signal from me as to what we should do.

"John, I'm going to get myself some coffee," I said, at last finding the nerve to interrupt him. "Would you like me to bring you some?"

"Yes, I would."

I opened his door and was immediately handed two cups of coffee before I could even step out into the hall. I handed John his and explained that I thought I should go back to my dressing room and begin to get ready for the performance. He agreed. As I got into my costume, John and I continued conversing through the top of the thin wall that divided our dressing rooms. I came out dressed, and was then informed by the stage manager that Bob Courier was now in not much better condition, circling the barn and roaring insults toward Mr. Carradine.

"Should we keep him out?" the stage manager asked me.

"For God's sake, yes," I said, realizing later that Bob had no intention of coming in. He just kept circling and yelling. Finally someone came in with a message from Bob.

"Can he get onstage," he asked, "as I am about to open the house."

John, meanwhile, had never stopped talking to me from behind his closed door.

"Colleen, come in. I want to talk to you," he called. He had been talking for nearly half an hour. I entered, standing once again to his left in front of his mirror, this time squeezed in my hoops between him and the wall.

Unbeknownst to me, Mr. Cahill, the critic from the Portland paper, who had missed last night's opening, had arrived and let it be known that he wished to come backstage for an interview. Mr. Cahill was the one point of dispute between Bob Courier and me. Whenever Cahill came to the openings, Bob always insisted that I go out with him and a few others afterward for dinner. It was important to the Playhouse, Bob thought, that Mr. Cahill be deferred to in this way. I couldn't stand Cahill and referred to him all that summer as "the upper-arm squeezer." He was shorter than I, and whenever we went out he would invariably grasp my upper arm and knead it like a piece of dough. The only bearable thing about those evenings was that I could order anything that I wanted to eat, lobster and steak, which I did and of which Bob would gently remind me each time he asked me to join in this post-opening ritual.

That night, Mr. Cahill did come backstage and was quickly ushered to the opposite end of the backstage area, away from Mr. Carradine and me, to speak to the other actors. As he walked through, obviously looking for the star and me, he passed John's door, which was ajar. The next day, the stage manager told me that through the door you could see me standing next to Mr. Carradine just as he reached his "sentimental" stage. Never before this exact moment had John ever expressed a bit of lechery toward me. Whatever else he was, he was always a gentleman. However, just at this moment, as Cahill passed, John had laid his head tearfully on what would normally have been my shoulder but, as I was standing beside him, turned out to be my bosom.

Mr. Cahill took one look and quickly exited into the theater. By now, it was about twenty minutes to curtain and we had to seriously figure out if John could get onstage. I could hear the audience taking their seats.

"I'm fine," John said, looking up at me. "I will not let you or anyone in this company down." He turned back to his mirror and began to put on his false beard, one hair at a time. I realized as I watched this process that he was now deliberately trying to sober up, and putting on the beard would buy time.

Curtain was usually at eight o'clock. At about eight-fifteen, the audience began clapping. By eight-thirty, they were clapping and stomping. Bob Courier was still pacing outside the stage door, hurling various and sundry threats. The curtain finally went up at eight-forty to a full house, as Mr. Courier had made it clear to everyone what was happening offstage and no one wished to miss what was to follow onstage.

The Heiress ran about half an hour longer that night. Mr. Carradine never missed a line but seemed to speak each vowel as if it were a word in itself.

"O-o-o-o-o-oh daugh-ter mi-i-i-i-ine. I wish to speak to yo-u-u-u-u-u-u-u-u."

That evening, after the performance, no one came backstage to say hello. A few of us did, however, go back with Mr. Carradine to his suite at the Colony. There we were told once again about his love for his ex-wife and of his despair. It was not something that any of us found amusing. It was evident that this man was lonely and feeling without hope.

Mr. Cahill's review of *The Heiress* was not good and took a particularly snide view of my and Mr. Carradine's performances, even though he did not mention John's condition. But for the rest of that week, John was a definite part of the company, both on- and offstage.

Toward the end of the run, the cast was invited to a large costume party in Ogunquit. John chose to go as Abe Lincoln and simply wore his costume from *The Heiress*, complete with stovepipe hat. That night, we moved from house to house and party to party, as the whole town seemed to be invited to whatever was going on. I remember John saying over and over again at one house, "I don't know where the hell I am, but I'm staying close to Dewhurst because, with her at my side, I know I will eventually get home." And so we went, John sticking close by. At some point, as is usually the case in an evening like this, we lost him and returned to Kennebunkport, assuring each other that John had probably gone on ahead and forgotten to tell us.

The next day, while in rehearsal for the next week's show, someone reported that he had seen John at about two o'clock in the afternoon being driven back to his hotel in a convertible driven by someone nobody recognized. No one saw John until a half hour before curtain for *The Heiress*. But that evening, John gave a wonderful performance. The only thing missing was his stovepipe hat which, it seems, was not returned with him to Kennebunkport by some mysterious stranger from Ogunquit.

7

"The name Helen Hayes meant nothing to you? Love, Mother."

Over the next five years, from 1949 to 1954, I worked in a number of summer stock theaters in the East. Each September, after Labor Day, I would come back to New York to search for a new apartment, as I could never afford to keep the old apartment unoccupied over the summer. In 1952, Jim and I had made one of our most successful moves apartment-wise, finding a cold-water flat on West Fiftieth Street for twenty-six dollars a month.

Thirty-five years later, I watched in amazement as my son and his lady moved into an apartment in the Village for a thousand dollars a month, to say nothing of what they paid the broker who managed to find it for them. When I entered their apartment, you could have blindfolded me and I would have tripped over the bathtub in the kitchen on my way to a small front room overlooking the back alley, and a tiny six-by-seven-foot room that they referred to as the bedroom. The only amenities that seemed to have been added from when Jim and I were in a similar situation was a toilet behind a door—inside the apartment, as opposed to out in the hallway—and a small radiator in the small room. And for a thousand dollars a month, they thought this was a find.

For Jim and me, in 1952, twenty-six dollars in rent was about all we could afford. At this time, I began to study at the American Theatre Wing with Joe Anthony and with Joe Kramm, who had written *The Shrike*, a big hit of the previous season directed by José Ferrer. The school at the American Theatre Wing had been established under the GI Bill for servicemen returning from the war who wished to make the theater their career. Women were regularly interviewed and auditioned for the Theatre Wing's school to work with the returning vets. Those accepted could take scene-study classes at no cost. It was wonderful for both the men and for those who, like myself, could not afford to study with other teachers anywhere else.

So upon my return from the wilds of summer stock each year, I would begin classes at the Theatre Wing while, once again, making endless rounds of agents' and producers' offices in the city. In those years, unlike today, actors could get a great deal of casting information from the *New York Times* and other daily newspapers, which would occasionally announce that a particular star was already cast in an upcoming production, as well as what roles the producers were now looking to fill.

One night, while looking through the *Times*, I read that the ANTA group (American National Theatre and Academy), with Robert Whitehead as producer and Harold Clurman as director, was going into rehearsal with Eugene O'Neill's *Desire Under the Elms*, starring Karl Malden as Ephraim Cabot and Douglas Watson as his son, Eben. The *Times* went on to report that the role of Abbie Putnam, the old man's young wife, had not yet been cast. I desperately wanted a chance to audition for this role but knew that without an agent, I would never have the chance to read for it.

What was true then and is still true today, forty years later, is that while the actor is on the street looking for "the job" every day, he is also searching constantly for an agent. A good agent is much more than just a "ten-percenter." The ideal agent not only has the respect of producers, directors and, in today's business, the casting directors, but he also gives the actor a sense of stature and dignity. For the actor, the difference between having an appointment to audition and standing in a line of hundreds hoping simply to be seen is monumental. It's the difference between coming in on your hands and knees, begging for work, and entering a room where people have been told in advance that you have something to offer. You are no longer an invisible part of the cattle call. You are an individual who has already been spoken of highly and whose work is known by someone the producer respects. This producer knows that the agent fully understands what they are looking for in an actor, and that when he recommends a client, he is not wasting the producer's time because, frankly, the agent's own reputation rests on the fact that he or she can be trusted to send an actor who is not only talented but physically right for the role. The agent spares the actor the indignity of salary negotiation. The agent believes in your work when you are certain you will never work again. More important, the agent will bluntly remind you that you are not five feet two inches and cute when you are five feet eight inches and weighing in at roughly one hundred and forty. The best agent is one who is absolutely honest with you while having absolute confidence in you. The agent gives the actor access, opportunity and support. He opens the door. Walking through it is up to you.

I'm not sure when I first heard the name Jane Broder. But when I first arrived in the city, Jane was considered to be one of the best and most respected theatrical agents in New York. For a young actor, to have Jane Broder represent you meant you had something, that what you had to offer as an actor was unique.

At that time, it was not difficult to see Miss Broder in her office, located in the old New York Times Building, at Forty-second and Broadway. I began dropping by Jane's office, making rounds, as soon as I graduated from the American Academy. You saw Jane as soon as you entered the office. You'd open the door and there she was, sitting at her desk, facing you as you came in. She always looked very formidable to me, like a ship in full sail.

Jane Broder was a large woman but had wonderful legs and dainty feet, as many heavy women do. Her problem, as she told me many years later, was not her size but that she was "carrying a great deal of weight in my bosom." She was very much a woman of her time, perfectly dressed and never without her corset, stockings and black high-heeled shoes. Her hair was carefully done and if out of doors, she always wore a hat. This was the woman I saw as I opened the door to her office, awestruck, intimidated and barely able to say a word.

I was—and sometimes wonder if I still am—one of those actors who always began any conversation with an agent or producer in such a way as to let them very easily say to me, "There's nothing here for you." Nevertheless, Jane's statement to me that first time I walked into her office was the most positive rejection I had received to that point.

"Well," she said sharply, "I haven't seen you do anything and I know nothing about you, my dear. I don't handle people that I don't know and haven't seen. However, if you do something in town, call me and I will come to see you."

Months later, I did a scene from Tennessee Williams' *Orpheus Descending*, in a showcase presented by the American Theatre Wing and directed by Joe Kramm. Joe knew Jane quite well and, knowing that I wanted her to see my work, without my knowledge, invited her that afternoon to observe a series of scenes involving me and fifteen other unknown actors. After the performance, which I thought went well, he told me that Jane had been in the audience.

The next day, filled with apprehension, I went to Jane's office which, over the previous six months, she had moved to Madison Avenue. Her desk was no longer in the front office. Now, like most agents, there was a receptionist who greeted you. Jane's was her younger sister, Sophie, a very sweet, soft-spoken lady. In later years, I would learn that Sophie was the exact opposite of Jane in every way. Sophie constantly worried that her sister was being too harsh. While Jane was doing business, Sophie wanted to know if you had eaten. Jane always seemed to be securely in command. Sophie seemed as if everything had dropped off her desk just as she was reaching for it. Jane took charge of your life, Sophie took *care* of it. They were an unlikely, yet complete, team.

"I'll tell my sister you're here," Sophie said, after I timidly introduced myself to her and told her that Jane had been to see my work the day before. Sophie picked up the phone and, in the next moment, Jane appeared at the door to her office and silently indicated that I should come in. I sat down in front of her desk in silence, nearly frozen with fear and waiting for her to speak.

"Well," she said, "you're talented, but, of course, I can't tell too much from that scene." She paused. "Do you always wear your hair like that, dear? What you have to do is to get up in the morning and comb it." She stopped again and stared. I could feel her studying me. Finally she stood and came around the desk, abruptly saying, "Stand up!" As I did, she circled me, struck me in the diaphragm and said, "First thing you have to do is take off some weight! I'm an old-fashioned agent, Miss Dewhurst," she continued without apology. "I know times are changing, but I believe that an actress should look and dress a certain way."

With that said, she went back to her desk and told me to sit down. I could tell we were reaching the end of this conversation.

"If you get a part," she said, "come to see me. It would be unfair for me to sign you on as a client at this time, because I handle only a few people I know well and know what they can do. If anything should come in to this office that might be right for you, I will call."

It was certainly not what I wanted to hear, but was much better than what I had been hearing: "Nothing today." And on that note, I left.

I did not see Jane again for quite a while, but I thought of her that morning, six months later, when I read of ANTA and Robert Whitehead's upcoming production of *Desire Under the Elms*. Mustering up every bit of courage I had, I called Jane Broder and asked her to please get in touch with the Whitehead office and try to get me an appointment to read for the part of Abbie Putnam.

"My dear," she replied, "they are looking for a star for this. No matter how good you are, they are not going to cast some unknown." Undeterred, I begged her to try to get me a reading.

"Can you do this part?" she asked, finally interrupting my pleading.

"Yes, I can."

About an hour later, Jane called back to tell me that I had an appointment the following day at the old ANTA Playhouse on West Fifty-second Street, since renamed the Virginia and beautifully refurbished by the Jujamcyn Organization. There I was met by Jimmy Gelb, the stage manager, who took me into a very tiny room where I was introduced for the first time to Robert Whitehead, the producer, and Harold Clurman, the famed director of The Group Theatre. Both were sitting crunched behind a small desk. Mr. Clurman spoke to me for a few minutes about my background and what other roles I had played before asking me to read a scene with Mr. Gelb. When I finished, we sat for a minute or two, the three of us, staring at one another. It seemed as if I were about to be pushed off the edge of a cliff.

"Is there some scene you have prepared that you could do for us tomorrow?" Mr. Clurman finally said, breaking the silence. I suddenly felt as if I'd been pulled back to safety. I left the theater ecstatic and walked—practically skipped—back to my cold-water apartment, thinking all the way, "Oh, my God, they are thinking of me for this role!"

The next day, I went back to the ANTA, where I was shown into a large rehearsal room filled with at least ten people, including Mr. Whitehead, Mr. Clurman and Ben Edwards, the great set designer with whom I was to work many times in the future. I was a nervous wreck, but the scene went all right, not as well as I knew it had before, but not badly. Everyone behind the table was very courteous and, as I left, I was thanked for coming. I walked home in silence.

Two days later, I read in the *Times* that Carol Stone, a well-known Broadway actress of the time, had been cast in what I had thought for a moment to be "my role." I was terribly disappointed. The following day, Jimmy Gelb called to ask if I would like to be a supernumerary in *Desire Under the Elms*, playing one of the neighbors. I told him immediately that I would love to, and he gave me my call for rehearsal. I had worked on scenes from *Desire Under the Elms* in class and was very eager to be a part of this company, which was headed by Clurman and Whitehead, two men I already knew by reputation and with whom, it would turn out, much of my future career and life would be involved.

ROBERT WHITEHEAD

My first impression of Colleen? That was years ago, when she came in as an extra and understudy in a production I did of *Desire Under the Elms*. I remember her clearly because I wanted to take her to bed right away. I remember when we were staging the dance sequences. I couldn't take my eyes off of her. She was utterly delicious. I wasn't thinking of her at all then in terms of her talent. I was thinking of her looks and her body. She must have been twenty-one or twenty-two at the time. So I sort of kept her around and, later that year, hired her again as an extra in Tyrone Guthrie's production of *Tamburlaine the Great*. I think she may have even had a line or two. Her gifts as an actor were not revealed at that time. But she was lively and attractive and people seemed to enjoy having her around. That's about all that was required for what she was being hired to do.

Later, Colleen did some productions off-Broadway and some very early work for Joe Papp that I became aware of. I could tell then that she had range as an actress and many qualities besides her beauty. But the theater is always all very much a part of all of that. It's surprising who catches your attention and for what. But from then on, I followed her career very carefully and we became good friends, particularly years later after Zoe [Caldwell] and I built the house in Pound Ridge. Colleen and, for a while, George [C. Scott] were living not far away. And in the last twenty years of her life, our families saw a good deal of each other. I haven't thought of Colleen, the young girl, for quite a while. But as I think of Colleen today, I remember her as someone I've been close to most of my life.

It's funny to think back on Colleen as an extra, and then to recall her magnificent performance in *A Moon for the Misbegotten*, as well as other productions she starred in, including a play that Zoe directed her in, *An Almost Perfect Person*. I thought she was very charming in that. Zoe actually got her to comb her hair. She had been doing too many of those "wind blowing through her hair" roles before that. Zoe helped her discover a whole different human being. I liked that. She also, years before, eventually did *Desire Under the Elms* with George at Circle in the Square. I was so attached to the play that it was hard for me to be objective and let the experience of that new production wash over me. But I remember thinking that she was good.

Oddly, for all the work Colleen did in the theater, as well as all the plays I've produced or been a part of, after hiring her as an extra twice, I don't think we ever actually worked together again. But we saw so much of each other outside the theater that we developed a relationship of considerable confidence. She would discuss many things with me, of a professional and a personal nature. She often sent me scripts to read that she had been sent. She seemed to value my opinion of what she might consider doing. One thing many people overlook; in spite of all the laughter and hair blowing every which way, Colleen took her career very seriously. She took the process of being very good at what she did very seriously. Yet, at times, I couldn't help but feel that she also thought she was somehow just getting away with it, that she had fooled people into thinking that she was better than she actually thought she was. I loved her dearly—her vulnerability, her strengths, the strange sense of guilt that she seemed always to carry through her life. She was an extraordinary woman.

ೲ ೲ ೲ

I learned from Harold Clurman my first Jewish word. One day, as I walked past him in rehearsal I heard him say, "You are meshuga." I told Jimmy Gelb later that evening what Harold had said.

"He said you are crazy," he laughed. Oh. How could he tell? I'd barely spoken to him.

At our first rehearsal, in the scenes with the extras, particularly in the dance where we all appeared as neighbors, Harold gave each actor a character, so that we would be playing something specific rather than just filling the stage. When he came to me he said, "Colleen, you will be playing the nymphomaniac." I see. Perhaps *meshuga* meant more than Jimmy knew.

After playing out of town in New Haven and Hartford, *Desire Under the Elms* opened in New York to mixed reviews. "Let's be grateful for the stirring performance that opened at the ANTA Playhouse last evening," said Brooks Atkinson in the January 17, 1952, edition of the *New York Times*. But, countered Robert Coleman of the *Daily Mirror*, "There are those who contend that *Desire Under the Elms* is Eugene O'Neill's best play. They have every right to their opinion. I do not share it." In such a small role, the notices did not really seem to affect me. I was very happy just to be working in a company of actors I admired and for a producer and director I respected. Whatever its success and place—or lack of—in theater history, it was that job in my first production of *Desire Under the Elms* in which I made my first truly important connection, slender as it was, in the professional theater.

Three weeks after we opened, another play, also produced by Bob White-head and ANTA, went into rehearsal. Written by Mary Chase, it was entitled *Mrs. McThing* and was to star Helen Hayes. Even my limited association with Whitehead's office through *Desire* got me a reading, and I was offered the role of the "good fairy." I turned it down, however, because I was very happy to be working in O'Neill's *Desire Under the Elms*, even though only as a supernu-merary. I'd never heard of Mary Chase. The closing notice for *Desire Under the Elms* was posted on the night *Mrs. McThing* opened to rave reviews. The next day, I received a brief telegram from my mother.

It simply read: THE NAME HELEN HAYES MEANT NOTHING TO YOU? LOVE, MOTHER.

Many months later, long after *Desire Under the Elms* had closed, I was again offered the role of the "good fairy" as well as the role of the "bad fairy" in the touring production of *Mrs. McThing*, in which Miss Hayes was re-creating her Broadway success on the road. *Mrs. McThing*'s great success and several months of unemployment had made me very aware of the name Helen Hayes. Not wishing to make the same mistake twice, I quickly said yes and joined the touring company of *Mrs. McThing* in Chicago.

Before I left New York, I was informed that I would wear a wig and hat as the "bad fairy," but as the "good fairy" I was to be appear with my own hair, as a blonde. Terry Faye, then Mr. Whitehead's assistant and now a prominent casting director, took me to a beauty salon somewhere in midtown to have my naturally dark brown hair dyed. In one sitting, my hair was stripped of its true color, and the blond dye, an almost platinum color, immediately applied. I was terrified, as I had never been in a beauty salon and loathed the idea of being a blonde. When I walked back onto the street, four hours later, with platinum hair, I had no idea who I was and could scarcely recognize my reflection in the store windows I passed. When I walked into our cold-water flat, Jim was even more stunned by the sight of me and said that if I had passed him on the street, he wouldn't have known me—or wanted to. I spent the next few days furious and wrapped in a scarf.

Nevertheless, I played my first performances of *Mrs. McThing* in Chicago. The most prominent critic in Chicago at that time was Claudia Cassidy, who was known for being tough. All I can remember from her review of *Mrs. McThing* was that she referred to me as "the sticky ending." Years later, when I was in Chicago to receive an award, I repeated this story to an interviewer. Later, I received word from Miss Cassidy saying that she had read what I'd said and was quite upset. In her letter, she wished me to know that she had looked through all her reviews and could find not one in which she referred to me or anyone as a "sticky ending." I guess I must take her word for it. But ask any actor and he or she will tell you that as the years go by, you may not remember your good reviews, but the bad ones are imprinted indelibly in the mind forever. I stand by my story. Someone said it. I still think it was Miss Cassidy. "Sticky ending," indeed.

One reward of playing *Mrs. McThing* in Chicago was that my mother was able to take the train down from Milwaukee to see me. When she came backstage after the performance, I introduced her to Miss Hayes who was, as always, very gracious. Later that night, in my mother's hotel, we sat opposite each other on twin beds. Mother had not seen me before the performance and I had neglected to tell her that I was now a blonde—on- and offstage. Her first sight of me with platinum hair came with my first entrance as the "good fairy." She had made no comment at all since we returned from the theater, and said nothing still as she sat just opposite me on the bed. I couldn't bring myself to casually ask what she thought of my performance, knowing it could only lead to a discussion of my hair. So there seemed to be very little for us to say to each other. Finally she started to laugh.

"It's not that it doesn't look good on you," she said, completely dismissing any remark about the play or my performance, "but I think we do have to face that it isn't you." This made her laugh even harder, which really began to irritate me, sitting there as blond as Betty Grable but a lot less happy about it.

"At the very least," she continued, barely able to speak, "with this play, we both have been offered certain proof that you are not meant to be a blonde."

With that I finally began to laugh myself. In one way, I had found it fascinating. People on the street did not speak to me the same as when I was a brunette. As a blonde, it seemed I was never expected to join in any conversation that had meaning. I was there simply to decorate, and not with class but with glitz. Worse, I never felt secure walking around in daylight during the run of *Mrs. McThing,* as it seemed I was wearing some foreign ornament on my head that should only have been worn at night, and preferably indoors. Some lessons you need only learn once. For me, this was one of the few. I have never again been a blonde. And in more recent years, as I am now a regular at Thomas Morrisey's salon in New York City, I have never been gray, either.

Some time later, while in Milwaukee visiting my mother, I received a another call from Terry Faye telling me that Mr. Whitehead was to produce a very large and exciting production of Christopher Marlowe's classic *Tamburlaine the Great,* to be directed by Tyrone Guthrie, one of the theater's most beloved and respected directors. The production was to star Anthony Quayle as Tamburlaine, the Asian conquerer; Coral Browne as Zambina, the Turkish empress; Lloyd Bochner as Soldan of Egypt; and would feature a company of

Canadian and English actors. In addition, there was to be a chorus of fifteen American singers and six young American actresses who were to play the non-speaking roles of concubines and virgins. Mr. Whitehead was interested to know if I wished to be one of these six actresses. As the play was already in rehearsal, he asked that, if so, I quickly return to New York before traveling to Toronto to join the company.

I was very excited to be a part of what was thought to be a very important production of the 1956 theatrical season. The day after the company arrived in Toronto, I went to my first rehearsal with the other five actresses hired to play the virgins/concubines. We seemed to move always as a group. This was no doubt due to the fact that we had no idea what we were supposed to be doing. I remember walking with the other five into a huge rehearsal hall where the rest of the company was already working. We quietly took chairs and sat, watching.

I was fascinated by Mr. Guthrie, who was at least six feet four inches. He wore no shoes and literally skated around the room in a pair of red socks, directing and cajoling the actors in front of him in an incredibly booming voice. When the company reached the entrance of the virgins, Guthrie stopped and brought us from our chairs and onto the floor, quickly directing us as to how we were to enter.

There was a speech at this point in which one virgin pleads for the lives of her frightened and inexperienced companions. None of us had really noticed it, as I don't think any of us had read the play. These were nonspeaking roles, after all.

"Which one of you is Dewhurst?" Guthrie asked abruptly.

"I am, sir."

"Read the speech," he demanded. I did, at once.

Rehearsal continued and we, the six virgins, were dismissed until the next day when we came in for our first full rehearsal. When our cue came, we shuffled on as a group while an actor playing part of the pillaging horde pronounced our cruel fate. We all stood and stared as he reached the cue for "the virgin's plea." There was a moment's silence. No virgin spoke.

"Dewhurst," Guthrie's voice echoed from across the rehearsal hall.

"Yes, sir."

"Are you going to read it or not?"

"Yes, sir," I replied and proceeded to read. That night, I went back to the hotel and learned what now appeared to be my lines. In all the years since, I have never asked Bob Whitehead why I was chosen to speak, except that in this particular production, only Canadian or English actors were to have speaking roles. I have always assumed that Mr. Whitehead had told Mr. Guthrie that there was one Canadian actress among the virgins named Dewhurst who could speak or, at least, make a convincing plea for her life.

We opened at the Royal York Theatre in Toronto and played for two weeks. After Toronto, we embarked for New York, the stars traveling by plane and the rest of the company by train. I remember standing in the Toronto train station and suddenly seeing Mr. Guthrie, wearing a wonderful red woolen scarf around his neck, coming toward us with his wife. I couldn't believe that they would be traveling with us on the train. As we sped toward New York, Mr. Guthrie moved among the company, from seat to seat, conversing privately with each one of us. There was no doubt that this group, who already admired him so, now had a tremendous affection for him for this great courtesy.

In New York, the company went immediately into rehearsal on the stage of Broadway's Winter Garden Theatre, where we would play. *Tamburlaine the Great* was a tremendous undertaking, with a huge cast and complicated, over-sized sets. It was a spectacular in the old-time sense of the word. As one person commented to me, "I truly believed that at any moment elephants would walk across the stage." I believe to this day that only Tyrone Guthrie could have conceived and directed such a mammoth production, paying attention to every detail, even a detail or two I could have done without.

We were in the middle of rehearsing the rape scene for the first time in New York when from the back of the house came that by now resonantly familiar voice.

"Stop!" We all froze onstage in mid-rape.

"The only one," he raged as he came down the aisle, "who appears to be acting as though she is being raped is Dewhurst! She is the only one up there who is acting as if she is in danger of being fucked!!" I couldn't believe my ears. I wanted to die. Right then and disappear into the floor.

As staged to that point, I was about four "rapees" back from the front of the stage.

"Dewhurst," he continued, "bring your partner, come downstage and be raped in front."

Like every actress, I was gratified, of course, to be given such prominent focus but, as most actresses, also a little shy for having been recognized in this way.

I had also been asked, once we arrived in New York, if, in addition to my concubine/virgin duties, I would be interested in being an assistant stage manager and assist the three stage managers already working with the production. I gratefully accepted this job as it meant a slight raise in my salary. It became my responsibility to check the prop table before curtain and during intermission. Every night I was responsible for twenty-five or thirty knives, a like number of swords and many other smaller props, which were to be in place for the cast. For better or worse, I am notoriously bad with personal accessories—lighters, eyebrow pencils, glasses and such. There are some, I know, who become a bit nervous if I'm required to handle even a few props onstage.

How I got through placing dozens of knives, swords and spears backstage without incident I will truly never understand. And, not wishing to push my luck, I have never done it again.

We opened in New York to, at best, mixed reviews. *"Tamburlaine,"* wrote William Hawkins in the *World Telegram,* "ought to be proof enough for anybody that Marlowe did not write Shakespeare's plays." The *Times'* Brooks Atkinson wrote: *"Tamburlaine* is all in one key of violence and bombast. Even Marlowe is not entitled to more than two-and-one-half hours of American time." These are notices that are not "money reviews." As it was a very expensive production, playing under capacity in a huge house, *Tamburlaine* closed in less than a month.

So for four weeks, we virgins/concubines dressed together in one dressing room farthest from the stage. I had discovered to my despair, as we were fitted for our costumes, that as concubines we were to be very heavily clothed in long robes. While playing virgins, however, we wore scanty brassiere-like tops, covered by a see-through dress and veil that revealed only the eyes. Trust Mr. Guthrie to see his concubines heavily clothed and his virgins wearing gauze.

I love spending the hours before or between shows in my dressing room, but have always dressed very quickly after the curtain, and *Tamburlaine* was no exception. Many times, as I raced through the backstage hallways and down the stairs, often someone from the audience would assume I had just seen the show with them and would say, "Hi. It was a terrific show, wasn't it?" "Sure was," I'd reply. Despite my featured positioning as a pillaged concubine and my impassioned plea on behalf of all virgins, no one ever seemed to know that I was in the company or recognize me. I can only assume that it was because I was wearing either a burlap cloak or a see-through veil.

I believe that Tyrone Guthrie had a great love and respect for actors. He seemed to feel a kinship with them. Every so often in the few weeks of the run of *Tamburlaine,* he would climb all those stairs and knock on the virgin/concubine door, asking to speak to "Dewhurst," and I would come out into the hall where he would thank me for my performance. I would just stand there and stammer thanks as he would turn and go back down the stairs to another dressing room.

A year or two after *Tamburlaine* closed, I went to see Alvin Ailey at City Center. As I came out into the lobby during intermission, I saw Guthrie standing with two or three people. At first, I was apprehensive about going up to speak to him. But my great admiration for him helped me to overcome my usual shyness and I couldn't help but walk up to the group surrounding him.

"Mr. Guthrie," I said, "you probably don't remember me but—" He cut me off saying, "Of course I remember you, Dewhurst," and we chatted a little about Alvin Ailey before returning to our seats.

Sometime after that meeting, I was doing the "Scottish play" outdoors in

Central Park for Joseph Papp, in which I was playing Lady Macbeth. I had looked forward to playing this role for a long time but, no doubt, because of the curse on this play, it rained consistently. The stage would become too slippery for us to work. Performance after performance was canceled. One evening, before curtain, Joe came back and told us that Tyrone Guthrie was in the audience. We were all terribly excited and none of us could believe our bad luck once again, as, minutes later, it began to pour. I wanted more than anything to play this part with Mr. Guthrie watching. As the rain continued past curtain, some people began to leave the outdoor theater while others sat with umbrellas and newspapers over their heads, hoping for a reprieve that might allow us to begin the play. We were finally told, after holding for half an hour, that we were canceling the show, as only one person remained in the audience. I looked out and there on the bleachers sat Tyrone Guthrie, a lone figure with a dripping newspaper over his head. We would all have done anything to go on just for him. I wanted to do just one scene, the opening scene, anything, while he sat there. We could not.

Later, I was told that Guthrie had come that night specifically to see "Dewhurst" play "Lady M." I was astounded. These are the moments, small as they are, that keep actors alive. These keep them rolling through endless auditions and hungry days while trying to pile up twenty-six weeks of work in order to qualify for unemployment benefits. These moments help an actor to quiet the doubts that assail you from time to time, telling you that just possibly you will never be able to do what it is you love and make a living at it.

To be noted in any way by someone I admired (for me, men like Guthrie, Whitehead, Clurman or Papp), these brief moments of recognition kept me going in this profession of rejection. These small and possibly unknowing acts of kindness and concern give you a sense of dignity and keep you strong enough to come back onto that stage again and again, with the hope and conviction that one day, you will truly be recognized for your best work.

To this day, I remember the uncommon kindness of Tyrone Guthrie with great warmth and admiration.

8

"The essence of that girl was easy for you to find."

I was very nervous as I entered the lobby of an apartment building on Central Park West to attend the first class that was to be taught by Harold Clurman, the celebrated director in whose revival of *Desire Under the Elms* I had just appeared. The class began at eleven-thirty at night, as it was expressly given for actors currently working in the theater. I went to Harold and asked him if, even though I did not have a job at the time, I could be a part of it. I was very fortunate that he did accept me, solely on the basis of having seen something of my work and, perhaps more important, my determination to work in *Desire Under the Elms*.

That first night, Harold stood in front of the class, looking at the twenty-five or thirty of us sitting informally in front of him. At that time, we had all been trained in what had finally become known simply (and perhaps somewhat grandly) as The Method. The class was made up of actors who had studied at The Actors Studio or with Sandy Meisner, Joe Anthony or Stella Adler. We all arrived more than a little arrogant, believing that the way we each approached our work was the *only* way. Now standing before us was one of the founders of The Group Theatre and a true leader in that movement. As I sat waiting for Harold to speak and knowing that I was the only one in the room not currently working, I could feel any overconfidence I might possess evaporate through my shoes.

"You see this?" Harold asked, smacking the wooden floor of the tiny bare stage behind him. "It's not real. You see that door in the back of the stage? It leads nowhere. What *you* do on a stage is *act*," he said, pausing just long enough to see if what he had just said had been heard and, if heard, understood. "When you get up here," he continued, "I do not want to see the day your dog died. I do not want to see your little souls. If I ask you to do Hamlet or Lady M., I want to see the souls of kings and queens."

As he spoke, I could feel a shock going through each of us in the room. We thought that, as Method actors, we were "the chosen," assured of success and ready to claim our places in the theater. And now we were being accused of bringing only our "little souls" to our work onstage? "If you are to be actors, you must broaden your scope," he continued. He went on, telling us that as a generation of actors we had become self-indulgent. Not only were we ill-equipped to deal with certain playwrights, but in our great preoccupation with ourselves and our deepest feelings, we had forgotten the audience completely. We had to learn to project and to use our bodies. We had to develop the discipline to be in complete control of the instrument, the only instrument the actor has, himself.

"You are highly self-impressed," he said, "with this naturalistic acting. If you are having an emotional experience, the fact that the audience cannot hear what you are saying or understand what you are doing doesn't seem to matter to you. Let me assure you, that experience is not the least bit important to the man or woman who has spent their money and is sitting in the balcony, thoroughly bored with you and the play."

As he spoke, I realized for the first time that I had indeed fallen into just the trap of self-indulgence that he described, a trap that had nothing to do with the real Method. This was the middle 1950s. These were the years of analysis first being fashionable, almost hip. Everyone was in it or, at least, discussing it as if they were. I was no exception. Through this relentless concentration on self, this endless analyzation of supposed tortured personal history, I, along with many others, was fast becoming an actor whose persona always took precedence over the life of the character I was playing.

"You are all actors," Harold continued. "*Working* actors. But I will be the only one who critiques the work done in this room."

He then told us that instead of our choosing our own material, he would be giving us specific class assignments. He began to call out our names, one at a time, followed by the play and character on which he wanted us to work.

"Colleen Dewhurst," he said. "I want you to do Racine's *Phaedre,* the role of Constance in *King John,* and Catherine's 'waiting scene' from *The Heiress.*"

My God, I was so happy about *The Heiress.* At least I'd heard of it and played it before, in spite of myself, in summer stock. At that time, I didn't know who had written *King John,* much less who Constance was, and I had never heard of Racine or his *Phaedre.* But I wrote all three down as he spoke, being saved, only by the grace of God, in not having to ask him how to spell *Phaedre.* I wrote it down as it sounded to me, *"Fedre." Racine* I could spell only because I had lived near Racine, Wisconsin.

Jim and I were still living in the cold-water flat on West Fiftieth Street, between Ninth and Tenth Avenues. There was a wonderful library nearby, on Tenth Avenue, just off Fiftieth, where I went, at least once a week, to pick up books to read. I read constantly. It had become my favorite escape and, I must admit, drove Jim crazy. I became such a regular there that I had become friendly with one of the librarians, a woman who sat at the front desk. So I did not feel shy about presenting her with my list from Clurman and telling her of my predicament. She immediately disappeared into the stacks and, in a few moments, returned with copies of Shakespeare's *King John* (how embarrassing to admit today that I didn't know that) and Racine's *Phaedre.*

I worked on the scene from *The Heiress*, of course, first. It went well. Next, I moved on to Constance in *King John.* That, too, seemed to go well enough. I then turned to *Phaedre.* Harold had proved his point. It was now time for me to begin to "stretch." If I was to be a professional, I had to broaden my scope to include many facets of human behavior and, more important, find a way to play those women whose actions and desires had no connection to my every-day life. As Stella Adler once said, "You must study the period. What were the politics of the time, what were the clothes, and why were they designed and worn as they were? Who were the artists? And what effect did the history of the time have on the character you are about to play?"

I studied *Phaedre* for weeks, rehearsing a monologue at home that seemed to go on forever. I became more and more filled with panic as the evening I was to present this piece in class approached. I had no idea what to do and couldn't imagine simply standing still and delivering the lines. Figuring that you could not hit a moving target, and in desperation, I filled that long but simple speech with so much business, I must have seemed like a woman in a kitchen some-where, preparing a meal and talking incessantly. That night, I brought two shopping bags of props to use, anything to keep myself from having to stand still and deliver what seemed to me an interminable speech.

When I was through, I stood on the stage, still for the first time since I'd begun to speak. There was silence for a minute before Harold began to describe a great French actress whom he had seen play the role in Paris, years before. He told, as only he could, the excitement of that evening and of the moment when the actress, as Phaedre, entered and stood, absolutely still and delivered the entire monologue to the audience from center stage, never mov-ing until she exited.

"This," he said, "was one of the most electric and wondrous moments I have ever experienced in the theater."

Harsh criticism was never Harold's way, as it was (and still is) for many teachers. I had seen some acting teachers actually seem to relish being able to demean and destroy an actor in front of a class. Harold made no further state-ment beyond this single recollection. No one else spoke.

"Thank you, Colleen," he said. I gathered my myriad props, came down from the stage and sat. He never spoke to me again about what I had done, but it was very clear what he wanted to say about my ability to act in a way that speaks directly to the audience. I never did the scene again. But Harold had proved his point, not only to me but to the entire class.

Not every play was suited for "kitchen drama." Not every scene needed to be filled with action in order to convey emotion. As a consequence of this, I began to read all of Shakespeare's plays and to investigate, for the first time, various other classical playwrights.

It was in Harold's class that I first played Josie Hogan, in a scene from Eugene O'Neill's *A Moon for the Misbegotten.* I had first discovered the plays of Eugene O'Neill in college and loved them from the first reading. I had prepared a scene from *Desire Under the Elms* in Joe Anthony's class at the American Theatre Wing, and had, of course, been with Harold in his recent production of the play. My affection for the work of this playwright was evident. I was delighted when Harold asked me to prepare a scene from the play with Jeffrey Lynn, whom of course I knew from summer stock.

Jeffrey and I worked on the scene outside of class. After we presented it and had sat back down in our seats, Harold began to speak about Josie, about the loneliness of the human soul, and about going through something that is truly devastating, yet surviving.

"Sometimes," he said, "one's capacity for love surpasses what the human illusion of love is. This makes that character capable of giving love that does not think of itself. Josie loves, without holding back, without asking anything in return. This is love in its purest of forms."

Harold was incredible in moments like this. Often a scene would set him off with such enthusiasm that he would jump up from his seat in the middle of a sentence, throw himself back into the seat with the next thought, miss it completely, and keep right on talking. There was much spitting and waving of arms, but always such love for the actor and for the profession itself that, through it all, he would give you a feeling of dignity and self-esteem. On any given night, I may have entered class knowing I was flat broke and without a job, waiting on tables to pay the rent, and, at best, hoping to get twenty weeks of stock in order to get unemployment. But, hours later, Harold left me with an undeniable feeling of dedication and self-worth. Harold's very presence somehow taught me that this was not a "taking" profession and, best of all, that I had something to give. Harold could put you on a plateau and make you walk out of the door on air, in love with the world and understanding the wonderful double image of having the complete freedom and daring in your work that comes with also having a discipline about yourself and your talent.

Harold Clurman, to me, came the closest to fulfilling what a man and a teacher should be. He loved the theater and life. If I could not be all that he was, if I could not absorb all that he offered, at least Harold gave me a glimpse of something I knew, from then on, I could be a part of.

Over the next two or three years, I attended every class that Harold gave. In one of the last, he turned to me and said, "Colleen, I want you to do *The Glass Menagerie.*" I thought to myself, The Glass Menagerie? *I don't think I want to do the mother in that."*

"I want you to do Laura," he said.

"Laura?" I replied, stunned.

"Yes," he answered. "In the 'gentleman caller' scene."

"Laura?" I said again.

"That's right. I want you to do Laura. Amanda Wingfield's daughter." I felt the entire class was thinking, *"He wants her to play Laura? Not even when she was twelve. He's got to be kidding."*

I read Tennessee Williams' play again as soon as I could get to the library and get my hands on it, remembering, as I read, the original production with Laurette Taylor and Julie Hayden that I had seen with my mother in Chicago. As I read it, Laura seemed to be just as I remembered, a frail, inhibited and frightened young girl, living in a world of her own.

Why am I doing this part? I thought. *I can't believe he's asking me to do this. This is crazy. No one in his right mind would ever ask me to play this.*

A wonderful actor, Chuck Aidman, played Jim, the gentleman caller. As we rehearsed, I found to my surprise that I loved working on the scene. The night we presented it in class, when we finished, there was one of Harold's now-familiar pauses.

"Did you find that easy to do, Colleen?" he finally asked.

"Yes."

"Of course," he continued, "you will never be asked to play it. But remember, the essence of that girl was easy for you to find."

Harold had often told us in class not to be afraid to approach a role that comes easily. "Do not feel you must complicate it to make it worthwhile," he said. "Let it come naturally."

To this day, I have often thought about why Harold asked me to play Laura in that particular scene. I can only assume that he wanted to tell me that I would be cast, because of my looks and voice, as what would be described again and again as "formidable" and "strong" women. I have come to hate those two words. Nevertheless, that night Harold told me, in a way that only he could, that inside my formidable and strong exterior was that shy and frightened girl.

My fondest memory of Harold came years later, at the last curtain call on the opening night of the 1975 Broadway revival of *A Moon for the Misbegotten*. As I turned to start offstage with Jason Robards and Ed Flanders, suddenly up the house stairs, directly from the audience, came Harold. I stood there startled but will never forget how he looked at me right there onstage, in front of the rest of the audience filing out of the house. Harold reached out and we held each other in a tight embrace.

"Well, well, my dear," he said to me, "that is the lady I will never, never forget." For me, it was a moment that I will likewise remember forever.

During the Broadway run of *Moon*, Harold continued to drop by the theater, always unannounced, between a matinee and evening performance. One of my favorite times in the theater, possibly in life, is that time between afternoon and evening shows. I never leave the theater. The house is absolutely quiet and the stage looks wonderful in the glow of the work lights. Backstage, everything is in its place, waiting for the curtain to go up again. Somehow, during those two hours or so, from about five to seven o'clock, I always feel safe. I know I'm not going to be late or miss the performance, because someone will wake me if I fall asleep while everyone else is out to dinner.

At the Morosco, during the run of *Moon for the Misbegotten,* I had two small rooms: one I made up in and dressed in and the other, next to it, had a cot and one small chair, which was all that could fit in there. After a certain amount of time during a long run such as *Moon,* your dressing room begins to resemble a cozy library at home, piled with books and scripts, notes, letters and magazines. There, it seems, nothing can touch you. There, in that time between shows when you are nearly alone, you can dream without pressure, nap without fear.

It was in these moments that I would hear footsteps coming up the back-stage stairs and down the hallway toward my dressing room. I would sit up just as Harold appeared at the door. Always looking very dapper, he would look in solicitously and ask if he was interrupting me. He would then take off his hat, sit down across from me and proceed to talk, taking off on some subject or another and nearly carrying the entire conversation himself. I would lie back on my small cot, my head resting on my hand, as we spoke and laughed of things past and present.

"Are you tired today, Colleen?" he asked me one day. "Is it too much doing two performances of this play in one day?"

"Oh, no. It's exhilarating, and in some ways, rather cathartic," I replied before launching into some discussion about how I felt about O'Neill and Josie, the woman I was playing. Harold sat through about two minutes of this monologue before he interrupted me, nearly without my being aware of it, to ask if I knew anything of Jeanne E's performance of Sadie Thompson in *Rain.*

"No, not particularly."

"Well," he went on, "she was magnificent. But as she continued to play the role, her life outside of the theater began to disintegrate, in the usual way for us, drinking, carrying on and the like. And," he continued, "as usual, this, combined with the demands of her performance, did not work."

I sat there startled, wondering if this statement was why he had come by and what brought it to his mind as he was strolling down West Forty-fifth Street, looking up to see the name of one of his students emblazoned in lights above the Morosco Theatre.

"Colleen," he continued, "the physical and emotional mechanism of the actor must be cared for. It is not a natural strength that can be taken for granted. It must be kept fresh and constantly renewed. Energy," he concluded, "is the actor's greatest asset."

Energy had certainly always been one of Harold's greatest assets. I began to laugh as I remembered Harold, those many years ago, in class, galloping off into one of his many dissertations about acting and the theater. I could see him standing against the stage and speaking, his arms flailing, staying put for just a few moments before sitting down for ten seconds, then getting up again and talking, still more about energy. Above all, he wanted to see our energy.

"That's what I want," he would say, "I want energy on this stage. Come in here with energy. I don't care if you are dying. I want you to die with energy!"

Harold asked me why I was laughing.

"It's not important, Harold," I replied, coming out of my reverie and looking at the man now sitting there quietly in front of me.

"Well, then," he asked, looking at me as if he was not entirely convinced that it wasn't and slightly changing the subject, "do you think it is a good idea to play both a matinee and evening performance of a play as demanding as this?"

This question truly surprised me because I thought that Harold, more than anyone, believed that as an actor, you did what you were asked to do in the theater, without question and without false temperament. That you met the demands of the play with as much danger and creativity as you could, each time you performed. When I didn't immediately respond to his question, he let it drop without further comment. In that moment, much was left unsaid and unanswered.

We spoke for a bit longer about other things, small talk, before he finally got up, came over and gave me a kiss. Picking up his hat, he took a look at himself in the mirror and said, "I mustn't stay any longer. You should get some rest in order to play tonight with energy!" And with that, he left.

I fell back on the cot, listening to Harold's footsteps disappear down the hall. As I lay there, staring upward, looking at those wonderful pipes running across the ceiling that let me know I am in the dressing room of a Broadway theater, I thought about what Harold had said and about what was going on in my life, here in the theater and outside, at home. I realized that no matter how much time had passed or how much success might come and go, Harold considered each of us who had been his pupils as *his* actors, somehow, his children. And I thought again, for the first time in years, of his quiet response to my work as *Phaedre*, how he made his point simply and then asked that we both move on. I understand today that Harold was compelled to pass on to us all everything that he knew, all that he had experienced and seen. His love for actors and the theater was boundless and complete. And his gift was in how he unselfishly shared that with so many.

Don't get the wrong impression, Harold was not by any means a goody-goody. He had, like most in our profession, a tremendous ego and vanity and could make some of the most devastating remarks about what he saw onstage. He loved to be the center of an adoring group in the lobby of a theater, between acts, holding court, smoking his cigar and glancing at you quickly to be sure you had caught some bon mot he had tossed off. And when you laughed, letting him know that you had, how he could twinkle and preen before taking another puff of the cigar.

I remember Harold calling me, after *Moon* had closed, to ask if I would take part in a symposium he was to conduct on the relationship between the critic and the actor. In addition to his work as a director and teacher, Harold was, in later years, one of the theater's most respected newspaper critics. We were to discuss, he said, what theatrical criticism is and what we on the actor's side of the footlights felt about being criticized. I thought this was a wonderful idea and marveled that Harold, in his infinite wisdom, understood that many of the men and women there, both performers and critics, did not truly understand what the art of criticism is.

I cannot say that I remember much of what was said that day. I do know, however, what a gift Harold possessed for fair and honest theatrical criticism. When you read Harold's reviews, you read a man who could be as excited and enthusiastic as a child when he witnessed a play that moved him. Likewise, the review in which he had been disappointed in either the playwright, the actors or the execution of the play was always written with a sense of sadness. No matter what the experience had been, Harold's reviews were always stimulating. He brought to them his own incredible intellect and joy in being alive. Above all, he brought an understanding of not only that evening but of hundreds of years of theater history, as well as what the theater is and what it should be.

Harold's reviews could be devastating, but he never lowered himself to sniping, or worse, cruelty, taking potshots at actors or playwrights for the sake of his own amusement or to show off his own facility for language and the well-turned phrase. Harold provides a true contrast in this day of destructive critics, who are dangerous because of the combination of intellect and anger that makes them eager to hurt and destroy rather than illuminate with constructive observation, to both audience and actor, of what they have seen.

If, in his view, a play or performance had been a disaster, he stated it very clearly. In fact, I can distinctly remember Harold's to-the-point critique of me in an early play in which I had opened that he was assigned to review.

"I do not feel," he wrote, "that Miss Dewhurst is quite ready yet to take on this role."

I thought about that one for a good, long while. What did he mean? What had I not done? I felt much better, years later, when Harold wrote in his review of *A Moon for the Misbegotten* in *The Nation:*

> *I am rather pleased to relate that Colleen Dewhurst, now in the role [of Josie], was asked to play it for me while she was still a beginner, in one of my private classes, before I had ever seen the play. Colleen Dewhurst brings*

a powerful womanliness to the part of Josie. She is of the earth, warm and hearty. She looks and sounds like a person who can do her own and her father's hard work; one, moreover, who possesses the vast sexuality she boasts of, as well as a woman chaste through the very force of that sexuality.

No matter whatever had gone on before, Harold was finally saying, *yes,* I had grown into being able to play a woman and had become the actress who could fulfill such a role.

The last time I saw Harold was in September of 1980 when I went to see him at Mount Sinai Hospital in Manhattan. I had heard that he was very ill, possibly dying, but had been seeing visitors. I was very nervous. When I entered his room, Harold's wife was sitting in a corner, away from the bed, reading. The room had a large window, nearly the length of the room, facing out over Central Park. The sun was streaming through. Harold was lying on his side, facing the window. His eyes were closed. His wife stood and greeted me when I entered, very kindly walked over to Harold and, bending close to his ear, whispered softly, "Harold, Colleen is here to see you," before bringing another chair from against the wall and placing it next to the bed. I thanked her and sat down facing him. Harold seemed to me to be very small. But his face was very smooth and clear, without wrinkles.

"Colleen?" he said, opening his eyes. He began to speak in a whisper that I could not hear. I had to lean over quite close to him.

"Your hair looks beautiful with the sun behind it," he said.

I thanked him very politely, as if we were at a tea and he was someone I had just met. There was nothing about Harold that indicated that he was in any pain, but it was clear that it took great effort for him to speak. I felt there was nothing for me to say. So we sat, for a time, across from each other, in silence, looking into each other's eyes, out the window, and then back to each other again. I stayed another fifteen minutes during which there were such long silences that I thought he might have gone back to sleep. But then, without warning, he would open his eyes again and, without hesitation, look directly into mine.

"You'll never leave the theater, will you." His words seemed more a statement than a question.

"No," I replied. We sat again in silence for a while.

"Do you know Aaron Copland?" he asked.

"No."

"You should. He's very American. Like you."

A week later, Harold was gone. I know, with a great certainty I feel about little else, that Harold Clurman will never be gone from me—nor his influence from the American theater.

9

"Line first, business second."

One late afternoon, as I was sitting in the apartment on West Fiftieth Street, the phone rang. I picked it up.

"Hello?"

"Colleen Dewhurst?" the voice on the other end asked.

"This is she."

"My name is Joe Papp," he continued, "and I'm starting a small Shakespeare company in a church on East Sixth Street. My wife, Peggy Bennion, is in the class you take with Harold Clurman. She's suggested I call because I'm going to do *Romeo and Juliet* and I would like you to come down so we can meet."

"What role are we talking about?"

"Juliet," he answered.

"Have you ever seen me, Mr. Papp?"

"No."

"Well," I replied, "I couldn't do Juliet when I was thirteen."

Joe asked me to come down to see him anyway, and I was happy to do so. The theater, at the Emanuel Presbyterian Church on East Sixth, was very tiny, shaped like half a teacup. Once we met, Joe also realized that I was not to be his Juliet. Instead he cast me in *Titus Andronicus* as Tamora, Queen of the Goths, a woman not known for her kindness, a killer in every sense of the word who, at the end of the play, ends up being fed, by her enemies, a pie into which her two sons have been baked. (Who would have known that several years later I would end up with two sons? This makes us all very tense.)

Roscoe Lee Browne was in the cast of *Titus Andronicus,* playing Aaron, the Moor. Meeting Roscoe in *Titus* began what has been one of the dearest and most important friendships of my life. The cast also included my husband, Jim Vickery, and a young actor, Clem Fowler, who today has a successful career as a character actor. It was so wonderful to get up in the morning and go down to this tiny church and work with people who were totally dedicated to what they were doing and felt that this was what the theater was about. *Titus Andronicus* was one of Joe's first productions to receive any notice from the mainstream press. *Variety* wrote:

> *Although a long way off-Broadway, the New York Shakespeare Festival's auditorium is nicely adaptable to Shakespearean staging. . . . There is little self-consciousness as the actors weave their way through the audience, except possibly when an extemporaneous hanging seems about to take place in the collective patrons' lap.*
>
> *The New York Shakespeare Festival is a non-profit organization chartered by the N.Y. State Education Dept. and the professionals participating sign releases with Actors' Equity and work for carfare. Among those using the showcase advantageously are Leonard Stone . . . and Colleen Dewhurst as a handsomely seductive Queen of the Goths, who handles the pentameters with provocatively offbeat emphasis.*

Not bad for the first time out.

One Christmas, about four years ago, Clifford Stevens, my agent and, more important, a beloved friend, brought me a gift. I opened it and there was a framed program of the 1956 New York Shakespeare Festival's production of *Titus Andronicus* by William Shakespeare, produced by Joseph Papp, directed by Frederick Rolf, designed by Bernie Joy, incidental music by David Amram and, as one of the "soldiers, Goths and citizens": Clifford Stevens.

This was the first time I worked for Joe, and I loved it. My theater career and my life, in the thirty-five years since then, have been closely tied to that of Joseph Papp, both onstage and off. Here, in 1956, was a young, attractive man who, out of nowhere, appears with a dream to bring Shakespeare to the people of New York City in its city parks. We, who started with him, watched with great amazement and awe as Joe won each successive battle against the city's greatest powers necessary to realize his dreams. Many thought these were all just steps to Joe's becoming a powerful producer in the commercial theater. This may be because so many of us, as individuals, were consumed by our own ambitions, where we were going, and how fast we could get there. Unlike Joe, we had no overall vision for the city, for the theater or its audience. In every age, there are men and women who have dreams that they pursue fanatically. They do not acknowledge the words *no* or *impossible*, as finally, one by one, every obstacle is overcome.

There is no need to relate what Joseph Papp has done for untried playwrights, unknown actors, nontraditional casting and the young because it is now all a matter of public record, not only in New York City but throughout our nation. Today, Joe Papp is acknowledged internationally as a champion of the theater and its artists.

But I love Joe, not for what he has done, but because he is still dangerous and has always done what he believed in and says what he feels must be said. God knows, he's stumbled and had his failures through these past forty years. He is known to be tough and arrogant. But there is another Joe who, back in those days, knew you were hungry and without the rent and saw that you were provided for in a way that made you think you hadn't asked for a loan. There are many of us out here whose life in the theater began with Joe, whom we knew as a friend of incredible loyalty. For us, it was Joe who finally made us aware of the importance of the theater and of its artists and who, most importantly, taught us that theater does belong to the people. Sometimes when I feel that I am only treading water or that there is nothing challenging out there, I find myself saying, "If only I could find a dangerous play." But what if I did find such a play; who in today's theater would care? I then feel a sense of security come over me as I remember that I have a home. I can still go to Joe. He'll let me try it. Joe doesn't believe in *safe*. Joe believes in the artists and the work and I loved him for it then, in 1956, and I love him for it now. I know now that when I picked up the phone that day and first heard, "Colleen Dewhurst, my name is Joe Papp," it was the most important introduction of my career and my life. Since that time, I have grown to love this man. There will never be another like Joe.

SOON AFTER *Titus* closed, I was asked to meet with Edward Everett Horton, the famous character-comedian who had been in hundreds of films, to discuss my playing three engagements with him in *Nina,* a three-character play, as his usual leading lady was ill. I had worked with Edward a few summers before in Kennebunkport and knew him to be as ornery offstage as he could be charming on. Nevertheless, at the meeting with Edward and his agent, I accepted the offer. Edward then told me not to speak as he informed the agent what my salary was to be, a figure that was double what I would have ever thought to ask. The agent then placed the appropriate calls to the Coconut Grove Playhouse in Florida, the Milwaukee Rep Company and the Barnesboro Playhouse in Pennsylvania, where all of Mr. Horton's demands, including that of my salary, were accepted. Mr. Horton then went on to describe what my costumes would have to be for the play and asked if I owned anything like what he described in my own wardrobe. Of course, I did not.

"Then," he announced, "*we* shall go shopping."

The next day, this peculiar twosome, myself and Mr. Horton, entered Saks Fifth Avenue. Edward asked for a particular saleswoman, who appeared at once. After graciously greeting her, he went on to describe just what he wanted for me. A number of dresses and several hats were brought out and, for the next hour, this kind saleslady and I gave Mr. Horton a fashion show. He picked out two incredibly beautiful outfits from the ones I had tried on, as well as a hat, a purse and two pairs of shoes. I was afraid to look at the bill and even more terrified of saying that despite Mr. Horton's enthusiasm, I could not afford to purchase the clothing. Just as I was about to stammer something to this effect, Edward touched my hand lightly and pulled his checkbook from his suit pocket.

"Of course," he said matter-of-factly, "as this is my choice, I will take care of it." To this day, I remember one incredibly beautiful dress of rose-red chiffon in which I don't think I have ever looked better.

In between fittings at Saks, Edward told me that he did not have a leading man yet, as he used to tour Christopher Plummer in the role but Chris was now too much in demand to work in stock. I asked if Edward would meet my husband, Jim Vickery, which he did, hiring him on the spot. So for the next couple of months, Jim and I worked together on tour with Edward in *Nina*.

I had first met Mr. Horton when he played *Nina* at Kennebunkport during one of the summers in which I had been a member of the resident company. As he had come to Kennebunkport with a leading lady, I had not, at that time, had the chance to play opposite him. Audiences loved him, and he always played to a full house. I first worked with Mr. Horton later that same season, when he returned in another play, the title of which I cannot remember—something with sheep—in which I played opposite him in a leading role.

At that time, I found him to be very irascible and short-tempered (particularly with the poor apprentices). Edward was a man who knew exactly what he wanted from each supporting player, down to the exact reading of a line of dialogue. One is not expected in summer stock to bring all of one's motivational "Method" approach to the work being done in rehearsal and performance. There is hardly time to learn your lines. But I did resent being told by Mr. Horton both how I was to read a line and how to play any bit of business.

Every day in Kennebunkport I came to rehearsal in jeans and a T-shirt, bare feet or sneakers. I quickly sensed that although Mr. Horton did not approve of me, he would not ever confront me. At the dress rehearsal for the "sheep" play, I was costumed in the perfect suit, hose and high heels, as befitted the very proper secretary I was playing. When I made my first entrance, Mr. Horton, who was already onstage, stopped midscene and said, "Well, look at this. Miss Dewhurst has legs," and picking up exactly where he left off, continued playing the scene, leaving me quite dumbfounded.

As many stars before him who came to play one week with our stock resident company, Mr. Horton had directed me very specifically. Looking back on it all now, I can understand how strange it must have seemed to these stars to play the same play with a new cast every week in a different theater, and how frustrating to have a bit of business or laugh line play terrifically one week and then be lost the next due to another actor's inability or weakness. It was no wonder that our directors often served only as figureheads while the stars quickly moved us into the places that had worked with the previous week's cast and would work again the following week, after we were through.

Edward was no exception. In a scene in which he was dictating a letter to me, he would speak, "Dear Mr. So and So," and I would type it out. His next line in the letter began with the word *I.* He told me that I was immediately to hit one typewriter key for the *I* before he could complete the sentence. He then instructed me to stare at him, waiting for the next word. I thought the whole bit of business was silly, but did as I was told. At that moment on opening night, the audience fell over laughing. The longer we stared at each other over the typewriter, neither of us moving a muscle, the harder they laughed, and as we held, Mr. Horton, with his upstage eye out of view of the audience, winked at me.

When we exited at the end of the first act, for the first time, Mr. Horton spoke to me offstage.

"You're a rock out there, aren't you?" he said smiling.

At the end of each performance, Mr. Horton would give a curtain speech, which the audience always adored and, by the end of the week, all of us could mouth with him from backstage.

"There is the sound of the wind and the trees and the waves on the beach, but nothing," he would exclaim, throwing open his arms to the audience, "is to the heart of an actor like the sound of applause." Except, Edward neglected to add, perhaps his paycheck.

All through our rehearsal period, it had been as if Edward never really saw me. I was something that had been handed to him, and his only hope was that I might be passable and, above all, would feed him his lines and business correctly. After finishing his curtain speech opening night, Edward came to my dressing room. He knocked and came in. I turned to him in my chair and looked at him. He stood there staring at me with what seemed to be a faint look of surprise.

"You are very good out there," he said, still with that look of surprise. "But allow me just to point out another moment in the second act."

The moment he spoke of was a line I delivered to him in anger, stamping on his foot. There had been a slight murmur of laughter that first night. But the reason it was not a *big* laugh, Edward now went on to explain, was that I was trying to do too much at once. Instead, he continued, I should complete the line first and then stamp on his foot.

"In comedy," he said, "it is always line first, business second." *I do not work in that technical manner,* I thought to myself as he spoke. But, as the typewriter bit—*I* spoken first, business hitting the key second—had worked so well, I simply said, "Yes, Mr. Horton" and, looking satisfied with himself, he turned and left.

Second night, second act. I said my line, and then stamped hard on his foot. At the exact point where the audience had only giggled the night before, that night they fell over laughing as we stared at each other; and once again, the wink from Mr. Horton's upstage eye.

We rehearsed *Nina* at the Coconut Grove in Florida, a beautiful theater in which Jim and I had a small apartment upstairs above the stage. Mr. Horton was staying, naturally, in a posh hotel nearby.

As I worked with Edward in rehearsals, I noticed that although I was playing his mistress, he never at any time touched me onstage in a romantic way. Although I would take his hand at times, we never embraced and, at the end of the first act, as he fell into a faint on the couch, he directed me, as his mistress, to simply kneel and drape just one arm around him. By the middle of rehearsals, I realized that Mr. Horton, who was probably about seventy at that time, felt that somehow it would be distasteful to his audience if there were any external display of affection between us. And who knows, perhaps there might have been. He'd certainly been right about everything we did onstage up to that point.

My favorite moment in this perfectly dreadful farce came the opening night of our Coconut Grove engagement. As the curtain came down at the end of the first act, to no laughter, and I knelt beside him, facing upstage, my one arm draped carefully over his shoulder, Edward whispered to me something that was not in the script and that he had never said before: "I am dying, Egypt, dying."

Thank God the curtain was coming down, because I, of course, had to turn my head to keep from laughing. Edward so loved my reaction that night that he did it at every performance for the duration of the tour. Years later, when playing Cleopatra for Joe Papp in Shakespeare's *Antony and Cleopatra* at the Hecksher Theatre, I always had a brief moment of fear as Antony, being held in my arms, repeated that famous line in its true context. Each night I would silently threaten myself with death if, thinking back on Edward's whispered rendition of the line, I would feel myself want to laugh. How kind and good this rascal of a man had been to me. And how odd to be playing Shakespeare's Queen of the Nile and remember every night as Antony died in my arms, "Line first, business second."

When we arrived with *Nina* in Barnsville, our last stop on the tour, I received another call from Joe Papp. I have no idea how he found me. He informed me that his production of *Julius Caesar* was currently playing outside in a park on the Lower East Side. It was a wonderful production, he said, and although they had sent out flyers to critics, newspapers, agents, producers and the like, no one had yet come down to see it.

The next production to go into rehearsal, he said, was to be Shakespeare's *The Taming of the Shrew*, directed by Stuart Vaughn. J.D. Cannon had already been cast to play Petruchio.

"And you," Joe said, "are my Kate."

Would I be able to come back to New York and do it? There would be no money, just carfare, he said, and possibly no one of importance to see it, but, as there was no admission, he could assure me a full house every night of the people who lived in and around that park and who really wanted and needed free theater.

Joe was right. The most beautiful crowd in the world showed up at that theater for *The Taming of the Shrew*. It seemed as if the whole Lower East Side came night after night, including many people who did not speak English but who came with copies of the play and followed the script as we spoke. This was an audience that became involved in what we were playing, listening and yelling back to us on the stage. To me, it seemed as if we were playing *Taming of the Shrew* to an audience much like the one that, three hundred years before, had watched the play's first performances in Shakespeare's London.

This was an audience that became completely involved in the action onstage, shouting to Petruchio to look out each time he turned his back on me—as I would be about to strike him again. One night, in the last scene of the play, after J.D., as Petruchio, had dropped me hard onto the concrete stage and was exalting to the audience his final domination over Kate, from somewhere in the back a man yelled out, "A-w-w-w-w-w, give her a pillow." The audience roared in agreement, and I had to roll over onto my upstage side to hide how hard I was laughing.

On another occasion, on a very, very hot night, as I was making my plea to the women about how we should behave to please our men, the laughter seemed much louder than it had ever been previously. I thought, *Well, I'm obviously playing this brilliantly tonight.* Just then, I noticed in my peripheral vision a little boy of about four or five standing next to me, onstage, staring up at me. He was wearing no pants, only a T-shirt. I paused as we stared back at each other. I reached down and he took my hand. We walked together back and forth in front of the audience to great applause as I continued my speech about how we women should take care of our men. All of them.

I will never have another experience in the theater like that of Joe's first production of *Taming of the Shrew*. Good actors working on a play that is considered one of the greatest in the English language for an audience that would come out of tenement apartments on hot summer nights to watch something that was being given to them. They became immediately as much a part of the play as the actors, reacting viscerally and without restraint while, at the same time, educating themselves. During the day, children from the neighborhood would hang around the edges of the stage and watch rehearsal. The young boys would become as fascinated by the actors' swordplay and the movement onstage as the little girls were entranced by the actresses in their long rehearsal skirts. None of us were stars, we were just one of them, part of the neighborhood, which, to all of us, made it seem like anything at that moment was possible.

Once we had opened, I asked Jane Broder to please come and see me do Kate. She said, without hesitation, that she would. So, one night, about a week later, Jane and her sister, Sophie, came down unannounced to the Lower East Side and sat outside in their starched summer dresses, in girdles and stockings, taking their places on those hard concrete benches among the locals in their T-shirts and jeans. After the show, I saw Jane for just a moment, but she did not say any more to me than that she and Sophie had enjoyed the production very much.

The next day, I went to Jane. Summoning all my courage, I asked her to take me on as a client.

"I have a feeling about you," she said, "now that I've seen you in a complete play. But," she added, "I don't know what I can do for you. Why should I tie you up if there might be other people who can handle you?"

I didn't have an answer. I only knew that I wanted Jane to be my agent. I wasn't interested in anyone else. I barely knew anyone else. Although disappointed, I could not let it go at that. "If another job comes up or someone else approaches me, may I call you again?" I asked.

"Certainly, my dear."

That's all I needed to know.

About two weeks after Jane and Sophie had come down to see *Shrew*, there was a tremendous thunderstorm during a performance, immediately following Kate and Petruchio's wooing scene. The audience ran for cover as the cast dashed into the huge maintenance building behind the stage. Suddenly a gentleman and his wife appeared, asking who were we, where had we come from, and who was in charge? That was when I first met Arthur and Barbara Gelb.

At the time, Mr. Gelb was on staff at the *New York Times* as a second-string drama critic. This summer evening, they had nothing to do and, as they had received one of the flyers that Joe had been sending to everyone in the theater for over two months, they had decided to wander in and see just what was being done. Although we could not continue the performance, Arthur wrote a very wonderful notice that appeared two days later in the *Times:*

> *It started to rain last night at 9:45. For most heat-weary New Yorkers, it was a blessing. But for 1,800 spectators and forty-five actors at the East River Amphitheater . . . the downpour had the effect of a slap in the face.*
>
> The Taming of the Shrew *was being lustily performed there against a background of tooting tugboats and flashes of heat lightning. Petruchio had just finished giving Kate a sound trouncing. The audience was leaning raptly forward on tiers of long wooden benches. If ever an audience was with a play, this one was.*

When Joseph Papp announced . . . over a loudspeaker that the show could not continue because of the rain, exclamations of dismay resounded in a blending of dialects that could only be heard on the Lower East Side. Many of the disappointed shouts came from children.

The merits of the performance must be judged on one act alone. But even from this abortive look, the production could be rated as a resourceful one. There is in particular a spirited and lovely Kate, played by Colleen Dewhurst.

Gelb had been so taken by the evening that he also went to Brooks Atkinson, perhaps one of the theater's greatest critics, who, at the time, was the chief critic for the *Times*. At Arthur's insistence, Mr. Atkinson came down to the Lower East Side to see us and wrote his own lovely review of *The Taming of the Shrew* that appeared prominently in the *Times* two weeks later. What follows here is the last two-thirds of Mr. Atkinson's review, in which he relates for his reader of 1956 the circumstances surrounding this production—circumstances that set the stage for the phenomenal success of the New York Shakespeare Festival:

Sometimes the theater is dismissed as a charming anachronism in a world of mass entertainment. But mass audiences would not continue to flock to the East River Amphitheater if they did not enjoy what they were seeing. The amphitheater seats nearly 2,000 people. It has been filled or nearly filled at every performance [of The Taming of the Shrew*].*

Nearly everything that is picturesque about outdoor Shakespeare in one corner of a turbulent city weighs against a theater performance. But at the Thursday evening performance . . . the audience sat through two and a half hours of classical farce with complete absorption, laughing not only at the horseplay but at the gibes in the dialogue. . . . The company that has been recruited under the management of Joseph Papp is as sound as the audience, with nothing at stake except an evening's good time.

Two months of Shakespeare in a park have cost $2,000 chiefly for costumes, scenery and amplifying equipment. Nobody has contributed as much as the actors, the dancers, the backstage crew and the staff. They have given skill, time and energy. But other people have given enough money to make this quixotic enterprise possible. . . . About three weeks ago the company found itself hopelessly in debt for $750 for expenses—chiefly for the amplifying equipment—incurred in this production of Shrew. *It looked as if the bailiffs would make off with everything and put a dismal end to a unique midsummer night's entertainment.*

When Arthur Gelb included that bit of gloomy news in his comments on this production in these columns, the catastrophe was miraculously avoided.

Herman Levin, producer of My Fair Lady, *sent his check for the full amount the next day. He made it possible for some actors to continue working for free. Next year Mr. Papp would like to raise $25,000 to put on his productions in several of the city's parks and pay the actors $40 a week which is the Actors' Equity minimum rate for off-Broadway actors. That seems like the least New York could do for a good deed in a heedless city.*

With Brooks Atkinson's blessing, our world changed overnight. Suddenly in our audience of neighbors in T-shirts and jeans appeared men in white shirts, jackets and ties, and ladies in summer dresses. Suddenly we were "the play to see" and everything changed. For the last two weeks of our run, it was different. We were in a hit that would have a positive effect on my career, as well as Joe's, but I missed the shouting. I missed the feeling of not knowing what might happen next or how that play would that night move an audience unafraid of talking back. I missed the little boy in the T-shirt.

During this time, I received phone calls from two agents I had never met, one of whom was considered to be "very big." This man told me over the phone that he had been very impressed with me and invited me over to meet him the following day. I'd never before seen anything like his office. It was huge and entirely different from Jane's rather drab but functional workspace. The phone rang incessantly during our brief meeting and he made much of telling his secretary through an intercom on his desk to "hold all calls while I'm speaking to Miss Dewhurst." I was very impressed. Another agent was brought in and introduced to me. This man spoke to me of the great movie career I could have and of his connections on the West Coast. The more they talked at me, the less impressed I became.

"We'd like to sign you right now," the first one finally said.

We all sat looking at one another in silence. It seemed that they were each waiting for someone to speak, and since there was no one else in the room but the three of us, it would have to be me.

"Thank you for your interest in me," I stammered slowly. "But I am actually on my way to Jane Broder's office. She is who I would like to represent me."

The second agent immediately launched into telling me that he had a movie being cast right then that he was certain I was right for.

"If you think I'm right," I said naively, "I'm sure Jane would be happy to speak to you about it."

The movie agent looked at the man who had called me in, as if he could not believe what he was hearing. Looking back to me, he smiled. "Jane Broder is a wonderful woman," he said sweetly. "There has probably never been a better agent. But Colleen, I don't mean to be cruel, but she is now old and tired."

I sat absolutely still, unable to take my eyes from him as he spoke, which he obviously intended to keep doing.

"But even if she were younger," he continued, "her only connections are here, in New York, on Broadway. And if you wish to really have a career, you will, of course, have to leave Broadway and move to Los Angeles. Colleen, let me tell you honestly, you will not be easy to sell to the movies. You need someone young who is a good salesman. You need us."

It suddenly dawned on me, as I listened to him, that neither of these "flesh-peddlers" had yet even mentioned my performance in *The Taming of the Shrew.* All that had been talked about were my looks, my presence and my voice. Nothing about my work. That thought helped me to stand up, cutting off the monologue that had been going on now for what seemed quite some time.

"Gentlemen, thank you," I said. "But I think I know now what I would like to do."

I went straight from there to Jane's office. I told her that I had just been to visit the other agent.

"How did it go?" she said with absolutely no nervousness or tension.

"I want to go with you," I said without hesitation. "I want to say that I am with you."

"These other agents," she replied, "there are many things that they can do for you. They must have told you that."

"I don't believe them."

Jane said nothing for a moment. I sat in silent fear, unable to know what to expect or what would happen to me now.

"You can come with me," she said, sitting back in her chair. I was thrilled. And for the next twenty years, Jane Broder was my agent. I will always be grateful to Jane for teaching me any morality I have about the theater.

A short time later, Jane made an appointment for me to meet Kermit Bloomgarten, one of the theater's most prominent and respected producers of new American plays. Jane and Kermit had known each other for years. They had fought, not spoken, made up, fought again, not spoken and made up all over. When Jane gave me the appointment, she also informed me that she would be coming with me.

When I arrived at Jane's office on the day of the interview, I was wearing slacks and a sweater. Jane took one look at me and said, "Colleen, you will not go like that. Go home, put on hose, a dress and a decent pair of shoes. I've worked with Mr. Bloomgarten for years. He has produced beautiful work in the theater, and you will show him the respect due to him by presenting yourself as a lady. As I told you," she continued, "I may be old-fashioned, but if you wish to be my client, that's how it will be."

I left and came back better dressed. When Jane and I got into the elevator that would take us up to Mr. Bloomgarten's office, I was nervous both about the meeting and going with Jane. I could barely look at the other people in the car, knowing they were probably also actors who had been sent over for an appointment—and were traveling alone. The doors shut and before I knew what had happened, Jane whipped a comb out of her purse and proceeded to comb my hair right there, in the elevator, in front of everyone!

"Don't do that, Jane," I said, trying to pretend that this wasn't happening.

"Don't do what?" Jane replied, as if indeed nothing out of the ordinary was happening. "Just let me straighten this out. You look just awful."

We finally arrived, freshly coiffed, and Jane and I entered Kermit's office and sat down. There must have been thirty actors in that room, all waiting to meet Mr. Bloomgarten, all with appointments made by other agents. Jane had made only one. Mine. Suddenly I was very glad that she had come with me.

We were among the first to be asked into Mr. Bloomgarten's office. I sat there silently as Kermit and Jane spoke of old times. Finally, he turned to me and said, "Well, Miss Dewhurst, it's very nice to meet you. I've heard a great deal about you from Jane and others. But I was interested in meeting you myself." He asked me a few general questions about myself and what I'd done before asking nonchalantly, "How old are you?"

"I'm—," I began to reply.

"Excuse me, Colleen," Jane interrupted, "I'll answer that question. Colleen will obviously answer any question that is asked her," she continued, turning back to Mr. Bloomgarten. "How old do you think she is?"

"Well, I don't know, Jane," he replied.

"Oh, yes you do," she answered. "How old do you think she is?"

Kermit finally replied with some age I cannot even recall. But Jane's answer I can remember clearly.

"Fine. So that's the age she is for you."

I didn't say another word, except perhaps, "Very nice to have met you, Mr. Bloomgarten."

DOING *The Taming of the Shrew* with Joe brought me immediately into my off-Broadway career, beginning with an infamously remembered and ill-conceived production of *Camille.*

There was a gentleman I had worked with named Wayne Richardson, who loved the theater. While I was doing *Shrew,* he spoke to me about doing *Camille,* a stage version of the well-known Alexandre Dumas book and Greta Garbo's classic MGM film, at the Cherry Lane Theatre in Greenwich Village. I was thrilled. I had never read the play but had, of course, seen Garbo's performance. What could be more perfect? After eleven years of starving and hanging around, I was being offered the chance to play Marguerite Gautier, one of the great women's roles in theater. For some reason, unknown to me now, it never entered my mind that I could also be completely wrong for it.

When we went into rehearsal in early September of 1956, I was still very tan from playing Kate in *Shrew* outdoors that summer. An alarm must have gone off in my mind somewhere, because I did ask Adri, the woman who was designing the clothes, to be sure that all my gowns had sleeves in them. I didn't mind how low-cut they were, or if my shoulders were exposed, but I knew that my bare arms looked more like they belonged to a running back on the Giants than to a woman dying of consumption in eighteenth-century France. Unfortunately, the producers must have run out of costume budget when they got to building my ballgown, because I ended up wearing a strapless gown with nothing—no netting, no lace, nothing—covering either my arms or shoulders. With the exception of Armand, my lover, I was taller than every actor in the show and looked as if I could floor any of the other women with one quick blow. The reviews following opening night reflected my unspoken fears in every way.

"My suggestion to Colleen Dewhurst," wrote Richard Watts in the *New York Post*, "is that she forget Armand and run away as fast as she can with his father."

Most plays receiving reviews such as these would have closed in a night. And you can be certain that no one in the cast, after reading these notices, wished ever to step on that set again. Closing would have been a blessing, to say nothing of the fact that no one was rushing to buy tickets to see it. In response to this, the producers in their ultimate wisdom decided to give out free tickets at the USO. What better group for *Camille*? For the two weeks of its run, *Camille* played to full houses of soldiers and sailors, just off ship or on leave. And as we danced, flirted and gaily laughed across stage, our audience screamed with laughter and called out every imaginable—and unimaginable—remark. This carrying on continued through the entire first act until Joseph Barr, who had played my father in *Taming of the Shrew* and was now playing M. Duval, made his entrance in the second act. When Joe began this scene with me, in which, as Armand's father, he tells me never to see his son again, the house was still rolling with laughter. Joe had the first line. Every night, it was the same. With my back to the audience, looking out the window, I could feel Joe enter and stand there, leaning on his cane, studying me in character and waiting for the audience to get quiet before he spoke. For me, that scene was the one saving grace of this entire experience. Every night, with Joe's entrance the audience became quiet, remained quiet, and at the scene's finish, applauded. I learned two things from this production. One: Never do *Camille* again; Two: True conviction will shut up even the rowdiest house. If you, as the actor, believe in what you're doing, you can make them believe. *You* control the audience because they will want to hear what's being said, if something is really happening that's worth listening to.

You've heard of "Out of the frying pan and into the fire"? After *Camille*, I was immediately offered the role of the Queen in a revival at the Actors' Playhouse of Jean Cocteau's *The Eagle Has Two Heads*, a play that had been produced years before with Tallulah Bankhead playing the role in which I was now to appear. This part was another that required me to die in the second act. Not having learned my lesson with Garbo and *Camille,* I eagerly stepped into another famous play and a famous role played by an equally infamous actress. There's not much to say about this production. The review that appeared in the *New York Times* will suffice.

COLLEEN DIES AGAIN AT THE ACTORS' PLAYHOUSE, read the headline. "This play keeps disappearing like the target the Queen shot at," the review read, before closing with a final jab: "Will someone give this girl a decent job?"

After the opening night of *The Eagle Has Two Heads,* Jane Broder was waiting for me, standing on the sidewalk in front of the theater. Without any greeting, she said, "I am supposed to be your agent. Now, according to my lights, agents do not sell actresses. They are supposed to guide their careers. That's what *agent* meant when I started in this business. I do hope, Colleen, that nobody knows that you are signed with me because from *Camille* to opening tonight in the horror that I have just witnessed, I would want no one to think that I was guiding you to this!"

I told Jane that I thought *Eagle* was an exciting play and that I had wanted to do it.

"Colleen," she answered. "I am speaking to you honestly. You must realize that I will always speak to you honestly though, God knows, I am not making a penny off you playing in these two plays, down here, off-Broadway. If you don't want to know what I think," she continued, "then tell me now."

"No," I answered. "I want to know."

"Well," she replied, "you'll be very lucky if this play closes in two nights." Which it did.

If I learned nothing else through this period, it did become clear that I was better off playing a truly unruly wench than delicately dying of tuberculosis behind a fan.

10

"What about George Scott?"

Joe Papp was very aware of what kind of role I should have been playing. So perhaps it should come as no surprise that after the winter of my Camille, the following summer, I appeared onstage in Central Park as Lady Macbeth. Roy Poole was to play Macbeth in a cast that included J.D. Cannon and John McLiam, as well as Anne Meara as the Second Witch and Jerry Stiller as the Porter. I had always wanted to play the Lady M., and I very much enjoyed working on her. Coming off of *Taming of the Shrew* from the previous summer, Joe had now captured the attention of both the general public and the theatrical establishment with the vigorous, unique productions of Shakespeare that he was presenting free of charge in New York City's parks.

"There is something so very comfortably consistent about the productions of the Shakespeare Festival," wrote Paul Beckley in the *New York Herald Tribune*, "whether it be comedy or tragedy, that regardless of this actor or that actress, one must finally conclude some firm but sensitive hand has had much to do with the shaping of what, by and large, is about the most virile Shakespearean series we've seen presented in some time."

"What three elaborate Stratford theaters in as many countries have been attempting with varying degrees of success over a period of years, Joseph Papp and his colleagues accomplished in last night's *Macbeth* on the green in Central Park," wrote Robert Kane in the *New York World-Telegram and Sun*.

I should tell you here and now that after the rude receptions I received from the critics in both *Camille* and *The Eagle Has Two Heads*, I decided never again to read a review, until, at least, after the play had closed. What I discovered over the years is that once the play has finished its run, the reviews no longer hold any importance. So, from that point, with *The Eagle Has Two Heads* in 1956, until today, I have never read another review of my own. The truth, of course, is that whether you read them or not, you get the gist of what was said very quickly—especially if the play closes in one night. My favorite comment is always that made by some earnest friend, who blurts out over dinner, "I didn't agree at all with what so-and-so said. I thought you were wonderful." Immediately you want to know what so-and-so said, but by that time, the clippings have disappeared into some file somewhere at Lincoln Center.

I mention this only because, from this point on, I am now reading for the first time many of the reviews that will be quoted in this book. I can tell you that some of them are making me furious. What does someone mean when writing that an actress is "not perfect" for a role? Christ, that's annoying. "Not perfect," indeed! I'd be the first to tell you I was certainly "not perfect" for the role of Shen Teh in *The Good Woman of Setzuan*. It was a hateful experience to begin with and has now been thrown up into my face again this past year with the controversy around Equity's decision—or should I say, two decisions—regarding the casting of *Miss Saigon*.

But I digress. The truth is the good review is often as damaging as the bad. Often the critic will mention a particular scene or moment and describe in detail what it meant to him or her. You then find yourself approaching that moment or scene thinking, *This is where I was great*, and trying to repeat it, forgetting both the play and your fellow actors. I read the notices for *Taming of the Shrew* and was gloriously happy for myself and everyone concerned. When I did *Camille* and *The Eagle Has Two Heads*, I looked forward to reading the notices, expecting to be recognized as the next Duse. You have no idea how difficult it is to walk down the street and run into someone you know after reading DEWHURST DIES AGAIN AT THE ACTORS' PLAYHOUSE.

But, as I read them today, it is a small comfort to see that my notices for *Macbeth* were kind. "Colleen Dewhurst, who was the Kate in last summer's *Taming of the Shrew*," wrote Brooks Atkinson in the *Times*, "plays Lady Macbeth with equal skill—bold, cool and ceremonious in the court scenes." This is wonderful. But I never felt during rehearsals or performance that my Lady M. was ever fully realized. I left that production hoping that somewhere, someday, I would have the opportunity to play her again. But, unfortunately, I never did.

Nevertheless, I never cease to be reminded of my performance in this production of *Macbeth*. In these years since, I have been to many gatherings and parties only to be greeted—from across the room—by Anne Meara, upon seeing me, screaming, "Who's the best fucking second witch you ever had!" You, Anne, the best and the only. Some experiences you never forget.

The following December, I was called at the last minute to go to Washington, D.C., to replace another actress as Mrs. Squeamish in a revival of William Wycherley's Restoration comedy *The Country Wife*, starring Julie Harris. Upon arriving in Washington, I was sneaked into the National Theatre and seated in an aisle seat close to the back of the house. At the end of each act, before the lights went up, I was tapped on the shoulder and escorted out. I was caught in the middle of the actor's nightmare of being called in to replace another actor who had no idea that she was being fired. I can remember very little about the experience of going into a production that is already playing to paying audiences with a cast you have not rehearsed with, which tells me today that it must have been ghastly. But later on, what I can remember as exciting, once I was comfortable with the role, was to share stage with Julie Harris, Laurence Harvey and Pamela Brown.

Two months later, in February of 1958, I was cast in a revival of a play at Circle in the Square called *Children of Darkness* by Edwin Justus Mayer. Mr. Mayer's drama about the inmates of eighteenth-century England's Newgate Prison had a brief run on Broadway in 1930. Since then, there had been a loyal group who felt that this tale of intrigue, infidelity, and treachery had been underrated in its first production and now, nearly thirty years later, deserved a second look. This now eagerly anticipated revival of *Children of Darkness* was to be produced by Ted Mann and directed by José Quintero. I was very excited because, at that time, these men were the best of off-Broadway. They had already presented Geraldine Page at Circle in an acclaimed production of Tennessee Williams' *Summer and Smoke,* and Jason Robards in an equally successful revival of O'Neill's *The Iceman Cometh.* Both of these now-celebrated productions were revivals of plays that had failed when originally produced on Broadway. The success of both restored Williams and O'Neill to the prominent positions they hold today as two of America's greatest playwrights.

After *Taming of the Shrew,* I began to be offered work off-Broadway for which I did not have to audition. Such was the case with *Children of Darkness.* I was very excited to be working with José Quintero, whom I did not know personally at that time, but whose work with Gerry Page and Jason I had much admired. Rehearsals began on the stage at Circle in early February of 1958, with the first weeks going along very easily. José and I were kindred spirits from the first moment we met. I trusted him implicitly, and have done so ever since. I was very happy to be working in *Children of Darkness* because I was once again in a cast with Joe Barr, Arthur Malet, and, above all, J.D. Cannon, who had been my Petruchio in *Taming of the Shrew.* In these last few years, during which we were all struggling, J.D. and his wife, Alice Cannon, had become my closest friends. To have all of us together again only enhanced the rehearsal process for me. Unlike any previous productions, we rehearsed on the stage that we would be playing on. This was the first time that I felt that I was in a womb, that the theater was a safe place. Everything else was closed off. The atmosphere at rehearsal was one of dim lighting and a feeling of absolute security as we began to immerse ourselves completely in the script.

After three weeks of rehearsal and a week away from the opening, José came in one morning with our producer, Ted Mann, and announced that the gentleman who had been playing the part of Lord Wainwright would be

unable for personal reasons to continue. This role was of tremendous importance to the play. Wainwright did not enter until the third act, but he was the
catalyst that brought the play to its grim and disturbing resolution. José asked
us gathered there to quickly think of anyone we knew who might be right to
play the role, as the part had to be filled at once. J.D. and I were standing
together with the rest of the company listening to José.

"What about George Scott?" he whispered to me.

"No," I replied.

I had never met George but knew his work and held a slight grudge
against him. My husband, Jim Vickery, had not been cast in another of Joe
Papp's productions after he had first worked with us in *Titus Andronicus* at the
Emmanuel Presbyterian Church on East Sixth Street. I had never brought it
up, but it was always painfully clear that Joe was not interested in Jim. This
did not make life any easier in my house at that time. At the same time, Alice
and J.D. began to talk about another young actor named George C. Scott
whom Joe had recently hired for a production at the Hecksher Theatre on
upper Fifth Avenue. I was not interested in hearing about Mr. Scott. I was
angry and more concerned that Jim had not been auditioned. Nevertheless,
one night a few weeks before rehearsals began on *Children of Darkness*, Alice
and I went to see J.D. in Joe's production of Shakespeare's *All's Well That
Ends Well* at the Hecksher. It had never occurred to me that the much talked-
about George Scott was also in the play. When George entered, Alice leaned
over and whispered to me, "There's your Antony." There had been talk about
my doing *Antony and Cleopatra* for Joe, but no one had come up with a suitable Antony.

"What? Who?" I replied.

"There," Alice whispered under her breath. "That's George Scott."

"He's too short," I hissed back at her, never taking my eyes from the stage.
I could tell out of the corner of my eye that Alice was furious with me, and she
turned away in a huff.

Back at *Children of Darkness*, I quickly suggested the name of another actor
I knew to play Lord Wainwright.

"George C. Scott," J.D. called out after me, ignoring my objection. José
looked at me and J.D., turned to Ted, and said, "Call them both. And hire
whichever one is home."

Later, I discovered that the first call was placed to the actor I had suggested
but that there had been no answer. Ted then called George, who was at home,
answered the phone, and came over to the theater at once.

When George entered rehearsal, we were all politely introduced to one
another. By now, I was quite irritated that the actor I had suggested had not
gotten the role.

"Mr. Scott," José said, "we will begin with the third act, and I apologize but, due to the shortness of time, I will walk it for you before you begin." We did the act, with José walking through the role of Wainwright. When we were through, George stood and with script in hand proceeded to rehearse the act with us, never once faltering or taking a false step. When it was over, J.D. and José both looked at me with what I can only call a " thumbs-up" expression. My irritation was forgotten. I could not deny that George was terrific, and one hundred times better than the actor originally cast and, perhaps, just as Alice had said weeks before, a perfect Antony to my Cleopatra.

It was like we had never lost step. George knew his lines the following day, and in one week, we were ready to open on schedule. Our opening night performance played smoothly to an enthusiastic audience. At the party afterward, Jane Broder was ecstatic. At last, I was in an off-Broadway play that she approved of.

"The show is wonderful and you're wonderful in it," she said, coming up to me and taking my hands. "But what is the name again of that actor who enters in the third act?"

"George Scott."

"Well, my dear, he is brilliant. He comes onstage and just wraps up this play and takes it away with him."

Suddenly I was irritated again.

"*Children of Darkness* is sure to surpass its previous stay on Broadway," wrote Frank Quinn in the *New York Daily Mirror*. "Mr. Quintero has given playwright Mayer a most sparkling revival."

"This is one of the Greenwich Village Group's best off-Broadway productions," wrote John McClain in the *New York Journal-American*, "taking its place beside *Summer and Smoke* and *The Iceman Cometh*."

As I read reviews of *Children of Darkness* now, they were generally wonderful for all of us. "Jack Cannon is the most successful," wrote Brooks Atkinson in the *New York Times*—even if my own ranged from raves to pans. "One must stand in honest awe of Colleen Dewhurst's sultry-mouthed, stony-eyed trollop," wrote Walter Kerr in the *New York Herald Tribune*. "As bad girls go, she is a beaut to be remembered." But then there was also Mr. Whitney Bolton, of the *Morning Telegraph* who wrote, "Finally, there is Colleen Dewhurst as Laetitia, the gaoler's wench . . . I liked her Laetitia no more than I liked her Camille and I liked that scarcely at all." Oh, well.

But whatever their feelings about me or the play, none could ignore George's performance. "Mr. Scott is rapidly becoming our most admirable stage villain," wrote Walter Kerr. "George C. Scott, black-wigged and black-lipped as the lord who is imprisoned for poisoning his wife and a son of doubtful heritage, is terrifying as he drops icy word after icy word with glinting amusement," wrote *Variety*. "He fills the play's final moment with chilling humor."

Jane was right. *Children of Darkness* was a respectable hit, not of the caliber of *The Iceman Cometh* or *Summer and Smoke,* but we all, as actors, had done well and been recognized by most of the critics for our work. But no matter what the papers thought, audiences left the theater talking of George. *Children of Darkness* was another success for Ted, José and Circle in the Square. More important, it was the start of a number of relationships that were to change my life both onstage and off.

Children of Darkness played to full houses through the spring of 1958. The cast got along very well together onstage and, as we settled into our run, we fell back into our separate lives offstage. One night after the performance, as I was getting ready to go home to Jim and my flat on West Fiftieth Street, I realized that I had forgotten my apartment key. I wasn't worried, as Jim was always home. I went to a restaurant/bar next door to the theater where all of us in the cast hung out and met friends who had come to see the show. I used the telephone to call home, but there was no answer. The only thing I could imagine was that perhaps Jim had gone to a movie, so I sat at an empty table near the phone and had a glass of wine, certain that in an hour or so, Jim would be back. As I waited, I noticed that George was sitting by himself at the bar. After more than an hour had passed, with no answer from Jim on the phone, I went up to him and explained my dilemma.

"Would you mind if I sat with you? I feel a little uneasy by myself for so long."

"No, of course not," he replied.

So we sat and chatted. It was the first time George and I had ever really spoken to each other at all personally or about anything else other than what we said to each other onstage. Finally, after trying to reach Jim every fifteen minutes or so, still without success, it was closing time and we had to leave. I decided the best thing to do would be to go over to the apartment and wait outside for Jim to return. George offered to go with me and when we reached the apartment, there was still no response when I rang to get in.

"I'm going to call J.D. and Alice," I told George. "I know they'll let me stay there." George accompanied me back downtown to the Cannons', where he said good night. I went upstairs and spent the night. Later, Alice told me that when I came upstairs and told her where I'd been and who I'd been with, she had said to J.D., as they went back to sleep, "I think that's dangerous." It turns out they were quite right.

During the first few months of the run of *Children of Darkness,* José Quintero had been asked to participate in what was to be called the Spoleto Festival. Gian Carlo Menotti, the legendary composer, had chosen Spoleto, Italy, for a festival of the arts to be given every summer. This was to be the first. Menotti had asked José to choose and direct an American play for the festival's theatrical presentation. José had asked me, for the first time, to do Josie Hogan in *A*

Moon for the Misbegotten, along with Richard Kiley as James Tyrone, Farrel Pelley, and Paul Milikin.

We rehearsed *Moon* during the day at Circle, and I played in *Children of Darkness* at night. I will always remember the day when I arrived close to a half hour late for a morning rehearsal. As I rushed into the theater with my excuse ready, José saw me, looked at his watch, and simply said to the cast, "All right, we're ready to begin." This had a more devastating effect on me than if he had screamed at me, for then I could have screamed my excuse back at him. There was no excuse. The memory of José's obvious disappointment in me and his courtesy to the rest of the cast, to this day puts me in agony if I am even ten minutes late and have, in doing so, kept another cast and director waiting.

About the same time, I received a call from Jane Broder, saying that Fred Zinnemann was directing a movie of the book *The Nun's Story.* Although I had read the book, I had no idea at that time who Mr. Zinnemann was. Jane clarified for me that he was the very talented and highly respected director of such films as *High Noon* and *From Here to Eternity.* So Jane set up an appointment. Fred was a very nice man and very attractive. I didn't read from a script. I didn't do anything. I just sat there and talked with him. The interview took, at most, fifteen minutes. The next day, Jane called to say that we had an offer. *The Nun's Story* was to be my first film. I was ecstatic, I couldn't believe it. It was to be a big movie, starring Audrey Hepburn and, Jane said, I was to play the "Archangel Gabriel."

The Nun's Story was to be shot in Rome. I was needed for only a week to ten days. Wonderfully, these dates coincided perfectly with the performances of *A Moon for the Misbegotten* in Spoleto. I remember getting on the Alitalia flight to fly over first-class for the film, knowing that the rest of the cast of *Moon* would be following me a week later in coach. Such was the difference between film and theater.

This was my first trip to Europe. I was awakened by the pilot's voice announcing that we were just passing over Ireland. Everything, the villages and the fields passing below me, looked very strange, yet somehow vaguely familiar to me. I thought this is what death must be like. You just leave one dream and awaken peacefully entering another. Suddenly I was circling over Rome, and in the last bit of daylight, saw the Coliseum and the Forum, places that I had only seen in books. Everyone I knew, it seemed, had been to Europe. At last, I was there. And how was I there? Acting. I couldn't have been happier as the plane touched down.

I was met at the airport and driven to the Hotel Pariolli on the outskirts of Rome. When I entered, it was evening. There was a little note at the desk, a very sweet note saying that the other actresses who were in the movie were all outside in the trattoria and I should join them.

There must have been eight actresses, six of them from the States, two from

England, sitting there when I arrived. The girls were wonderful, but it was difficult for me because it was as if someone had picked me up in Greenwich Village and set me down in the middle of Rome with seven complete strangers. My time clock was off, and I suppose I was frightened to death. Everyone was kind, however, and soon I was made to feel a part of the company.

After an hour or so, the temperature of the table changed as, at one point, one of the actresses began what can only be described as a not-too-subtle attack on Beatrice Straight, another one of the actresses sitting right there with us. Beatrice was and is one of the most beautiful women I have ever met. She has great warmth and humor and was blessed with lovely coloring and beautiful red hair. This other actress proceeded, at first, to attack the New York critics for their recent assault upon her in a particular play. But somehow her thoughts shifted, and Beatrice became the focus of her anger. The critics, she said, being male, were influenced by the beauty of a woman such as Beatrice and not by her talent. This went on for a good ten minutes. I was stunned, and could not understand what was happening. The young actress speaking was not particularly attractive, that was true. But interestingly enough, she became only more unattractive as she continued to speak. Beatrice never reacted in any way except to smile and behave as if this were perfectly normal conversation. She jumped from there to the comment that Fred Zinnemann was known to cast simply by instinct. When he met an actor, it was said, he would immediately know what part he was right or wrong for. As proof, she pointed out that everyone at the table was playing a nun, including herself. But that she had been cast as the only mean nun. At last, I had reason to speak, pointing out that I was not playing a nun. I would be the "Archangel Gabriel." Yes, she said, a schizophrenic, catatonic and violent girl who tries to kill Audrey Hepburn. To this day, I occasionally wonder what it was that Mr. Zinnemann saw in the first fifteen minutes of our interview.

As we left that trattoria, Beatrice and I were walking together.

"What happened in there?" I said. "Why was she so angry?"

"It had nothing to do with me or you," Beatrice replied with great kindness. "It has to do with women who, without men, feel unattractive and unloved. The sad thing is that once you determine that about yourself, that can be, unfortunately, the very role you play."

I had left a wake-up call at the front desk for the following morning, and went to bed exhausted, falling into a deep sleep, as by now, I must have been up a good twenty hours. The next thing I knew, there was a heavy knock at the door. It was Beatrice, telling me that the car that had come to pick up the actresses for the day's call had come and gone. I immediately felt sick to my stomach. This was my first day in a big film with one of the biggest directors and biggest stars in the world and I was late. Beatrice got me organized and tried to get a call through to the studio to explain. Finally another car came to pick me up and I arrived. Nothing was said, as the previous scene being shot was going over schedule and, fortunately, my absence had not yet been noticed. I was made up and dressed in costume in plenty of time.

A while later, Mr. Zinnemann introduced me to a gentleman, a doctor from what appeared to be an insane asylum, who was there to observe the scenes within the institution where Miss Hepburn's character had been sent to work. The doctor asked me if I wished to visit the hospital in order to observe the actual patients who were insane and in a catatonic state. I said no, I didn't feel that was necessary, as I had been in a situation where I had been able to observe that condition firsthand. This was not true, but there was no way I was going anywhere near an actual mental institution—particularly in Italy. I felt that I would have no problem portraying this condition.

When it came time for the actual shooting, I was put into a cell that held only a cot. Mr. Zinnemann asked me if there was anything that I needed to help me prepare for playing the scene.

"No," I said, "except that if you can lock the door, lock it. Let me hear you lock it."

I went over to the cot, lay down, and heard the cell door close and the bolt catch. That day, we played the first shot of the scene in which I ask Miss Hepburn for a glass of water. After shooting, through an interpreter, the doctor congratulated me on my excellent portrayal of the catatonic state. I kept reminding myself that this was meant as a compliment.

That same day, José arrived in Rome with the cast of *Moon* to begin rehearsals. I would shoot *Nun's Story* during the day and rehearse *Moon* at night in a beautiful little jewel of a theater in Rome. I had not felt it necessary to inform Mr. Zinnemann that I was rehearsing *Moon* at night since, technically, that was my free time. Also, I figured rehearsals for *Moon* would not be difficult, as we had already rehearsed for three weeks in New York while playing *Children of Darkness* at night.

Somehow, Mr. Zinnemann heard about this arrangement. When I came in the next day, he took me aside and explained to me that women who wanted a career in films needed rest and had to take very good care of themselves. He was disturbed to hear that I was tiring myself by rehearsing a play in the evening and that it would have to stop.

I was taken aback by his comments. I felt that in this particular situation, working on *Moon* was in no way affecting my work in the film. I was even more stunned when he dismissed my attempt at explanation and told me that I should go and lie down and rest.

Cinecittà was a very large studio. As I was resting, I suddenly heard announced over the loudspeaker that Mr. Zinnemann would be moving on to another scene, as "Miss Dewhurst is resting." That night, at rehearsal, I told José about what had happened at the studio, and he understood. But as there were only two or three more nights of rehearsal, we continued as planned.

I was very fortunate in filming the fight scene with Miss Hepburn, as she was wonderful and highly disciplined. We worked on it as you would a dance, and it was shot quickly and without incident. The following day, I left the movie studio and, with our little theater troupe from off-Broadway, proceeded to wonderful, exotic Spoleto.

We opened *Moon* in the most beautiful theater in Spoleto. As we played on a most stark stage set, all we could see around us was this golden, sparkling architecture and an audience similarly dressed and bejeweled. I was very nervous because by opening night I understood what an important international event this actually was to be. I had been warned by Gian Carlo and José that in Italy, members of the audience came back during intermissions between the first and second acts if they were enjoying your performance. I couldn't believe this and threw what can only be called a fit. If there ever was a play in which I needed some isolated time between acts it was *Moon*. But, as warned, at the end of the first act, into my dressing room came a number of incredibly beautiful women accompanied by equally beautiful Italian men, none of whom I'd ever met before. Gian Carlo would then introduce them, each with wineglass in hand. They were very complimentary about the first act and when the stage manager called five minutes, they went back to their seats, as I took my place in the wings.

Every evening after the show, we'd all go over to a café reserved for the company, their guests, and the aristocrats and hoi polloi of the audience who could get in. There, José and I would dance madly. It was exciting for me to see the other performers who came into the club, to go to Menotti's apartment and be with people like Thomas Schippers, the marvelously handsome musician and conductor, and Ben Shahn, the painter, and so many others I'd only heard about and never expected to meet. This was a world of money and aristocrats beyond my dreams. Everything seemed extraordinary and nothing was out of reach. Being invited to palazzos in Venice and Rome, wonderful conversations late at night in restaurants and cafés, seeing the amazing artworks and paintings in Assisi, Michelangelo's *David* in Florence. It was a most wonderful time, marred only by having flyers dropped from planes over Spoleto that decried the debauched behavior of the artists. One, which also appeared as an article in an Italian magazine, reported that Signorina Dewhurst had danced nude in front of the *duomo*—in front of the cathedral. I had danced in front of the *duomo* one night, during which two members of the orchestra from the club had come with José and me and several others. We all danced in the moonlight. It was wonderful. But I was not nude.

What happened to me in Spoleto was magic. At night, I played a wonderful show, after which I entered into an exotic wonderland. I understand that there were bets being placed among the beautiful people as to whether Josie Hogan was or was not a virgin. Finally, in order to settle the bet, I was asked. I proceeded to go into a long and rather philosophical explanation that I thought virginity was "in the eye of the beholder." The Italians seemed to love this response. Although I must say that I have always believed that you must play Josie as if she is. I don't think the Italians were as concerned about Josie as they were about simply asking me the question.

I CAME BACK to New York and two days later flew out to Yakima, Washington, to see George Scott, who was making his first movie, *The Hanging Tree,* with Gary Cooper. After four days there, I returned to the city and resumed playing Laetitia in *Children of Darkness.* This was a period for me of complete self-involvement—having done *Children of Darkness,* which was a success, meeting and falling in love with George, appearing in my first movie in a foreign city with a famous director and star, and then moving on to Spoleto, where I was treated as a prima donna in an environment that to me seemed more fantastic than any I could have imagined. I believe now that I was out of control. I was riding a very fast roller coaster. Like so many who find themselves in such a time, everything seems centered dramatically on you. Everything is breathless and exciting, nothing can go wrong. You feel as if you're running the ball game. Then, one day, you become aware that you are not in charge, you are not the center of the universe and, with an abrupt jolt, life becomes very real.

In the years following, Joe Papp would call me from time to time. George and I played *Antony and Cleopatra* for him in a concert production at the Hecksher Theatre on East 103rd Street, which I played again, two years later, at the Delacorte—that time with Michael Higgins as Antony. Unfortunately, my indelible memories of this production are of the weather. Playing outside, as you do at the Delacorte in Central Park, is always risky. You are at the mercy of the wind and rain, not to mention the routing of planes coming into LaGuardia and Kennedy airports. During this second production of *Antony and Cleopatra,* it rained several times just as we reached the final scenes of the play. I began to testily notice that it never seemed to rain during Antony's death scene. But the minute I said, "Give me my robe and my crown, I have a mortal longing in me," and I clutched that asp to my breast, the skies would open in a downpour. I was aware, as those six nubian slaves carried me offstage in the rain, that the Egyptian queen's eye makeup was fast dissolving and running all over my face and shoulders in rivers of black.

Despite the occasional rainstorm, I had moments playing for Joe outdoors that were magic. I would be standing high on some parapet above the stage, not speaking for several minutes, looking out over the trees into the sky. With the wind blowing and the clouds sailing past the moon, I had no sense of time or that I was in the middle of one of the world's largest cities. Nothing around you tells you where you are but, somehow, perhaps because you are in the middle of this play, you feel safe. Nothing can touch you; whatever your reality is outside of the theater just disappears. In those moments, I somehow felt quiet and at one with everything around me and had the greatest sense of peace I have ever experienced. I've never had that feeling on any stage except at the Delacorte in Central Park.

One day a number of years later, in 1972, the phone rang again. It was Joe.

"Honey, I know you'd like to do all the Shakespearean women. Well, I'm going to do *Hamlet* this summer, and I'd love to have you play Gertrude."

"I don't know, Joe," I said, "let me think about this."

Fifteen minutes later, the phone rang a second time. It was Joe—again.

"What would you say if I told you," he said, "that James Earl Jones will play the king?"

"OK, Joe," I replied. "Let me go reread the play." Two hours later, I called Joe back and agreed to forgo Nova Scotia and play Gertrude to Jimmy's Claudius. Stacy Keach played Hamlet, with a wonderful cast including Barney Hughes as Polonius and Kitty Wynn as Ophelia, directed by Gerald Freedman. Rehearsals went smoothly, with the exception of the fit of my costumes. It has taken me a while to realize that some designers simply sketch the gown they have decided is correct for the period and the character. They do not really pay any further attention to who is actually to play the role. I have always been very insecure about my costumes. So much so that many times I am nearly unable to bring myself to say to a designer, "This won't work for me." In *Hamlet*, what was often just a point of insecurity was more of a disaster than usual.

Now I feel is my last opportunity to correct a fanciful story about my behavior during *Hamlet*, that seems, over the years, to have gone the rounds and keeps coming back to me to this day. What follows is the truth, at least, as best I can remember it.

Because we were playing the play in a period in which women's breasts were flattened, my costume for Gertrude fit very, very tight across my bosom. My problem with this was simple: I couldn't breathe. I was bound so tightly in this costume that I could not get out a full sentence on one breath. It was annoying, to say the least, devastating, to speak creatively. Thus began, bit by bit, the releasing of the binding across my chest, which was ultimately never truly successful. Topping this, to use a pun, was the crown that I wore in the last scene. It never sat on my head correctly and, as I drank the poisoned wine in one of my more dramatic moments, as I slowly died it would slip over my eyes and nose, coming to rest upon my chin. Although the cast might have been amused, I was not.

I complained bitterly about the crown, but nothing was done. By the final preview before opening night, when it occurred once again in front of an audience, I had had it. I came off the stage, took the young woman who was my dresser by the hand, and led her to the edge of the lake behind the Delacorte.

"And now, my dear," I said, "we will never have to worry about this damn crown again," tossing it into the lake and watching it sink out of sight into the water and mud. My dresser was terribly upset, almost in tears. I assume she figured she would, at least, be blamed for not keeping me from tossing the god-awful thing and, at worst, might be expected to retrieve it.

"I'm certain someone will do something about this now," I assured her. The designer, who was and is brilliant, was terribly distressed, and I was some-what sorry for that. But the story that comes back to me now, years later, is that I walked off the stage to the lake, tossed the crown, threw the shoes, stripped down to my bra and panties, and dumped the entire costume into the lake. Even though that was what I wished to do, I am here to say today that this is not true. I knew who I was working for. I remained fully clothed. I was open-ing the following night and did not want to have nothing to wear or to throw the entire production into a furor. I simply wished to make a statement. I dare say, I did. And just for the record, I was given a better-fitting crown.

I have learned since then why actors ask for certain designers. For example, I would like always to have Jane Greenwood design anything I wear onstage. I first met Jane through José Quintero and have worked with her in many pro-ductions, from period costumes in *Long Day's Journey into Night* and *Ah, Wilderness!* to a chic, political woman's wardrobe in *An Almost Perfect Person*, to farm girl in *A Moon for the Misbegotten*. Every time, she has always known, without comment, what to cover and what to reveal. And, as the years go by, that becomes terribly important. Even more, Jane reads the play, understands what the actor will be called upon to do physically and always makes certain that what you are wearing is easy to work in and that you are "at home" in it. Jane knows that I hate to be fitted and will often hate, in the initial stage, what-ever she has designed. But trusting her, through gritted teeth, I've found she has always proved to be correct.

JANE GREENWOOD

From when first we met, I have always felt that I could uncon-sciously get on the same wavelength of how Colleen wanted to play a role. I would watch her for a while, or imagine her on the stage, and then go away and pull the clothes together, and no matter how she put it all on, it invariably seemed to work. Costumes were always a bit troubling for Colleen. She hated fittings because she really didn't like looking at herself in the mirror very much. This is somewhat odd behavior for an actress, but more common than you would think. Colleen was, in some ways I think, always a little discontent that she wasn't some other physical size, yet it was that very solid and earthy physical presence that she had that made her so remarkable. But somewhere inside her, I think there was always the wish to be something else.

In her personal life, Colleen was very uncomplicated about what she wore. It was simply not an issue that she thought about much. I'd be working with her on a project and from out of nowhere she'd say, "Oh, dear, I've got to go to this dinner (or this benefit) and I don't know how to get dressed up. What am I going to wear?" she'd practically moan. Nevertheless, she always managed to find something that had some sort of exotic or ethnic quality to it that on her would look sensational. Yet it was never what anyone would call high fashion.

There was so much about Colleen that was contradictory. I remember when we were working on *Ah, Wilderness!* at Yale, she was giving lots of lectures to the young students, who were all hanging on her every word. For those acting students to have Colleen spend time with them was as if they had died and gone to heaven. It was particularly interesting to observe how the young women related to her. Colleen really had a great natural rapport with young women coming into the business. She clearly never had forgotten her own difficulties, not being typically beautiful, and she was very encouraging and easy to talk to.

I was also talking to the design students while we were there, and I remember telling them how important it was for actors to be in the right costume for the period they are playing in. So, of course, for *Ah, Wilderness!* I said to Colleen that for this period, she really needed to wear a corset. "Oh, my God," she said. "Do I have to?"

"Let's just try," I said, trying to assure her that with proper fittings, it would become familiar to her and feel like a part of her performance. So here we are after the first dress rehearsal, when Colleen had worn the corset once and then said, "I'm not going to wear this again. It's too uncomfortable." *Oh, dear,* I thought. So much for my saying how important it is for everyone to look and feel exactly right in these period roles—and there's Colleen throwing her corset in the garbage. But for all that, Colleen was the kind of actress who could make you believe she had on a corset, which a lesser actress couldn't do.

For all the costumes of every kind that Colleen wore onstage, I don't think she ever loved any piece of clothing more than that very simple wash dress she wore as Josie Hogan in *A Moon for the Misbegotten.* Josie, of course, was a very simple girl with no real interest in clothes. Even when she made a tremendous effort to pull together what modest clothing she had, to meet Jamie Tyrone for the evening, when it didn't work, I can still see Colleen pulling at the neck of her dress as if she had to destroy it. I remember Colleen taking her shoes off again and again; she wanted to play much of the role barefoot. Those were small details that she worked out very carefully with José Quintero, the director, but they helped me pull the entire costume together. We found that old dress she wore in the first act of *Moon* in stock at Brooks. Colleen wore it through the entire run, from the Kennedy Center through New York and on to Los Angeles, over a year and a half. She scrubbed the floor of that porch so many times in it, that by the time we got to filming *Moon* for television, that original dress had been repaired and mended so many times it was practically worn through. They built Colleen a duplicate costume for the taping, but she wouldn't wear it. She insisted on wearing the old one.

I have a little bottle that Colleen gave me that I've always kept. Colleen loved to give gifts, and she always gave curiously odd little things, very personal things, on all kinds of occasions. She knew I loved little boxes and bottles. This was, I think, from an opening night. It's an old Liselle's sachet bottle. It came with this note: "For Jane, because I love you and because you know what to do with me." And this is so typical of Colleen: That beautiful sentiment is written on the back of some old scrap of paper, God knows what. I've always kept her note inside the bottle because it so reminds me of her.

∽ ∽ ∽

At least ten years passed by as my career gained some momentum both artistically and, fortunately, financially. In addition to working in the theater with regularity, I began to enter the arena of television and film.

One night, at about midnight, the phone rang at the Farm. I picked it up and it was Joe, terse and abrupt as always.

"Colleen, can you come down here tomorrow morning at about eleven?" he asked?

"Joe, what is this about?"

"I'm doing a play and I want you to look at it."

"Joe," I said, "I'm going away in about two weeks to do a TV film on the coast and—"

"Just meet me tomorrow morning," he interrupted.

"OK," I said, and hung up.

I drove into the city the next morning, went to his office at The Public Theater on Lafayette Street, and explained to the woman at the desk that I had an appointment with Mr. Papp. She said, "Oh, yes," and handed me a script. "Mr. Papp would like you to read this now."

I sat down and proceeded to read a play called *Taken in Marriage* by Tom Babe. When I finished reading, about an hour later, I informed the receptionist that I had read it. Minutes later, Joe appeared, escorting me to an empty rehearsal room that had about four folding chairs and two gentlemen I had not met before, who were apparently waiting for me.

"Colleen," Joe said, "this is Tom Babe, the playwright, and Robert Allen Ackerman, our director."

Joe and I sat down in the two empty chairs, about six feet apart, as he proceeded to tell me that the actress who had been playing Ruth Chandler, the part of the mother, was being released and that he wished me to take over the role. Mr. Babe and Mr. Ackerman never spoke during any of this. I had the feeling then that they were unaware of what was about to happen.

"Joe, this is not really a part that I'm interested in," I began to explain tentatively.

"Yeah, yeah, I understand," Joe said nodding. "But," he added, "I wish that you would do it."

I reminded Joe again that I was due in Los Angeles to begin filming *And Baby Makes Six* in just over two weeks, and that I didn't know how I could begin rehearsals at this time and open in a play.

There were a few minutes of silence.

"How far along are you in rehearsal?" I finally asked.

"First preview is tonight."

"Good God, Joseph, that's impossible."

"I'll hold previews until you are ready," Joe replied.

"Who is playing this part now?" I asked. Joe told me the actress' name. "What's wrong?" I continued. "She's perfect."

"I will cancel the play," he said, "if you don't do it."

I felt at that moment that this was news to the playwright and director sitting across from me, as their silence was deafening.

At this point, Joe managed to slide his chair over so that we were practically knee to knee. We sat like this, looking at each other. No one spoke.

"Joe," I finally asked, "is this business or friendship?"

"Friendship," he replied.

More silence. No one moved.

"How long can you give me?" I asked.

"How long do you need?" Joe replied.

"I don't know . . . five days?" Joe got up, walked across the room, opened the door, and shouted, "Call the *Times*, the previews are postponed five days, Colleen Dewhurst is in rehearsal." This says all that needs to be said about another side of Joe.

The cast of *Taken in Marriage* was made up of five women: Dixie Carter, Kathleen Quinlan, Meryl Streep, Elizabeth Wilson, and now, me. When I came into rehearsal the next day, the four ladies seemed equally stunned, and it was fortunate that I knew Liz Wilson very well, Meryl and Dixie slightly and, although I had not met her before, had heard wonderful things about Kathleen Quinlan's work. Being the superb actresses and pros that they all are, these ladies rallied quickly, as it became very evident that the next five days were going to require great effort and high concentration. For me, it was all about cramming lines into my head and finding out where I was standing and how I was to move at any time onstage.

José Quintero once said, "You must try never to give Colleen any props to handle within at least her first five minutes onstage, as her complete lack of physical coordination is most frighteningly apparent during that time." This remark had been made because José had once directed me, in the first moments of a play, to snap the ends off of string beans, toss the ends into the garbage, and drop the beans into a pot of water. I had managed to do this without incident throughout rehearsal. In our first performance before an audience, however, I was so nervous that I tossed the beans into the garbage and the ends into the boiling water. I never realized, until the end of that performance, that, once again, an audience had proved its tremendous courtesy by not making a sound while this outwardly very assured woman proved to one and all that she knew beans about beans.

In *Taken in Marriage,* I was not onstage for more than four minutes before I was to set a table completely while talking interminably. At the first preview, I rolled along with great outward assurance, setting each place. At the end of the first act, I was informed by the rest of the cast, who were highly amused, that I had managed methodically to set the entire table, piece by piece, backward, knives to the left, forks to the right, etc. It was only through their own first-night jitters that they had been able to observe this and not laugh, keeping a high concentration and thereby assuring the audience that this was quite normal for my character.

Taken in Marriage opened to good reviews (although by now, I had stopped reading them) and ran to excellent houses for quite a while, although due to my film commitment, I only previewed, opened the show, and played ten days. What I most loved about the entire experience was the dressing room in which all five of us made up together each night. It was taking a chance that these five women would get along—and we did, famously. The laughter from that dressing room could be heard throughout the building.

Joe had promised me that he would find a replacement as quickly as possible and he did, bringing in a terrific actress, Nancy Marchand. I was told later by Elizabeth Wilson that she was brilliant and, even more important, with her humor, fit perfectly into the coven of the five laughing witches.

11

"Ready to go on, are you?"

When George and I returned from Yakima, Washington, we made the painful decision to live together. We found a small, two-story house, behind an apartment building off Hudson Street in Greenwich Village. Both of our previous partners, my husband, Jim Vickery, and George's wife, actress/singer Patricia Scott, obviously felt that our relationship, which had been going on since *Children of Darkness,* was disaster for all involved but that, in the long run, it could not last. At this time, none of the four of us was well known outside of our professions or of any interest to the public. So it was only within our own circle of friends and coworkers that our affair was known or discussed.

Within that circle—and rightly so—George and I were looked upon by many as being not only scandalous, but in some ways reprehensible. This was primarily because George had a baby boy, Matthew, who was about a year old, and, as we had learned almost immediately after we began seeing each other, his wife, Pat, was pregnant again. For me, it was a different story. My marriage of thirteen years to Jim had been a failure from the start. Jim and I had impulsively married when we were very young, barely knowing each other. Soon after the union, it became clear that in many ways—many critical ways—we were not at all compatible. Nevertheless, we stayed together in what became essentially a platonic relationship.

When I met George, the contrast in personality between him and Jim was extreme. The strong draw of George's passion and aggression, as opposed to Jim's almost sullen passivity, was undeniable. Prior to George, no one had ever overtly come between Jim and me. There was simply an unspoken acknowledgment of what was wrong with our marriage and how the two of us, in our very different ways, took care of our separate needs and lived a lie. Consequently, my friends looked upon George as someone who could pull me out of this relationship once and for all, and from there I would go on to another more stable relationship. No one, however, looked upon what was happening with George as the first steps into another marriage.

The first year that we lived together was tumultuous, and many times we were on the brink of breaking up completely. In spite of our relationship, George remained close to Patricia through her pregnancy and the birth of their daughter, Devon. We both bore guilt about the pain that we were certainly causing our spouses, particularly Pat. But for George, because of Matthew and Devon and the true affection he did feel for them as a father, it was much worse. I, on the other hand, could assuage my guilt with the relief of being finally separated from Jim. If nothing else, this was a great gift that George gave to me.

About this time, George's career and mine began to take off. I had moved so quickly from one off-Broadway production to the next that I was known, at one point, as the "Queen of Off-Broadway." This title was not necessarily due to my brilliance but rather because most of the plays I was in closed after a run of anywhere from one night to two weeks. I would then move immediately into another.

At the same time that I was working for next to nothing in small theaters and lofts downtown, I was beginning to be called to work in television uptown. Initially, I appeared in a number of local Sunday-morning productions, such as *Sunday Morning Live, Camera Three* and *Look Up and Live.* These programs were live half-hour morality-based programs, tailored to a Sunday-morning audience. This work was a great initiation into the pace of television production for me and many young actors then starting their careers. Even though the shows were slanted toward that very specific audience, I can remember playing Roxanne in a scene from *Cyrano de Bergerac* (a role I would never have been asked to play in a full production), and having the opportunity to read work from many great poets.

From there, I began to be cast in a series entitled *Play of the Week*, produced by David Susskind for Public Television. Unlike the live Sunday morning shows, these were quality productions of plays that had been adapted for television, produced on a respectable budget, and taped for broadcast.

In these, I began to work with actors and actresses I had long admired. One wonderful experience was working with Dame Judith Anderson in Susskind's production of *Medea,* directed by José Quintero. Betty Miller, Jacqueline Brooks and I had been cast as the female Greek chorus.

One of the things you learn very quickly in the theater is that one actor does not ever cue another actor in rehearsal, particularly if that actor is the star. When an actor "goes up" (forgets his next line), that line is given to him by the stage manager or, if working in film, an assistant director or script supervisor.

Miss Anderson had already received great acclaim for her portrayal of Medea onstage and, of course, knew the role inside and out when we arrived for the first rehearsal with José. One morning, in a run-through of the infamous scene in which Medea demands that a messenger describe to her, in detail, the death by fire of her husband Jason's new wife, a death that she herself has orchestrated and to which she responds with great sensual and ecstatic delight, Miss Anderson "went up."

Poised, arms in the air, Dame Judith simply stopped and stood motionless and silent. The three of us, Betty, Jackie, and I, standing six inches from her, froze. The entire room seemed to be holding its breath while we waited for the assistant director to cue her. No one moved a muscle, including Judith.

Standing there, we could hear José trying to subtly and quickly find this missing A.D., who was not on script as he was supposed to be and for whom José had already developed an antipathy due to his ineptness.

This silence went on for what felt like hours as Miss Anderson stood, frozen in silence, her arms up, absolutely not moving. Finally I couldn't stand it any longer. I whispered the line. Miss Anderson picked it up and went right on as if nothing had occurred, and we continued through the rehearsal.

As we were getting ready to leave the rehearsal hall, Dame Judith passed by me.

"Good night, Miss Anderson," I said.

She paused, glanced at me, and said, "Ready to go on, are you?"

In those days, when taping a show for broadcast, you shot one act at a time, in sequence. The act could be thirty minutes long, but you couldn't stop. There was no going back. If an actor went up or anything went wrong during taping, everything was stopped and the entire act began again. The director could not technically stop tape, back up, and cut in from where the scene had gone awry.

I had several close-ups in *Medea* and, to my great dismay, the one fly in the studio had taken a great fascination to me. Even in scenes where Betty, Jackie, and I were standing together, this fly favored me.

As we got to one scene in particular, in which the three of us were standing onstage with Judith, about twenty minutes into the act, this fly found me and would not leave my side. I could not brush him away or, in the best of all worlds, kill him. My great anxiety was not for myself but for Dame Judith, who was in the middle of such a strenuous performance. They would let the scene run for a few seconds, hoping the fly would disappear. He would not.

"*Stop,*" José would finally call. The fly had become the complete focus of the scene. We would have to return to the beginning of the act, and Miss Anderson would have to re-create this magnificent performance again.

This occurred at least three times, and although by the third time I was in the depths of despair and just waiting for Miss Anderson to explode, never did Dame Judith express what had to have been her extreme frustration and anger.

This was another learning experience for me that a star, but more important, an actress, never lost her temper. Dame Judith never blamed another actor for something that was beyond his or her control or let such an incident interfere with her own performance.

When I had arrived at the studio on the first day of taping, I was given my dressing room number and proceeded down a long hall, stopping at a door to the room I assumed to be mine. I opened it, and to my embarrassment, Miss Anderson was sitting in a chair, with her back to me, facing a mirror. Her makeup and hair man was standing beside her with what looked like a steel clamp in his hand, pulling Dame Judith's hair back and away from her face, at the same time pulling her facial skin up and taut. There were already three or four of these clamps in place at her hairline. A wig hung on the side of the mirror ready to be placed over them.

I stopped dead in the doorway. I could feel my whole body and face redden (I have always been a terrible blusher) and, starting to back out, mumbled, "Oh, I'm terribly sorry, please excuse me."

"No, no, dear," Miss Anderson said, "please come in. Sit down and let me show you what I'm doing." I sat down and she explained the procedure, as a teacher might to a schoolgirl. "These clamps," she began, "are to pull the skin on my face taut, in order that, with the wig on, I will appear ten to fifteen years younger."

I do not remember much else of what she said or how I left the room. But in thinking back, I realize that a great actress had just graciously acknowledged me as one who would belong in the profession. Dame Judith had, in her way, told the future.

I know now, thinking of these two incidents, that this is what is meant, in our world of the theater, by a true professional. And obviously, the day has come that Miss Anderson's advice has become very useful. With her expert technique and a very good wig, I could possibly drop back to, shall we say, fifty?

I did a great many of these television adaptations for David Susskind. One morning, I was sitting at home in George's and my small rented house, when I received a call from Jane Broder, telling me that there might be a change in the casting of a TV show currently in rehearsal. There seemed to be a problem between the actor playing the lead and the actress opposite him. Mr. Susskind had called and said that as the gentleman was the bigger star, he thought they would have to replace the leading actress. While Jane could not say what it was before a decision was made, she acknowledged that it was a very good show and the role was excellent. The final decision was to be made at lunchtime. David had asked Jane to alert me in order that, if they did replace her, I would be ready at once to come to rehearsal.

In those days, all of the big television productions rehearsed at Central Plaza, located on Second Avenue and Eighteenth Street. Most actors had a good idea of what was in production there at any given time. After Jane's call, I sat at home waiting, knowing that in all probability it had to be *Don Quixote,* and the only part a star actress would be playing was Dulcinea. Shortly after one o'clock, Jane called and said I was to go at once to the rehearsal. I would indeed be playing Dulcinea in the television adaptation of the Cervantes *Don Quixote.*

I was a nervous wreck as I took the bus across town to the rehearsal hall. What was I walking into? What had gone wrong, and would I later be taking the bus back home, also replaced? When I came out of the elevator at Central Plaza, I was met by Susskind and his director, Sidney Lumet. The star was Lee J. Cobb and I was told, quietly, that the problem had been that both Mr. Cobb and the woman I had replaced were "Method" actors, taking long pauses with each line they spoke. Both had complained about this trait in the other to the powers that be. The first direction I received was simply to "talk fast and answer immediately on cue." I was introduced to Mr. Cobb and we began to rehearse.

There didn't seem to be any immediate problems. People then were afraid of Method actors because they were known—unfortunately and in many cases incorrectly—as actors who required a long thought and emotional process before being able to speak or do anything onstage. The misperception was that if such an actor didn't feel properly motivated, he didn't speak. Many of us were trained, and continue to be trained, in what is known as the Method, or Stanislavsky school of acting. But this particular cast, like all good actors, Method or otherwise, understood the medium in which they were working and that their study and preparation was to be done at home.

Acting in television is so much about technical problems. Time is of the essence. The actor who breaks rehearsal, again and again, to find "motivation" only holds up the process. Such motivation must be found in private study or in simple, instinctual reactions while playing the scene.

I remember, years later, when I first began to work in television and film in Los Angeles, that I would come onto a set the first morning and realize that the director and actors around me were often nervous. This was because they knew of me, by reputation, as a Method actress. Their fear was that I would enter into interminable discussions, often combative, about each and every scene before being able to proceed. If you have weeks of rehearsal for a film or even just one week before you shoot for television, it is a gift. Then you may improvise, learning about your character and those playing opposite you, finally entering that wonderful world of discovery where you are led by instinct to enter each scene, aware how your character will react, moment to moment. It is a luxury not often given, especially in television, even if such time would make the actual shooting faster and the results richer.

You know when you enter certain shows that you are being paid for "fast."

They trust that you will study on your own time and be prepared when you enter the set. The Method became a dirty word only after so many actors misused it, at the expense of the script and their fellow actors. I am not a Goody Two-shoes. If I disagree with a director completely, I know, in my own way, how to handle it. If the script stinks, I know it before I arrive. I want the money. I trust I am being hired to flesh out this cardboard cutout of a woman and make her, at least, appear to have some depth.

It took me years to realize that we are in a profession in which the mind and body, our souls and emotions, are one complete instrument. That instrument must be tuned and taken very good care of if we are to be able to call on it to react as quickly as possible to whatever the material demands. Nothing is more boring than to enter a set where you recognize that some actor is determined to show off his or her great knowledge of internal motivation. But it happens, and in those cases, it helps a lot also to have been trained as a Method actor so you can see one coming at you.

So, reading from the script with Mr. Cobb, I followed direction and spoke as fast as I could. It was a wonderful script and cast, especially Eli Wallach, who played Sancho Panza. Not only was Eli wonderful in the role—he was also very kind to me. I had met Eli before and knew him slightly. But his kindness and humor quickly put me at ease and made me feel a part of the production, instead of an outsider.

Don Quixote was a huge production, very complicated, with many sets and a large cast, including horses. Since this would be a live show, dress rehearsal was most important. When we were finally in full costume and on the set, the cameras moved in as Mr. Lumet and the producers moved into a control booth, becoming just disembodied voices speaking to the cast through a loudspeaker.

Each camera has a red light. When that light is on, it means that particular camera is taking the picture that will be broadcast. I began to realize that in my scenes with Mr. Cobb, when the light would go off behind me on the camera that had been shooting him, he would actually turn his head and look back into the camera shooting me.

This strange behavior went on for a while until I could vaguely hear a voice from the control booth speaking into the earphone of one of the cameramen. Taping stopped. "OK," he announced in reply, "we put the camera where the money is," and with that, we resumed.

It took me a while to understand, but I eventually realized as we continued what the cameraman meant: Mr. Cobb was the star and he was making it clear by his actions that the camera was to remain on him. Not yet being wise in the ways of certain stars, I was unfamiliar with what that would ultimately mean. It became obvious in the final scene, at Don Quixote's death. Eli was on his knees, facing Mr. Cobb at the bottom of the bed, and I was on the other side in the same position, but it was clear that however truthful and touching our characters' reactions were to Don Quixote's death, there was only one camera with a red light on and it was shooting Mr. Cobb.

It was as exciting doing live television as it was to do theater because it's an opening night. All of your adrenaline is flowing, and you'd better be on and ready. On the day we taped, I remember standing off camera in what was like a courtyard as Mr. Cobb made his entrance on a horse and promptly fell off of it. A wave of horror ran through my body, as well as everyone else's, as we were only at the very beginning of the show and it seemed that the lead was in no condition to go on. That's live television. Fortunately, Mr. Cobb, like a true trouper, rose in all his armor and continued.

After we had been playing for maybe ten minutes, I noticed that none of the cameras seemed to have working red lights. Also, in the final scene, as I looked at Mr. Cobb on his deathbed, slowly but surely from behind the bed appeared a camera sneaking its lens through the drapes. I was certain there had not been a camera there in rehearsal. But we continued. Don Quixote died, and in the end, everyone was very pleased with the production.

I hurried home to meet J.D. and Alice Cannon, who were waiting with George for me to arrive.

"How was it?" I asked. They said it was terrific. Naturally, after such a traumatic experience, I wanted them to tell me every little moment that they had enjoyed. As they spoke I realized that it had been decided in that control booth to keep the red lights off so that none of us would know when we were on camera. By the description of various scenes, I now knew that Sidney Lumet had been very good to me.

There were many wonderful television productions that were done very quickly by young actors who were then coming up very strongly, trained in the discipline of the theater. I had, at last, managed to be recognized by the producers of live television in New York. Consequently, I also managed to have the distinction of playing in the final productions of these classic plays as one by one, live television shows were discontinued in New York and everything moved to the West Coast.

On the other hand, I understand that on the way to the airport the next day, Mr. Cobb, accompanied by Mr. Susskind, said, "David, you fucked me."

ALTHOUGH WE were both working with regularity, George's reputation as an actor was growing by great leaps. You could tell that he was on the verge of some sort of major success; all he needed was the right break. And it came in a film called *Anatomy of a Murder,* which was to be directed by Otto Preminger. George loved the script but was not particularly interested in the small supporting role that he was being offered. I read it and agreed. It was a good role and a wonderful opportunity just to be working in any Preminger film, but

George was quite right. He was perfect for the leading role of the prosecuting attorney. This was the part that would explode him into the public's eye. This was the role with which he could create a sensation.

Over the next few days, as George's agent went back and forth with Preminger over George's request to play one of the leading roles, I received a call from Jane Broder, telling me that Otto wished to see me about a small part in this same film. Jane and Otto had been very close for quite some time but, for some reason, had had a recent falling out and not spoken to each other in the last couple of years. This occurred, no doubt, over one of Jane's "morality stands" which, of course, is exactly the reason a man like Preminger loved and trusted her so. Nevertheless, business being business, it was also invariably the reason why some directors and producers would end up not speaking to Jane from time to time.

In spite of this feud (or perhaps just because of it), Jane came with me when I went to meet Mr. Preminger. I was very nervous, because Preminger was legendary for a cruelty that made strong men cry. I was fascinated with the idea of meeting him. He greeted Jane and me cordially but without any particular warmth. However, within a very few minutes, he knew just the right buttons to push in order to engage me in a conversation about my work and the theater. Jane sat by silently. At one point, he began to discuss the small, ingenue-like role for which he was considering me, and the people he had already engaged for the leading roles, such as James Stewart, Ben Gazzara and Lee Remick. I knew from reading George's copy of the script that I was not right for the role Preminger was considering me for, particularly as I would be playing a sweetheart type in the same movie with Lee Remick. No one would believe it. At any age, next to Lee Remick, I'm nobody's ingenue. Finally, after listening to Preminger's description for what seemed an appropriate amount of time, I spoke up.

"Mr. Preminger, I just don't think I'm right for this role." Jane sat by, still saying nothing but with a look on her face that seemed to say, "You heard her." Otto was a little perplexed by my remark but continued talking about the entire project, the locations, the story, his stars. He was clearly enjoying himself. Gradually Otto's attention turned away from me and to Jane. As the meeting came to a close, they were speaking to each other again, as if there had never been a problem between them. Suddenly and without warning, Otto turned to me and said, "Do you know the work of an actor named George Scott?" I remained silent. Neither Jane nor I looked at each other.

"Yes, I know his work," I answered.

"Having read the script, do you think Mr. Scott could play the role of the prosecutor?"

"I think he would be perfect for it," I replied. Preminger then turned to Jane and said, "Have you seen his work?"

"Yes," Jane replied.

"What do you feel about it?"

"Otto, if he's right for the part, you'll never find anyone better." They continued to chat for a few minutes more, about their work and how good it was to see each other—whatever one says to someone one hadn't been speaking to after engaging that person in a totally delightful conversation—before Jane and I got up to leave.

Later, Jane told me that Otto had called her after the meeting to say, "Jane, just what do you do with a client who tells you in front of the director that she's not right for the part?" I asked Jane what her response was and she said, "Who knows better than the actor if she's right or not?"

Jane was right on that count in more ways than one. After much maneuvering back and forth between agents, George was offered the role of the prosecutor and gladly accepted. *Anatomy of a Murder* was shot in Ishpeming, Michigan, where the actual case the movie was about took place. George and I agreed that two weeks or so into shooting, I would come out and visit him for a week. When Jane heard of my plans, she went crazy and gave me some lecture that to this day I've never quite understood—about crossing state lines to sleep with someone while being married to someone else. I had never paid much attention to geography and wasn't going to start now over that.

Before my arrival, George explained to Otto the nature of our relationship. Otto, true to being the great gentleman I have always known him to be, immediately took over making all arrangements, explaining to all concerned that he was having "this actress"—me—"fly out for a week to discuss a role."

From the moment I arrived, everything was taken care of "at Mr. Preminger's request." I was introduced by Otto to cast members and crew in a way that indicated to all that I was there at Mr. Preminger's invitation, thereby putting his stamp of approval on my relationship with George when, soon after, it became obvious why I was there.

It was a fascinating time. I had never been on a movie set with such wonderful actors as James Stewart, Lee Remick, Ben Gazzara (with whom I would, years later, do *Who's Afraid of Virginia Woolf?*) and Joseph Welch, a judge in real life who had became so well known and admired for his stance against Senator Joe McCarthy during the infamous Army-McCarthy hearings. When I arrived, the company was shooting in the courthouse. I made a point of never sitting on the actual set, but stayed behind in the judges' robing room, which was much like a small locker room with a couch, table and chairs. The actors also used it as a place to relax in between takes.

So as not to distract George, I tried always to be as inconspicuous as possible, sitting on the far corner of the couch and reading whatever book I had brought. During that time, I was introduced to the actress who was playing the role I had turned down. We spoke for a few moments before the door opened, and one of the assistant directors escorted in an actor who was having his first day on the set. Introductions were made all around. After the A.D. left, the three of us stood there for about five minutes, long enough for me to realize that the actor I had just been introduced to was completely taken with the other actress in the room and completely uninterested in me.

Quietly, without anyone noticing, I went back to my corner of the couch and began to read, but not missing a word of the fascinating conversation that began to ensue. The actress began to explain in a flourish of detail that she had to finish shooting very quickly because she was pregnant and her breasts were swelling. Soon she wouldn't be able to play an ingenue convincingly, as she would, in her own words, "just be too sexy-looking, don't you think?" Just then, the door opened to the chamber and Jimmy Stewart entered the room. I kept my head buried in my book to save him the embarrassment of perhaps not remembering who I was. After greeting the new actor and the actress, he moved around the corner to his locker and began to change into a fishing outfit. As he did, the other two continued their conversation, consisting now of the story of the delivery of her first baby a few years before, sparing no anatomical detail. The actor hung on her every word, which only seemed to encourage her to embellish the story with even greater seductive detail. I continued to pretend to read, desperate to ignore what was going on around me. Finally the A.D. interrupted and called the two of them back onto the set. I continued to read, now vaguely ill at ease that James Stewart and I were alone together in this room, both having overheard this bizarre conversation.

Out of the corner of my eyes, I could see him pulling on a pair of hip-length rubber boots. As he fit his foot into the second boot, he looked over to me and said, "I suggest you get a pair of these, because we're in it up to our asses." As I glanced up at him he winked and walked out.

Many months later, *Anatomy of a Murder* was shown at a single preview in Detroit, Michigan, three weeks before its official premiere in Los Angeles. George and I flew to the Coast and were driven in a studio car to the theater that night. We entered very quietly, taking our places unnoticed in the seats that had been assigned to us. No one paid any special attention to us. No one in this Los Angeles audience knew who we were. Who had ever heard of *Children of Darkness* or even off-Broadway, for that matter? The lights went down and the film began. It was truly wonderful, and George was magnificent. The audience loved the movie, and as it played to its conclusion, you could feel the excitement that was building in the auditorium for George. Who was he? Where was he? When the lights came up and we rose from our seats and began to move up the aisle toward the lobby, people immediately recognized him and began to move toward him. Soon George was being stopped every step of the way by people wanting to shake his hand and tell him how wonderful they thought he had been.

As we reached the entrance to the lobby, we were surrounded and pushed from every side. It was an electrifying and slightly terrifying experience. Suddenly, I felt a hand on my arm. It was Mr. Stewart.

"Why don't you come with me?" he said, ignoring the crowd and stopping us for just a moment. "Is that all right George? She can sit with my wife at a small table we have in the lobby. She'll be more comfortable." George nodded and was soon swept by the crowd into the lobby. Jimmy led me in the opposite direction and toward the table where his wife, Gloria, sat. He introduced us and then turned back into the crowd that was now also trying to reach him.

As flashbulbs exploded throughout that night and I watched George go from being an actor to being a star, I realized that Mr. Stewart had put me in the safe position of not having to be identified by the press or having to explain my relationship to George (which in those days was highly unacceptable). At the same time, Mr. Stewart had done me the courtesy of putting me with one of the most highly respected women in the industry, his wife. This was an unexpected act of kindness that has remained with me for over thirty years.

12

"Could that be taken care of for Miss Dewhurst, please?"

G eorge once said to me, "Colleen, I believe it is the responsibility of any actor in a leading role to do exactly what you are doing—no matter how bad it gets, you hold and never break the line." At the time George made this remark, I was furious, seething and in a rage. And although I loathed seeing actors blow up in rehearsal, I was feeling about at the end of my rope and was just about ready to blow. "Nevertheless," George continued, "you are not an egotistical or temperamental actor who simply disrupts a rehearsal in order to prove his own strength. If you, as the leading actor, are in a situation where you know that you are working with someone destructive, than you damn well owe it to the cast to do just that—speak out! That's not breaking rank. That's your duty!"

You can go through life ignoring a lot, forgiving inadvertent slights, giving people—who often don't really deserve it—the benefit of the doubt. But I cannot bear to watch any director deliberately sabotage an actor's performance. Some do it deliberately because they have tremendous ego problems of their own. Some are very intelligent and, as if to entertain themselves, are quite deviously quick to find an actor's professional or emotional Achilles' heel and exploit it throughout the entire rehearsal period. It is a very dangerous and destructive game.

Thankfully, I have rarely found myself in a company led by such a person. But unfortunately, one sad exception was with director Alan Schneider in *The Ballad of the Sad Café*, the beautiful theatrical adaptation by Edward Albee of the haunting Carson McCullers story.

I was thrilled when I was cast as Miss Amelia Evans in *Ballad*. It was one of the first times, after the success of *All the Way Home*, that I was to have a leading role. I had always loved the story. I adored Edward's adaptation. Before being cast, I had never met Mr. Schneider, about whom, with the theater being as small and close-knit a community as it is, I had heard a number of conflicting stories. Some actresses worshiped him. Others spoke of him as a demon, deliberately cruel and lacking in compassion and understanding. I tried as best I could to enter the rehearsal period without any preconceived notions. With a cast that included Lou Antonio, Roscoe Lee Browne, Enid Markey, William Prince and Michael Dunn, I felt overwhelmed by my good fortune as the first day of rehearsals approached. And for a time, all seemed fairly calm.

One of the pivotal characters in *Ballad* is a dwarf, played by Michael Dunn. From the start, he was wonderful. It was extraordinary to look at Michael. I remember George telling me how creepy it was to see him sitting on the edge of the stage with me standing not far behind him. As we spoke, George said, you could not take your eyes off Michael, and what initially seemed to be a distorted appearance became strikingly handsome. And the more handsome he became, the more dangerous the scene felt. I loved Michael. He had a beautiful tenor voice. He told me, over the course of rehearsals, of his mother and father—how they raised him to mingle and play with other children. He was very well educated, at one time studying to become a Jesuit priest. But there was also a sad isolation about him that was very hard to reach through. Michael told me once, over a meal after a rehearsal, that he did not expect to live past forty. I do not know how old Michael was when he died alone in some Italian hotel, but I suspect he was not much past the age he predicted.

As we came closer to previews, which are always a treacherous time even for the most well adjusted and secure among us, I began to go home at night seething with anger. To my mind, Mr. Schneider was beginning to show signs of cowardice. He was frightened by the material, and to relieve himself of his fright, he began to put Roscoe, Enid and especially Michael under his thumb.

My dear friend Roscoe is a brilliant actor with a mind as sharp as a knife, or at least much sharper than Mr. Schneider's, which I'm afraid caused the latter some consternation. But I could not stand especially when Alan began to snipe at Michael. At first, I may have stupidly felt that way because of some old-fashioned notion that you must never attack those who are vulnerable. But as I grew to know Michael, I realized this was not the case. He was capable of protecting what was most precious about him. But even the strongest of us can be broken bit by bit, and that's what Alan began to do instead of thanking God every day for finding such an extraordinary man to play this extraordinarily difficult role.

And then there was Enid, a lady who had been a star in her day and now, grown old in the theater, seemed almost like a girl again. I loved her. She was particularly vulnerable, not because of her age but because, I believe, she had never in her many theatrical experiences met a man who was not a gentleman.

In spite of it all, we made it through early rehearsals and entered our run-throughs before previews. At this point, at the end of each rehearsal a director will usually give notes to the actors together. Each director, of course, gives them in his or her own manner, but most will simply speak to each actor, in front of all the others, about a point he wants clarified. Sometimes a director, particularly a sensitive one like my dear José Quintero, will, at the end of this session, draw aside an actor and speak to him or her separately. This is occasionally done privately, often because the director will ask you to change your approach completely, without your fellow actors knowing it, in order to force them into an improvisational response.

From the start of run-throughs, Mr. Schneider would call us all together to give his notes, and before beginning would look at me and say, "Colleen, you can go to your dressing room. I'll give you yours separately." My first reaction was that I had been doing so badly that he didn't want to embarrass me in front of the others. But these private sessions proved to be rather mundane, with nothing particularly embarrassing or sensitive about them.

"Alan," I finally said at one point as he indicated that I could retire to my dressing room, "that's all right. I can hear my notes out here along with the rest of the cast." He didn't like it. Perhaps I should have taken him aside to tell him that I would prefer to stay with the others or should have mentioned it during one of the private sessions. But I didn't. And it was the beginning of an unspoken battle between us.

With each succeeding day, the tension mounted. Worst of all, a feeling of fear began to invade the cast. This was not the usual subliminal fear that we all experience as we move toward an opening; it was a quiet, yet debilitating, fear of being unexpectedly humiliated by some unprovoked or snide remark from Mr. Schneider. He was never direct. Instead, what he said was tossed off in such a way that it would divide me from the company or set other actors off balance with each other. I drove home every night frustrated with the tension and my seeming inability to do anything about it.

As we got closer to the first preview, the question of why Miss Amelia had chosen to marry and what had happened on her wedding night still had not been addressed. No matter how hard I tried, I could not get Alan to work with me closely on this. Finally at the end of a rehearsal, I asked if I could meet with Edward Albee, Mr. Schneider and the producers in my dressing room. This time, being away from the company seemed completely appropriate.

"I need help here," I began. "In what direction do you want me to take Miss Amelia? We have to have some explanation about the nonconsummation of the marriage." I aimed my questions at Mr. Schneider and watched him closely as I spoke.

"This play is beautiful, Edward. It follows the line of the novella exactly. But, Alan, I need to have some direction. I know this wasn't answered in the written story, but we have to deal with this in a dramatic form. I need some help here understanding what you think has happened if I'm going to be able to play anything that makes sense, if only by intimation."

Each time I asked Mr. Schneider a question he would put his head down and, looking out from under the brim of his baseball cap, glance quickly to Edward, clearly trying to read what he wanted him to say. If Edward shook his head, Alan said no. If Edward nodded, Alan would immediately say yes.

"Is she a lesbian?" I countered. "I don't see it in the novella or the play, but someone has to attempt to determine this lady's problem on her wedding night!" No one spoke, and I knew I was never going to get an answer. Was this such an unspeakable possibility that we couldn't even discuss it?

That was when Lou Antonio and I began meeting at the Farm after rehearsals to work through scenes. We were able to work out a great deal between us. But one scene that kept eluding us was the climax of the play. The fight. It is very difficult to have an honest fight between a man and a woman onstage and make it believable. We had a marvelous choreographer come in and put us through moves that were excellent in terms of covering space and movement. But as a fight, a dangerous, brutal battle, it was not believable.

In desperation, I asked George to come in and watch a run-through to which we could invite friends. Afterward, George, Lou, and I drove back to the house. On the way home, George gave us excellent notes in terms of character and motivation, the sort we had never received from Alan. But George wouldn't talk about the fight. I kvetched and yelled and generally released a lot of anger that didn't really seem to help me or anyone else. George quietly continued to give us notes about what he thought was wrong. Once we arrived home, Lou and I were fixing something to eat in the kitchen when George called from the living room.

"Colleen! Lou!" he shouted. "Come in here."

We looked at each other and walked in. George had pushed all the furniture from the center of the room to the walls.

"The danger is missing," George said. "It's not your fault," he added. "Most people won't ever believe a fistfight between a man and a woman is possible."

We began to play the scene as we had performed it that night at the theater. "It's not about destroying each other," George said as he changed and modified what had been originally directed. "Get ahold of each other. Force yourself on the other. Force the other to listen." George continued to work out moves that began with us striking out at each other but moved very quickly into wrestling, releasing, holding, escaping. He worked with us for a long time. It was exhausting, but Lou and I, under George's careful direction, began to feel comfortable and in that comfort began to have the look and feel of brutal combat between a man and a woman.

The next day, I went into rehearsal still appearing to operate under the old rule that the director is the director; he knows what he's doing. Although by now, in my heart, I knew it was not true. We began to work through a number of spots and different scenes that needed some polishing. Then we came to the fight. Previously we had begun by circling a table three times. After working with George, we circled only twice.

"Stop!" Alan shouted from the house. "You circle the table three times, Colleen."

"It wasn't working, Alan," I replied.

"Circle three times," he repeated. "It works."

"No," I said. Finally, suddenly and for the first time, Alan and I entered the arena. We weren't circling. We were engaged.

It was a shouting match. I screamed, "No!" and Alan screamed, "Yes!" back at me at least ten times. What looked to be possibly mortal combat dissolved into a children's fight. Out of the corner of my eye I saw Lou, who had been standing beside me, sit down on the edge of the stage.

"When I saw your body begin to shake," he told me later, "with the first *no*, I knew the fat was in the fire and I may as well get comfortable for the fireworks."

By the time I got to the last *no*, the entire company was on the stage. Seeing them, I couldn't stop myself. Everything I had been feeling over the previous weeks spilled out.

"You're a destructive human being," I screamed, almost out of breath. "And I don't want to have anything to do with you again!" I turned around and stomped off to my dressing room.

José Quintero and I have a theory about actors who "blow," as he calls it, having been in so many plays together and having watched so many actors explode. Everyone, José believes, even under the best of conditions, blows for a specific reason. It releases tension. It's necessary. José says I can always be counted on to blow about costumes.

"One way or another, Colleen," he says, "at some point you are going to march onto the stage during a costume call and begin screaming about the snaps, the zipper, the cut . . . something."

After José brought this to my attention, I realized that he had always sat quietly in the dark until I had wound down. Then I would hear a voice simply say, "Could that be taken care of for Miss Dewhurst, please? Colleen, dear, that is going to be taken care of." And I would slither offstage into my dressing room, having released all my fears about my performance onto an unwieldy snap.

José and I have continued this discussion over the years and have come to the conclusion that there are basically two types of actors—accepting, of course, our original premise that we all "blow." The first are those who blow up, leave in a rage and stomp off to their dressing room, slamming the door. The second are those who blow up, take a long march down the corridor to the stage door, which is then kicked open and slammed behind them. With the first, the dressing room door slammer, his or her problem is solvable. The one who marches out the stage door is usually lost forever.

But back to *Ballad*. Being a dressing room escapee, I went in and sat down, shaking. We were only about three hours from the curtain going up on our second preview and I was still in a rage, wanting nothing further to do with the play or, at that moment, caring what was going to happen to it. This feeling always frightens me because I know it only to be purely destructive. Worse, I hate to have the object of my fury know that I am out of control. Slamming doors is out of control. And once I have gone to that extreme, my anger with the person seldom abates.

There was a knock on my door. I wouldn't answer it. There was a knock again.

"What?" I snapped. The door opened just a bit. Lou put his head in, looked at me, gave me the *OK* sign, and smiled.

"I love you," he mouthed without actually voicing the words. Nevertheless, for the next hour and a half I stayed in my dressing room alone. There was another knock on the door.

"Yes?" I said. It was Michael Dunn. He opened the door and stepped into the room.

"Could I spend a few minutes?" he asked. Before I could respond he hopped up on the chair next to mine, as he always did, and looked at me in the mirror.

"Thank you for what you said to Alan." He held his gaze on me in the mirror. "I didn't know what anyone thought about anything anymore," he continued. "It's been pretty discouraging."

"You're terrific in this, baby," I said, holding his reflected image in the glass.

"You, too," he replied before jumping off the chair and leaving the room, pulling the door shut behind him.

In short succession there were three notes slipped quietly under the door from actors playing smaller parts, each telling me that they agreed with me. This didn't make me feel much better at this point. I was wondering how I was going to continue, having called the director a son of a bitch and, in no uncertain terms, having told him never to speak to me again.

"Half hour," the stage manager called. I began to dress.

"Places," he said, thirty minutes later, adding a rap on my door.

I walked to my place onstage. As I did my eyes met those of other cast members, who grinned at me. I grinned back. We touched each other, wished each other luck, and that night, for the first time, went on to perform the play with a unity we had not reached before. We began to find moments with each other that we had not found before. The fight worked—minus the third circle. It took me a long time to figure out what had happened. We had found a common enemy. If we were not united as an ensemble by him, we would be united as an ensemble against him.

This is not an acceptable solution to this problem. But it was the first time

I had ever encountered such a situation. I had worked with José Quintero, Harold Clurman and Arthur Penn. It would never have occurred to me, not even for a second, to do more than discuss a point with any of these men. They were each directors who understood fully the play and the psyche of an actor. They truly held the reins. Every actor dreams of the director who will take him to that place he feels he can go but has a little fear about going there alone. These directors, these men and women, lead you. They are worth their weight in gold.

One of the saddest statements I have ever heard before going into rehearsal for a play was this: "Who's directing you?" a friend I had worked with many times asked me over the phone. When I told him he said, "Oh, that's OK. He'll leave you alone."

Now I know what he meant. If you don't have a director who can take you by the hand, it is better to have someone who just directs traffic and lets you find your own way. The worst, as I have recounted here, is the one who doesn't lead you *or* leave you alone, but instead grabs your hand and leads you around until you are so inhibited that there is no way ever to find your way or understand his. Sometimes this can't be avoided. What I learned in *Ballad* is that if ever someone who calls himself a director begins to operate on me, it should be stopped sooner rather than later. If not, sooner or later, I blow.

And not over a zipper.

BEN EDWARDS

I knew Colleen before I ever did a play with her. She was one of the pretty girls walking on in the first Broadway production of *Desire Under the Elms*. That was so long ago I've forgotten what year it was. But the first time I worked with her as a leading lady would be *The Ballad of the Sad Café*, of which I was the set designer and coproducer. She was great. There were some tensions during rehearsals and backstage, but that happens in a lot of plays. An actor will just sort of side up against the director and the director takes it out on a particular actor. Everyone's nervous, everyone's insecure. Half the time it's a part of the rehearsal process. This case was a little more extreme, and as we all became aware that Alan Schneider and Colleen didn't much get along, no one really wanted the job of stepping between them. Including me. I'm not one to pay much attention to those things. I liked Alan very much. I adored Colleen. But deep down, I knew Alan had a very dark sort of distrust of everyone and everything around him that caused him to stop and start and fiddle around with everything and everyone until it just became ridiculous. And still, he'd be uncomfortable. He about drove the poor lighting designer mad, although it turned out to be very beautiful lighting. I'm certain Colleen sensed his basic distrust of everything and as a result felt very unsupported by him and annoyed with his constant worrying.

To be perfectly honest, the problem between them began well before rehearsal. When we first started working on a dramatization of *Ballad*, Alan had gotten Geraldine Page to agree to play it. Edward insisted in his contract that Colleen had to play it and Alan was very annoyed. I wasn't so sure about it at all myself at first, but Colleen very quickly won me over. I don't think Alan was ever very happy about it and took his displeasure out on everyone. Amelia was a very hard part, but Colleen ultimately made it work despite her great dislike for Alan and in spite of whatever support she felt she didn't get from him.

The *Ballad of the Sad Café* was a troubled production all around. It got decent reviews, despite some quibbling from Walter Kerr in the *New York Times,* and made some money, running for about five months. But the play seemed cursed with a run of bad luck with one terrible thing after another weighing us down that really had nothing to do with the production itself. First we played the Martin Beck Theatre on Forty-fifth Street across Eighth Avenue, just as an apartment building was being built on the corner. This blocked the street in a way that you could barely see the marquee. Then there was a newspaper strike which knocked out our advertising, and a series of terrible snowstorms which knocked out the box office. None of this was helpful in building an audience. To top it all, we were running the day President Kennedy was shot, which just took the heart out of everyone. One terrible thing after another and this odd but beautiful little play barely stood a chance.

I felt particularly bad for Carson McCullers, the writer of the original novella on which the playwright Edward Albee had based the script. I had known her for a number of years, I guess since she first came to New York. By this time she wasn't well and came to see the show in a wheelchair. I so wanted it to be a hit for her. Afterward, she pulled me toward her in the chair and said, "All I want to see is the SRO [standing room only] sign. That's all I want." Sadly, that was not to be. Although Edward's adaptation was excellent indeed, I'm afraid she felt a little discarded by the entire experience. It was sad, really. We closed soon into the new year, 1964, with very little fanfare. Colleen was nominated for the Tony for Best Actress later that spring. She lost to Sandy Dennis for *Any Wednesday.*

I worked with Colleen again most happily ten years later when I designed the set for the Broadway production of *A Moon for the Misbegotten,* and still later, for the revival of *A Long Day's Journey into Night* that she did with Jason and José. Colleen would always surprise you. Something would go wrong, for which another actress would scream at you for hours, but Colleen wouldn't have any problem at all with it. She just hated to waste time with that sort of thing. If you were honest with her, she was eager just to work through it. She was quite a lady. I still think about something she said about me once. "Whenever Ben builds a set," she once told a reporter, "I know where I am." For a set designer, it can't get much better than that.

ROSCOE LEE BROWNE

I met Colleen the day that I became an actor. It was the last day of auditions for the inaugural season of the New York Shakespeare Festival. We all auditioned in front of one another. Because I had never been to an audition before, I had none of the terror that the other actors had. They knew how difficult this moment could be. I did not know. Now, I *know* this to be a terror. Then, I thought, *How nice to have other people here.* Among all these others, sitting way in the back were Colleen, Jack Cannon and Joe Papp. I did some turn in the audition, that as I think back on it now, could only be termed *plebeian.* You see, we were told in the audition announcement to know a speech from *Julius Caesar* and to be prepared to read anything that the director might ask us to read. I prepared a speech of Cassius'. They were very responsive.

"That was wonderful," the director Stuart Vaughn said. "Wonderful. But I don't think we can have a colored Cassius." I stood there in silence while he thought about it some more and said, "Mr. Browne, can you read the soothsayer's lines?"

"Well," I said, "he *is* an exotic." There was a rumble of laughter from the house and I began, "Beware the ides of March"—or whatever it is.

"Wonderful," Stuart said. "Now you understand, there is more you can do. You can come back as another character. You can play Pindarus. Yes," he said thinking aloud, "we *could* have a colored Pindarus." Well, by this time I am getting quite fed up with what he thought he could and could not have colored. But Roscoe says nothing.

"Are you ready, Mr. Browne?"

"Yes."

"Now this is very important. You enter and must set the scene for Marc Antony's entrance. Remember, you are running onto the fields at Philippi."

"I know," I said. And somehow he worked the word *colored* into his last bit of direction one more time before saying, "Enter, Mr. Browne!" which I did, putting a shuffling southern dialect on Shakespeare's "Fly further off, my lord. Fly further off. Marc Antony, he is *in* your tents! Fl-y-y-y-y-y further off." Colleen was howling. Stuart was dumbfounded and Joe came right down to the lip of the stage. "You're new to me," he said.

I said something in reply, hoping he could hear me over Colleen, who was still shrieking with laughter.

"You're in," he said. It was my first day as an actor and the first time I heard that glorious laugh. Our eyes met as Joe walked away from the stage, and Colleen and I were friends on the instant.

Sometime later, Joe was doing *Titus Andronicus.* This was after the great success that Colleen had had as Kate in *The Taming of the Shrew,* in which she had been just staggering. I'd done a couple of other things by then, somewhere off-Broadway. Joe had seen them and called one day, asking me to replace the actor who was then rehearsing Aaron, the Moor. So there I am, still very new to this business of being an actor, suddenly playing opposite Colleen's Tamora and we are lovers—Shakespearean lovers. You have to remember, of course, that Roscoe is still relatively new to the theater. The director had the notion that a particular scene—during which Aaron does most of the speaking—should be a lovemaking scene. We thought it was silly, but we both adored the idea of being wrapped in each other's arms and rolling on the stage. I didn't really realize how difficult it would be to be rolling around and trying to speak lines at the same time so that they could be understood. It was not going well for me. One night, Colleen wrestled me into submission and held me so that I couldn't move. In my ear she whispered, "Now do the lines, darling. You are facing downstage." I had been talking upstage. No one could hear me. What did I know? I was newly an actor. Every night thereafter she would do the same, roll me into position and whisper, "Now, darling." And each night I laughed and went into my speech, which made her laugh and I'm sure that the audience thought we were the most delighted lovers, Aaron and Tamora, when, in fact, we were simply delighted with each other, Roscoe and Colleen.

Colleen and I worked together again in 1963 in Edward Albee's adaptation of *The Ballad of the Sad Café*. I was the narrator. Colleen's first entrance in *Ballad* was a very difficult one, as she had to enter laughing. Now for any good actor, life onstage doesn't begin when you enter, it begins just before. I was already onstage, as the narrator, setting the scene with one of those interminable monologues we couldn't cut. When I mention her name—Miss Amelia—the lights would come up on the scrim behind me, and you'd see Colleen looking out the window of the second floor of Miss Amelia's General Store. As I exited stage left, Colleen would pass by me on the way to make her entrance. Now—Enid Markey was a delightful apple dumpling of an actress in the company, who had some amusing lines to say as one of the villagers. I also knew how bedeviled Colleen was with that first entrance. One night, early in previews, as she came down the steps on the back of the set, I whispered, "Colleen, do you know who played Jane to Elmo Roper's Tarzan in the silent film?" as we passed in the dark.

"Who?" she said.

"Enid Markey!" I whispered. Colleen howled and stepped out onstage, laughing just as Miss Amelia should. From then on, it became a part of every performance. "Enid Markey," I'd say every performance, and Colleen would laugh as if hearing the answer to that question for the first time: "Enid Markey." Before long, it was practically all I had to say in the dark. "Enid Markey!" And it's true! Enid *had* played Jane years before. Colleen would howl every time, perhaps at the idea of Enid playing Jane or perhaps just hearing those names together—Elmo Roper and Enid Markey—and step out onstage laughing as only she did. I have no idea if anyone was aware of this little exchange, but I think if my understudy had replaced me for a day, Colleen would have shot him if he had not known to ask her that question.

We never talked about this during the run of the play, fearful, I think, that laughing about it outside of that very moment backstage would destroy its spontaneous magic. But one night, after the play had closed, she looked up at me over dinner with George and said, "Roscoe Lee, how did you know that?" And without needing any explanation of what she was talking about, I replied, "It's in the *Playbill*." It so staggered George that I would know what she was talking about that he hit his fist on the table. We paid no attention. But he banged it again. This time, my fork bounced off the table onto the floor. Colleen and I both reached down to grab the fork and our heads knocked together under the table, at which point George slammed the table again.

"Well, G.C.?" Colleen said as she sat up.

"For two people who are known for the clarity of their speech onstage, in real life you two fucking well mumble! But what bites my ass," he says, "is that I'm sitting between the two of you and I don't understand a fucking thing you're talking about!"

Now, of course, George is the only person who could be sitting with two people at a round table and assume that he is the middle. By that time, we were all in hysterics. George was right. Colleen and I really did mumble in a way that would complete each other's sentences. Maureen Stapleton said we would *begin* each other's sentences.

One afternoon, Colleen called to ask if I would meet her for dinner at Downey's after the performance. I'm not sure what she was doing at the time, and I was in something off-Broadway that came down later than she did, but I said I'd meet her there. When I arrived, she was already sitting with Maureen. As I approached the table, Colleen's eyes met mine and she beamed. As I sat down, I said, "Oh my dear, is *that* what you wanted to tell me?"

"I'm sick of you two!" Maureen said, with a force similar to the way George had slammed his fist, and pushing away from the table, got up to get herself another drink at the bar. Now, Colleen hadn't said a word yet. But she looked over at me and said, "What, Roscoe Lee?"

"You're pregnant," I said, quite matter-of-factly. Colleen got this look on her face where her chin stuck out a little and she glared back at me.

"Don't you dare," she said. "Don't you dare."

"Isn't that what you wanted to tell me?" I asked.

"*No,*" she said, "I wanted to tell you something amusing that Jane [Broder] had done." And she did, and we ate, and Maureen might have even eventually come back from the bar. The next day, Colleen called.

"How did you know?" she said, without saying hello.

"Know what?"

"Do you remember that it was only two months ago that I had Alex?" she said rather impatiently.

"Yes . . ."

"Well, I've just come back from the doctor and I *am* pregnant again. How did you know?!"

"It was in your eyes, dear. Like it or not, some part of you was telling me you were pregnant." Nine months later, I visited Colleen in the hospital, where I was first introduced to Campbell.

Once, when I had too much of a good thing under the care of Dr. Feelgood, I called Colleen shortly before dawn and said something like, "Help!"

"Don't leave the apartment," she said. "George is in the city, and he'll be there in fifteen minutes." G.C. was there in about ten, and he whisked me and all my hallucinations off to the Farm in South Salem. I had not slept for seventy-two hours, so I fell into a fitful exhausted sleep in one of the bedrooms on the second floor, waking only when Colleen or Elsa Raven would come in to pour orange juice into me, Elsa saying, "Blood sugar."

During my stay, three or four days, Colleen had made plans to speak to a local Girl Scout troop. As I slowly came down the steps from my bedroom one morning, I heard Colleen on the phone. "Oh, I really wanted to speak to the scouts, but I have an emergency that I must attend to." Colleen's back was to me. Just then she turned and saw me standing at the foot of the stairs. She smiled. "I'm so sorry," she continued, "I want to see the girls but I need to be here today." I could see that Colleen was having a difficult time trying to explain why she had to cancel, since she couldn't be specific about the nature of her emergency.

"Tell them," I said with as much returning wit as I could muster, "that you're tied up with a crumbling Brownie."

Colleen roared, literally roared into the phone as she tried to explain to this poor woman that she truly did have an emergency on her hands. "I'm so sorry," she said, trying quite unsuccessfully to contain her laughter, "but my friend just said something very funny about what's going on. Darling, I will come another day. Yes," she added after listening for a moment, "I think we'll be all right." And with that she hung up the phone and sat down in the middle of the kitchen in hysterics, repeating to herself as she looked over at me standing at the foot of her stairs in this sad bathrobe and slippers, "crumbling Brownie . . . crumbling Brownie, oh, my God. You're getting better, darling."

A few years later, Colleen was in Rome at the same time that I was in Spoleto to do a play. George was there shooting that dreadful film *The Bible*, for Dino De Laurentiis, who had put Colleen and George up in some splendid villa. Before I left Spoleto, Colleen rang up saying, "Please come down and stay with us at the guest house. I'm here with the kids—and please come, Roscoe." So I did, and by the time I got there, everyone knew—what I assume had been going on all during filming—that George was having an affair with his costar, Ava Gardner. The Italian newspapers were filled with it, screaming it in unbelievable headlines every day. It was a dreadful time for Colleen. So one day I announced, "Colleen, we're going to lunch—"

"No, Roscoe . . . I don't—"

"Yes! We are," I explained. "Today! Now." So, I called our dear friend Leontyne Price, who was there recording an opera, and asked her to join us in a well-known restaurant in Rome that had all these faded pictures of people who were favorite movie stars, opera singers, anyone—whoever the current diva was. But they had the best food. We sat at a table against the wall, Colleen with her back to the wall. Leontyne and I facing Colleen. At some point, Colleen began to speak to us about what was happening. She was "finished," she said, "this is it." But as she spoke, her voice caught and she seemed just about to weep.

"Don't you dare!" I said.

"Don't I dare *what?*" she said.

"Don't you dare cry," I said.

"Roscoe!" Leontyne said, "if this sweet girl wants to weep, she must. Honey," she continued, "you go right—"

"Colleen!" I interrupted, because she was really ready to go. She stops and looks at me and I indicate with my eyes the wall behind her. She turns, looks above her head, and there, in a frame, is Ava Gardner! Colleen looks back at me and then to Leontyne and starts to laugh. We could not stop howling at the insanity of it all. I thought we would be thrown out. There I was with these two beautiful women and we could not stop laughing. And then, as Colleen and I continued to laugh, Leontyne began to sing a beautiful aria from *La Rondine*. Then Colleen began to weep, but it was all right because it seemed she was weeping for joy and the beauty of this voice, as were many others in the restaurant. It was all very Italian and perfect. I had noticed the damn photograph after we sat down, and I ignored it, figuring Colleen would never turn to see it. But then I thought, "No! I cannot have Ava look down on her as she weeps." So we laughed and laughed and laughed as Leontyne sang a song of joy

One day, about ten years ago or so, I went off to get an honorary doctorate at Lincoln University. Colleen called me the next year. "Say, darling," she said, "I'm going off to get my own honorary doctorate at Lawrence University." And we laughed about it. "Darling," she said. "I know what I wanted to ask you."

"What is it, Colleen?"

"Can we use these doctorates?"

"Colleen," I replied. "There are people—and many of them you've met—who love to say, 'I'm Doctor So-and-so,' 'Doctor This-and-that.'"

"Oh," she said, a bit confused.

"You and I may use them only once," I said.

"When?"

"The next time I'm up for an award," I told her. "I won't show if you promise you'll accept for me and promise to say, 'Dr. Dewhurst is pleased to accept for Dr. Browne.' And the next time you're up for one, I will go for you and say, 'Dr. Browne accepts for Dr. Dewhurst.'"

Colleen never left my heart nor I hers, but there was a time in later years when we did not see very much of each other. I was in a bit of trouble again and Colleen was heard to say, "If he wants to commit suicide, I will not be a part of that." It was withering. But I discovered that even after this episode was over, she was being told some really awful stories about me by others, many of which, as those things go, were not true. So, after much time, I called her.

"Can we dine?" I said. "At Jezebel's." So we did, and we discussed all that had happened, and all that people had said and how it infuriated us so much to hear stories about each other that we had been unable to speak to each other. We were both furious at everyone and had been missing each other. But with that dinner, all the trouble was over. We were still absolutely unshakable in our love for each other. And even during all that time of discomfort, if either of us had had the sense to call the other and say, "Come," the other would have said, "I'll be right there." So at this dinner, as we spoke and laughed, Colleen reached over the table and just held her hand on mine. Just then I noticed this waitress who had been watching us very intently. "Roscoe," Colleen said. "Why is that girl staring at us?"

"Because you are beautiful and I am interesting," I replied. Finally, this sweet woman came over and said, "I'm so sorry to interrupt, but I have to ask you a question."

"Go ahead, my dear," I said.

"I've never seen a man and woman finish each other's sentences the way you two do," she said. "Are you married?"

"For eternity," Colleen replied, not taking her eyes from mine. "We are so married," she then added, looking up at the waitress, "that we cannot be divorced."

And we laughed.

13

"I think you're pregnant."

Motherhood had never been a part of my thinking in terms of my future or as a part of my life. It was not something that I had ruled out, but it was certainly not anything that I had ever dreamed of, thought of as a goal, or felt a need for. Therefore, I realize now that I entered motherhood as I had always entered the most important stages of my life—rather casually.

George and I wanted a baby and so I got pregnant. First with Alexander, and then just months after his birth, with Campbell. I went through both pregnancies easily. I enjoyed them tremendously. I looked rather like one of those huge dolls that are shaped like a vase with a small neck swelling out to the bottom, the kind that you could have such fun pushing over and rolling around on because they always come back standing up. For neither pregnancy did I have books around the house advising me as to what I was supposed to do with this child once I had it, although I think not two weeks after I had Alex, I bought the famous Dr. Spock. What I remember most clearly is that during both pregnancies I was working.

When I carried Alex, I was playing Caesonia in *Caligula* opposite Kenneth Haig and directed by Sidney Lumet. After I was cast and when I realized I was pregnant, I went to Sidney and told him I thought I should pull out of the play. He told me that there was no reason to, I was not showing. I was delighted. I ended up with a costume with a rather wonderful belt that came around the back of the waist and then down to a point on the front just below the belly, just below Alex. My pregnancy was kept a secret for a long time.

I also asked Sidney that we not tell Kenny Haig, because I felt it would make him tense in his scenes where he was to strangle me, his mistress. George, however, took it upon himself to inform Kenny toward the end of the run that I was pregnant and, as I feared, Kenny became terribly nervous and somehow my strangulation never had the nerve that it had had originally. Unfortunately for the play, we closed in four months. Thankfully for me, and particularly for Kenny, who seemed to be having a more difficult time with me each passing week, this meant I was not strangled beyond my fourth month.

It was while I was pregnant with Alex that Nana came to us. Once *Caligula* had closed, I realized that if I was to continue in this profession, I was going to need someone to help me take care of the baby. Nana's name was Christine Davis. She had worked for the actor John Marley and Stanya, his wife, where she had taken care of their home and children. It was a God-given day for me when Stanya, who knew I was pregnant, said that she and John and the children were moving to the West Coast and that Christine did not wish to go with them. Would I not like to meet Christine, she wondered.

I remember the day that Christine arrived at George's and my little house hidden behind an apartment building. I loved that house. It consisted simply of a living room with a kitchen unit at one end and a fireplace at the other. There were a bedroom and a bath upstairs. At the appointed time, there was a rap on the door. I opened it, and there stood this incredibly beautiful black woman. She looked like a queen, but a queen with a most warm and lovely smile. I asked her to come in. We sat together and talked and I, who in many meetings will never really get to the point, quickly became fascinated with this woman sitting across from me. We talked for a very long time. Finally, Christine got up with great dignity and, while I continued to babble on, wandered about the living room.

"Do you have a broom?" she asked.

"Oh, sure," I replied. "I must. Let's see, where do I have a broom?"

As was to be indicative of our whole relationship, Christine found the broom and, as I continued to talk, proceeded to sweep the living room floor. From that day, indeed from that moment, Christine—who would in time be christened Nana by the boys—became a part of the family, making it possible for me to have a career but, most important, bringing great love into the family.

From the start, Nana could not wait for Alex to be born, and I remember the day as if it were yesterday. Nana had gone home the night before and, like every evening when she left, she said to me, "Well, maybe tomorrow." I went to the hospital at about six o'clock the next morning. Alex was born at about ten, and George returned to the house at eleven. Nana was there already, out in the courtyard sweeping. She was astonished to see him, assuming that we were both sound asleep upstairs.

"Oh, my God," she said seeing George, knowing at once that something had happened.

"We have a baby," George said. "A boy named Alex." Nana clapped her hands. "Thank you, God," she cried, pulling George into her arms for the kind of embrace you never forgot. And never for a moment since then have I ever believed that George meant anything but that we three—Nana, George and I—had a baby. Nana came to the hospital the next day with George, and we came home with Alex.

Nana was one of those women who paid close attention to what they dreamt. When Nana dreamt of fish, someone was pregnant. Therefore, Nana knew I was pregnant with Campbell before I did. Two months after having Alex, I was packing to go to Boston to open in the play *All the Way Home,* which was to come into the Belasco Theatre in New York in November. Naturally two months after you have a baby the last thing that enters your mind is that you are going to have another. As I was packing Nana looked at me.

"I think you're pregnant," she said.

"No, that's silly. I can't be," I replied. And off I went to Boston. Within a month, I called to tell Nana she had been right. I was carrying Campbell. Nana, the great seer, had seen it first. I was very excited to be working with the director Arthur Penn and a marvelous cast that included Lillian Gish, Arthur Hill, Clifton James, and John Megna. There are so few scripts that you open up and, as you begin to read, know it is a wonderful play. As adapted by Tad Mosel from James Agee's beautiful book *A Death in the Family, All the Way Home* was such a play. I had been called in to read for Arthur Penn only after they had been unable to cast a well-known actress.

I read four times for Mary Follet, one of the leading roles in this story of the Follet family of Knoxville, Tennessee. One night, after the second reading, I gave George the script and asked him to read it aloud to me. He had only read a dozen pages or so before he looked up at me, silent for a moment, and said, "I think this is a great play," confirming my initial feelings of its depth and beauty. By now, I wanted this role very badly. Two more readings and finally there was a call from Jane Broder telling me that the producers, Arthur Cantor and Fred Coe, had called to begin negotiations. I was thrilled. Although I had done other things, *All the Way Home* really began my Broadway career, if for no other reason than I was finally in a great critical success that ran nearly the entire season. *All the Way Home* won the New York Drama Critics' Award for Best American Play and the Pulitzer Prize in 1961, and I won the Tony for Best Supporting Actress. Now, truth be told, I was not a supporting actress in this role. I was the leading actress, onstage practically every minute. But due to the somewhat silly rules surrounding such things, since my name was not above the title of the play on the marquee, I was not considered a leading actress and was therefore nominated for Supporting. I'm very grateful to have won, but I did feel bad for Rosemary Murphy, who should have won the Best Supporting Actress award for her work in *A Period of Adjustment.* She was wonderful and the role was clearly a supporting character.

But back to Boston and Nana's prediction. Once we came into town and opened, I gave the producers "act of God" notice. They were not eager to let me go. Since I was pregnant as Mary, the character in the play, they thought there was no reason why I should leave. Ultimately I agreed. What no one considered, however, were a few of the lines that referred to Mary's condition. Lines when we started like, "You don't show, Mary," were, as we continued the run, changed to "You're showing a little, Mary," and finally to "You're show-ing, Mary."

By New Year's Eve, I was into my fourth month with Campbell. George and I were living in the Village and George was playing in *The Wall*. That night, Nana, who had been with us for a while, was unable to be home with Alex. Both George and I had evening performances, so rather than find some-one else—for there was no one else like Nana—I carried Alex uptown to the Belasco Theatre and put him in a basket in my dressing room. Many times that night while onstage, I would casually glance off into the wings where the stage managers, Pete Van Zandt and Bill King, were standing. When they could see me look their way, they would fold their hands palm to palm, press them against the sides of their faces and close their eyes to assure me that Alex was still sleeping peacefully through his first play on his first New Year's Eve.

I played in *All the Way Home* until the beginning of my eighth month. Like sweet Kenneth Haig in *Caligula*, the men in *All the Way Home* became much more preoccupied with my pregnancy than did many of the women. This is not to say the women didn't care. They did and were wonderfully supportive. However, the men, particularly my two dear stage managers, were, as I began to show more with each passing month, watching my every step. The set for *All the Way Home* was a house, built to be open to the audience. Upstairs, ele-vated on the stage, was a bedroom where I spoke to the audience. This second floor had no guard or fence in front of it on the downstage side. Each night, I would stand and move quite close to the edge, without looking at it, to speak. It was a scene I loved and in which I felt quite comfortable. Not Pete and Bill. More and more often I would see them in my peripheral vision standing on the side of the stage wildly holding their hands up, as if telling me, pleading with me to back up. One night, they weren't waving. I could see them standing quite still, side by side, often one holding his hands clasped tight as if in prayer, and the other looking straight ahead and holding the side of his head with both hands. It was not the first time I had gone too close to the edge. But it was one of the first times that I ever felt I had two such wonderful guardian angels.

I had both boys during the summer, Alex on August 1, 1960, and Campbell on July 19, 1961. A Leo and a Cancer. Both boys were born after the start of one of the great loves of both George's life and mine: the Broadway Show League. George played both summers, and I could see no reason why my preg-nancy should keep me from going to the games. I love baseball.

The first summer, when I was carrying Alex, everyone would have to stop the game as I came lumbering across the field in Central Park, trying to look inconspicuous and move as fast as I could. Of course, when I turned up in exactly the same condition the next summer, there was a good deal less rever-ence toward me and a lot of comment about the obvious medical miracle, that somehow I had managed not to deliver the baby and was now pregnant for two years and looking none the worse for wear.

The summer I was carrying Alex, there was one game played for charity in which the ladies were "allowed" to play. (Yes, can you imagine today telling the ladies in any Broadway company that they were just to watch the men play? George objected strenuously to my playing, but I wanted to very badly. So I did. I was terribly excited when I got a hit and made it to second base. The batter after me hit a very nice single, which could have easily brought me home if I had been in shape. But as I was lumbering to third, I took a look behind me and, rather than stopping safely on base, started for home plate, mustering as much speed as I could.

"Stop! Stop, goddamnit!" I could hear George screaming from the dugout. But it was too late. I was on my way home as an outfielder whipped the ball to the shortstop, who fumbled the ball for a second, making my safe race for home plate possible—if I slid.

"Oh, Christ, she's not going to!" screamed George again from the dugout. By this time, he was up and charging toward me as the shortstop fired the ball into home. I pushed with my last burst of top-heavy speed and slid into home. I got there just as George did—and just ahead of the ball. Safe! I was thrilled. The crowd went wild, by now quite excited by the action of the game and, I guess, the drama on the sidelines. It took days for George to speak to me. Like me, Alex has always loved baseball and plays quite aggressively. We can assume there is something to be said for genetics and a baby's experiences in utero.

Alex and Campbell are quite different, as their sun signs, Leo and Cancer, are different as fire and water. Alex from the first was gregarious, loved everyone, and couldn't wait for people to come to the house. He always wanted to be with people, was quick to talk, and eager to get on with it—whatever *it* was. Alex was the baby who, when he began to rise to his feet, made me conscious of everything in the house that had corners on it. Campbell came in rather like the moon; sometimes you'd see it, sometimes you'd see only a sliver. Then there are those times that he decides to shine completely and beautifully. When Campbell rose to walk, he never fell again. Campbell, I realized, had made a quick study of what could happen if you rose too soon or went too fast.

Unlike Alex, Campbell for the first year of his life screamed if anyone came into his room or looked into his crib. Only Nana, his father, his brother, and I were allowed entry. Only we four did he want anything to do with or wish to see. I think it was very fortunate for Campbell that he grew up in the kind of house he did, because there was no way that he was going to be able to avoid throngs of people, and happily he grew to adjust to it.

Alex loved to have parties when he was little, especially birthday parties with cake, presents and friends. He also loved to give orders, organizing everything as he thought it should go. Whatever the game, Alex wanted *everybody* to play, but *he* wanted to win. When we gave Campbell his first birthday party at the Farm, we planned carefully. All his friends came over and put their little presents in front of him. Campbell was horrified from the start and never spoke, from the moment the first guest arrived until the last guest left. He would not open his presents, would not play any games, and did not want to blow out the candles on his cake. I felt very sorry for him, but at the same time, could not stop laughing. Poor Campbell was in such a state of shock at having these people thrust upon him that he was literally in a trance. It's so strange now, because I know Campbell has come to love the Farm in some part for just these kinds of special celebrations.

When the boys were young, George and I often disagreed about how to observe various holidays. George's point was that he did not want them to be encumbered with so much fuss about Santa Claus and the Easter Bunny, the Tooth Fairy and that crowd. He felt that it was much too much of a disappointment when you removed those fantasies from them after you personally had made such a point of convincing them to believe in them. I, on the other hand, insisted that we had to have them, because, as it had been explained to me as a child, these were symbols of love. I believed any disappointment in eventually finding out the truth about Santa would not mark them forever, but that as they grew up they would simply replace these early fantasies with other real images and people.

And now, many years later, as I sit here and think about both my sons— now handsome young men with ladies of their own, Campbell with Annie and Alex with Irene, as well as his own two beautiful children, little Campbell and Christine—I feel most confident that Alex and Campbell have done just that.

14

"I would say that on your list of worries, fear of being elegant is last."

I live in an old farmhouse about fifty-five miles north of New York City, to which I came kicking and screaming. I was a city girl and had always been a city girl. When we first moved up here, George maintained that I continued to live as if I were still in an apartment in Greenwich Village, except with a car. Every day, I would go out the door, get in the car, drive to the city, come back, come in the door, go to bed, get up the next day, go out, get in the car, and repeat the entire routine all over again. I felt isolated and wanted nothing to do with my new surroundings, particularly if it snowed. Then I was furious. My first spring on the Farm, I didn't do much more than walk to the door and think, with very little conviction, "Oh, how pretty," before getting into the car and driving to the city, still furious for having been uprooted. I was not happy nor was I making those around me happy, either.

My city mentality did understand, however, that when summer came, other city people would be eager to come to the country to visit. They certainly did, and gradually, as more of our friends came up and stayed, I began to see what was even then becoming known as "the Farm" through their eager eyes and less through my anger. By the time spring came around again, what had initially felt imposed and forced upon me had become my home. And as I went out the door—yes, still to drive to the city, though not every day—all that surrounded me now began to embrace me in a way that eased me into my new surroundings. I looked forward to coming back each day, and found more reasons not to go into the city if I wasn't working.

I wouldn't leave the Farm now for any reason—love nor money, as they say—and I realize that setting new roots down here was the best move that ever could have been made for me and my children. This house is the only reality, the only constant—although it is a completely unruly place—that I have in my life. The Farm, no matter where I am in the rest of the world, is my center. The theater is my soul. But this place, this bit of land and house that always seems to be moving and collecting things and people and, God knows, animals, is my heart. The Farm was not my beginning (nor even my idea), but after all this time, after so much joy and through so much trauma, it will surely be my end.

It's impossible to tell any sort of complete or chronological story of the Farm, since it is a rare place that is always in flux, with very little attention paid to such things as time and order, clear beginnings or tidy endings. The Farm, God knows, is casual. I still wonder how this came about. My mother ran a rather formal home—formal in furnishings, formal in feel and always very lovely. But you were *invited* into the apartment. You did not *ever* simply arrive. I cannot remember any time when I was growing up, except possibly in an emergency, when anyone just dropped over. Whereas here, we have drop-overs, drop-ins and drop-outs. And I love it that way. It is exactly what I would have liked my house to have been when I was a child.

When we first arrived, the boys were six and five. One of the reasons George had insisted we relocate was because we wanted Alex and Campbell to go to public school, as we both had. We agreed that if we stayed in the city, they would at some point end up in private schools. So Alex entered first grade in Lewisboro. In the middle of December, his teacher called me to ask a favor. Every year, she said, one of the parents would come in and play Santa Claus for the day. I couldn't believe what I knew she was about to ask. Poor Alex was already nervous about his mother doing anything strange or different from the other mothers. I had already flunked the required baking of homemade cookies that each child occasionally brought in from home. Now I was being asked to show up in drag.

This teacher swore she hadn't been able to get anyone else to do it. I didn't agree until the next day when a peculiar little Santa suit arrived, lined with white tassels that looked like they had last been seen on kitchen curtains. No wonder she couldn't find anyone. Word was obviously out to everyone but me about the costume. I kept my upcoming participation a secret from Alex and explained to his teacher, in advance, that if he seemed upset by my appearance, I would leave at once. As the afternoon of my debut approached I was in agony. I literally threw up before leaving the house, worrying if I was going to ruin my oldest child's experience of first grade and perhaps scar him for life. An opening night on Broadway was nothing compared to this.

A neighbor drove me over to the school. As I met her in the driveway she nearly doubled over the steering wheel, unable to believe that I was going to do this—pillows in the front, pillows in the back, and those damn white tassels hanging everywhere. Upon arrival, I informed the teacher that I would not be saying, "Ho, ho, ho." (I could just imagine her thinking, *Oh, she* is *difficult to work with.*) No, since these children were not going to believe for a second that I was Santa, I thought I should introduce myself as "Santa's helper" and thereby not be stuck with any particular "Santa script." As I entered the school, the principal met me just inside the door.

"Here are your bells," he said.

"Bells?"

"You need these so they can hear you coming down the hall," he replied. *Oh, God.* I thought one of the best things Santa, or any of his helpers, had going for them was stealth, getting in and out quickly, without anyone noticing. Not wanting to disappoint or risk having given someone else another "She's difficult" story for the next PTA meeting, I put on the bells, careful not to tangle them in the tassels. Mommies and teachers were all lined up curiously in the hall. Just as I was ready to enter what I thought was Alex's classroom, the principal pulled me aside and asked if I would mind going to all the classes. "The other children will just feel terrible if Santa doesn't stop by to see them, too," he added.

"Santa's helper," I reminded him.

"Of course."

By now I was nearly hysterical, and my friend who drove me was paralyzed with laughter against the hallway wall. But down the halls I went, bells ringing, tassels flying, and pushed open the first door.

"Oh, children, look who's here," the teacher exclaimed as I entered. There were cheers all around as I introduced myself as "Santa's helper, sent by Santa himself," said hello to all the children and left cookies, made no doubt by the mothers crowding the hallways. I was a smash and continued to the next few rooms, embellishing and enjoying my performance as I went. But as I entered Alex's classroom, my stomach tensed with worry. Miss Scofield, Alex's teacher, kind of smiled at me and said, "Look who we have here, it's—"

"Santa's helper," I interjected. I didn't go over to Alex right away. But as I talked to the other children, I kept sneaking a peek his way. He didn't seem to recognize me at all; in fact, he seemed too engaged in his own conversation with his little friends to much care who had just arrived. I worked my way around the room, child to child, speaking to them all. When I got to Alex I said, "Oh, what a handsome shirt you're wearing." He looked up at me, and when his eyes met mine they froze. For the first time since I'd entered the room, he said nothing, and I moved along to the next child. When I left, I looked over toward Alex. He had put his head down on his desk. *Oh, dear,* I thought. I made a few more visits to other classrooms, came home, tossed Santa's suit back in the bag it came in, and waited.

I was sitting upstairs on the bed when I heard the school bus arrive. The door to the kitchen slammed and Alex ran straight up the stairs to me. "How could you do that?" he said before he was even in my room. "That was *you!* That was *you!*" he said standing at the foot of the bed.

"That was me what," I answered, hoping against hope that I might be able to squirm out of this.

"You were Santa's helper!" he yelled, before running into his room and slamming the door. I was nailed. By morning, Alex seemed to have recovered from the trauma of his mother making an unannounced personal appearance. Nevertheless, at lunchtime, I called the principal to make sure that Alex was all right.

"Oh, yes," he assured me. "In fact, I've overheard him say, 'That was my mom' any number of times today." We both figured that I was forgiven and that Alex's place in the first-grade social stratum would survive me.

"But, please, no more costumed visits," I asked before hanging up. "It's going to be bad enough when he and his brother figure out that I do this for a living."

I HAVE SPENT my life trying to organize this house and the fact is, there are just certain things you can do nothing about, so you're best off to adjust to them. This is one of them. I will never have an organized home. I was, however, so excited once to read in the *New York Times*, no less, that "shabby chic" was "in." They described how suddenly it was now chic not to have a decorator's touch, that it was somehow fashionable to have a chair that looked like it had been chewed by a dog. "Distressed," they called it. I have a few of those. And that it was all right to have an old, old rug on the floor in faded colors, although it seems they stopped short of spots left by the occasional untrained puppy. Got that, too. Earth colors, lots of pillows, and old books scattered about, worn places in the wallpaper, suddenly all of this—a look I had been clearly cultivating for years—was "in."

Not long after this appeared, a friend called asking if I'd allow the house to be part of the PTA house tour. Someone had backed out at the last minute, she said. *Someone has come to his senses,* I thought. Now, I love to go into other people's homes and look around, but I had never allowed my house to be on such a tour. However, she was desperate, so I finally agreed. The day of the tour we all tried to whip things into shape, putting flowers around to hide what was falling apart, sweeping up, stacking what could be stacked, hanging up what should be hung up, chasing the animals out of rooms and off of furniture that they had long assumed was rightly theirs and, most important, closing off the upstairs. When everything was ready, I left. I had no intention of being a part of the tour. When I returned, I was told that all had gone exceedingly well, although one woman was caught with one leg over the barricade at the foot of the stairs to the second floor.

Afterward, I was amazed by the mail I received from women saying how wonderful it was, after seeing houses that were beautifully done, to get into a house that looked lived in. One woman even wrote that she was overjoyed to see, peeking out from under a chair, just one sneaker. We probably still haven't located its mate. I never knew whether to take those letters as congratulatory or as a slight put-down. I just hoped they had read the same piece in the *Times* that I had.

If I'm not in a show, I'm a great one for just spending the day on my bed. Not *in* bed; not asleep or undressed, but spread out on the bed, in jeans and a sweater, with a lot of newspapers and magazines nearby, animals napping near me, and, inevitably, the television on. When the boys were young, every school day at about two o'clock I would hear the bus stop outside near the driveway. Then I would hear *troop, troop, troop* through the house, *troop, troop, troop* up the steps, and then a bang on the door. Five or six little boys would all come in and stand there staring at me.

"Would you mind taking your friends out of the bedroom?" I didn't mind the lack of privacy; in fact, I was glad that the boys were always comfortable enough to bring their friends home. But I did often wonder how many of them returned home saying, "Mrs. Scott spends all of her time in bed."

Many memories slip through my mind. I remember Alex and Campbell having some fights that were beauts. After one in particular, I found a note that said, "Dear Mom. I am running away. Don't worry, I'll come back. Love, Cam." It was dusk and raining. I went down and told Nana and Alex, who began to search for him up and down the road. Alex was distraught. He felt that it was his fault, and kept assuring me, over and over, that Campbell would never hitchhike. *He* would, but his brother would not. After an hour, as it got dark and began to rain harder, I became more upset and began to make calls to neighbors and to the head of the camp where he had been going, which was about thirty miles away. We called everybody. Still, no Campbell.

People whom we had called began calling us back to ask if we had found him, making us even more tense. Finally, I announced that if we had not found him within the next fifteen minutes, I would have to call the state police and his father to say that he was missing. Nana and I were standing downstairs, trying to pretend that we both weren't extremely upset, when Alex suddenly appeared at the top of the stairs yelling, "I found him! I found him!" I can still feel Nana hugging me and then see her hugging herself and saying, "Thank you, God. Thank you, God. Say it again, boy," she shouted up the steps.

"I found him! I found him," Alex shouted again and again.

We went racing up the stairs. Alex motioned me into Campbell's bedroom and then into his bathroom, where we had all looked before. The shower curtain was closed. Alex pulled it back and there was Campbell, lying in the bathtub, fast asleep with a tiny suitcase on his chest. I woke him up. I was crying.

"What's the matter?" he said. "What's going on, Mom?"

"I found your note, Cam. I thought you ran away."

"Oh, no," he said. "I was going to, but I was hiding here until you all left. I guess I fell asleep. I'm sorry, Mom." Alex was very happy to see his brother, and whatever had happened between them before was long forgotten. Later,

Nana and I agreed that it was just like Campbell to get himself in a snit, decide to run away, and fall asleep before he could leave.

Alex was on his first Little League team, playing second base. George and I went to a game after Alex had only been playing a month or two. At that game, the ball came straight at him, hit the ground, took a bad bounce, and hit him in the mouth. It happened so quick I could barely see it—just that he had scooped up the ball and thrown it to first. Then I saw blood. I started to rush from where I was in the bleachers onto the field. George reached across me and took my arm. "No, no," he said. "This is his coach's job. Alex doesn't want you out on that field, only his coach." I sat there in agony as I watched Bob Sawyer, his wonderful coach, bending over to talk to him and looking at the lip, which I could see was blowing up. Alex continued to play until the end of the game and then came off the field and let me hug him.

"Oh, my darling, let me see your teeth," I cried. "Are your teeth still there?" He had lost a little chip. "That must hurt," I said, pulling Alex into me for another hug.

"I got him out at first," Alex announced proudly, looking over to his dad and then up at me.

"You sure did, Beany," George said. "You remembered what you were supposed to do. You got him out at first."

Fortunately, the boys were not brought up alone in a house with just their mother, even after George and I divorced. There were always people around to love them, to teach them. But my secret weapon was Nana. Nana's instincts were always loving: to hold, to cuddle and to be there. I don't remember ever receiving a call from her when I was working to report on anything about the boys or their friends that was distressing. I'm sure there were distressing times, but if they happened while I was away, she took care of them. They would be reported to me later upon my return, but I would never let the boys know that Nana had told me anything or do anything that would diminish Nana's authority or the clear bond of trust she had with each of them. Alex and Campbell loved Nana dearly. It was with Nana that their great and wonderful growing up process began.

After Nana, there were many people: Tony and Stuart; Elsa and John and Leon; Gerry and Nana's son, Bobby. Many came through this house, some who stayed for years or simply reappeared again and again until they became family. Alex and Campbell grew up knowing that they could be loved by many people, yet were solely responsible for the love that they would receive in their lives. I think they grew up learning to love without guilt and not to be afraid to love many different kinds of people without having to explain themselves. My only hope is that this extraordinary environment has made up for other things in their upbringing that were overlooked. But something is always to be gained from what is lost. There is always an exchange of circumstances that can turn

Colleen, mom and dad at the beach.
(Author's collection)

Colleen, summer at the lake.
(Author's collection)

"Biddy."
(Author's collection)

Colleen, after school, 1937.
(Joan Warburg)

Colleen, on her way to school,
1937. *(Joan Warburg)*

Mrs. Frances Dewhurst.
(Author's collection)

Colleen Dewhurst—first actor's resume
picture. The inscription reads, "To my
darling Mother. Love, your Colleen."
(Author's collection)

Center stage in summer stock. *(Michael A. Shalhoup)*

Mr. and Mrs. James Vickery leave
"The Little Church Around the Corner,"
June 1946. *(Mrs. John H. Esser)*

Colleen, as Kate, and J.D. Cannon, as
Petruchio, in *The Taming of the Shrew.*
(George E. Joseph)

Joseph Barr, Colleen and neighborhood children during a break in rehearsal at the Lower East Side Amphitheatre, New York City. *(George E. Joseph)*

Colleen and J.D. Cannon in the Circle in the Square production of *Children of Darkness*, 1958. *(Bert Andrews)*

George C. Scott and Colleen in the New York Shakespeare Festival's production of *Antony and Cleopatra*. *(George E. Joseph)*

George C. Scott and Colleen (pregnant with Alex Scott) in New York City's Central Park for softball with The Broadway Show League. *(Author's collection)*

Colleen and playwright Edward Albee during the run of *Ballad of the Sad Café*, 1963. *(Alix Jeffry)*

Mr. and Mrs. George C. Scott— July 4, 1967, the second wedding. *(Barbara Mae Phillips)*

The Scotts—Colleen, George, Campbell and Alex—and guest, July 4, 1967.*(Barbara Mae Phillips)*

Colleen and George at home.
(Alex Scott)

Colleen, coach of the Fireflies. *(Jill Sawyer)*

Colleen in *All the Way Home*, 1961. *(Arthur Cantor)*

Colleen greets
Eleanor Roosevelt
backstage at the
Belsaco Theatre
during the run of
All The Way Home.
(Arthur Cantor)

Colleen Dewhurst,
publicity photo prior to
leaving to do *A Moon for
the Misbegotten* at the
Spoleto Festival.
(Author's collection)

Colleen, Pamela Payton–Wright and Stephen MacHattie in the Circle in the
Square production of *Mourning Becomes Electra*. *(Bert Andrews)*

Colleen Dewhurst, *Mourning Becomes Electra*.
(Bert Andrews)

Doctor Dewhurst and Doctor Browne. *(Alex Scott)*

Jason Robards, José Quintero and Colleen Dewhurst,
Photograph by Richard Avedon
June 16, 1988, New York studio.

Colleen Dewhurst and
Jason Robards in *A Moon
for the Misbegotten.
(Martha Swope © TIME, Inc.)*

Vivian and Colleen at the Farm, 1984.
(Alix Jeffry)

Leon and Nana. *(Barbara Mae Phillips)*

Colleen Dewhurst and Ken Marsolais.
(Alan Markinson)

Colleen, Maureen Stapleton, and Charles Durning (back to camera) in the kitchen at the Farm. *(Joan Warburg)*

Peter Lawrence (seated far left), George Hearn, Colleen, Rex Robbins, Zoe Caldwell (all seated on couch) and the Broadway company on the set of *An Almost Perfect Person*. *(Cliff Moore)*

"An almost perfect person?" *(Betty Chamberlain)*

Colleen in rehearsal for *Artichoke* at the Long Wharf Theatre, 1976. *(William B. Carter)*

Jason Robards, Colleen and the cast of *You Can't Take It with You*, 1983. *(Ken Howard)*

Colleen on her birthday in her dressing room at the Plymouth Theatre during the run of *You Can't Take It with You*. *(John Handy–Betty Miller)*

Ellen Burstyn passes the gavel to the new president of Actors' Equity Association. *(Equity News)*

Colleen, in hot rollers, going over her notes at her desk in the president's office, before a meeting of the council of Actors' Equity. *(Tom Viola)*

The cast of the New York Shakespeare Festival's production of *Taken in Marriage*. Left to right: Colleen, Dixie Carter, Elizabeth Wilson, Kathleen Quinlan and Meryl Streep. *(George E. Joseph)*

Director Colleen Dewhurst, John Vickery (seated in tux), Buzz Cohen (sitting on floor), Peter Michael Goetz and Ken Marsolais (both kneeling, center) and the company of *Ned and Jack*. *(Martha Swope © Time, Inc.)*

"All right, I laughed. So shoot me." Colleen and the company of *Queen and the Rebels*. *(Martha Swope © Time, Inc.)*

Clifford Stevens and Colleen. *(William Gibson)*

Ben Gazzara, Colleen and Richard Kelton in *Who's Afraid of Virginia Wolff?* *(Barry Kramer)*

Best friends since childhood, Colleen and Joan, 1988. *(Joan Warburg)*

Colleen Dewhurst and Alex Scott, 1988. *(Alex Scott)*

Campbell Scott and Colleen Dewhurst in *Long Day's Journey into Night*, 1988. *(Peter Cunningham)*

Candice Bergen and Colleen Dewhurst as Murphy and Avery Brown. *(CBS, Inc.)*

Colleen in the one-woman show, *My Gene*, at The New York Shakespeare Festival. *(George E. Joseph)*

Marilla, *Anne of Green Gables. (Sullivan Productions)*

grief into strength and sadness into joy. There have been many imperfect times, but I do not feel guilty, nor do I feel that my sons have been marked any deeper than most of us have been marked in life. Life is a learning process. There is no prize for being perfect. My feeling about myself and the boys is that difficulties are to be lived through. It is strictly in the living of it *all* that makes any of it *at all* worth it.

ONE AFTERNOON at the Farm, I brought Maureen Stapleton into the living room to show her two new chairs that had just been delivered. I wasn't really sure how I felt about them now that they were in the room. "Well, Mo," I said. "What do you think? Do you like them?"

"Yeah," she said, "I like them."

"You don't think they're too, well, too elegant, do you? The Farm is so casual that I don't want anything to make it stiff or formal."

"Elegant?" she said. "Elegant?! This is a house in which all the animals run outside all day to leap and bounce and then come back into the house to shit, Colleen. I would say that on your list of worries, fear of being too elegant is last."

We have always had lots of animals at the Farm. There's no way to think about this house without thinking about the animals. At present, we have three dogs and nine cats that live in the house, and a peacock, chickens, two goats, and a couple of sheep that don't. And Boris, the cockatiel who rules from his cage in the den. We fully expect he will outlive us all. The population has varied over the years but has probably always remained about the same in number. It is simply not true that they all proceed, as Maureen so elegantly claims, to relieve themselves inside the house. No, for the most part, all make "pee-pee in the woods," as Ken is fond of saying. But, it does occasionally happen, especially if it's very cold or one or the other might not be feeling particularly well that day. But who can blame them?

My friend J.D. Cannon and his wife, Alice, had come up to stay for a few days when we'd first moved up from the city. One night we had steak. Rusty and Go-Go, the two German shepherds that lived with us, kept wandering around the table, eyeing us all. Finally Jack looked up from his plate and said, "Should I just take the bones and throw them over my shoulder? Or do they keep patrolling back and forth until one of *us* is fed to them?"

I've tried never to have a dangerous dog. But, since any dog takes his home quite seriously, I suppose on occasion one of them might seem a bit ominous to a stranger. But again, that's what dogs do. Once, a French photographer came by to photograph me. When he was greeted in the driveway by Rusty and Go-Go, he immediately asked if they could be shut away somewhere.

"Oh, no," I assured him. "These guys will never bother you as long as I'm with you. They'll see that you're all right." He reluctantly agreed and went about setting up his camera. Soon he was ready for me. I stepped in front of the camera without a hitch. Rusty and Go-Go couldn't have been less interested. "All right," he said, "would you mind if I shot you with the children?" I was caught a bit off guard, but reluctantly agreed, calling for Campbell and Alex. As soon as the boys joined me in front off the camera, Rusty, from about two hundred yards away, tore across the yard and without a sound, grabbed the photographer's arm and would not let go. He froze. I immediately ordered Rusty to let go, but I was nonetheless fascinated that she must have sensed my discomfort with the situation and chose to step in and stop it.

Rusty and Go-Go had puppies at the same time; one a litter of four, and the other a litter of six. We had ten puppies in the house that winter and, of course, our fair share of yapping, scampering and pooping before good homes could be found for them all, after one of the boys put up a sign in the yard: FREE PUPPIES FOR SALE. But for the life of me, I could never get one of my beautiful shepherds to mate with another shepherd. Never. We would take them to meet some wonderful, chic, masculine male, shut them in the garage together, and wait. Nothing would happen outside of the occasional growling over food and sleeping space. We'd bring them home again, and both of them would fall in love with whatever they could find on the road, some damn mutt, and we'd be painting another sign offering "free puppies." The girls' lack of discretion, while I hope not a reflection of their surroundings, did result in a rather extreme measure of doggie birth control. But even after their operations, they still had an eye for the road and always ran to sniff whatever wandered by. I fear word was out among neighborhood dogs that Rusty and Go-Go were always up for a good time.

EACH ONE of us, in our own way, has a rather mystical feeling about the Farm. The actual property seems to have a life and personality of its own, one that changes with the people who enter it and those who stay. It has seen many, many faces. Some people have taken refuge here, others have run from here, but always the house seems to close around those who need it, for however long they need it. I really believe that this house has become my eye in the storm, and I have watched as it seemed to know when to hold on to someone and when to release. No matter where I am, the knowledge that I will ultimately go back to the Farm makes whatever is happening all right. The Farm stands here not always cared for as it should be but always, always loved.

Once, when we had fallen on not particularly good times, the house was peeling badly. It had obviously needed a paint job for a number of years. All of us had gotten more or less used to the look, but I found out later that the neighbors were very conscious that things had fallen into disrepair. About this time, I had gone to the West Coast to make some film or other and was gone for two months. Before I flew back, Ken called to say that he would pick me up at the airport. As we came down the road, I began to look for the familiar white farmhouse that I knew would soon pop into view as we wound up the road. Suddenly, I looked up to see that the house had received a beautiful, spanking new coat of yellow paint. As I got out of the car, I was met by Alex and Campbell and some of their friends. I couldn't stop talking about what they had done. What a wonderful surprise, especially knowing they must have done the job themselves, as we had been given estimates which were, for then, way beyond anything we could afford. We all stood very proudly and looked at the house. I was ecstatic as I walked through the side door and into the kitchen. I was home.

Two days later, when I had gotten myself somewhat organized, I walked out through the back door to look at the patio Ken was working on. I went back where the animals were, to visit the two mules, Buckle and Christmas, and the coop full of chickens. As I turned to start back down the hill to the house, I stopped dead in my tracks. The back of the house was still white. I began to laugh as it became apparent that the only part of the house that had been stripped and painted this new yellow was the part of the house you could see from the road or as you entered through the kitchen door from the driveway. The back we are still waiting on, but it doesn't seem that important now. I couldn't have been more happy with their surprise and now, at least as far as the rest of the world is concerned, good times and a good paint job have come to the Farm again.

The Farm is like a child's dream to me. Obviously there is no color scheme or order, just anything and everything we love strewn across and through it. One night, I sat with Elizabeth Wilson, a wonderful actress and dear friend, watching some program about communal living. Different couples were being interviewed, along with their children, many saying that this was a new experiment in living. You would have men, women and children in residence, not all necessarily related to each other, lots of commotion, animals. Most of those being interviewed felt it was particularly good for the children, as they would have many different role models. "Isn't that interesting?" I said to Elizabeth. "Look at that. Now that's a good idea."

"Colleen," Elizabeth interrupted, "how do you think you're living here? This was a commune long before any of these people thought of it." And she was right. People seem to just come and go here—sometimes without me even knowing. I can't tell you the number of times I've come down in the morning to find one or two people making breakfast who I didn't realize had dropped in sometime since dinner. Oh, they were on their way to New Haven from New York, decided they couldn't make it, and stopped. I had gone to bed but they had sat up with whomever and still hadn't made it to bed. This is one of the reasons that I chose dogs rather than a gun for protection. I'm afraid that at some point, one of these good friends is going to arrive at two in the morning and I'm going to come down shooting.

You never know how the mix of who and what are here at any given time is going to react. I remember once a gentleman came by who was going to be directing a film that I was to do. We had met only once before in California, under rather chic circumstances. He had flown out just to have dinner before we were to begin shooting. I was out when he arrived, but as I entered I asked him how he was, and began making the usual small talk.

"The house is wonderful," he said. Just then one of our mules trotted by the large picture window. He just stared—the director, not the mule.

"Oh," I said, trying to break the silence, "have you met our mules?"

"Yes," he replied, "in fact, one of them kicked me as I got out of the car." The offending mule ran by again. This time in the opposite direction.

"Well, he may have to be gotten rid of," I said, hoping it would be some sort of comfort. "He has been hard to get along with since he was forced to let the Virgin Mary ride him at the Christmas pageant in town last year."

"Some people just don't appreciate being forced into show business," he answered. I was never quite sure what he meant by that but the next year our mules sat out the pageant.

WHEN HE was quite young, Campbell once said to me, "Mom, this is a holiday house."

"What do you mean?" I said.

"It's just right for all the holidays," he replied. "I mean, even the Easter bunny comes."

I have friends who have lost their minds, because if they are trapped with me on the eve before Easter, they must help me write the poems that lead everyone from one egg to another before we finally get to the big nest of eggs. At two or three in the morning, it is often very easy to come up with nonsensical rhymes but difficult to remember where you have hidden the eggs for the hunt the next morning. Inevitably we would lose a few eggs, only to find them over the next few days, half eaten by one of the dogs, or worse, a raccoon, whose appearance would cause hysteria throughout the house's entire animal population.

I AM A compulsive inviter. Finally I realized that if I was going to continue along this way, I needed a dining room table that would seat a crowd. If I have invited two people to dinner, then in the meantime I see two other people whom I enjoy or find interesting, I see no reason why I shouldn't invite them as well, and this goes on until sometime in the afternoon when I say, "Now let's take a count."

"Fifteen," somebody chimes in.

"That's impossible. We were just going to have Mary and Blumphy over tonight." Well, yes, but "Mary" and "Mr. Blumphy" have been joined by "Whosey" and "Whatsit," who brought along "Bunny" and "Buffy," and then there's all of us. Fifteen it is, and I think I really like it that way. I like a house to have an atmosphere of being open, with a feeling that most homes only have in the summer, when screen doors swing open and someone comes in. I like the idea of people feeling comfortable. That's what I wanted for the boys. That's what I wanted for me.

Now there have been times as the boys got older that I have considered abolishing the open-door policy. I have been awakened by the telephone at seven or eight in the morning—and sometimes, at two or three in the morning, depending on the circumstances—to have a rather tense mother's voice inquire as to whether Bill is there, or Greg, or Peter, or Don, or Jeff. Whoever. My attitude on the phone is always an immediate show of control of the situation. I respond that if she will wait just one minute, I will check. I then put down the phone and proceed to go through the house, room by room, pushing open doors, walking over cats, examining tufts of hair and closed eyes, until I can distinguish that this is Peter or whoever is momentarily missing and unaccounted for at his own home. I cannot always make a positive identification, but most of the time, if I'm lucky, I can recognize them.

I've come to understand that the boys in the living room are the losers in whatever subtle game of choice for bed space has gone on the night before. I assume they are the ones who usually go home, but for reasons best unknown, have not done so that night. If I have not located the son of the mother who has been hanging on the phone by now for ten minutes, I proceed to go outside, in all kinds of weather, and climb the stairs into a large studio above the garage. It started out years ago as a wonderful library with a lovely pool table and fireplace. When the boys were teenagers, it became an area about which they always said, "No, no, Mom, don't come up here. It will hurt you to come in here, Mom. We're cleaning it up now. Don't worry about it, Mom." On the mornings when I was forced to enter, the sight of that formerly lovely spot, where guests from the city could find moments of quiet, could on occasion bring me to tears. But I also took comfort in hearing the reverberations of the boys playing pool and hanging out with their friends, even if I knew that the laughing and chortling, the running up and down the stairs to get to the refrigerator in the main house, would probably go on until three or four in the morning.

By the time I should have returned to the telephone to inform Mrs. Whomever that indeed her young man is in my house, I usually thought better of it. Instead, I would simply awaken the heir in question and inform him that his mother was on the phone and would he please take the call, as I don't want her to think that somehow I am not right on top of whatever is going on in my house. For years, I have sat and watched flashed on the television screen quite ominously every night at ten o'clock: "It's 10:00 P.M. Do you know where your children are?" Most of the time, I do. They're here with their friends. And I have always liked it that way.

I only need one place in the house that is just mine, usually the bedroom. As long as I can retreat there and be alone, no matter who is with us, I don't mind how many people come and go wandering through. We're all in this thing together. And after over twenty-five years, the house still stands, with the feelings and ghosts of dozens of people—and animals—who have come to stay for some short or not so short period of time and were invited, just by their immediate ability to be comfortable here, to make this a haven.

ALEX SCOTT

There were two cartoons that were framed and hung in the bathroom on the main floor of the house at the Farm. One was of a young guy standing on a wharf. He looks like a young Errol Flynn, staring out to sea from a dock that looks like Boston Harbor in Revolutionary times. There's an old guy watching him, standing nearby. He looks like the old man of the sea. "You know why that ship you've been waiting for hasn't come in?" he says to the young guy. "Because they don't use this wharf anymore." The other is a *New Yorker*-like cartoon of a king in a very ornate bed. He's talking to his wizard, who is standing at his side. "Now, wizard," the king says, "today I want a very nice day, approximately 70 degrees with a nice southwesterly wind and I want only nice smiling faces all around me and throughout my entire kingdom." The poor wizard has a look on his face that says, "This could be tough." I think those two cartoons—just cut from magazines and framed—pretty much sum up how my mother saw herself at the Farm. The Farm was a very special spot. My father took her up there kicking and screaming. My mother had long fancied herself a big-city girl, while my father had this image of himself as the gentleman farmer. He also thought it would be a better place for Campbell and me to grow up. My mother swore she would not budge from Greenwich Village. But she did and, of course, she fell in love with it.

Even though many people first think of her as this big talker or they always go on and on about her laugh, in fact, Mom was a great listener. I think people who came up to the Farm for any length of time did so because they felt like she was really listening to them. And she was. In many ways, it was her favorite thing to do. She loved listening to people and helping them out. The Farm became a manifestation of that, as well as her heart and her talent. That's probably what made her a great actress as well, her capacity to listen. Like all the great actors, it's not when they're carrying on on center stage that's important. It's when and how they listen that sets them apart.

People would come up to the Farm from whatever show my mother happened to be in. Like most actors, she was a gypsy. Each show was like a ship filled with people who would become very tight with each other for six months or so. And, of course, when you were on ship with my mother, you came to the Farm. Some docked and stayed for quite a while. This drove my father crazy.

He was basically a quiet, very shy guy. He didn't like a lot of people around him. But every time he'd get up to go downstairs, there'd be someone new in the kitchen. My mother, on the other hand, loved it when people came to visit. All these people were outside stimuli, but I think it was a problem for her, needing this constant activity around her. She avoided thinking about herself by surrounding herself with really fascinating people. Now, of course, if you happen to be living in the house, this means that you also had to have these fascinating people around. Until we sold the Farm, after my mother's death, I always thought that was how I was, too, that I needed to bicker with people, have constant crises and carryings-on. Until recently, I had never lived with just one person. Now I do and I realize I'm not really that constant-stimuli kind of guy at all. I loved the Farm, but in some ways, it also made me insane.

A lot of incredibly talented people walked through those doors. It was a circus, but it was a really unpretentious place because my mother was an unpretentious person. There was always a flavor of congeniality and eccentricity. Everything and everyone was an eccentric mix. We were all mismatched, but it worked because it was a comfortable place. You could sit anywhere. Of course, there were the dogs and cats all over the place. They drove me crazy. But my mother loved them and that's what counted because it was her house. As a kid, I used to sit in my favorite spot at the top of the stairs when everyone thought I was asleep and listen to them talk. But eventually, it became too much and she drove my father out with all these lunatics, one after another, coming up or moving in.

I can't talk about the Farm without thinking about Nana. Nana was a woman from Alabama. She was my mother, too, and very close to my heart. Nana was also the only clairvoyant person I have ever known. If she dreamt about fish, somebody was pregnant. When we got to be of an age, she'd come downstairs into the kitchen and start looking at us all, me, Campbell, her own son, Bobby, who also lived with us, and whichever of our friends were there. "Now I don't know what you boys are up to," she'd announce, "but somebody's in trouble here because I keep dreaming about fish. And I'm gonna keep dreaming it until I find out the truth!" And she was always right. She dreamt about Bobby Kennedy being shot the night before he was. She was incredible. My mother met Nana when she was living with my father in New York. She had just had me, and Campbell was on the way and she needed help. Nana picked up a broom during their interview and never left, quickly becoming the mainstay of the household. When we moved to the Farm, Nana came with us, even though she always kept her apartment in Harlem which she went to for the weekend at least every other week. When we were young, Nana cooked and cleaned and took care of the entire house. She raised Campbell and me when my folks were away working. It's an awful cliché to say your "help" is part of your family, but in this case, it was true. Nana was not only part of our family, she was its rudder. Mom depended on her in many, many ways. Everybody adored her. If you came to the Farm, you paid homage to Nana. And if she didn't like you, forget it. You were out, man. Out with us and soon out of the Farm.

Nana was always playing the numbers. She'd play blackjack and keno. She was lucky as hell and always winning. Nana was also the only person in the house who had a gun. Thank God. Or at least one that looked like it worked. I don't think it had any bullets, but it didn't matter. Believe me, seeing Nana coming at you through the window with a gun was enough to get anyone off the property immediately. She never let us play with it, and since it was Nana's gun, we didn't. But she could scare the shit out of you, gun or no gun.

I was a hellion kid, but Nana and I had a good rap. Nana never told on us. She never ran to my parents. If something happened, she would straighten it out herself. It made for a very special relationship between us. I do recall, however, one time when my parents were away that I was very rude to her. Whatever I said had hurt her feelings. I can't remember now what it was, but I must have really been a particular asshole. Somehow this got back to my father and just the fear of him was enough to keep anyone straight. I remember coming home from a football game, still in my uniform. Dad had just arrived. He was in a suit. That alone startled me because it was rare to see him at home in a suit.

"C'mon, Alex," he said. "We're going for a little walk." I thought, *Holy shit, is this about last night and me mouthing off to Nana?* We walked up to the field behind the house. *This is it,* I thought, *he's gonna whoop my ass.* My father could be very loving but he was also a scary guy, and even at age eight, I knew that if you crossed him you were in trouble.

"If you ever are rude to Nana again," he said, "if I ever hear about it again," he repeated, "you will regret the day you came into this world. OK?"

"Yes," I whispered.

"That woman has nurtured you since you were a baby and you are to treat her at all times with the utmost respect." He was really in my face. I was glad to come back from the field alive. But my father was right. I never forgot what he said and from then on, I always tried to be aware of Nana's feelings. One thing: Nana adored my father. As far as she was concerned, he could do no wrong, even when she knew that he had. My father was an excellent gambler. He and my mother were real broke at one time and owed everybody in town; the hardware store, the grocery, everybody. They owed Nana a year's wages. A year! Why anybody extended credit to them in the first place nobody knows. The only thing that can possibly explain it is that they liked Mom. They liked Nana. They liked my father. You have to understand that, in those days, the sixties, this area around South Salem, Bedford and Katonah, outside New York City, was much different from what it is now. There were no muni-bond traders living here then; no Wall Streeters. It was all blue-collar and farmers. I went to school with plumbers' sons and carpenters' sons. My brother and I were like the gypsy kids, actors' kids. The whole celebrity thing was much different. I think people understood that even though my parents had periods of success, they had come from nothing. Their roots were just the same as everyone else's in town. And I guess if they really needed any proof, we were broke. But now my father gets into a crap game. Nana loved to tell this story:

"One day," she'd say, "your father comes home. He walks up here to this room we're sitting in now and puts the money on the bed. He just laid all this money out on the bed!"

And she said to him, "Mr. Scott, what happened?"

"Nana," he says, "I had me a few good runs with the old dice."

"Lord have mercy," she says. "Is Si gonna get paid?" Si was from the market and Nana had to have it right with the market.

"I've just come from paying Si," my father says. "And what's there is for you."

"Oh, Lord have mercy, good God," she'd say, recalling the whole scene. "You got some money, Mr. Scott. I didn't know how we were gonna go on!" That's a true story. Nana would tell it over and over, laughing and just as pleased as if it had happened yesterday.

As she got older, it became more and more difficult for Nana to do things, so, basically, she'd just cook. The old joke is that it was Maureen Stapleton who said, "Colleen, you're the only person with a maid who makes only cameo appearances." None of us cared. I'm certain that in my mother's mind, Nana had taken care of all of us when we needed her most, so now she was glad just to take care of her. Nana died very suddenly. Her death was very hard for us all, taking us by surprise in a way that nothing else ever had. Her funeral in Harlem was unbelievable. Everybody was out on the street. It was hot, about a hundred degrees. Roscoe [Lee Browne] did the tribute, a eulogy. It was a magnificent and incredibly sad afternoon. My Nana was a very special person. When she got hold of you, she never let go. She still hasn't. I love her very, very much.

In the early sixties, Stuart Jensen and Tony Di Santis had an antique store in Greenwich Village. They were big friends of Terrence McNally, the playwright, and Bobby Drivas, the actor. I'm not sure what exactly went down, but suffice it to say that one day my mother went into their store and they were friends for life. Now, as I understand it, after my parents moved to the Farm, Stuart and Tony ran into a little trouble and had to close up shop and get out of town in a hurry. Of course, they didn't have any money and Mom says, "Come live with us, until this blows over." So once again, my dad comes downstairs and there are two new people in the kitchen. Stuart and Tony proceeded to redesign the Farm. In those days, we had very little money to fix anything and Stuart and Tony were quite resourceful. Everyone settled in for the long haul.

Now, you have to understand that Stuart and Tony were a gay couple and this is the late sixties in South Salem, so their presence was a big deal for a lot of people. But it wasn't long before they became Uncle Stuart and Uncle Tony to just about everybody and, with Nana, became part of our family, playing very big roles in my and Campbell's growing up. They were everywhere. Tony used to pick us up at elementary school in a '67 Dodge Dart, red with a big white stripe. We loved it because he'd do "donuts" before pulling out of the school yard. The principal would call home and say, "Mrs. Scott, Uncle Tony is taking the kids and doing donuts in the Dart. Would you please ask him to stop." So she would and he would . . . until the next time. Uncle Tony was cool. He would take us to the movies or into Foodtown and then try to embarrass us. At that time, the theaters up here would play the national anthem before the movie. Tony couldn't just sit there when the national anthem came up. No, he would stand up, put his hand over his heart and sing. This is both hilarious and highly embarrassing when you're twelve. He'd make a scene no matter what public place we'd go to. But Tony was also incredibly talented. He was a visual genius and had the ultimate eye. Although he and Stuart had that antique store, Tony was an interior designer by trade. He could look at anything and know exactly how to redesign or fix it. So naturally, his big ongoing project became the Farm.

Stuart, on the other hand, was another kind of genius. He was a book genius. He read everything. He could tell you about the plumbing, talk to you about Tennyson, and then explain how to put your central chimney in. Whenever we would have contractors come in, they got the message real quick not to mess with Stuart. He and Tony were both fiercely protective of my mother and the house. If anybody came in and was disrespectful or crude, they would reduce that person to shreds. It was just awesome. Summers, they would take us to Canada and all my buddies would go along. The parents all trusted Stuart and Tony with their kids. There was never any question, because they were endearing, loving people. Wherever Tony went around town, the liquor store or the gas station, the clerk or the mechanic all wanted to know, "Hey, Tony. What's up?" And it was a lot more difficult and unusual in those days to be gay. Talk about people being "out." These guys were never "in." But they were very secure about themselves as human beings, and people just went with it.

My mom loved them both and I think they, perhaps more than anyone who came to the Farm, provided that stimulus that she seemed to need. Tony was the one who would say, "Let's go, Colleen. We're going to Westport to pick up draperies." They'd drive to Westport and spend hours talking about us or this project at the Farm or some crisis that a friend was having. Tony provided a fun outlet for her. They were buddies. Stuart was more cerebral. Mom would sit with Stuart when she needed to talk to somebody about why Nixon was such a prick. She wouldn't talk to Tony about that. She'd say to Stuart something like, "Why are bonds going up? What are bonds, anyway?" And he'd explain them to her. Stuart could talk about things that my mom had no idea about. Stuart and Mom were more like brother and sister.

My mom would also challenge Stuart. She wouldn't challenge Tony. And that's an important distinction in their relationships. If she had too much to drink, she'd go after Stuart because she knew Stuart could handle it and, more important, she knew that he could give the same back to her. She would never go after Tony. For as tough and crazy as he was, she knew she could hurt Tony and damage their relationship in a way that couldn't be fixed. In the last few years of her life, my mother didn't drink at all. But in those earlier days, when she did, she could get mean. Not often; most of the time she was a good drunk, a happy sort of Irish drunk, but if she got mean, she would choose the person who could most handle it and go for them, and that was usually Stuart. But these men, Stuart and Tony, stood up *for* my mother, too. You know, with all the people in and out of the house and all the inherent craziness—everyone was drinking quite a bit then—there were some very bad nights. Stuart and Tony went to bat for my mother at crucial times. She never forgot that. Like Nana, with my mom, they raised us and helped us survive. I can't even remember how long they actually lived at the Farm, probably about five years before they moved out and then lived just up the road for another ten, before moving out to California in the late seventies. They were wonderful men.

Mom met Leon Doffman when she was in California. He was going door to door, in Malibu—quite an unusual thing to be doing in Malibu—looking for housecleaning work. She opened the door and there he was. "I clean houses," Leon said. I think Mom was immediately enamored and felt a bit sorry for Leon.

"Come back tomorrow," she said. And he did. He came back and cleaned like such a demon, in such an almost-on-the-edge sort of way, that Mom took to him immediately. Leon ended up coming back to the Farm with my mother, where he took on all the responsibilities that Nana could no longer do. Stuart and Tony were gone by now, and my brother and I weren't really around much anymore. So it was hard for Nana to keep things up. But in short order Leon adored Nana and Nana adored Leon. Leon was built like a rail but he could eat, and Nana could sure cook. So they were in heaven together. She'd make pork roast and collards. Incredible things. Leon would eat for three. So he came and filled the spot that had been Stuart and Tony's. My mom needed him. Leon could vacuum the carpet and talk to you about Schopenhauer. He was from England, and before he came to America, he had been a photographer's agent. He could paint and was also a writer. Leon was incredibly intelligent and he filled that need my mother had for discussion. Mom was a big idea discusser. I grew up in a house where there would be no activity for months except my mom lying on her bed reading or talking with whoever was around. Then she'd be gone for two months or rehearsing for twelve hours a day, eight days a week. So there was always a lot of discussion in the house and a lot of nothing getting done. But in another way, it was a house that was filled with ideas about art, theater, politics and all kinds of human endeavor, all discussed with great humor. And Leon could keep up with the best of them. I think Leon also inspired my mother to do some of her best work. He inspired me. Leon loved talent and he adored my mother for that and for all her human qualities. He also loved her because she became his analyst.

My mother was everyone's fucking analyst. There was this couch in the den off the kitchen. Anybody who had anything to say would go to that couch. Now, like the people on the couch, the couch changed over the years because the dogs and cats would rip it to shreds. But there was always a couch and Leon spent a lot of time on it. My mother would sit in a chair, with Leon on the couch, and they would go for hours, back and forth about whatever they were going through. Leon liked big women. That's probably the reason he loved Nana. He was big on big women. But he was also gay. The more you tried to analyze Leon, the more you realized you should never try to analyze anyone.

But Leon also had the goods on us. He'd say things that he knew would get you going. He came in one day and I was lying on the couch, drunk or hungover, and he said to me, "How come someone with so much talent can't get off the couch, baby? Your mother, your father, your brother. Baby, it's not about any of that. It's about this garbage that you're supposed to take out and you're not because you're so drunk you can't get over there. Is it a matter of courage, baby? Why is it that the heir-apparent to the Scott/Dewhurst family has to lie on the fucking couch all day? Who are you trying to destroy, anyway? We know the truth now, don't we, baby." Well, the truth was he didn't know any more than I knew at that time. But he'd come in like that and drop some remark like a depth charge. That's pretty much how Leon was. He would just lay it out there as he passed through. Mom would go after it every time. "That's just bullshit, Leon," she'd say.

"I don't think so, Colleen," he'd reply. And they'd be off. My mother shouting to him from the couch and Leon doing the dishes in contractor's boots and a purple robe. Leon was a very special dude. He's living back in London now.

My parents had a lot of fun together. They were and are funny people, really funny people. I really don't remember their divorce the first time, because my father continued to live with us anyway. I don't think I was even told about the first divorce. If I was, it didn't mean anything because he would show up anyway. When people talk about my old man, they always talk about *Patton* and about his rage. But his genius lies in the fact that he is very funny. He could do Patton and then do Noël Coward. That's the side of him that most people don't see. And that's the side that my mom was most attracted to. She was attracted to his incredible talent but also to his humor, to this big-bear sort of cuddliness that was my father much of the time. But that's the part of him that he doesn't let many people see. I know that the time my parents spent together was a very special time in both of their lives. Those years at the Farm were a special time for all of us. For Nana, for Stuart and Tony, Gerry, Bobby, Leon, the neighbors and just about anyone who found a haven there. It was a time of great craziness and great artistic accomplishment. It was a time of two people, Colleen and George, who loved each other very much.

I remember hearing them through the wall running lines together in bed. A lot of people feel they have to have separate bedrooms when they're working. That's not how it was with them, especially if they were working together. I would be in my room and hear them talking or running lines for the next day's rehearsal and then I would hear them laugh. You could tell in those moments that they really adored each other. I think the key to understanding their relationship, besides the fact that they had incredible respect for each other's talent, was that they were also charged for each other in a physical sense, which, of course, is a very big aspect of any relationship. But it was their humor that kept them together. Even in the worst of scenarios, there was always a bit of humor.

It was a rash decision when they decided to get married again. I remember the day. It just happened all at once. I recall someone calling the neighbors and saying, "Come on over. Colleen's getting married!"

"Who's she marrying?" they asked, a bit surprised since they hadn't heard of anyone else being around.

"George!" came the reply. So the neighbors ran over. A few people came up in a hurry from New York and the wedding was that very afternoon in the yard. I think José [Quintero] was there. I'm not sure who else. These very talented people had an intense, fascinating and at times dangerous relationship. But you've got to also understand that there was a tremendous amount of love.

LEON DOFFMAN

In 1978, I had been living in Los Angeles for about eighteen months. I was a bit down on my luck and had been working on a construction site and doing some housecleaning to make ends meet. It's very difficult to find work in L.A. if you don't know anyone. So I was putting photocopied sheets of paper advertising my services under front doors in Malibu. For some reason I will never be able to explain, I ended up ringing the bell at one of the houses. This very handsome woman in some kind of flowing robe actually came to the door.

"Yes?"

"I clean houses and thought you might—"

"Oh, good. We're leaving here soon. So I actually need someone to clean up. Can you come by tomorrow?" I had no idea who this woman was. But she had a look that you didn't see much out there—strong and statuesque. I was struck by her uncommon beauty. Of course, it was Colleen.

I came back the next day and dove into cleaning this house, which was not dirty but quite untidy. There was a lot of stuff piled up in the kitchen and newspapers and magazines everywhere. They obviously had been having themselves a jolly time. I wasn't there long before I cut myself on a broken lightbulb on the kitchen stove. I'm afraid I gave the first impression of being one of those furious cleaners who ends up damaging himself in an effort to be thorough. Alex told me much later that Colleen had said, "Now there's a desperate man." I remember thinking how unusual a thing to say that was, but also how very perceptive. I didn't feel desperate just then but I suppose I was. Later, when I went to leave, my car wouldn't start. So that was my first day: a cut hand and a dead battery. I guess I did seem more desperate than I realized.

The next day, I came back to find the kitchen in about the same state it was in the day before. After I'd been there a few hours and cleaned it up, Colleen offered me some lunch. This was the first time I ever tasted Nana's cooking, which was delicious. She had prepared some kind of chicken and potato salad. As we ate, Colleen saw me looking at Nana as she moved around the kitchen.

"Isn't she beautiful?" she said.

"Yes," I replied. Colleen smiled. After we finished eating, I went back to work. Everyone seemed to go about their own business. Ken [Marsolais] was there, lying on the bed reading. Alex and his girlfriend went down to the beach. Colleen asked me to take a drink to Nana, and then she disappeared. I don't know why, but I thought at that time that Colleen was a writer and had probably gone off to work. It wasn't until the following day that she told me she was an actress. She also told me that she needed someone back East to clean and look after the Farm. "Do you think you would like to do that?" she asked. I couldn't reply. "Well," she said, "why don't you think about it and write to me."

Colleen went back East soon after, and I remained in Los Angeles, thinking about the offer. The more I did, the more I realized that it was not only a good opportunity but perhaps my last chance. I needed to get out of Los Angeles. I was born in Birmingham, England. I'd been an actor, then a photographer, and then a photographer's representative before coming to the States in 1976. I ended up serving behind a bar and doing a number of other terrible jobs before the people I knew in New York from London had obviously had enough of me. So I got a free one-way ticket to Los Angeles and just got stuck out there. Colleen must have sensed that, or perhaps it was just a habit of hers to pick up strays. Either way, they seemed like a very nice kind of middle-class, bohemian group of people who I suppose, like me, needed looking after.

A few weeks later, I wrote to say that if she still wanted me to come, I would. Colleen called to say she was coming back out to Los Angeles for a few days' work and would meet with me at the Chateau Marmont, a wonderful old hotel in West Hollywood that she loved, to discuss the arrangements, which were quickly agreed upon. I packed up the little I had, mostly clothes, and flew East.

My first impression of the Farm was that it was painted yellow and had these large lampposts on the driveway. I don't know whatever happened to them but they somehow disappeared. When first I arrived, Colleen made me toast and marmalade and sat down to talk with me in the living room. She was very sweet and didn't have any specific instructions. She seemed more concerned that my room on the side of the house was all right, which it certainly was.

The next morning, I started work and realized that like the house in Malibu, there was a lot to be done. I came through the doorway off the kitchen and started cleaning out the sink in the laundry room. Every day, I did a little more, having this stupid idea, of course, that everything would stay clean and neat. It never did. I worked for weeks and weeks, before I got through the whole house, cleaning out the cupboards and painting the living room. Colleen didn't pay much attention to what I was doing, but I was very thorough.

I stayed at the Farm nearly nine years, through 1987. Nana was there but spent most of her time in a bedroom upstairs because she couldn't do the kind of work she used to, except cook, and that was extraordinary. I ate very, very well. Colleen adored Nana. We all did. Whenever Nana would feel well enough to come downstairs, the two of them would just sit for hours and talk. There were a whole pile of other people there, always in and out, and the house was filled with incredible things that Stuart and Tony had found over the years. But what I remember most fondly was all the conversation. We all talked a lot, especially Nana and I. It was very magical just talking with everybody about whatever was going on that day. Other than that, it settled into a kind of ordinary job.

Of course, it didn't stay clean. But how could it, with all the animals? Colleen loved animals, but then it just grew and grew and there were so many of them, it was stupid. I never quite understood what Colleen was doing out in the country. She was no more a country girl than I am. She belonged in the city, but someone had the idea to drag her off to the country. But I guess that's what city people think they have to do when they have children—move to the country.

When I first arrived, I saw a lot of Colleen. There were two years where she did almost nothing, barely left the house. She just sat on the couch, talking with whoever was there or she spent the day upstairs in her room, reading and watching television. Day after day it was like this; she was nearly always in her dressing gown. It was just a slow time and something that happens to all actors. Then she got involved in The Actors' Fund. That was lovely. It got her moving again and became something she looked forward to going into town to do. Not long after, she began to work again and just as she got busy doing a number of films and television things that took her away from the Farm for weeks at a time, she also got involved at Actors' Equity. Since there was a sofa in her office at the union, we began to see less and less of her at the Farm during the day, and soon after, in 1987, I went back to London.

If you ask me, life is largely very mean, but that was a very generous time. In a way, Colleen was my best teacher. By that I mean that I was constantly astonished by her, by what she said and by what she saw in other people. It was fascinating to watch Colleen in a crowd of people, how she studied them. I remember one Christmas when there was a houseful of people streaming in and out. I realized that whenever someone entered, Colleen wouldn't watch them come in; instead, she was watching all those who were already in the room to gauge their reactions to whoever just arrived. A lot of actors talk about doing this sort of thing, but Colleen really did it, and not because it was part of her work but because she couldn't stop herself. She was endlessly fascinated by those around her. I mean she was flying by the seat of her pants most of the time, but her assessments of a situation were always surprising; even when she got it wrong, even then it would at least be interesting.

Colleen could talk incessantly. I'm not very articulate all the time. I can be, but when I'm not feeling comfortable, there are many awkward gaps in a conversation. Colleen could fill those in for me until there wasn't ever a need for them again. Colleen made me feel wanted and marvelous. I was happy to take care of whatever material needs she or the family had because, in essence, she did just the same for me. She was always looking after everybody. That's why she was always in some kind of financial trouble.

She was a very smart woman. There was one thing she used to say to me and the boys: "You can't expect more from others than exactly what they can give. So that's what you try to understand. People can only do what they can, and can only give what they have, most of which you can't really see or count. You'll be happy if you can keep from expecting more than that."

I dream of Colleen occasionally. We talk, like we used to. I suppose I just don't know that many smart people anymore. I certainly don't know anyone who gave so much, and so much of herself to other people. You know, she had the most incredible kind of eye. Every Christmas, she bought everybody clothes, never really knowing anyone's size or thinking to ask. But whatever she bought always looked good on them. I still have a beautiful coat she gave me and a short-wave radio. She gave me the radio on my first Christmas at the Farm because she thought I was homesick. Now I look at it today and think of her.

PETER DUSENBERRY

I played Little League baseball with Al and Campbell when we were kids. Colleen would show up most games with Uncle Tony and Uncle

Stuart and at the end of the season, they had us all over for a party. So that's when I met Colleen, but I only knew her as Al and Campbell's mom, who was very vocal in the stands at the softball games. She was in girl's softball as the coach of the Fireflies but, of course, I never got to see her there. She was quite an athlete herself and I heard from my sister that she was very spirited, well-liked by her own team, and a bit awesome to the others.

I didn't really start hanging around the Farm a lot until a few years later, when we were out of high school and all of us started drinking together, at least me and Al. We had a lot of friends in common, and since I was hanging around the house a lot with Al, I just hit it right off with the family. Colleen told me later that the reason she liked me right away was because one of the first nights I was over, we were all sitting around with her watching television in the room off the kitchen. A friend of Colleen's, another woman, came in through the back door and when she came into the room, I stood up. I don't know why, I just did. Colleen liked that, I guess. So if she took to me, how could I not take right to her?

The Farm was one of those places where most people became comfortable right away, but there were certain people it held very close and I guess I was one. Colleen was always asking me to stay for dinner. It took me a while to accept but once I did, especially with Nana's cooking, I seldom missed a meal. After Leon left to go back to London, I began to help out around the house, mostly because with Colleen coming and going as much as she did, someone had to be there every day to take care of the animals. So I moved in, very gladly. And it was as if I became part of the family. In some ways, it was a very difficult time for me; I was working but getting fired a lot by my friends. Al and I were running around a good deal. My family was pretty fed up with me, but Colleen offered a lot of understanding and encouragement. I love my mom and dad, of course, but Colleen really stood up for me at a very important time in my life.

It took years, but ultimately she was instrumental in my getting my act together at all. By that time, even though I was still doing some work around the house, I was barely holding on because of all the drinking and drugs. I remember she took me out to dinner on Valentine's Day and said, "We have a couple of options here, but you have to do something." One of the options she offered me was to go into rehab. When I came back a month later, Colleen welcomed me back. In fact, she came with Al and Irene to hear me speak on the ninety-day anniversary of my sobriety. That's when they all met Jenny, and it was really cool. I had brought a number of girls around but Colleen immediately liked Jenny, and after she came by the Farm the first time for Thanksgiving dinner, Colleen told me she thought Jenny was "a winner." About the same time, Colleen also began to encourage me to explore studying anything I might find interesting. She'd send me off to talk to people or suggest things for me to read. The last Christmas that she was around, she didn't make any big deal about it, but she told me that there was a card up in the tree for me. Inside it said that she was paying for my first semester at school. She wanted to be a part of that with me, she said. Colleen died the following August just before I started. But this May, I'll be graduating with a B.A. in architecture. It's taken five years, but it feels as if she's been with me through it all. I know she's always right there when I have to make a presentation. I'm not much of a public speaker, but knowing I'm doing some of this because of and for her gets me through. Jenny and I still miss her and probably think or talk about her every day.

BOBBY ANDERSON

I met Colleen and George when Nana, my mother, began working for them when they were still living in Greenwich Village, before Alex was born. I as about twenty-two at the time and was in school taking an industrial arts course. When Colleen heard this, she decided that she had some antique wooden furniture that she wanted me to refinish. Not long after the furniture was completed, George [C. Scott] asked me to help him finish a small room in the courtyard behind their apartment in the Village. One project led to another, and as I continued to work for them, we became very friendly. Before long Nana and I were practically family. Somewhere during that time, I bought a car. Colleen and George didn't have a car at that point, neither of them were working regularly yet, so I began to drive them around. In a way, this was the first car in the family. But soon things started to get a little better, particularly for George. There was more work, a little more steady money, then, as the years went by, better work and finally some real money. By the time Colleen, George and the boys settled into South Salem, I was working full-time as George's chauffeur-bodyguard. With Nana, I helped Colleen and George keep the household in order.

Once we all got to South Salem, I taught Colleen how to drive. It was quite an experience. Although she certainly knew how to drive a car and had driven considerably, she had never bothered to get a New York State license. We had to take care of that once she moved out of the city, so we set about having a few lessons. She was a good student, learned fast, a little bit of a heavy foot on the gas pedal, but we survived and she got through all the little tricks you need to know in order to pass the road test, which she did with ease.

I loved Colleen. I love the whole family. But there was an amazing bond between her and my mother. Colleen adored Nana. They became partners in everything that had to be done at the Farm, everything from raising the boys to trying to keep their weights down. My mother was heavy, Colleen much less so. But, as I said, they did everything together. There were a few years where every other Wednesday or so I'd drive Colleen and Nana into Manhattan, where they'd march in to see some doctor who prescribed for them (and a lot of other people at the time) some kind of pills that Nana and Colleen referred to as "vitamins." They'd come back to the Farm, after one of these doctor visits, and tear the house apart, cleaning everything in sight. It was a sight, those two cleaning and talking for the rest of the afternoon, like everything that had to be said in a lifetime had to be said right then, for there would be no tomorrow. Needless to say, the Farm was very clean for a day or two, but no one lost much weight.

Although Nana always maintained her apartment in Harlem, as I continued to work for Colleen and George—and then just for Colleen—I ended up living for years in a little house that was connected to the main house on the Farm. I was there with the family for nearly twenty-one years. What a time. I was there for both weddings. The first was a quiet, private affair after Alex was born. The second time around, over seven years later, they threw quite a party at the Farm. We were all pretty much taken by surprise when they decided— at what seemed like on the spur of the moment —to marry again. Colleen and George had been separated for a while and Colleen had just purchased a house down the road from the Farm. We all had set about getting the house in shape and helping her move in when one morning she said, "Stop everything! We're gonna get married again!"

At the Farm, George was very private, much more than Colleen. He wouldn't come downstairs when someone rang the bell. He stayed very much to himself. Colleen moved around a lot more, laying around the pool with friends, inviting people over for dinner and to play bridge. There was always someone at the Farm and always some drama.

The house was very quiet for a while once George left at the end of the second marriage. Colleen tried to keep everything going as it was for the boys, but it was a very difficult time. It seemed sad but inevitable. I knew what was going on simply because I always was around. George and I were together all the time, driving in and out of the city, in much the same way that Colleen and Nana were always together at the Farm. We were in the car together when George specifically asked me to stay with Colleen, "so the boys will have a male image. What I'm asking you to do," he said, "is stay with the family and help your mother take care of them because I'll be starting a new life." So I did. I'd known the boys since they were born. I was like their big brother and, I guess, once George left, a little like a dad. I was there until Campbell finished college.

You couldn't separate Nana and Colleen. After my mother passed in June of 1985, Colleen seemed lost for quite a while. My mother's death was sudden. I had spoken to her at her apartment in the city on a Thursday. She was very pleased with a recent paint job. The following Saturday I went by but there was no answer and the night chain was still on the door. I kicked the door in—but she was gone. She had died. It was an awful shock for us all. I called Colleen immediately. She was devastated. Everything changed. And I have to say for a while it was like the whole house fell apart. Nothing was getting done and Colleen seemed not to have the spirit to do anything about it. She was heartbroken. It took us all quite a while to heal. Some days I think I hear Colleen's laugh. I can still see her floating around her pool on an inner tube with her drink on a little float beside her.

"Bobby!" she'd holler, "this is so good. I feel rich!" I was always glad to see her happy. When she was happy she wanted everyone to know it and everyone to be happy around her. She was like a second mother to me. I was thrilled to be in her company and, with Nana, a part of her family.

CAMPBELL SCOTT

Initially, I was more aware of what my father did for a living than what my mother did. I think with the children of theater actors, it really just seems like a job, like anyone's parents might have, only the hours were stranger. It's not like being the child of some celebrity or famous television or movie star where there are media trucks around your house all of the time. So none of what they did ever seemed so out of the ordinary to me. My mother would drive off to work in the afternoon, and when I was in grade school, come home after I was in bed. When I got a little older, I began to go into the city with her, which was always shocking to me. Being raised on the Farm, I was really a country boy. It was very exotic to see my mother on television the first few times. My friends would sometimes make a big deal out of it but I would say, "I'm just as shocked as you are!"

I was thirteen the year Colleen won the Tony for *A Moon for the Misbegotten*. We had been through the "your parents are actors" thing with my dad when he began to make movies that people recognized. But this was really the first time for her that we could tell. It was an extraordinary time. It was the first time that I ever associated a real location or place with where she went when she went to work. Both Alex and I spent a huge amount of energy playing down all the excitement it created in our lives. But I do remember realizing that something had happened that would sometimes change the perception of people standing with us in a room. I began to tell people that my parents did other things, such as my dad, "John" Scott, was in advertising and his wife was a homemaker. But it was also about this time that I began to like going to the theater. Going backstage was fun and soon became a very comfortable and social experience. Alex and I couldn't have cared less about being in the audience. The plays bored us to tears. But we loved coming into town, sitting through the whole play backstage, playing cards with Ed Flanders. That was the first time I realized that my mother was doing her job and her job was at a theater. I remember we were at a friend's house the night of the Tony Awards. I was very excited to be able to stay up until midnight. She addressed us in her speech. "You can go to sleep now," or something like that. The night was very exciting, but we never could figure out what all the hullabaloo was about. Both Alex and I had seen it a number of times and at twelve and thirteen years of age thought, *Could this boring play be any longer? All this talking and nothing happens,* we thought. The part of the show we liked best was when Ed Flanders would push John O'Leary into the mud. Of course, as I got older—fifteen and sixteen—I didn't want to be a part of any of my mother's life in the theater or, just as suddenly, it would become a very big deal—the usual adolescent stuff. Although I never considered being in the business myself at that point, I realize now that it was a very good conditioning.

Colleen was much more perceptive as a mother than I think anyone ever gives her credit for. You would think that she wasn't paying attention to anything, and then she would make some remark off the cuff and you'd think, "Wow! How did she ever figure that one out?" She was very comfortable dealing with people who didn't really know her. She understood exactly what it was to be a public personality. If she wasn't emotionally involved, she was incredibly good at finding out just what was troubling someone and being very clear about what to do about it. But if she was caught up in it with you? Watch out. Of course, she would think—and tell you—that she was being as perceptive as she was in more impersonal situations, but she could be just wildly off base about some things.

Growing up at the Farm was probably extraordinary 95 percent of the time. The other 5 percent was spent wondering what the hell were all these people doing here, and it was that way for as long as I can remember. Sometimes I'd go over to a friend's house and think how strange it was that everyone ate at the same time or that there wasn't a lot of insane talk that I didn't understand. But if I was ever away from the Farm for some time, I would actually miss everything that made it such a circus.

There are many aptly titled "circus households" in this business, probably more than in most other careers. I know that the cliché is to think that all of the hullabaloo exists to fill in for something that isn't, like love. But I truly believe that that wasn't the case in our house, for all its craziness. In truth, I think it was just that great collective feeling of love that pulled so many people—Nana, Stuart and Tony, old friends, new friends, other actors, drunks and friends who were pregnant or in some kind of trouble—to the Farm at the times in their lives when they really needed something they weren't getting anywhere else. For all its insanity, the Farm was actually a very safe place. Because everything was so informal, it gave people who might be having difficult times some comfort and a sense of joy. I really believe that it helped some people heal in some way or find the best of themselves again, and then they would move on. Of course, there were some real crazies but they never stuck around long because the Farm wouldn't make room for them and for some reason or another they would have to leave. I know it all sounds very strangely mystical but that's how it felt. For many people who were really dear and good—and who also inherently understood that you had to know when to leave my mother alone—there were huge amounts of love. I think for that reason and that reason alone, no matter how disorienting it became—and it did—it also gave Alex and me some sort of center that can't be taken away from us today as adults.

I'm not sure that if my parents had stayed together, that would have been the case. They were both such powerful personalities, especially back then, that after a while it did seem that only one of them could live at the house. The house became much less strict once my dad left. Not because he was tyrannical; he was actually very quiet much of the time. When he left, I think we all went nuts for a while, which often happens when a father figure moves on to deal with his own life. Alex and I both went a little crazy then, but in our own ways. I withdrew. Alex tried to step into whatever he felt was missing from the role my father played. I just wanted everything to be smooth. Although this could make me seem well behaved, it's not such a great path, either. I often envied Alex for being able to make his feelings known immediately. It took me years to say what I felt about some of what went on and some of the people who were in and out of there. You always knew right away with Al.

But I am very happy to have been raised by my mother, because she had an uncanny ability to shroud the household with a feeling of safety. I don't know how she did that because, let's face it, she was at a loss most of the time in her own life. She couldn't find anything—the car keys, her glasses, messages, money. She never knew where she last put anything. She was seldom prepared for any of the practicalities of life. Once, when she had been cast in one of those television biblical miniseries that she would do when she was broke—I think it was *A.D.*—she got on a plane and flew to Tunis with just twenty dollars and her passport. She said later she just figured that once she got there someone would take care of her.

Yet, as far as her work went, she was always totally professional. It's the Gemini thing; she could be two completely different people in different areas of her life. She was both extraordinarily private and yet willing to give so many people so much of herself. Once my father had left the Farm, she created for my brother and me a tremendous sense of safety while also giving us a great deal of freedom that could be misconstrued by someone who didn't know anything about us as neglect.

Isabella Rosellini told me a story once when we were working together on a film that her mother, Ingrid Bergman, had once told her. Mom and Ingrid must have been working together in New York on *More Stately Mansions* when Ingrid—like everyone else my mother ever worked with—came up to the Farm for a couple of days. That first night, it was probably Sunday after the matinee performance, everyone had partied. They wouldn't have to be back at the theater again until Tuesday night. Ingrid was introduced to Alex and me, and she thought we were charming and all, but it was basically an adult affair. Isabella said that her mother remembered waking up the next morning and from the guest room hearing some clattering in the kitchen. *Great,* she thought, *someone's making breakfast!* She came downstairs, walking past snoring behind closed doors and into the living room, where there were others from the night before lying on various couches in front of a coffee table filled with empty glasses and bottles with a few last cigarettes smoldering in the ashtrays. No one was up, except me and Alex, and we were busy in the kitchen making the noise she had heard. Now I don't remember this but I'm sure it's true. Ingrid told Isabella that when she saw us, she froze and didn't make a sound. She just quietly watched us getting ready for school, making our lunches, putting on our sweaters, checking each other out, and then walking out the door to school. She thought this was extraordinary. But it was just how we lived at the Farm.

There was a great sense of humor and irony about life that I got from my upbringing that I wouldn't trade for anything in the world. And now that I, idiotically, have chosen this same profession as well, it helps. As I get older, I find myself reveling in the more usual aspects of life, which I probably would have been sick of had they been drilled into me. My home today is very quiet. It was rather depressing after my mother died because Alex and I attempted for a year or two to re-create that sense of the Farm at our own separate homes. It was a huge strain as we were trying to do something that didn't have a center or the kind of energy my mother had that would help it to occur naturally.

Looking back on it now, I realize that my mother was incredibly responsible and kind to all of us, including my father, when they divorced for the second time. She told Alex and me that it was a very personal thing between the two of them that was in no way our fault. She never said a bad word about him to us. She made it clear then, and even as I think back on it now, that whatever failings there were in the marriage were theirs together. She never said or implied that he was the problem. I know from friends of my parents who were around when they were first together that they were great colleagues and lovers, but the worst two people to put into a house together. They probably should have been best friends—and were. But for these two overwhelming personalities to be together all the time was just too much.

Colleen worked with an actor named James Ray in Edward Albee's play *All Over* in the late 1960s. James was a very interesting guy, slightly psychic, or at least very perceptive. He had observed them both, separately and together, before getting to know my mother well in the play. One day he was at the house and said something my mother never forgot.

"You know, Colleen," he said, "I'm going to tell you something for your own good."

"Well, what is it?"

"You really shouldn't be married to George," he replied.

"Why?" she asked.

"Do you want to know the present reason or the one from the past?" Jimmy asked. He was always very interested in past lives.

"The past," she replied. "I've had about all I can stand of the present for right now."

"Because you have been brother and sister time and time again, and in some cases, royal brother and sister. You are like a prince and a princess who are bound to each other but cannot both rule together." Mom loved that and thought the whole notion to be terribly fascinating. I'm not sure that it really explains much of anything. But they were certainly bound to each other both in strength and weakness. It was almost too powerful for either of them. But I believe that their bond was the most unique for both of them in their lives. They recognized something in each other very early and brought the best of it out in each other for quite a while. But life continues and becomes more complicated. Mistakes are made, sometimes what seem to be unforgivable ones. They were married for seven and then six years with a break of about eight months in between. She used to say to me, "I don't know why we got back together. I guess for you and your brother. But I think we both knew it was a mistake." Nevertheless, they managed for another six years. It was thirteen years altogether, and while in some ways not always the best, they were certainly the most fascinating years of all our lives. Thirteen years that I know we each will carry with us for a lifetime.

∞ ∞ ∞

Naturally the boys have experienced and observed great pain in what we know as "romantic love." They are not only the children of divorced parents, but they have seen friends of their parents and now themselves suffer the loss of relationships. I had a woman come to the farm to interview me several years ago and when the article appeared the first line was "Miss Dewhurst's walls are covered with pictures of George C. Scott." Bloody fool! We do have at the Farm a long wall with pictures of family and friends, as well as beloved cats and dogs pasted up and covered with Plexiglas. If the interviewer had been more observant, she also would have seen a picture of me on my wedding day to Jim Vickery, my mother and father, George's father (the boys' grandfather), etc. Every three or four years, or whenever we feel energetic, we remove the glass and update our lives with other pictures. The last time we took down the glass, up went pictures of Ken, the recent menagerie and Leon, new friends and partners. Did this interviewer not understand that G.C. *is* the boys' father? Was I to go through and cut his face neatly out of all family shots (as I have heard of husbands and wives doing) and remove pictures of him in some of his best roles?

My sons loved that wall. When they were young and new friends entered the Farm, I would see the boys take them over and proceed to show them every picture. It was—and is—their history and their inheritance. God knows there have been agonizing and painful times for them. And I have found that as much as I wanted to protect them, they each had to learn the way that is right for them as individuals. All I hope is that they understand that their mother and their father loved them and wanted them and that we love each other. Yes, that is now a different kind of love than made us want to marry, but from that remains an affection and respect for each other that will never change. It is important to a child of divorced parents to know that either parent can be spoken of with love in front of the other. It was very hard for the boys for a while, but as they grew to be young men, I think they began to know that, in spite of many faults, they were fortunate to have the father they have—a man who is one of the great talents in his profession because he has a brilliant mind and can be a wonderful human being because of his generous though often aching heart.

I love to laugh and enjoy life. Life without joy would be unbearable. But life is not all laughter. For myself, I am very secretive about my pain. I cannot ever seem to be willing to communicate it to anyone. Is this false pride? I don't know. I do know that it is better for me to deal with it alone. Not to deny it, but simply to allow myself to feel completely the very core of it, with the knowledge at the same time that someday the whole experience—no matter what it is (except death)—will be very funny to me. I have great admiration for those people who can scream and verbalize their pain until they literally wear it out. For me, I just *thank God for the stage.*

I want the boys to step out into a world vulnerable always to the joy that awaits them because of the depth they've gained from the pain they've experienced. Besides a love of life and all that it encompasses, I want my sons—Alex and Campbell—to never stop learning, but also to understand that they must listen *to hear* and observe closely if they are to recognize the chaff from the wheat, the destructive thought from the giving.

Oh my darling boys, I grew up in a time when the rules and morality of living were very clearly but rigidly defined. Today I find myself living in an age where so many of those rules no longer apply, and in many cases rightly so. Although the rules have changed, priorities and values have not. But these are all the more difficult to live by now, because without rules to force them upon us, they can only be taught by example.

As they grew up, I wanted the boys to know that they would always have a home at the Farm. I would always be there for them. Nothing would ever stop my loving them, but there were and could be times when I could stop *liking* them. As importantly, I wanted them to believe that there were and would be many people out there who would also love and support them. That is all I hope they will carry through life: that it is good to love and trust others without, as my mother said, putting chains around and suffocating the object of that love.

This is the part of the Farm that I hope will remain with them always, long after the property is sold and these photos under Plexiglas are lost forever.

15

"I hadn't noticed before, but it is a very good job."

My career really began with Joseph Papp and José Quintero. As I mentioned, I first worked for José in *Children of Darkness,* at the original Circle in the Square at Seventh Avenue and Sheridan Square in Greenwich Village. With Ted Mann as the producer, Circle had had a great success with Jason Robards in Eugene O'Neill's *The Iceman Cometh,* and with Geraldine Page in Tennessee Williams' *Summer and Smoke.* It was after *Children of Darkness* closed that José asked me to do O'Neill's *A Moon for the Misbegotten* at the Spoleto Festival. It was a great success.

I did O'Neill's *Desire Under the Elms,* again with José and at the Circle in the Square (downtown), with Ted Mann as producer. Franchot Tone was to play Eben in a cast that included Cliff Powell, Lou Frizzel and Rip Torn as his sons, with me as Abbie Putnam, Eben's new young wife.

I loved that part, but we had not been in rehearsal more than four days when Ted called me one evening to say that Mr. Tone felt that he was not in good enough health to do the role, because even though he was to play an elderly man, the emotions were too demanding and the role too physically strenuous.

Ted asked me if I thought that George would be willing to replace Mr. Tone. George was on the West Coast at the time but coming home in a few days. I said I didn't know if he would do it, but, as I had dragged him into various things before, it couldn't hurt to ask. So I called George and explained to him that he would be playing a character much older than his actual age. George seemed unconcerned about the age difference but went on to explain that he did not feel comfortable with O'Neill, the playwright. Of course, George was the perfect O'Neill actor.

By the time he arrived back in New York, Ted, who was a close friend, had gotten him to agree to take over for Tone. We opened to very good reviews and a successful run. Prior to that time, I had never had any real physical problems that would keep me from giving a performance. Suddenly, one morning at home, I sneezed and went into a back spasm that left me literally bent over and crawling around on all fours trying to get to a phone to call for help. I had to go on that night. I had never missed a performance. I had to find a doctor who could quickly adjust whatever I had blown out of whack.

We called a doctor who, I now realize, didn't know what was wrong but pumped me up with some kind of painkillers that left me feeling absolutely nothing but the determination to go on. Resolute, I arrived at the theater assuring everyone that I would be fine. That night, I came onstage standing straight and feeling very strong. I gave what I thought was probably one of the more magnificent performances of my life. As I moved in the dark with the rest of the cast to our positions for the curtain call, I whispered to George, "That was really a great performance. We all were really on." Just before the lights went up, I felt George squeeze my hand. "Really on?" he said. "You must have added twenty-five minutes tonight!" And with that news, I took a very careful bow, as by now, it seemed some of my miracle cure was wearing off.

"You took so long to get a sentence out," George continued once we were both safely offstage, "that I thought we would be here until tomorrow morning, and so did the audience." By now, I was considerably dismayed to find that the wonderful time I had observing my every move had not greatly enhanced my performance. Just an hour before, the every movement of my little finger had seemed so creative. My every syllable entrancing. What a shock now, not only to be feeling the pain again, but to realize that my performance may have been equally painful to the audience.

I did learn something that night. There is no greater sin than actors' self-indulgence, where they are literally observing themselves, fascinated by the brilliance of their own work, so that they feel they do not need other actors on-stage with them. They act without discipline or concern for what their fellow actors need from them in order to perform. There are two things in this world that enrage me almost beyond self-control. One is driving a car in which I am dealing with some stupid driver ahead and wish I had a tank. The other is to be trapped onstage, night after night, with an actor who has no regard for the audience, the rest of the cast and, most particularly, the play. Instead, he sets everyone out of rhythm while he marches to his own different and unrehearsed drummer. I have also wished then for a tank.

Desire Under the Elms had a very successful run. If it is done well, O'Neill is always a fulfilling experience because his women are not cardboard cutouts. You cannot read them and say, "Oh, this is that kind of woman and this is the way she will react to this kind of situation." No. These are women of great intensity who do not look at what the consequences of their actions might be. They act and then deal with the consequences.

I was quoted once as saying that I was wary of people who never made a move out of impulse. It made me nervous to be around people whose whole lives were determined by their own emotional preordination of what the results would be. Even with the best planning, how can we know? God knows, I don't.

Maybe this is why I have an affinity for the O'Neill women. They feel, they need and they act. Their greatest mistakes, which often create great tragedies, always have as their basis, love.

Sometime later, I again received a call from Ted Mann, who by now was ready to open Circle in the Square (uptown) on West Fiftieth Street and Broadway. I was doing a play in Paramus, New Jersey, called *The Great Coca Cola Swamp in the Sky*. It was a two-character play that I had done up at Westport with Chris Sarandon. Paramus had lost another play and quickly booked *The Great Coca Cola Swamp in the Sky*, grateful to have something to fill the hole in their season, and especially grateful that it required only a cast of two. I had played there once before with James Daly in *Who's Afraid of Virginia Woolf?* and had broken their house attendance record. When we came in with *The Great Coca Cola Swamp*, we broke the record in the opposite direction. Needless to say, I was very happy to hear from Ted. We were to open with another O'Neill play, *Mourning Becomes Electra*, and went into rehearsal, with Ted directing, as soon as I returned from "the Swamp."

It was a difficult period. Perhaps, when you consider the depth of the emotion of O'Neill's writing, it should not ever come as a surprise, but it always does. We began with Janice Rule playing Lavinia, the daughter to my Christine Mannon. Janice had a very painful neck condition at the time, and after ten days or so into rehearsal, she had to leave due to the trauma caused by the great physical action between the two women. Janice was replaced by Pamela Payton-Wright, who is a wonderful actress and who was to become a dear friend. All told, *Mourning Becomes Electra* was a wonderful experience in terms of the actors involved, particularly Pamela, Alan Mixon and Steve McHattie, who played my son and Pamela's brother.

PAMELA PAYTON-WRIGHT

I was in California, trying to get some work in television or films, when rehearsals first began for the Circle in the Square production of *Mourning Becomes Electra*. Janice Rule had originally been cast as Lavinia but was unable to continue. So two weeks before opening night—which was also going to be the opening of Circle's new theater—Ted Mann, Circle's artistic director, who was also directing *Mourning Becomes Electra*, called and asked me to fly back to New York to join Colleen and the company, who were already in rehearsal.

I'd never met Colleen before and, at that time, had not seen any of her stage work since she and George had done *Desire Under the Elms* at the old Circle in the Square (downtown) in the early 1960s. I didn't remember her performance as much as I could recall seeing her on that stage in a wash of moonlight and being struck by the sense of her physical presence. She was quite mesmerizing. I can still see her like that. But, ironically, what I remembered most at the time of Ted's call was having recently seen her in an episode of *Bonanza*. Colleen played the mother of two outlaws who were big, strapping boys. With her voice and all that wonderful raw energy that practically overwhelmed whatever was going on with the Cartwrights on the Ponderosa, I thought she had to be six feet tall. So when I came into rehearsals, I expected to meet someone enormous. I'll bet Colleen was only about five feet eight inches, but she seemed taller, she had such a bigness of being. I have always been struck by that.

Yet, once I worked with her and got to know her, it wasn't her larger-than-life qualities but the little things that she did that I remember so fondly. Like so many others, I loved her gravelly speaking voice and that outrageous laugh. But she also did this vocal thing—a low, guttural growl—when she didn't like something that was going on. When she sensed something wasn't good, she would literally make this low, quiet growl from somewhere in her throat, like a dog. It was totally unique to her and reflected the way she took on the world. I've never heard anyone else do it. And I heard it a number of times during the course of those rehearsals and subsequent performances of *Mourning Becomes Electra*. I would see what was going on around us and listen for it.

Mourning Becomes Electra's opening night and the official opening of Circle in the Square (uptown) was a very big, big party with a lot of celebrities and press and everything that comes with that sort of thing. Colleen was right there in the middle of it all, and she was wonderful, onstage and off, with all this commotion and craziness going on around her. I don't know how she did it, except to think that perhaps she thrived on it.

The actor who was playing my father liked to have a drink, you might say. I remember standing on the porch with Colleen at the end of the first act, waiting for him to come home, to come on. Colleen and I were playing this very chilly relationship between a mother and a daughter who worships her father, and we're waiting for him to come home in his uniform. Well, there were at least two nights when he never showed up, in spite of the script, because he had become somewhat indisposed in his dressing room. I would just go crazy inside, but I swear Colleen lived for this sort of thing. There was another scene in the second act where this same actor is now dead and we've laid him out on a table in the middle of the stage and played the scene around him. Night after night, he would start to snore. I guess he would have had too much to drink and would fall asleep. But the man was supposed to be dead! So there Colleen and I would be, in the middle of this drama by Eugene O'Neill, all this emotion flying around on this thrust stage with the audience all around us and a snoring corpse. I'd hear the first little snore and see Colleen's eyes begin to dance. I'm very good about not breaking up, but I knew she was just rumbling inside and if she went, I knew I wouldn't be able to resist. Thankfully, she never did. But there were a few times she came offstage and would howl with laughter backstage at this poor actor who couldn't keep it together, dead or alive.

I only worked with Colleen in that one production. But she did me many good turns in the years to follow. She was one of those people you were more likely to see if you were in need of something. She was just so involved in helping so many of us, personally, as friends, and then also through her work at The Actors' Fund and Equity. If you really needed her, she would be there. At one point, I was in the middle of a very difficult divorce and custody case that had left me in complete despair and crying in a way that I had never cried, before or since. To make a very long story short, the opposing lawyer was arguing in family court that I should not be allowed to raise my son because he would be exposed to an unstable environment being brought up around people in the theater. Colleen heard about this and came to my rescue, helping to find a brilliant female lawyer to replace the male one I had originally, who seemed unable or unwilling to argue against such an outrageously damaging premise. Later, my lawyer told me that Colleen had called her and after telling her of the situation I was in just added, "You've got to take this case because it needs someone with heart." And, thank God, she did and thankfully we won.

Colleen was one of a dozen character witnesses. She testified to working with me in the theater and observing how I behaved as a mother and actress working to raise a young child. It was unbelievable the way she just jumped in for me in court. I remember her arms going around me on the day she appeared to testify. I was never so glad to see anyone. When called, she rose and took the stand, speaking not only of what she observed of me raising a child and working in the theater but also shared her own experiences as a working actress and mother of two sons. For the first time in all the while I had been sitting in that courtroom I had a sense of safety and well-being. I took such loving comfort in her presence that day. No one could have denied the truth and goodness in her testimony. I still believe she made all the difference in my winning the custody case and being able to keep my son. Colleen's heart had gone out to me on any number of occasions in the years since we first met during those last weeks of rehearsal for *Mourning Becomes Electra,* but I will never forget that day in court. She helped save me from the darkest fate.

TED MANN

Colleen and I knew each other for years. I first worked with her in *Children of Darkness* and *Desire Under the Elms* at Circle in the Square (downtown) and then in *Mourning Becomes Electra* when we opened the new Circle on Broadway. There are just some people in this world who, when they're onstage, you know, as a director, you're safe. Coming into a massive, three-and-a-half-hour play like *Mourning Becomes Electra* in a new theater that had not had all the wrinkles worked out yet was a very generous thing for Colleen to do for me and for Circle. She had enormous dedication to whatever she did professionally and wouldn't give up. That spirit helped many of us get through that experience, which at times was quite hair-raising. Circle (uptown) is in the basement of an office tower. When we first opened, you could hear the policemen walking their horses on the street above, cars in the garage next to us, or drunks in the stairwells. Bells would suddenly ring like a fire alarm when the wrong door would be opened. It was a nightmare. Those kinds of difficulties didn't throw Colleen; she thought they were funny. Her good humor got us through some very dark days. The challenges were enormous and at times daunting. As others, like myself, occasionally shrank under the weight, Colleen became more and more a rock of support and inspiration. Most important, she did this while also giving us a performance that still echoes twenty years later.

We were great friends for a very long time. Our families were quite involved with each other. When she and George first got married and George began having some success in movies, I was their manager and tried to keep them on a budget. Can you imagine? I tried to help them organize their spending. That didn't last long. When Colleen and George met it was like thunder. Everything else and every other relationship they had changed. As a couple, they were larger than life. They were gargantuan in their personalities. Certainly there was an intense sexual attraction. But there was also an immediate identification between them that the other was someone to be contended with. Someone who must be paid attention to. It's amazing that they stayed together as long as they did. Yet, when they divorced, they were both very depressed, so much so that I was not surprised when they married again. It seemed fantastic! But as much as she loved George, it must have been a very difficult thing for her, because he was impossible to live with. And she was not easy, either. So they ended up living without each other for a long time. And that was probably hardest of all.

In a personal crisis, Colleen was very needy. She was intense and very lowkeyed. She needed to talk and to be talked to. As an actress, she was never as needy. She would move forward. She never became blocked; she just did it. She moved gloriously on the stage. In many ways, she also moved gloriously through life and had hordes of people around her. Personal crisis was especially hard for her because she had to move very slowly. In the theater, there are natural time constraints—union rules, dress rehearsal, opening night. None of these ever seemed to bother Colleen. She was very practical. She would get there. Moving through difficult times in her personal life took more time and much more thought.

I recently drove by the Farm again. The structure hasn't really changed, but it looks different nonetheless. That house just burst with Colleen in it. I think that's why it ultimately couldn't contain both Colleen and George. But there was certainly a vibrancy and vitality of life that she brought to the place that was clearly no longer there. She was a tidal wave, but there was also an overlooked softness. For me, she was the epitome of womanhood: strong, sexy, attractive, flirtatious, and always the center of attention. She is proof that actors are our royalty today.

PAUL LIBIN

When I arrived in New York in 1951 as a young actor, I firmly believed that the theater was defined by Broadway. But after seeing productions at Circle in the Square and other off-Broadway theaters with actors like Geraldine Page, Jason Robards, Rip Torn, George C. Scott and Colleen Dewhurst, I realized the boundaries were changing, and that off-Broadway was becoming an undeniable force in the American theater.

My first recollection of Colleen Dewhurst is from 1958, when she starred with George C. Scott in *Children of Darkness* at Circle in the Square in Sheridan Square. Bowled over by the intelligence, wit and passion of these talented actors, I knew immediately that I was in the presence of two dynamic artists. Similarly, I recall with burning clarity their stunning performances in the 1963 production of Eugene O'Neill's *Desire Under the Elms*. Married, unmarried, remarried—it didn't matter—seeing Colleen and George's volcanic performances is forever etched in my memory.

Having joined Ted Mann at Circle in the Square in late 1963, I was privileged to work with Colleen again in 1972 when Ted and I opened the Circle in the Square on Broadway with Eugene O'Neill's *Mourning Becomes Electra*. While Ted, as artistic director, was busy directing Colleen as Christine Mannon, my role, as producing director, offered me little time to spend at rehearsals. Nevertheless, I vividly recall a quiet, investigative Colleen, carefully watching all that was going on around her in the theater. It was an extraordinarily complex time, opening a new theater with a production as intense as this Eugene O'Neill play. But as we drew closer to the first performance, both Colleen's ideas and voice in the creative process gradually grew more powerful. By dress rehearsal, her artistic authority was unquestionably apparent and her love for the entire company was unmistakable.

During the run of the play, Colleen and I disagreed over whether or not to perform on Thanksgiving Day. She felt it inappropriate, and I foolishly decided to challenge her. She set me straight quickly, however, never really offering me an opportunity to make any other choice. "It's about family, " she said. "Family! So we will not perform on Thanksgiving Day." Such was Colleen's strong, gentle and principled nature onstage and off. And you can be sure that the next time we worked together on *Queen and the Rebels* in 1982, I made certain there were no holidays in the schedule!

Queen and the Rebels had originally been scheduled to play at the Circle in the Square on Broadway, but we were already enjoying an extraordinary success at that theater with George C. Scott starring in Noël Coward's *Present Laughter*. When we broached the subject with George of moving *Present Laughter* to a Broadway theater so that we could do *Queen and the Rebels* at the Circle, he wouldn't hear of it. "What do you want to do that for?!" he said. "Get another theater for Colleen. We're here, we'll stay here, and she'll do *her* play in another theater." Well, that's so sensible, I thought, I wonder why Ted and I hadn't thought of it already. So we shared our new plan with Colleen. Fortunately, we were able to secure the Plymouth Theatre, which the Shuberts had beautifully restored after *Nicholas Nickelby*. When we took Colleen to see the Plymouth, she was thrilled to be there, returning once again to Broadway.

It was just before *Queen and the Rebels* started previews that Colleen came to the Circle to see George in *Present Laughter*. By this time, they were no longer married. After the performance, Colleen came backstage and as they were leaving, Colleen turned to George and said, "G.C., how do you feel about me walking out with you?" As always, there was the usual throng of press and fans outside taking pictures and asking for autographs. "Hell!" George replied, "we've married twice, and I don't give a damn what anybody thinks about us walking out of a theater together!" And of course, cameras flashed and people tried to ask them questions, but they just walked off to dinner.

Colleen always talked about actors with great passion and compassion and fittingly became president of Actors' Equity. At the time, I was president of the Off-Broadway League, which negotiated the off-Broadway contract for the producers with Actors' Equity. I remember the first day of negotiations when Colleen explained the Actors' Equity position on salary, after which I stated the producers' position. Of course, we were miles apart. But Colleen simply looked across the table at me and said plainly, "Paul, it's your job as producers to get the money to pay the actors. It's simple. Just get the money and then we can agree." Remembering how she felt about working on Thanksgiving Day, I knew better than to negotiate with her right then. On top of all her talents, Colleen could talk off the cuff better than most anyone could read from a text prepared by the greatest speechwriters. It was amazing. She could articulate a problem, a need or a commitment in a way that would instantly force opposing sides to finally move from posturing to serious negotiating. While she never actually hammered out the minute and painstaking details, she was undoubtedly on the side of the angels, and she was able to move the negotiating process forward in a way few others could.

I remember overhearing young women who were student actors at Circle in the Square Theatre School talk about Colleen. They would say again and again: "I want to be an actor like Colleen Dewhurst." I'm not sure any of them knew exactly what that meant, but somehow their perception of Colleen's dedicated work ethic and commitment as a professional, her integrity and fun as a friend and, of course, her great robust laugh, made her someone they all aspired to become. And, all told, you really couldn't do much better.

In 1995, Cherry Jones won the Tony Award for Best Actress for her perfor-mance as Catherine Sloper in the revival of The Heiress. *In her brief acceptance speech, she thanked two people: her grandmother and Colleen Dewhurst.*

CHERRY JONES

When I was studying acting at Northwestern University, they took us to Lake Forest to see one of the early previews of *A Moon for the Misbegot-ten*. I was barely eighteen, but I have never forgotten the raw energy of Colleen's performance. I remember the lights came up and there she was, cleaning the floor of the porch on her hands and knees. I remember seeing her calves, her hands and feet, and the color of her hair, and then hearing the sound of her voice. It was an overwhelming sensory experience for me. I was sitting in the front of the mezzanine of the theater and, honest to God, I grabbed hold of the railing and didn't let go for three hours. All these years later, I can still see her smile, that incredibly mischievous broad grin that was so completely unique. I've done the role myself since, so I know the play awfully well and remember Colleen's performance through that understand-ing now, but as a young girl, it was just so startling to see a woman of such power and charm. She was so tough and seemingly big, yet had *woman* stamped all over her in a way that wasn't about some perceived femininity; it was an honest womanliness that could be strong, seductive and sensual with-out having to be pretty.

Colleen was gracious enough to come out and speak with us afterward. No easy feat, I can tell you, after three hours of O'Neill, but she did it. Somehow I found the courage to raise my hand to ask a question. "How do you keep your performance fresh?" I asked. Colleen just threw her head back and laughed that huge laugh.

"You don't," she said. "You just get good enough so that you can fake it well." Can you imagine, saying this to a class of acting students? But seeing her that evening was truly a turning point in what I came to believe one could do onstage as a woman. We all went out to a pub afterward, and in this crush of people, we all ended up sitting at a very long table. Colleen was sitting at the head of it, and I was way down at the other end, so I never got a chance to really talk to her. But there were a couple of times that we caught each other's eye, and I have always fancied in my own romantic mind that some wonderful con-nection was made there. It was just a generous glance that has meant the world to me since, as if she was saying, "You'll make it, kid, you'll get through."

∞ ∞ ∞

I am an actress who adores the professional Broadway stagehands, the crew. From my first show, *All the Way Home*, when those two big, burly men indicated that six-month-old Alex was still asleep, to today, there are none better to share backstage with. You will understand then why, during *Mourning Becomes Electra*, I felt I wanted to pay back a good turn to another member of the crew.

There was a moment in *Mourning Becomes Electra* where I came offstage to kill myself. There, a stagehand was to meet me and fire a pistol. This had been a tense rehearsal period, so when I found our propman, Spike, standing there during our last dress rehearsal ready to pop a paper bag for the shot, I was quite surprised. Later, to cover its own mistake in failing to provide the prop, management accused Spike of stealing the gun, an antique pistol. I threw a fit and said if Spike was fired, I would go to his union and agree to testify on his behalf. At that time, I didn't even know what the unions were, but it sounded good, and I was ready to go up before one, wherever that was. Everybody soon calmed down and another pistol was found in order that I could go out with more than a pop from a paper bag. To this day, if I go backstage at the Circle, someone on the crew from that time will ask, "Hey, when are you coming back, honey?" I would love to go back and do *Mourning Becomes Electra* again. Because it is really only now—with the passage of a good many years and much water over the dam—that this is a woman I can really understand.

At that time, and during the run of *Mourning Becomes Electra*, for one week each season, a basket was passed around in each Broadway theater for donations to The Actors' Fund. One actor was always asked to come out between the acts to give a speech as the basket was passed. Most actors didn't want to give this speech. It wasn't that they didn't want to help the fund. It just seemed odd to come out after the first act in which you had just attempted to throttle somebody and suddenly there you are, out of character, but in costume asking for donations.

That week of appeals, I was asked to be the one who spoke up for The Actors' Fund. I agreed and decided the best way was simply to speak about my own experience receiving assistance. So I came out at intermission and explained that a few years before, when my teeth were in terrible condition, I had gone to a dentist. This dentist, who understood the importance of good-looking teeth to an actor and had been recommended by friends in the business, suggested I have caps.

At the time, I had no money, but as all this dentist wanted was his lab fee, it was suggested to me that I go to The Actors' Fund for assistance. I had no idea such an organization even existed. I then learned that The Actors' Fund was the nation's oldest social-service agency for people, providing emergency assistance and social services for all who worked in the entertainment industry. So I went up there, embarrassed to be going to some charity organization on my knees, begging for teeth. Instead, I was ushered into a very nice room where a very kind gentleman came in and asked me what my problem was, which I explained. Three days later, I received a phone call at home saying that a check had been sent to my dentist and that he was waiting for me to call to make an appointment. I soon had caps and, more important, all of the self-confidence good-looking teeth will bring someone who feels self-conscious about her smile and even more awkward about asking for help.

They were very happy about the speech. I think we did very well that night in donations. The only problem was that when I came back on in the second act in character, I felt that as I would turn in each direction people were studying my smile or, if I opened my mouth to scream, they were sitting up for a closer look. Circle in the Square is a small thrust stage. It could have been my imagination, but I swear at one point I heard one man whisper to another, "Good job. I hadn't noticed before, but it is a very good job." The teeth, mind you, not the performance. Here we are in the middle of the Civil War and half the audience is captivated by how well the teeth were doing. I never gave that speech again.

16

"Which is real? Out there or up here?"

A reporter who had interviewed me at the Farm one afternoon was introduced to my two sons as she was leaving. She leaned down and said to Alex, who was then about twelve years old, "Tell me, have you seen your mommy in *A Moon for the Misbegotten?*"

"Have I seen it?" Alex replied. "First I saw it in Lake Forest. Then I saw it in Washington. I saw it here twice, and it is boring, really boring." I laughed rather giddily, took her by the arm, led her away from Alex, who I was afraid was just getting started—and thanked her for coming as I showed her out the door. I waved sweetly as she backed out the driveway. Then I came back in, slammed the door and said, "Alexander! When someone comes to interview your mother and has the misjudgment to ask you or your brother what you think of something she's done, the answer is always *wonderful, terrific* or . . . whatever. But above all, we never, *ever* say that Mother is boring!"

Well, Alex had a point. The boys had seen *Moon,* as they called it, from first to last, from Lake Forest to Broadway. In June of 1973, Alex and Campbell joined me at a Ramada Inn in Lake Forest, Illinois, where I was appearing in *Moon* with Jason Robards and Ed Flanders, directed by José Quintero at the Lake Forest Playhouse. After seeing the performance, Alex informed me that Campbell had slept through the entire show. Campbell yelled that he had not slept through the whole show, only through the intermissions. The highlight of the boys' trip was the room service at the Ramada. *A Moon for the Misbegotten* is a long play. I would come home and find that they had ordered two Cokes at a time, six times each evening.

The next time they saw it, as Alex reported, was in Washington, D.C. The highlight of that visit was that they were each allowed to bring one friend, who would share their room at the Watergate Hotel. To make Mom happy, they dutifully sat through a performance at the Kennedy Center, but informed me the next day that for the rest of their visit they would be glad to stay with their friends in their hotel room. I was asked a few evenings later by the concierge, upon my return from the theater, if he might speak to me for a moment.

"I'm sorry to bother you, Miss Dewhurst, but we have a slight problem. While you were at the theater these last couple of nights, they've been throwing snowballs from their room at cars in the parking lot below."

"I'm sorry," I replied.

"Well," he continued, "I wouldn't bother you with this at all, but in the last evening their aim has greatly improved and they're now hitting the drivers, as well as the parked cars. And—"

"I'll take care of it. Thank you." For the remainder of their stay, Alex, Campbell and cohorts had a wonderful view of *Moon* from backstage.

By the time *Moon* reached New York, it suddenly became clear to the boys—in the joy that pervaded the house, the laughter, the phone calls from friends—that, "boring" or not, something was different about this play. Something was happening at that theater in New York every night that hadn't happened ever before that they could remember. "Mom's got a hit! Mom's got a hit!" I heard them shouting back and forth to each other one morning as they got ready for school. And they were right. But *A Moon for the Misbegotten* was much, much more than just that.

Months before, in the spring of 1973, I was nowhere and looking for somewhere to go. A friend, sensing my great frustration and fear, asked why didn't I put together some kind of theatrical package for the summer. I could go out on the stock circuit, play all summer, and make enough money to live. I relayed this suggestion to my dear friend director José Quintero. "What can I do?" I asked him.

"I'll think about it, Colleen." I really did not expect to hear any real response from José. The suggestion seemed far-fetched, even to me. But the next day, he called back. "Why don't we do *A Moon for the Misbegotten?*"

"What?" I said back into the phone. "José, O'Neill . . . in summer stock?"

"Why not, Colleen? We can try. Let me see if I can reach Jason. If we could get Jason, we could finally do it the way we want to. The way we can."

As mentioned, José and I had first done Eugene O'Neill's *A Moon for the Misbegotten* in Spoleto, Italy, the year the festival had opened. We did it again in Buffalo, New York, for the opening of the city's new Studio Arena Theatre. But neither of us had ever been satisfied that, without Jason Robards playing the part of Jamie Tyrone, we had done it properly. José called an hour later to say that he'd reached Jason on the West Coast and that he very much wanted to do it. Just months before, Jason had had a dreadful car accident and the doctors were still working on his jaw and face. He could not leave Los Angeles; he needed to be near the doctors. So we would rehearse out there. "Well," José said, "that's the three of us. What do we do now?" Through an agent, we contacted a number of companies on the East Coast that booked "packages" for the summer. All initially turned down *A Moon for the Misbegotten* and, I must say, I was not too surprised. This was some offer we were making—a play by Eugene O'Neill that had never been successfully produced and no stars who would matter to a typical summer stock audience (meaning not from television or the movies). Also, on a strictly business level, we were starting late since most companies had already set up their entire program for the summer. I did not expect to hear about *Moon* again for quite some time. Then, as quickly as we had been turned down by all the others, Marshall Migatz, a producer with a theater in Lake Forest, Illinois, called José to say that he very much wanted to present Jason and me in *Moon*, not just for the usual one-week summer stock engagement, but for three. "It would be one of the highlights of my career," he told José, "if I could present this production."

We were thrilled and dumbfounded, and could scarcely believe the good fortune we had in finding Mr. Migatz, a man who loved this play enough to risk nearly all he had to see it come alive on his stage in Lake Forest. Negotiations began. José flew to Chicago, met with Mr. Migatz, and returned, happy to report that we were in good hands. Contracts were signed. Mr. Migatz was eager to see that the production was given a first-class presentation. Two days later, I received a phone call from Jane Broder, my agent. "Colleen, Marshall Migatz has been killed in a car accident. I'm so sorry." We were devastated by Marshall's loss. Although we barely knew him, he seemed to have exactly the qualities you would hope for in a man producing something you loved, if only because he seemed to love the idea of the production so much himself. "Somehow, this seems so O'Neillian," José said to me over the phone. "It has put me into a terrible depression." But just days later, fortune turned back to us again when the board of directors of the Lake Forest Theatre determined that rather than cancel the signed contracts under the "act of God" clause, they would continue and honor all arrangements made for our production of *A Moon for the Misbegotten* as a memorial and tribute to Marshall Migatz.

José and I left for California to rehearse with very mixed feelings. Gordon Davidson had been kind enough to offer us rehearsal space at the Mark Taper. It was an interesting and rather bizarre first day of rehearsal. There we were, brought together by a man who had died before we could begin what he put into motion. Here was our director, José Quintero, whom I loved and will love forever, looking very handsome and together. José's career had been interrupted for several years because of a drinking problem. I would rather be directed by José Quintero drunk than most directors stone cold sober, but he was now on the wagon (where he has remained throughout all these succeeding years). José seemed more alert and alive than ever. Jason entered, also looking very handsome. I had been afraid to see him because I knew that his accident had ravaged his face and brought him as close to death as one can come. I was overjoyed when I saw him enter with his wife, Lois. We hugged. I pulled back to look at him, still clasping his shoulders, as if to see for certain that it was really Jason. He stood before me, smiling, as if to say, "I'm all right. Let's begin." Then there was me, so broke that I could just manage to get myself from the East Coast to the Chateau Marmont, the hotel I loved in West Hollywood, and too embarrassed to ask when we were going to be paid for the first time. Such a ragged and fateful threesome came together that day.

The hiring of the actor who was to play my father, Phil Hogan, had been done over the telephone. All we knew was that it was to be a man named Ed Flanders. He came highly recommended, but none of us had ever seen him. Once Jason, José and I got settled that morning, I noticed a young man sitting to the side in a suit and tie. I nodded to him. Someone's agent, I thought, or a production assistant. We all continued to make small talk as eleven o'clock, our call to begin a first read-through, came and went. We sat, waiting for the actor who was to play my father. Finally, José stood up and announced that if the gentleman playing Mr. Hogan could not be there on time for the first rehearsal, he didn't want him. We would find someone else. I heard someone clear his throat behind me and turned to see the very natty man in the suit rise. "I'm Ed Flanders," he said. "I'm the actor who is playing Phil Hogan. I couldn't understand who we were waiting for." We all stared at Ed for a moment and then started to laugh.

"Oh, yes, ahhhh, Mr. Flanders," José said, "of course, you're here." We were all in a state of shock. Ed Flanders, who would be playing my father, looked—shall we say—at least a generation younger than Jason and I looked.

A year later, we were all at a pre–Tony Award taping. Tony Randall was interviewing each of the nominees in their various categories. I was sitting in the Green Room chatting and half-watching the television monitor. Out of the corner of my eye, I caught Ed come onscreen with Mr. Randall. "I'm terribly sorry," Tony said to Ed, "I haven't seen you in *A Moon for the Misbegotten*, but I understand you play an old man. That seems amazing to me, looking at you sitting here. How old a character do you play?"

Without missing a beat, Ed responded, "Well, it depends on how old Colleen feels that night!" The room burst into laughter and applause. Later that evening, I asked Ed just what does that mean . . . depending on how I feel. "Just what I said," he replied. "I adjust it up or down from when you come on." I will never fully understand what Ed adjusted, but he was brilliant and a joy onstage and off. He knew how to break any tension in rehearsal, and onstage never made a false move. Ed wore the mantle of Phil Hogan, Josie Hogan's father, as if he had been playing it for years. But it wasn't just a coat of characterization; there was a core to Ed. Whenever I looked into his eyes onstage or turned to him to speak, he was truly with me. There was such compassion and understanding coming through those blue Irish eyes. It was like having a wonderful tree to lean against, knowing it would always support me.

Everything about Ed Flanders was "father"; for me, he was all that I wanted in a father.

As rehearsals progressed, it was fascinating to watch the show develop. Because he is so strong, so passionate and almost overwhelming, O'Neill makes a demand for commitment from an actor unlike any other playwright. This is why, in the wrong hands, some audiences feel that he is corny. When José and I had done *Moon* earlier, there were two other actors playing Jamie, and although both men were good, there was a complete block for both of them in certain areas of the play. With Eugene O'Neill, this is not unusual. When we reached those sections, these other actors balked, stopped, and discussed (sometimes for hours) how to do it, and then how to get past it. When Jason walked into rehearsal, he didn't discuss a thing with José. He entered those same areas without pause, without intellectualizing, holding a script, walking with it across the rehearsal hall, never asking a question, just listening quietly to the few gentle suggestions José would make. My eyes would meet José's as Jason came to these dangerous sections of the play. Jason just began, he simply did them and, in doing so, became Jamie Tyrone. Obviously it never entered Jason's mind that there was anything to fear or that there was anything unusual about what was happening between us up there. With Jason, I could also make the commitment to O'Neill that allowed me, as Josie Hogan, to step off the edge of the cliff and into an abyss with the firm conviction that there was solid ground around me, in the words, in the actors onstage with me and, of course, in our director, José.

I love José Quintero and in many ways there is nothing more that needs to be said. But I particularly love José as a director, because he is so nondestructive, so understanding of the human condition, so passionate in a world that fears passion because it so often must break the rules. Other directors hold you. They don't want to let you go for fear that their own reason for being will disappear. José does not have that fear. He lets you fulfill yourself, he wants you to go beyond yourself, he encourages you to achieve what you always dreamed you could achieve. So he would sit watching us for quite a while without speaking, watching what Jason means by love and what I know of hurt. From these, Jose helped us create Jamie and Josie's tender affection. José knows just the moment you need to feel someone's hand; then and only then he steps in to say, "You may be right, but let's try it another way just once." And suddenly there is a spark that allows you to hear a line as if for the first time. José allowed Jason and me to be transparent with each other. He gave us moments of absolute breathing, where everything we were playing became one thought: Eugene O'Neill's.

Those three weeks of rehearsal in California were magic and spontaneous. There was that "Mickey and Judy" feeling of "Let's put a show on in the barn!" that you have when you first work in the theater. You've joined a group, found a play you love, and say, "Let's put this on. It's wonderful and I know it will succeed."

We left behind the rehearsal hall in Los Angeles and flew to Chicago, where we picked up the two actors who were to play Josie's brother and neighbor, and proceeded toward our first public performance. The board of the Lake Forest Theatre could not have been a warmer, more giving group. They seemed to sense just how important this play was to us and how much it meant to Marshall Migatz to bring *Moon* to what had been his home. They did everything in their power to make our stay pleasant and our production the best it possibly could be.

Marshall's spirit must have been with us for, much to our surprise, we played to full houses and enthusiastic audiences in Lake Forest, even though no one would ever have mistaken *A Moon for the Misbegotten* for your standard summer fare.

Over the three-week run, friends came in from New York and encouraged us to find a producer who could book and run the play elsewhere. One night, Jason, José and I sat in the lobby of the Ramada Inn and discussed the possibility of us assuming rights to *Moon* and trying to raise the money ourselves. We felt we belonged to the property and the property belonged to us. This was a very short meeting as we soon realized that none of us, least of all I, had the resources or could raise the investment money necessary. We refrained from even pursuing the idea or trying to reach friends who might have access to such sums. Raising money is a distinct talent. You either have it or you don't. And the talent is in not being embarrassed to ask and then being clever enough to ask in just the way that will appeal to the person you're asking. In both arenas, particularly the first, I am useless. So at the end of three weeks, we took our final bows and each took a plane, José to New York City, Jason back to the West Coast, and I went off to Prince Edward Island in Canada to spend the rest of the summer with my family. It seemed to be the end of *Moon,* and especially for José and me, the end of *Moon* for the third and last time.

While I was on Prince Edward Island, Elliot Martin, a New York producer, called Jane Broder. He had recently purchased the rights to *Moon* and wanted to present it with me and Peter O'Toole on public television. I told Jane I would not ever do *Moon* again with anyone but "the triumvirate": José, Jason and me. I did not expect Jane to hear from Mr. Martin again. In September, I flew off to Israel to work in a television film called *The Brothers.* Jane cabled to say that Mr. Martin had changed his mind. There would be no television production of *Moon* with Peter O'Toole. He had decided instead to produce the play, as done at Lake Forest, with José, Jason, Ed and me. We would open at the Kennedy Center in Washington, D.C., in November, then try to add a week or so in other cities before coming into New York for a six- to eight-week limited engagement.

We went into rehearsal in the autumn of 1973—with José, Jason, Ed Flanders, Edwin J. McDonough, John O'Leary and me. At that time, I did not know that Elliot Martin had not received any interest in *Moon* from the road beyond Washington, D.C. In desperation, he finally approached Lester Osterman, managing director of the Morosco Theatre on West Forty-fifth Street, a jewel of a playhouse in the heart of the theater district, and asked if he would come in as a partner, and since the theater was dark at the time, allow *Moon* to play there directly following our Kennedy Center engagement for a limited run. Martin hoped that if we got any decent reviews, then there was always the possibility that other theaters outside of New York would be interested in booking the production.

A Moon for the Misbegotten officially opened on Broadway on Saturday, December 29, 1973. In his review of the play in the *New York Times*, Clive Barnes wrote:

> *There are some performances in the theater, just a few that surge along as if they were holding the whole world on a tidal wave. I felt that surge, that excitement, that special revealed truth while watching Eugene O'Neill's* A Moon for the Misbegotten *at the Morosco Theatre.*
>
> *This is a landmark production that people are going to talk about for many years. The play has been staged by José Quintero, making a directorial comeback as assured as it is welcome and stars Jason Robards, Colleen Dewhurst and Ed Flanders. It seemed to me an ideal, vibrant cast—a cast that listened acutely to the realities and tonalities of O'Neill's voice—in one of the great plays of the 20th century.*

It was the most wonderful Christmas and New Year's I had ever celebrated and the best time of my life, of my career. The reviews were wonderful. We were happy. We were selling out. The producers were happy. Our supposed limited run became an open-ended run. The year 1974 was truly a happy, happy new year. Doubly so because never in our wildest imaginations had any of us believed that *A Moon for the Misbegotten* could be a commercial hit. Suddenly, with the new year, a group that just six months before couldn't be booked in summer stock had become the cast of a hit Broadway show, "a landmark production," as the *New York Times* said and as our grateful producers splashed across our ads for months to come.

Not long after we opened, someone nicknamed us the "Resurrection Company" and it is easy to understand why. For various reasons, none of us—José, Jason nor I—had been on the scene for a while, and suddenly it was as if we appeared in this enormously popular and critical hit from out of nowhere. At last, a play I was in ran long enough for that theater literally to become my second home. During the weekend, the dressing rooms would be filled with children. Alex and Campbell would come in on the train, go to a movie with friends, and run back to the theater to watch the last few minutes of *Moon* from the wings before driving back with me to the Farm for the night. Jason's children would drop by and sit with him. Ed's son came in. I can still see Ed sitting the boy on his lap and talking to him before he got dressed to go home. It was a place and time where the company not only became like a family but that feeling reached out and included our children and friends. It was a rare and beautiful time, and six days out of every week—for a few very blessed months—I was exactly where I wanted to be, doing exactly what I knew I could do. It was a joyous experience.

A Moon for the Misbegotten is not a play about which you can come into the theater at seven-thirty thinking, *OK, I have a date at eleven-thirty, so let's get this over with.* It's not a play that you do in between living the rest of your life. It becomes the living. From the moment I opened my eyes in the morning, I knew that eight o'clock was coming. The kids may be getting furious and there are a host of things that come with a great success that you know you should be dealing with. But you're split, split between home and theater, family, friends and career. Everybody and everything is cheated a bit and all you want to do is the play . . . and sleep. But you've got to do this thing eight times a week. Some nights feel as if you are pushing a freight train up a hill. And other nights are gloriously exciting, when you can feel that the audience is truly experiencing the play—this masterpiece by Eugene O'Neill—as one person.

Although it encompassed over a year and a half of my life during which many things occurred, including many problems, those seem inconsequential as I look back on those days now. Never having had such a success before, I didn't realize the pressure. I always thought, *Well, gee, if I could ever have that big success, I could just lie back and say, "OK, that's it!"* But you begin to fear that the audience is coming in with their arms crossed, saying, "So what's so good? Let's see what I paid all this money for and waited three months to see!" So now you come onstage even more nervous than you were before you were deemed such a success. At least when I was in failures, again and again, I'd just go out, play the show, and people would come back and say, "I don't know why everybody hates this." When you're in a flop, anything you do is terrific, as far as people were concerned, because they knew you were dead.

But the exhilarating success of *A Moon for the Misbegotten* was never and will never be repeated in my life. And I am very thankful now that it came to me when it did. Such a success didn't mean the same to me at forty-nine as it might have meant at thirty. It's like water dripping on a stone; you're hard enough to survive it. Fortunately, I'd been around long enough and have been through enough good times and bad to know that 1974 was my year. The next year always brings somebody else.

The boredom that can come from playing for a long period of time a role that has no depths to search, no significant facets to investigate and reveal is the actor's purgatory. Doing *Moon* was a great opportunity, not only to be in a play that was a solid hit and took care of me financially for over a year, but to be in a play that I so loved, that gave me the chance each night and every matinee to reach into myself farther than I had the performance before. Eugene O'Neill gave me just what I always dreamt of finding in the theater: a play that would consistently reveal itself to me, just as the character I played revealed a depth of me to myself that I had seldom before dared to uncover. This is a very special gift and one I shall carry in my heart forever. To do *A Moon for the Misbegotten* was the fulfillment of all those years of walking up and down Broadway in the West Forties, looking up and seeing the marquee of a beautiful play with wonderful actors in it and praying, *Oh, God, I would give anything to be up there tonight.* Sometimes prayers are answered and you discover that there is nothing you're expected to *give up;* all that is asked is that you *give back.*

For her performance as Josie Hogan in A Moon for the Misbegotten, *Colleen won the 1974 Tony Award for Best Actress in a Play. She was nominated with Jane Alexander in* Find Your Way Home, *Julie Harris in* The Au Pair Man, *Madeline Kahn in* In The Boom Boom Room, *and Rachel Roberts for her work in* The New Phoenix Repertory Company. *Upon accepting the award from Al Pacino, Colleen said:*

> *Well, José was right. It isn't a dream, it did happen to us. First I would like to say when I left the house today—this will be very brief—I would like to thank my family at home, my children and everyone. This is the speech they have asked me to give. I want to thank them for their understanding. I'd like to thank them for being an inspiration to me during this very trying period when their mother had a hit. And now, my darlings, as we all know, it's very late. Go right to bed!*
>
> *I know that what I hold in my hand is for* Moon, *for the total. What has been most fantasy-like, I guess, is that it was us all, it was the theater. No actress could be more lucky than to be with supermen: my sweet Jason, Edward, John, Edwin, that great man Mr. O'Neill, and that great Irishman of them all, José Quintero.*
>
> *Most of all, I want to thank you all for a joy you may never know you have given me, the joy that theater is alive and well and living inside of us all.*

KEN MARSOLAIS

Colleen and I met when José hired me to come in as assistant stage manager and understudy on *A Moon for the Misbegotten* once it came into New York. I had worked as a stage manager with José once before, on a huge, colossal off-Broadway flop called *Gandhi*. Despite the show's failure, it was quite a fortunate personal experience in that it began a close friendship with José. As those kinds of jobs go, *Moon* wasn't difficult. Jane Neufeld was the stage manager, you had a cast of five, all very professional people of the theater, so you weren't dealing with prima donnas. I just supported Jane in whatever needed to be done. There weren't many cues, so Jane and I took turns calling the show just to stay awake. Of course, Colleen, Jason and Ed were a very interesting group of people to spend time with offstage. Despite the depth of what was happening onstage every night, there was a lot of joking, card playing and horsing around backstage, but people did their jobs.

I had only seen Colleen in one other play, Albee's *All Over* with Jessica Tandy. I was in school then. It was a great play and beautifully done. I ended up seeing it three times, not especially because of Colleen but simply because the whole production was so extraordinary. When I finally met Colleen on *Moon*, I certainly had a great deal of respect for her. Personally I've been in awe of a lot of people, but that awe doesn't frighten me. Some you then get to know, and others you don't. Some you find you want to know, and others you don't.

One night—I don't really know why—I just hollered up the stairs to Colleen's dressing room, "Do you want to have a drink after the show?"

"Wait a minute," she shouted back. "I think I have some plans but let me see if they're gonna happen." After the show, Colleen came over to me and said, "Let's have that drink." We went over to Jimmy Ray's on Eighth Avenue. It's not there anymore—it burned down a few years ago. But in those days, it was a real neighborhood theater bar where a lot of actors would hang out for hours after their shows. Jimmy's was too dark and dusty for tourists, but it was perfect for the likes of us. I don't think a place like that exists around there anymore.

Now this certainly wasn't a date. At least, I wasn't thinking about it like that when I shouted up the stairs. But Colleen and I stayed there quite late that evening and somewhere in there things shifted a bit and I guess some people would say we did end up a little more than casual. So we continued seeing each other, but kept it low-key. You know this community, especially a small backstage community. Ultimately there is no such thing as a secret, just a general unspoken agreement about when something is to be officially acknowledged. So there was a lot of tiptoeing. But it was fine. By the time we were ready to open up most people had figured it out. This was around April. Eventually I began to spend more time at the Farm, where I was introduced to Alex and Campbell, who were twelve and thirteen at the time, as well as Stuart and Tony, whom I got along with really well. We all shared a very similar sense of humor, which is probably essential for anyone who spends much time with Colleen. It was just fun. Wild and crazy, but fun.

The first time we went out together publicly was in June, for the Tony

Awards. Colleen was nominated for Best Actress in a play and won. It was a wonderful evening but just a part of what had been an electrifying six months.

Opening night was extraordinary. I don't think anyone could ever figure out why what happened with that show happened, but, without doubt, lightning struck. It was unbelievable. Once the reviews hit, everyone in the business came to see the show. You could feel the audience's excitement and anticipation every night.

For every one of us, it was a time like no other, a great time, a very heady time. Obviously it thrust me into an arena that I had never been exposed to before, but one in which I became comfortable. And Colleen felt comfortable having me there with her, which was most important. So *Moon,* or to be quite specific, an evening at Jimmy Ray's, was the beginning of eighteen years that we spent together.

As many will say, Colleen was quite a remarkable woman. But there was much about her that many people wouldn't expect. She had an outrageous humor which came from a sadness that she held very close, and she had tremendous courage precisely because she knew great fear. With just that, and there was so much more, how could I help but love her?

ꝏ ꝏ ꝏ

One year later we found ourselves where we began, when *A Moon for the Misbegotten* opened at the Ahmanson Theatre in Los Angeles for a limited run to a subscription house. It was a very lucrative agreement for the producers and the actors. We could have played *Moon* for another year in New York City, but the agreement with the Ahmanson had been made prior to our opening, and because it was so financially attractive, it made sense to do it. I loved going back out to California. I took a house on the beach and when school was out, Alex and Campbell joined me. It was like a wonderful summer vacation for us all. But we all knew what we were in for.

José and I had opened the Ahmanson a few years before with O'Neill's *More Stately Mansions,* starring Ingrid Bergman and Arthur Hill. It is a huge theater and very difficult to play in. When we first entered the theater to rehearse, I could see that the other actors were shocked as they looked out into that vast expanse of auditorium. *A Moon for the Misbegotten* at the Morosco was a shared experience for those onstage and in the audience. The stage of the Morosco seemed to embrace the house and hold the audience. There was no barrier between them and what was unfolding onstage. *Moon* was not a play that could be observed from a distance and experienced completely. To understand this play, the audience had to feel it shared in the life of the characters for those three hours we were together. This kind of theatrical experience was impossible to achieve at the Ahmanson. Yes, the play was successful there. We had wonderful audiences, but the company never again felt the play and the absolute transference between ourselves in the unfolding of story and those who came to watch it unfold. To this day, when people say they've seen me in *Moon,* I become tense if they tell me they saw it in California, because I have always felt that *Moon* could have no real impact in that sterile barn of a theater.

I do love opening nights in Los Angeles, though, because the evening is truly star-studded, like you imagined as a kid, these evenings were supposed to be. I never cease to be thrilled when I am introduced to people who for years have been legends to me. The opening-night party for *Moon* was no exception, and because we arrived as such an anointed hit, the excitement was especially wild. But I never felt more like Alice falling through the rabbit hole than at this opening-night party. As I entered the room, a woman whom I'd never met but felt I'd known for years because of her work in films rushed toward me, holding a napkin filled with hors d'oeuvres. "Colleen," said Joan Crawford, "I've saved these for you because you and I know that by the time the actors get to a party, everybody has eaten everything. Look at that table over there," she exclaimed, "there's nothing left but a deviled egg and an anchovy!" I stood looking at Joan and thought, *Here is one of the great stars, running over to make sure I have something to eat, and doing it quite matter-of-factly and with humor.* I gladly took the napkin and thanked her for thinking of me.

Later in the evening, just before we left, Joan came up to me again and said, "Colleen, I did not want to disturb you, because this is your night and there are so many people who want to talk to you, but may I speak to you privately for a moment?" We moved over toward the windows that looked out over the pavilion. I rather prepared myself, thinking that she was going to discuss how wonderful she thought we were. Taking my arm, she lowered her voice. "Dear, I'm speaking to you as a woman who has worked a great many years. I know about this business. The first thing is," she said, looking conspiratorially around the room, "you must never, never, ever work with this director again."

I turned and looked at her for a minute nonplussed, not so much that she would say this but *why?* "I'm going to tell you why," she said, as if reading my mind. "Because any director who would allow you to come out in that dress you wore, faded and not fitted at all to your body, is not your friend." I was speechless. "But Colleen," she continued, turning us farther away from the crowd, "then to permit you for the first ten minutes of the play to scrub a porch floor, getting yourself filthy, with your ass shoved toward the audience— which, my dear, is not the most attractive part of any actress over thirty—was for you a completely destructive move."

I stood there with my mouth hanging open—not the most attractive look for any actress of any age—but managed to say, "Ah, yes. I see your point. Thank you, Joan, for telling me." But she was not through. As we walked arm in arm back into the party she continued, "I don't know if there is anything you can do to remedy it in the next eight weeks while you're here, but if you can, I would simply take the reins and change that entire piece of business. Insist that the dress be redesigned and fitted." And with that, Joan Crawford took her leave and rejoined the party.

I love the nerve and survivor's instinct that prompted Joan to speak to me so unguardedly. In fact, it was genius of José to direct me on my knees, scrubbing the porch for the first ten minutes of *Moon*. This simple direction left me and the character completely vulnerable, feeling very unattractive and with no corner to hide in as a woman. By the end of those ten minutes, when I stood up again as Jamie came in, the insecurity, the sense of being a woman that no man could truly love or be attracted to, was complete and never left me throughout the entire play. Even in that barn-like Ahmanson, as a woman, Joan Crawford felt this discomfort, and, as another actress, one with a sense of power in this arena, felt it was her duty to correct it for me. I adore the story, but I love the very real feelings that drove the behavior.

When we finished the run in California, we immediately went into rehearsal for the taping of *A Moon for the Misbegotten* for television. It was reassuring that each time we came to what seemed to be the play's end, we went on. After the Kennedy Center, we knew we were on to New York. After New York, we knew we had California. And after California, we knew we would go to tape. We finished taping while I was still living at the beach. It was not like a closing performance and particularly not like a final performance of a play in New York. We went out more with a whimper than a bang—much as we had begun over a year and a half before in Lake Forest. My only regret is that we did not come back to New York to complete the run. *A Moon for the Misbegotten* belonged on the stage of the Morosco Theatre. It is one of the reasons it so broke my heart when it was torn down to make room for a tourist/business-class hotel.

You can never account for what people will say to you when they see you after a performance. One evening, a woman came up to me in a restaurant and said, "Oh, I'm so glad you got this play because that thing you did by Albee, *All Over*, stunk." Really! She had no understanding that when I did *All Over*, it too was a labor of love. It would be like somebody coming up and saying to you after a lover has disappeared, "Well, he was always so—" And you reply, "Don't! It's all right for me to feel that way just now, but don't *you* say it." When you're involved, plays, like lovers, are a wonderful experience. Some end quickly, some go on for quite a while. But I wouldn't have been involved if I didn't think that both, the play or the lover, were worth the experience.

One of the most exhilarating memories I have of *Moon* is the mail I received during its run. We opened just at the end of what was considered yet another very bad period for the theater. There was much talk that the young were not interested in going to plays, that once again Broadway was no longer a welcome home to the American playwright. When we compared our letters,

Jason, José and I saw a pattern develop. There was, of course, typical fan mail, which is always welcome to an actor. But there were also letters that were unusual and touching in their depth and, most reassuringly, an astounding amount coming from teenagers and young adults in their early twenties. These letters revealed a great deal about the life of the writer. There were expressions of gratitude, not for the actors particularly, but for the experience they had watching the play. After much thought, I realized that many of these young people were finding some kind of answers in O'Neill to questions they had about life. They did not seem at all concerned with the age difference between themselves and the actors onstage or that they were watching a play that had been written well before they were born. I think—I hope—they saw us simply as human beings who, at whatever age or state in life, knew loss and agony and love, loss of that love and then, most important, redemption. I truly believe that these individuals knew instinctively that they were in the presence of a playwright who demanded that an actor strip down to the most vulnerable core of the self, and do it without embarrassment, without masks or tricks. We, as actors, were challenged to say, this is the joy and this is the agony of life. O'Neill takes loss and presents it passionately, always with passion. Emotion is not something that is thought out or instructed. We each react completely to the stimuli that come every day of our lives. It is all living. And finally and ultimately it is not to be judged. It simply *is*.

Jason and I often discussed theater ghosts. We never felt it necessary to clarify this for each other in any artsy-craftsy or spiritual way. But we both felt the presence of another at various times. Every night, as we came into the last scene of the last act, as the lights went down on an exhausted Jamie, I would reach out as Jason would adjust himself into my arms and go to sleep.

On one particular night, as the lights faded to dark, as I reached out I said softly to Jason, "Which is real? Out there or up here?"

And in the last seconds of the play, before the lights went completely to black, Jason whispered, "Up here."

JASON ROBARDS

The first smile I ever got in New York City was from Colleen Dewhurst. It was 1946. I had just been discharged from the navy and was going into the September class at the American Academy of Dramatic Arts. Colleen was in the class just ahead of me—the spring class. On my first day, I walked into the Academy's greenroom. I didn't know anyone and didn't speak to anyone. Colleen walked in. I didn't know her either, but when she saw me she smiled, that big grin that just lit up her face. It was the first time in this city that I felt even remotely comfortable.

Colleen was a senior and you know how it is when you're a student. We thought that all those people ahead of us, the seniors, were all so fucking marvelous. Some were. Some weren't. Colleen was. I remember seeing her in two plays, *The Shining Hour* and *You Can't Take It with You,* which we did together on Broadway nearly thirty-five years later. Colleen played the same role.

After we all graduated, we would see each other around the neighborhood in the Village, but not with any regularity. I'd worked downtown at Circle in the Square in *An American Gothic* and then with José Quintero in *The Iceman Cometh.* But it really wasn't until Colleen did *Children of Darkness,* also for José, and with George, that I caught up with her again. I would hang around to see José, and I knew George. That's when I first heard, from José, in fact, that George was crazy about her and she about him, and was until she died, I think. She had left Jim Vickery by then. I don't know what happened with him. But no wonder George adored her. Colleen had such a quality about her, and she was beautiful. We would all go out together for drinks at Donahue's or some other theater bar, all the actors. In those days, it was not all about getting drunk; it was camaraderie. All that time is gone.

George and I admired each other as actors. One night, I ran into him and he says, "Come with me! I'm going to Jack Delaney's to kick the shit out of this guy, Richard Kiley."

"What for?" I asked. Turns out George had just heard that José was taking Kiley and Colleen to do *A Moon for the Misbegotten* at the Spoleto Festival in Italy, and George was jealous. They weren't married yet, but he was jealous. I called ahead to Delaney's. "Listen, José," I said. "George and I are coming down, and you better get Kiley out of there." José spent the rest of the evening trying to talk George out of beating the shit out of him. I remember thinking, *Well, this must be pretty serious between Colleen and George. . . .* I got the hell out of there and went on to someplace else. Those were the days when we were all just wandering around. Somehow, José ended up being the peacemaker and Richard went to Spoleto in one piece with Colleen and José to do *Moon.*

By the time they came back, Kennedy had been elected President. I don't know how it came about, but someone asked José to direct Colleen and me in a scene from *Moon* for his inauguration in Washington. Kennedy loved O'Neill. Danny Kaye conducted the symphony, Freddie March did something, and we did a section of *A Moon for the Misbegotten.* Colleen did *Moon* a number of times, with Kiley in Italy, and I think again with Jim Daly in Buffalo. But I never expected to play it. I really thought the play was dead. There'd never be another Broadway production.

Oddly enough, during all those early years, I really didn't get to know Colleen that well. We'd see each other at various gatherings, or she and George would invite me to parties at the apartment in the Village. This is before they moved upstate. Or we'd be sitting around with a lot of other people in a restaurant or bar having a drink. We had friends in common, many people who all worked with one another at one time or another. So I talked to her occasionally but never got deeply involved with her until we did *Moon* again in Lake Forest, Illinois.

That production initially came about without any fanfare at what was a difficult time for all of us. José had not been doing a lot of good work for a while, but had gotten sober. I had just come out of a car accident that nearly killed me. I think Colleen felt that her career wasn't going anywhere, and since she had just divorced George for the second time, she was pretty much adrift. I hadn't heard about the second divorce. José had been best man for them both times. "If they get married again," he said, when we finally talked about it, "*you're* it! I'm not going there again."

Colleen was under a lot of strain by the time we all got together in Los Angeles to rehearse for what we thought would just be a three-week summer stock engagement of *A Moon for the Misbegotten* at the Lake Forest Theatre outside of Chicago. As we were getting ready to close in Lake Forest, we all thought that was it. Three weeks, no more. But Sam Peckinpah, the movie director, sent me some money and said, "Buy the goddamn rights and keep it." I had worked with Sam a couple of times. We were old friends. He had been best man at my wedding. So we threw money back and forth. I had saved a project for him once, so this time it was his turn. "Take your goddamn money," he said, "and hold on to it [*Moon*], for Christ's sake. I want you to have it!" So I talked to some people about it and everyone else discouraged me. "Don't beat a dead horse," they said. "It's not going anywhere. Forget it." So I sent the money back to Sam, and *Moon* closed in Lake Forest. Next thing I know, Elliot Martin read a review of the production in *Variety* that had been written by some stringer in Chicago. On the strength of that review, he bought the rights and tried to mount a television version of the play with Colleen and Peter O'Toole. I understand Colleen told him to go to hell and somehow it all came back around to the three of us: José, Colleen and me.

When we opened in New York, after playing in Washington, D.C., it was supposed to be for a five-week run at the Morosco Theatre. That was it. Five weeks. In and out. But we got tremendous reviews. Soon after we opened, Colleen says to me, "What do you suppose this is all about? What the hell is everybody talking about?"

"I'll tell you what," I replied. "Since I don't come on in the first act for thirty minutes or so, I'll stand in the back and watch what's going on." Colleen thought that was a good idea. So I watched her and Ed [Flanders], hoping I would get some idea of this magic that was supposed to be happening onstage and came backstage just in time to make my first entrance.

"So what's going on?" Colleen asked afterward.

"I don't know," I told her. "It's the same old shit we did at the American Academy."

"That's what I thought," she said. "It's the play. We believe in it. That's all." And, in a very basic way, I think Colleen was right. An actor doesn't change thought, theme or mood unless the character does, and the character only does it within the words of the play. You don't need to bring a lot of your own shit into something so beautifully written. If you know it well enough, have rehearsed it hard enough, and you know all of the attitudes, the play takes off and you don't even know that you've been there. That's the magic of the theater. That's what happened with us at times. Not always, but when it was there it was like O'Neill had stuck his hand in and said, "Go on. Keep going." I know that's the way it worked for Colleen and that's the way it worked for me. Whatever tears came out of this or whatever magic supposedly happened just occurred because of the combination of us all with the play. Colleen never worried about her performance. I worried all the time. I don't think it was until about two-thirds of the way through the New York run that I really got it right. Colleen knew it. We had been playing for months and one night when it went dark in that scene where she's holding me she says in my ear, "I believe we have been studying all weekend?" At the same time, I will never forget listening to Colleen screaming, "Father, Father, I love you." It just broke my heart hearing it every night. But, in such a marvelous situation, that is the kind of work you can do and the kind of fun you can have. What the hell are you going to do? Play this play every night for a year and go home and tear your heart out? No! The play tears it out for you. And the rest of the time, you might as well have a good time out there.

JOSÉ QUINTERO

Colleen was my true sister. I have a sister whom I am close to by blood, but Colleen was my sister by design. We seldom talked about how we felt about each other, but we understood each other completely. In some ways, I cannot imagine her sitting down to write a book about herself, because she was very discreet about private things, I mean to the extreme. People think that Colleen was an open book, but hardly. She was a great many books, and some were suitable just for her eyes. That is part of the beauty of the woman.

Long ago, after the great success of *Summer and Smoke* and *The Iceman Cometh* at Circle in the Square, I received a raise, making one hundred and fifty dollars a week, which was an enormous amount of money at the time. So I moved up to Commerce Street on the corner of Barrow in Greenwich Village. I was watching out my window one day when I saw a young man with an advertisement for the opening of *Camille* at the Cherry Lane Theatre nearby.

"Who is playing Camille?" I asked him.

"Colleen Dewhurst," he said.

I could hardly believe that. I had seen her play Katherine in *The Taming of the Shrew*. She was not Camille. But I stayed glued to my window, hoping to see her. And I did. As she walked by, on her way to the theater, she wore the street behind her like a mantle. She was at the height of her beauty and had a regal bearing that was of both the lowest peasant and the highest queen. I had to watch. Finally, after the third day as she passed my window, I said, "You're Colleen Dewhurst." She stopped and looked back to me at the window.

"I know who you are," she replied. She came over and we started to talk. And with that, I was hers. She continued to stop by after rehearsals, but always just to the window; she never came in. It was a most fitting beginning, because throughout all the years that I knew Colleen, there was always an element of flirtation between us. Colleen was a natural flirt all her life. It was one of the things I adored about her. Our meetings by the window were very romantic. And that begins my life with Miss Dewhurst. For over thirty years, as director to actress and as friend to friend, we were completely vulnerable to each other. We were intimate in our adventures in the theater, and many were not the easiest adventures. They were highly charged. But we knew that if we were to wound each other it would be forever. It was something that could not be, so we never let it happen.

Colleen's Josie in *A Moon for the Misbegotten* is one of the great performances, unforgettable and courageous, like Geraldine Page's performance in *Summer and Smoke*. Recently, Mercedes Ruehl wrote to me, to say she was thinking of reviving *Moon* and would I direct. Now, I think Mercedes is a wonderful actress and I have a great deal of respect for her. But I wrote her back and said, "If I were still directing, I would have to say no, but only because it would be most unfair to you." The image of Colleen in the role will never leave me. Never have I seen such a performance as Colleen's. It was so solid, yet you could see through it. Her vulnerability was enormous. It is probably the most exquisite performance I have ever witnessed, to such an extent that I separate myself from having directed it. It was her creation. Whatever I did, or pat myself on the back for, is with the understanding that all I could do was solve a problem for her here, suggest something there.

I directed Colleen in a number of plays over many years, including *Children of Darkness* and *Desire Under the Elms* with George at Circle, *More Stately Mansions* with Ingrid Bergman, and last, *Long Day's Journey into Night*. But *A Moon for the Misbegotten* was a joy. It was a revelation for us all—myself, Jason and Colleen—to be working together. Never had we expected to and never had we enjoyed the world so much. I think Colleen knew that she was good, but I believe she had no idea how really exceptional she was. She had no idea. The play is so universal. We don't think, so many of us, that we are worth loving really. It always comes as a surprise when somebody loves us. Like Josie didn't know this, Colleen didn't know that she was so exquisite. She just couldn't believe it, like she could never believe that she was that beautiful. That may be some of what made her so good in the role—that she never truly felt that she was a desirable woman, that she would be attractive to men. Somewhere she understood that when they told her she was, they had made a mistake. Likewise, Colleen knew that she had talent, that she could hold an audience. But she didn't know that she could provoke sheer amazement. After we opened on Broadway, she would say to me, "We're a success, right?" I would say, "Yes, Colleen, we are a success." Yet she would continue to question the outcome. Gradually I began to understand that what was happening to Josie in the play every night, was also happening to her. That is what fed her performance so. I do think there are certain parts written for certain people with certain talents and somehow all of that particular talent understands the depth of just that character in a way that maybe nobody else ever will again. Other actresses will play Josie Hogan and they will do a very good job of it, but that part was written by Eugene O'Neill for Colleen Dewhurst. Everything about her made Mr. O'Neill's creation larger.

It was so interesting to watch Colleen work with Ingrid Bergman in *More Stately Mansions*. At that time, and this is well before she hit so brilliantly in *Moon,* I think that Colleen had the wish of becoming a movie star. She never quite said it in those words, but I think that is one of the things she hoped for. Now, here she was in Los Angeles, working with one of the biggest movie stars there ever was. I do not think Colleen was quite prepared for it all, particularly since this was Ingrid's return to America after a long self-imposed exile in Europe. It came as a surprise to Colleen that Ingrid turned out to be as big a person as she was a star. There was tremendous pressure on us all. So when we began rehearsals, I felt there was a reserve from Colleen toward Ingrid. I sensed that there was a rivalry that I had never seen before in Colleen and that was coming from Colleen, not Ingrid. But neither of them ever said anything about it to me. Nevertheless, so as not to create a problem, I devised a way for Ingrid, Colleen and their costar, Arthur Hill, to take the final curtain call together when we opened in Los Angeles. Afterward, there was a write-up in one of the New York papers that Dewhurst stole the show from Bergman. I thought that this would be the end, as Ingrid had been very shaky about coming back to America in the first place. But Ingrid Bergman, like Colleen, was an exceptional woman. I received word from Ingrid's agent that she was not upset at all and indeed thought that the item was true. When I visited Ingrid in her dressing room, all she wanted to know was, "What must Colleen be thinking?

"José," she asked me, "would you take me to her dressing room?"

She knocked on the dressing room door. "Come in," Colleen said from inside. "Ingrid?" she said, clearly surprised to see her.

"I don't want you to feel badly about what they said in New York," she said to Colleen. "It is very true. Now I must just work all the harder to beat you and steal it back." I could see every bit of reserve melt away from Colleen in that moment. Ingrid opened her arms and they embraced and I know from that point became very fond of each other. Years later, when the O'Neill medal was given in New York to the Swedish Royal Theatre, I was supposed to give a speech about Ingrid. When I got there, Colleen came up to me and said, "Oh,

José, please let me give it." I did, of course, knowing why Colleen wanted to be the one to do it here in New York, and she gave a glorious speech, completely unprepared, about this woman she had come to love and respect completely.

Colleen was a constant surprise, that is why she stays in the hearts and memories of so many people. Many people who for whatever reason come into the public eye must always reinvent themselves to stay there. Colleen was an invention that did not ever need to be reinvented. She was a machine to last a lifetime and she left us with so many miracles yet to be performed. Learning of Colleen's death was the most shocking moment of my life. I did not even know that she was ill. I had just come back from giving a class and as it happened, as it always happens, I had just spoken of her as an example of expressive body language. Colleen always spoke with her body; she was like a princess, a seductress in that way. Her smile could turn her blank face into that of the most desirable woman in the world. I had just told the class about Colleen's first appearance in *A Moon for the Misbegotten;* how she washed the stage of the Morosco Theatre and with every stroke, she added a new layer to her character, simply in how she moved her body. When I arrived home, there was a message from Campbell. I called him back. It was a quarter to eleven. He gently and lovingly gave me the unexpected news that Colleen had passed on. To this day, she is still at the Farm for me. But Colleen was an enormously private person and dying is a private business. I know that selfishly I would have liked to hold her hand; that might have made losing her easier for me. But since I did not witness her completion, because I was not prepared for her physical demise, it seems as if she is only away, not gone. I believe it all happened just the way Colleen wanted it.

I don't think I have ever laughed with anybody as much as I laughed with that girl. But as much as Colleen laughed in life, she hid her wounds very quietly. Her laugh was explosive, her tears were quiet. She used to say that when we were seventy and we could both retire, we would get married. And then we would just dance. Colleen loved dancing. I will never forget the opening-night party at Delsomma's for *A Moon for the Misbegotten.* We danced all night, the rumba, the tango. Colleen was very light on her feet, so much so that no one would notice that she was improvising what looked like ballroom dancing. This wonderful girl could dance, and throughout her years as an actress, mesmerized hundreds of audiences and brought them to their feet, clapping.

Colleen was the person I trusted most in the world. This is the truth. I have never trusted anyone as completely as I trusted her. I found it easy to talk to her about being homosexual. When I told her, she just said, "Well, José, I knew it. But the important thing is are you happy?" At that time, I was ending a relationship with a wonderful young man whom Colleen loved very much. But once it was over, she made it a project to try to find someone new for me. Colleen had such respect for education and diplomas. I remember when she was going to introduce me to a young man who had a Ph.D. She was very excited by the prospect. "José," she said, "that doesn't come around very often."

"What?" I replied.

"A Ph.D.," she said.

"Yes, Colleen." Everything was open between us. We never had a question that waited. But we never barged into each other's privacy. She opened the door and then I went in or she waited until I opened the door and then she came in. I trusted her so because never had my private world been treated with such respect, such a sense that it was mine. She gave me back the right to my world. She made me respect my own privacy. Colleen helped me understand that I have a right to it, even though we were both in this profession in which you are expected to divulge everything. Colleen understood me. Sometimes when I would give her a direction she would say, "What an old world you come from, José." She would never say, "How do you know?" or "How do you come to this conclusion?" No, simply, "What an old world you come from." That is the greatest compliment that I have ever received from anybody. I still regard it so.

I feel like I've known Colleen's sons, Alex and Campbell, since before they were born. She was pregnant six months with Alex when George wanted to get married. Colleen wouldn't do it. She simply refused. Finally, George said to me, "Will you talk to her?"

"I don't know if I can," I told him. "But I will if the appropriate moment comes up." Well, somehow she brought it up, she opened that door. She said George wanted to get married before the child was born. "Why don't you get married then?" I asked her.

"I'm not going to go to a judge with a belly out to here and get married in some shotgun ceremony!" she said. She had projected the image of the wedding now and found it a cartoon. She would not make a caricature of her marriage, of herself, of this child, Alexander, who was beloved. I understood that. She was not going to inhabit a cartoon. No way. That was her honesty. That is what we were meant to understand about each other.

As close as I got to Colleen, never, ever did I hear her malign George. I gave her away at their second wedding. It is always very emotional for me to see George, although we don't ever mention Colleen, yet I know there was always deep respect and affection between them, in spite of everything. But every time we see each other or I see others, such as Elizabeth Wilson, it is like a Colleen Dewhurst movie flashing before me, and all of those years we spent together come back. I can hardly believe that Colleen is not still a part of my world. She is, for me, always alive. I don't have to see her. I know that she is there, still there, bursting forth. Colleen gave me courage. I think that had I not met her, had I not loved her, I could not have done the things that I did. As I said, she was my true sister.

17

"It's absolutely not too long."

There were many times when José Quintero, Jason Robards and I would be interviewed by a group of newspaper and magazine people on the subject of Eugene O'Neill. Whenever I would be thrown questions such as what did I feel was the influence of Mr. O'Neill's seafaring days or something or another, I would say, "Ladies and gentlemen, I know nothing about this. I have not studied O'Neill's life. I don't care to know any more about his personal life than I have to. Mr. Quintero and Mr. Robards are the experts on O'Neill. If you want to ask me about the woman I am playing, that is all I know at this moment. What you are handed is a script. If you like that script, you do it. If it is a good play, the playwright has given you all the information you need. Next question."

One of the points made by Harold Clurman and Stella Adler is that if the play takes place in a time that you are not familiar with, you should study what the politics were, who was writing then, who was painting, right down to why the costume you are to wear was designed that way.

In the case of O'Neill, I can no longer pretend to respond in the same way, having years later done Barbara Gelb's *My Gene*—a one-woman show in which I played O'Neill's last wife, Carlotta Monterey. To play Carlotta, it was necessary to understand in some depth more about O'Neill and his personal life. Going through the extraordinary and insane relationship of these two people, night after night, for over one hundred performances, I began to realize that in many ways, I instinctually did understand Mr. O'Neill and therefore, in many ways, his women. This only confirmed for me that just as within the text of O'Neill's work, as with any good playwright, the play written by Barbara Gelb held for me all the information I needed. I still did not need to do exhaustive research on his life beyond that play. An important part of my doing O'Neill will always be that a Panamanian named José Quintero had the instinctual understanding of this second-generation Irishman and his characters. His great talent is to be able to communicate to his actors the same passion, intensity and commitment that he felt for what O'Neill was saying about the human condition.

CLIFFORD STEVENS

Colleen and I met on a play, Shakespeare's *Titus Andronicus,* in late autumn of 1956. We were working for Joe Papp, down in a church on East Sixth Street between Avenues C and D, a very tough neighborhood, then and now. In fact, after the first rehearsal, we were told never to leave the theater in groups of fewer than eight. We were all just getting started. Joe was in his infancy as a producer, having been a stage manager at CBS, and *Titus* was one of the first productions of what would eventually be called the New York Shakespeare Festival.

I remember that it was very cold in that church; of course, we were rehearsing and playing in some place that wasn't heated. It was a typical Lower East Side, way off-off-off-Broadway situation, as still goes on today, probably in that same church. Colleen was our leading lady and absolutely magnificent-looking. I don't recall many of the other actors. Colleen's husband at the time, Jim Vickery, was one of the Romans, and there was Roscoe [Lee Browne], and a very good character actor, Leonard Stone, was Titus. I don't recall that any of the rest went on to fame or fortune. Now, I didn't really have any connection with Colleen in the production; after all, she was the leading lady and I was nineteen years old, in the chorus, and wearing body makeup and some costume made of red velvet that would have been too brief for Sabu. But since it was so cold, I came to rehearsals with a thermos of some lethal stuff called Old Overholt. It could take your face off, but when added generously to tea, certainly helped beat the cold. So when I wasn't onstage, which was often, I would slip off into a corner and sip away at this stuff. One day, Colleen must have got a whiff of it. The next thing I know, we're sharing the thermos and before long, I'm coming to rehearsal with tea for two. Even then, I was very much in awe of her. We would chat over the thermos and soon became friendly, like you do with fellow actors when you're in a play. After *Titus* closed, I went to see her in other plays. She did three in quick succession after that—I couldn't tell you what they were, but she met some terrible death in each. Around that time, there was a wonderful review by Walter Kerr in which he wondered if Colleen would ever do a play where she was allowed to live to the end.

After that early off-Broadway period in the late 1950s, I didn't see Colleen for a number of years. I was in Europe, living a whole other life. Colleen began to get more and better work onstage and in live television, in addition to marrying George—for the first time—and starting a family. Jane Broder was her longtime agent here in New York. Eventually, I got back from Europe and went to work for Bill Peters, one of the few independent agents at that time who had offices here in New York City, and in Los Angeles, where he represented Colleen for Jane. I had very little to do with her then, but that is where our paths crossed for the second time.

I remember going backstage at Circle in the Square to visit Colleen after seeing her in the revival of Eugene O'Neill's *Mourning Becomes Electra*, a production I think we would all rather forget about. But Colleen had always wanted to do it, so Ted Mann presented it as Circle's inaugural production when the company moved from downtown in the Village to its new theater on West Fiftieth Street and Broadway. Forgive me, but it's a perfectly dreadful play. Many of the early O'Neill plays are a problem; in fact, Jason says he'd only ever do the last four: *Ah, Wilderness!*, *The Iceman Cometh*, *A Moon for the Misbegotten* and *Long Day's Journey into Night*. So I went back after the performance, introduced myself, and reminded her of where we had met, over spiked tea, many years before. Colleen got that vacant stare in her eyes that we all know. She didn't know who the fuck I was. I didn't see her again until the revival of *A Moon for the Misbegotten* in 1973.

Now there are so many stories about how *Moon* got started, so let me tell you the true story. This is exactly how it happened. Jason called me in the spring. José Quintero was finally in shape again to get a job. He had been on the wagon, but his past had caught up with him long before. Jason is a good and loyal friend, and he wanted to do something for José. There was still a lively summer-stock circuit at that time, much more so than today, so I said, "What do you want to do?"

"*A Touch of the Poet*," he said.

"Well, I can't do anything with that," I replied. Then he says, "How about *A Moon for the Misbegotten*?" I thought, *Maybe.* I was familiar with *Moon*, because I had worked on the very first New York production of the play, starring Wendy Hiller and Franchot Tone, as a production assistant. So I started to call around to a few people. There was a very limited time where everyone would be available. Colleen had to go off to do some biblical television epic in Israel, and Jason was booked to do another play, so there was only a seven- or eight-week period where they both were free. I'd call these stock producers and say, "I have Colleen Dewhurst and Jason Robards," and they'd get very excited. Then I'd say ". . . in *Moon for the Misbegotten*," and the chill that would come over the phone was like ice. One producer, who is still with us so I'll spare him the embarrassment of naming him, actually came back with, "What? No, no. Can't they do *Plaza Suite*?" I thought not.

After calling nearly everyone, I had a moment of recollection of the Lake Forest Theatre in Chicago, where another client of mine, Brian Bedford, had done a number of interesting plays, like *Blithe Spirit* and *The Tavern*, during the summer. At this point, I had really given up on ever getting this done anywhere, but I called Marshall Migatz, the man who ran the theater, and was very aggressive with him on the phone, anticipating yet another "No!" or "Are you kidding?"

"Marshall!" I said. "I have Jason Robards, Colleen Dewhurst, José Quintero and *Moon for the Misbegotten*. Do you want it?"

"Who wouldn't want it?" he replied, practically gasping. Well, I wasn't going to answer that question. So I gave him the dates. Marshall had something already booked in the theater at that time, but was so excited he canceled it and flew immediately to New York to sign contracts with everyone. After Marshall died in a traffic accident, quite surprisingly, the production went ahead anyway. I had planned to go to Greece during the exact three weeks that *Moon* would be playing in Lake Forest and, mind you, at that point no one thought much of this production, so I didn't give up the trip. I talked to Jason during rehearsals by phone, long distance. He kept saying that all was going very well. Who knew? I still didn't think much about it. What's to go wrong in three weeks? I went to London after Greece and spoke to Jason again, who told me that *Moon* had opened in Lake Forest and had become something of a sensation. Maybe, he thought, we should do something else with it. But by the time I got back to New York, Elliot Martin had already snagged the rights. I didn't talk to Colleen about any of this until opening night of *Moon* in Washington, D.C. This time she remembered me, but the first thing she said was, "Is it too long?"

"No," I assured her, "it is absolutely not too long."

I didn't see Colleen again until *Moon*'s opening night on Broadway at the Morosco Theatre, December 26, 1973. Even though it was such a sensation in Washington, people were still hedging their bets on the show. Producers Elliot Martin and Lester Osterman chose to open on a Saturday night, giving them the option of closing the next day without having to pay anyone for even another week. But the evening was everything you imagine and wish an opening night to be. The company was upset because the producers refused to pay for an opening-night party, so Jason, José and Colleen had everyone over to Delsomma's, an Italian restaurant in the theater district that Colleen loved. When Elliot Martin got up to read aloud the *New York Times* review, which was an extraordinary rave, everyone went crazy, screaming, shouting and laughing. It was a night like no other since. Once they threw us out of Delsomma's, we all went downtown in fleets of cabs to some bar in Abingdon Square that Jason knew and assured us had never asked anyone to leave. Everyone got very stinko. I can remember sitting with my arms around Colleen and hers around me and just singing and crying and laughing and crying and drinking and crying. The front of my tuxedo was soaked with her tears. Don't ask me how any of us got home that night. But you know the rest. The show that practically couldn't be booked and that no one thought would run a week was a smash, a historic smash.

That was really the beginning of my professional relationship with Colleen. Colleen's dear friend and original agent, Jane Broder, was still alive, but she was at least eighty by that time and not doing very well. Nevertheless, Jane maintained a great deal of dignity, and Colleen very much wanted her to feel a part of all that she did. So, even though I would handle negotiations, we would conspire to include Jane in all of Colleen's professional decisions. Colleen would sign a contract for a job, and I would then say to one of my assistants, "Bring this to Miss Broder!" Jane would read it over and more often than not call Colleen to say, "I don't understand why you're getting all this money. You don't deserve this!" Colleen would then call me and just scream with laughter. Eventually, Jane's health failed her. She died while Colleen was on a cruise ship. When word reached her, Colleen was very upset and insisted on getting to the service. God knows what she went through, getting off the boat and onto a plane back to the States, but she arrived at the cemetery, literally as services were drawing to a close. There were only a handful of people there—Bob Whitehead, Peter Lawrence, me, and a few others. It was very sad but so perfect that Colleen arrived in that way. She adored Jane.

From then on, Colleen officially became my client. We sustained a professional and, of course, a considerable personal relationship. It was a very unique relationship that I have with few of my clients. But how could you resist her? Colleen had basically two groups of people in her life: those she loved and those she despised. She had a unique outlook on friendship. If she loved you and cared about you, you could do practically anything and she would excuse it. She would find a reason or a way to understand what you were doing. There was simply an incredible amount of love and warmth for those she let into her heart. At the same time, that laugh that everyone still talks about today masked a great deal that was not funny. That laugh could also be one step away from a howl of rage.

But laugh we did, especially whenever she would come to stay in the house I had on Fire Island in the early 1980s. I had given Colleen her own key so that she could go out whenever she liked during the week when I wasn't there. She loved the beach and was very comfortable out there in this house which wasn't fixed up in any fancy way and with people, gay men primarily, who knew who she was and were thrilled to see her but would let her move around with ease, without that feeling of being stared at that happens to celebrities when they're out in a place as public as the beach. Let's face it; there's too much else to stare at on Fire Island for any one person to grab all the attention. But there was one particularly infamous visit that she spent in the middle of the week with Guy Pace, one of the executives at Actors' Equity, that by the time I arrived on Friday, had already become part of the Island's colorful lore.

GUY PACE

I had been renting in The Pines on Fire Island for a number of years and had just gotten to know Colleen, who was by then president of Equity. We had worked together on two projects for the union, rewriting the regulations governing the relationship between actors and their agents, and leading Equity's lobbying efforts in Washington, D.C., to maintain miscellaneous deductions for actors in the 1987 tax bill. By August, we were finished with both. I told Colleen I was going off for a week to "the Island," as Fire Island is called, and she said that she was heading out there as well to spend some time at Clifford's.

Sometime that midweek, we met for dinner and had a wonderful time watching the sun set over the bay and talking about the union, plans she had and things she wanted to accomplish, just shooting the breeze over a wonderful meal. We sat for such a long while that by the end of the dinner, people began to recognize her. In fact, two friends of mine joined us from another table. That's when the wine came out. By the time we left, over two hours and more than a few bottles later, there were about eight people crowded around our table and no one—Colleen and myself included—was feeling any pain. As my friends and I walked Colleen back to Clifford's, she kept repeating, "Water. I need water," and would veer off the boardwalk and run toward the ocean, shouting, "Let's swim!" over her shoulder. Well, it was well past two in the morning. There was no moon. It was pitch black and Colleen is heading toward the surf. We ran after her and somehow convinced her that now was not a good time to take a dip, and we headed back home along the boardwalk.

Suddenly, Colleen stops. "I hear a pool," she says. And before anyone can stop her, she dashes up the walkway to this dark house, opens the front gate, runs to the patio. From the boardwalk, we hear a splash as Colleen dives into the pool. As we take off after her again, the lights come on in the house and someone shouts, "Hello?"

"Is this John's house?" I shout back, just trying to make something up to explain why we're there.

"No. Who the hell are you?" Just then, Colleen, who is still splashing around in the pool, bobs up for air.

"Anyone have any wine?" she shouts. "I need some wine." Now, Colleen's voice is rather distinctive and the person on the balcony—whom we still can't see—shouts back, "Is that Colleen?"

"It's me," she affirms.

"Red or white?" he calls back.

And before you can say *chardonnay*, Colleen and about six gay men are having a rather loud early-morning pool party, sipping wine, laughing and splashing about in the pool in various stages of drunkenness and undress. These guys couldn't believe that Colleen Dewhurst was floating around their pool, glass in hand, at three o'clock in the morning. Finally, at about five o'clock, we manage to get Colleen out of the pool, dried off and dressed. Everyone's kissing good-bye. "Thank you, thank you, thank you for inviting us." The guys who live there are saying this to *Colleen*, you understand, as we leave *their* house, staggering up the boardwalk in the dawn's first light. Now there was no way I was going to leave Colleen alone at Clifford's, figuring she would head right for the ocean again, or worse, someone else's pool. So we went back to my place, where I put Colleen to bed before falling asleep on the couch. I got up first, sometime around noon, and was in the kitchen slowly making coffee when Colleen emerged from the bedroom, wearing an old bathrobe she found, squinting into the light and rubbing the back of her neck.

"Was I bad?" she mumbled. I said nothing, just squinted back at her and carefully placed a mug of coffee in her two hands. "OK," she replied, answering her own question. It was a very late, very quiet breakfast. I heard from Clifford later that when Colleen went to meet him that afternoon at the ferry, her first words to him were, "I'm afraid Mother was very bad last night."

"What happened?" Clifford asked.

"I have no idea," she said, looking up from under her hand which was holding up her head. "You should ask Guy."

People just fell in love with her all over the island. She came out a number of times over the next couple of summers and ended up hosting a number of the very first AIDS benefits that were done out there. But I'm afraid her legacy, at least as far as Fire Island is concerned, will always be that early-morning, impromptu pool party.

18

"Yes, I could smell the booze."

Half hour, ladies and gentlemen," came the static-filled voice of our stage manager, Mark Wright, from the squawk box across the room from my dressing table backstage at the Music Box Theatre. "Half hour." I could hear Ben's footsteps above me, pacing back and forth.

"Fifteen minutes, ladies and gentlemen. Fifteen minutes." I looked at myself in the mirror. I was ready, in costume and makeup. I sat very still, my reflection staring back at me. My God, my lips were twitching. I had to bite them lightly to make them stop. I sat there quietly, feeling the tension move through my body, trying to relax my neck and shoulders, feeling myself only tighten more. I could still hear Ben's footsteps above me, walking back and forth, back and forth.

Finally, "Places, ladies and gentlemen. Places." I stood up and turned to embrace my dresser, Darthula, whom I dearly love and who had been with me through the great success of *Moon* and numerous other almost hits and full-fledged flops since an abominable production *The Good Woman of Setzuan* that I had the misfortune to be a part of at Lincoln Center. We hold on for a minute, each of us taking some little bit of strength and, I think, even courage from the other, and then I'm off. Down the stairs, across the back of the stage, hearing whispered "love" and "luck, Colleen" from the crew.

Ben Gazzara, my wonderful and intrepid costar in this just-about-to-open revival of *Who's Afraid of Virginia Woolf?* arrives just as I do. We embrace, standing in the soft glow of two little lights that William Rittman, the stage designer, has put outside the stage-set front door. We wait.

"Mark, what's the problem?" I whisper, when I can finally wait like this no longer.

"We have a hold out front," he says, meaning in the audience. I can feel Ben squeeze my hand. We are not looking at each other. Instead, we stare at the floor. I find myself glancing at the curtains in the stage-set window, noticing their pattern for the first time. My adrenaline is now pumping so fast that I can feel it in my temples. I am beginning to feel as if I might scream. My hand tightens around Ben's.

"Fuck the front!" Ben shouts, his voice ripping through the tense silence backstage. "Take up the goddamn curtain!" And without missing a beat, I hear Mark comply. "Curtain going up. Curtain going up."

We turn, walk up the steps, push open the door and enter, the first of Edward Albee's ferocious words spilling onto the stage.

IN THE summer of 1962, I was in a house on the beach in California with George and the boys, desperately trying to make some much-needed money, taking any work we could get, mostly forgettable episodic television. While there, I was sent a script by Jane Broder. I was astonished by its size. It looked more like a novel than a script. It was *Who's Afraid of Virginia Woolf?* I had been offered the role of Martha, in the cast that was to play the matinee performances. Unfortunately, I could not take the part because after months of looking for good work, George had just been offered a film that was to shoot in England and Ireland, and I was to go with him.

Soon after, I ran into Arthur Hill, with whom I had played *All the Way Home* and who had been cast as George opposite Uta Hagen's Martha in *Virginia Woolf;* he was just about to return to New York to begin rehearsals. I gathered up the courage to ask him for two tickets to opening night. I am usually loath to do this sort of thing, but I felt that this was going to be a very special night in the theater. Months later, as the opening of *Virginia Woolf* on Broadway approached, I received a message saying that Arthur had set aside two tickets for me at the box office. I couldn't believe that he had so sweetly remembered our conversation in the midst of what had to have been an exhausting rehearsal and preview period. There was an air of excitement in the audience that went beyond my wildest expectations. The performances by Uta, Arthur, George Grizzard and Melinda Dillon were as close to perfection as you could come. This was not just a special opening night. Both the playwright and the cast made theater history that night.

Years later, in the summer of 1975, I was at my beloved home on Prince Edward Island off the coast of Canada. I had finished doing *A Moon for the Misbegotten* four months before, and was searching for another play. Ken Marsolais and I had read and discussed many new plays, but kept coming back to one of our first considerations, *Virginia Woolf.* We felt that after twelve years, enough time had elapsed to do a revival. I had done *The Ballad of the Sad Café* and *All Over* with Edward Albee and knew that he was interested in directing. I thought we could create more excitement than might otherwise surround a revival of *Virginia Woolf* if it was directed by the playwright. In short order, an agreement was reached with Edward and with Richard Barr, the show's original producer, who would produce this time with Ken. We came back to New York very excited about the future.

We quickly ran into a problem that we had never anticipated. In the New York theater—then and now—there is a very short list of leading men of an age and caliber who could do the part of George: Jason Robards, George Scott, Ben Gazzara, Arthur Hill and Christopher Plummer came immediately to mind (and would again now, nearly twenty years later). We approached them all, but for various reasons, none could do it. By December, we were still without a "George," and returning once again to our original list, called Ben to ask him again. This time he agreed. We were ecstatic.

We rehearsed on the West Coast because Ben had been working on a film that was being edited there and he had to be in the vicinity for reshoots and looping. I was thrilled to be able to rent a house again on the beach and finally be in rehearsal for this magnificent play. To me, the first day of rehearsal is one of the most exciting and frightening experiences in the theater. You know what your destination is, but you're creating the map only once you've left port. We had gotten together a wonderful cast. Maureen Anderman, a beautiful woman and wonderful actress as well as a friend of Edward's, was to play Honey. The part of Nick was to be played by Richard Kelton. There we all were, finally, in the Masonic Hall on Hollywood Boulevard, ready to begin. Across the hall, Julie Harris was rehearsing *The Belle of Amherst*, with Charles Nelson Reilly directing.

"I'm looking forward to working on this with you," Edward said that first day, "because it is only now, after twelve years, that I think I finally understand what I wrote."

We had scarcely begun when Charles Nelson Reilly burst into the room announcing that "Julie and I are across the hall. Now I certainly hope you won't be blasting us out of there. I know we've got a roomful of shouters here. And there's Julie and I with this delicate, lovely, soft play. Try not to kill each other," he begged. "We scare easily." It was a wonderful scene and broke all of our first-day jitters.

There was something wonderful about being isolated in this old Masonic Temple, *Who's Afraid of Virginia Woolf?* coming back to life in one room and *The Belle of Amherst* being born in the other. Charles and Julie asked all of us to come to their first performance in a tiny theater in West Hollywood. That night Julie, too, had pushed bravely out to sea. It was lovely to see such a beautiful actress step onto this tiny womb-like stage and create an unforgettable illusion that would carry her across the country and finally to triumph on Broadway.

In the meantime, we were at it with Edward, always compassionate, allowing us free rein to try different things, until we got to the third act. Here he became very specific about the end of his play. There has always been much discussion about the imaginary child and what he meant to George and Martha. In that area, Edward was very much the director. He knew exactly what he wanted and exactly how he wanted it done.

During rehearsals, Edward stayed at the Westwood Motel. One night, he invited a few of us over for a game of bridge. Before everyone arrived, Edward took me to a lovely Japanese restaurant, well known for its sushi. Edward had introduced me to sushi in New York. Once again, he did all the ordering, being quite secretive about it all. He knew exactly what he wanted. Shortly, I was presented with a sushi tray the likes of which I don't expect I'll ever see again. I didn't ask what Edward had ordered. I simply ate, trusting his taste and judgment implicitly. It was delicious.

We returned to his apartment before the others arrived. I began to look around his motel suite, fascinated by the fact that, although we had been in L.A. for only ten days, the tables and floors were piled high with books and records.

"Did you bring all these with you?" I asked.

"No, of course not," he laughed. "They're from a few wonderful discoveries I've made." He went on to tell me of a bookstore, run by a fascinating man with whom he could talk about any and various publications, and other record and magazine shops he had wandered into. Apparently, while the rest of us were going home, falling into bed and studying the script, Edward was out walking the streets of Hollywood, listening to people and finding places that those who had lived there for twenty years didn't know about or ignored. I looked at his books—handbooks, obscure children's books, books of poetry and philosophy. I had only learned the quickest route from the beach to the parking lot beyond the Masonic Temple and the contents of his brilliant script. Edward's brilliance could not be contained in that repetition. He needed to explore and find much more, creating room in him for works yet to be written.

After three and a half weeks of rehearsal, we began our reentry into the real world, flying back East for a one-week stand in New Haven, Connecticut. There we were joined by Betty Miller, a lovely actress and longtime friend who had agreed to stand by for me, and my dear Jimmy Karen, whom I had met years ago, stood by for Jason in *Moon* and had agreed as a friend to stand by for Ben. Now we were faced with the reality that we were actually going to do it. Discovery was over. Now came the thrill and particular warmth that comes when they take the lights out in the house and the lights come up for the first time on that one and only set. We were now a company together on the road. There, far from home and everything familiar, everything accelerates. Intimate bonds are formed and formalities broken as you get to know each other strictly on the crest of your working together and now living together, eating together, drinking together, and sharing bits of yourself that would never need to be shared if you could retreat each day to the safety of family and home.

The New Haven Theatre, which at that time had seen better days (and thankfully, since our stint, has been renovated into actually living them again), was in a dangerous section of town. We were told never to leave the theater unescorted. It saddened me to see what had become of this once-beautiful home to so many successful productions, plays taking their first steps to Broadway and, in some case, making theater history. In this now-faded auditorium, great actors and actresses had played, leaving behind the brilliant memories and colorful anecdotes that continue to fire the imaginations of all who love a play.

After our first performance, Jimmy and I walked together to Benjamin's hotel room, where he cued us both. This gradually deteriorated into just talk—discussions of our children, what they are like, what we want for them, what we fear for them. This time ultimately turned out to be more important for our relationship onstage than the mere repetition of lines. Another night, after dinner and some drinks, again walking from the theater together, we spotted a lighted dance studio on the second floor of an old building. Up the stairs we went, Ben, Jimmy, Maureen and I, where we danced and carried on. Benjamin and Maureen could do quite an incredible tango.

Despite our offstage camaraderie, New Haven was not successful for us. We were still unsure and did not have the security onstage that we so badly needed. But that is what tryouts are for. The important thing is that we just kept at it, doing the real work, playing the play at night, rehearsing during the day with Edward, whose notes became only more precise and to the point.

We were all looking forward to Boston and a chance to play in the beautifully refurbished Colonial Theatre. It was waiting for us. We were ready for it. Now the honing began, the sharpening, the clarifying that would express the demons buried deep in Edward's script. We also began to see friends from New York who had come to celebrate or cry with us, whichever the case might be. If I wasn't seeing visitors, Benjamin and Jimmy would coerce me to join them in their carousings after the show. Most often, I could not last their distance and, at some point, they would gallantly return me to my hotel, bid me good-bye from the elevator, and disappear until morning.

After just such a night, I was awakened at five o'clock the next morning by bangings on my wall and bursts of laughter followed by footsteps receding down the hall. I gratefully rolled over and fell back asleep. At eleven o'clock, the phone rang. It was Jimmy, calling before I awoke, as he somehow often managed to do, to tell me of the doings of the night before.

"Did you hear us last night?" he whispered conspiratorially.

"Yes, in fact I did. Thank you for not knocking twice."

"We should have," he continued. "Guess who was with us?"

"Who?"

Jimmy started laughing, not answering my question.

"Who?" I asked again. "Don't do this to me."

"Clive Barnes," he answered, bursting, once again, into gales of laughter.

"Stop it. Now tell me who," I pleaded. There was a moment of silence in which I realized he was telling the truth. "You're joking." Jimmy proceeded to tell me how he and Benjamin had found Mr. Barnes in the Copley bar after depositing me in my room. Clive Barnes was at that time the drama critic for the *New York Times*. After doing a bit of the town, they returned to Ben's room for a nightcap. My mind reeled with horror as Jimmy continued to tell me what a great time they had and how he and Ben had a very deep discussion with Barnes about love and marriage, with Ben, of course, telling Barnes how to run his life. They then proceeded to discuss our play, which Jim said culminated in Ben ripping a rave review from a Boston paper that happened to be lying nearby and telling Barnes to study it well while he was in the bathroom. My end of the conversation consisted entirely of "Oh, my God," "Christ, no," and "That does it, we're fucked," and finally ended with me convulsed in hysterical laughter mumbling something like "Ken is going to kill you both."

I am still amazed at the fortitude of those two men. They arrived on time for a one o'clock interview—Jimmy rosy-cheeked, showered and shaved, Benjamin wearing what I began to call his "boiled bulldog face." I couldn't even look at them without beginning to giggle, wondering if Clive Barnes had much of a memory for what he read after long nights on the town.

If he did, Mr. Barnes never mentioned the incident.

Our thoughts began to turn toward New York. Soon into the run in Boston we settled into a fairly consistent interpretation of the play. We felt we were ready. One night, Clifford Stevens, who had been my agent since Jane Broder retired, came to see us. Afterward, as we were having supper together, he told me how much he had enjoyed the play and the performance. We sat together for a while talking. I only trust a handful of people to talk to me about interpretation of a role while I am working. One, of course, is the director. The other is a close friend like Clifford, who is willing and can honestly address the pitfalls I face as well as the assets I have as an actress. Clifford knows what he has seen and has the great tact not to offer any suggestions unless asked.

"Do you have any suggestions?" I asked him. "Anything that I am missing?"

"Just one small thing," he said. "I don't smell the booze."

I will never forget that comment. It was not some long-winded review. It was a simple observation, concise and even perhaps a bit obscure. But I knew exactly what he meant. I went upstairs and got into bed, thinking for over an hour about what he said, "I can't smell the booze." I woke up thinking about it and that night, came onstage feeling the soddenness of someone who had been drinking for a very long time, the mental dampness and the dull physical exhaustion that every drunk pushes through. It wasn't important if it was noticeable to anyone else but me; it gave me just the added edge that I wanted, that I needed, that I had not been conscious of. Drunk is an obvious characteristic to play, but if you live with it on your breath, on your clothes and in your hair day after day, that is quite something else.

Unfortunately, the handwriting on the wall first began to appear, but we all chose not to see it, to ignore it. I was beginning to be stopped in restaurants and on the streets by people telling me how they would love to see me work, but they had recently seen the film or a production of the play somewhere and just couldn't take an evening of *Who's Afraid of Virginia Woolf?* again. I misjudged the power of the film which had been perfectly done nine years before by Richard Burton and Elizabeth Taylor under the direction of Mike Nichols. By now, the material had become too familiar. Perhaps twelve years indeed wasn't a long enough time to bring in a revival, even with Edward directing. This we had felt would interest people who had seen it twelve years before and be an incredible opportunity for those who were too young to have seen the original production.

Nevertheless, our sights were now set on New York and on the very real joy of going to a theater and doing a great play night after night. As with every opening night on Broadway, it is like being hurtled through a dark tunnel. Nothing seen, nothing remembered, just catapulted along, until the curtain comes down and you are suddenly standing in the dressing room, watching, listening, laughing and crying. Faces pushed toward me. In the crush, I saw Clifford making his way to me. We embraced. "Did you smell it?" I asked.

"Yes," he replied. "I could smell the booze." The reviews were fair to excellent, but we were never really able to get rolling at the box office. Despite the excellence of the play and the good work of each of us in the cast, we did not catch the imagination of the theater audience. But before we closed, just four months later, there were nights I could sit offstage and listen to scenes that I was not in and be continually amazed and thrilled by something new. The complexity of Edward's play is infinite. The belly laugh is undercut by agony, the truth is discovered in old wounds and fresh blood. It was an incredible experience to play every night.

In July of 1976, the bicentennial year, we closed. Perhaps the nation was too eager for some sort of celebration—even a false one—to embrace so much of the ugliness and beauty of the human condition. Edward, Ken and Richard Barr tried their best to keep us running, but we could not.

I hated to lose this play. We were each so proud of having done it and of having one of those rare theatrical experiences, a play that you love, done with a company you adore. We closed on a Sunday matinee. Benjamin and I found ourselves again, but for the last time, standing in front of the door. Our door. Again, there was a hold out front. Last performances are sometimes as fraught as opening nights. We were sold out to the rafters.

When Mark called, "Curtain going up," Ben and I entered, filled with that adrenaline of wanting to make this performance the best ever. But as the courtesy applause turned into a theatrical farewell, we weren't sure what to do. We held for a moment, not looking at each other, before Ben, as directed, would walk across the stage. Normally, I turned and threw my coat to Benjamin. That afternoon, I walked across and handed it to him. Our hands met under the coat. We looked at each other and held on for dear life as we saw tears coming into each other's eyes.

And we exploded into performance, saying our good-bye to this most magnificent play.

DARTHULA MCQUEEN

I was Colleen's dresser. It was my job to help her with fast changes and see that all of her costumes were ready. But mostly, I just did whatever was needed to make Colleen comfortable, you know, so that she wouldn't have anything to worry about and could just mind what she had to do onstage. I was always in the dressing room.

I must have first worked for her over thirty years ago, in a production of *The Good Woman of Setzuan* at Lincoln Center. I was at the Vivian Beaumont Theatre at the time and had dressed a lot of people: Jessica Tandy, Pearl Bailey, even Sammy Davis, Jr. And oh my, each one of those people is a story all to themselves. But for this play, Colleen had to change from a woman to a man and back to a woman. There were some pretty fast changes in there. Well, we got on right away and just sort of fell in love with each other and from then on, I was her dresser. In fact, she even had me put in her contract for every show after that. Even if Colleen was in a show where she didn't have any changes, she would always make sure that I was the costume supervisor so that I could be there with her. I was very proud of that.

Now, some people will tell you some pretty crazy things about that play, *Good Woman of Setzuan*, but I thought it was fantastic. Every play Colleen did was fantastic to me. Colleen was very easy to get along with. She liked to do as much for herself as she could. She was always very independent. So I let her do it. I could see she didn't like people fussing over her. But if she needed something, I was always there for her.

Colleen hated to shop. She didn't like to buy clothes for herself. So, as I got to know her better, I would shop for her. She liked nice casual clothes. Jeans and things. Sweaters, mostly. She liked Saks. But it didn't really matter where they came from as long as the clothes were comfortable. She wouldn't wear anything that made her feel uneasy.

Colleen and I did a lot of shows together that I can't even remember anymore. But I will always remember *A Moon for the Misbegotten*. She was beautiful in that. Just great. That's when I started to call her the Earth Mother. Not for any fancy reason, just because we were becoming such friends and she always made me feel comfortable about myself.

But you know we didn't talk much about the plays. We both had sons about the same age, so we'd discuss our boys. We'd give each other advice, hope for the best, share a lot of what those children would get into. One of her sons was having some trouble once, just about the same time that I was having problems with my oldest boy. We were a comfort to each other at that time. We couldn't do much about what was happening. But we would talk about how we felt and how much we loved those boys. And we would pray. I talked to Colleen a lot about prayer. She had a great heart and whenever one of us would have a particular problem, we would pray about it and, you know, something always happened. It would work out.

I loved Colleen. She encouraged me to have confidence in myself. She told me I could do anything I wanted to do. And I did. I enjoyed being her dresser. She was such a caring person. During *A Moon for the Misbegotten* when there were so many people who wanted to come backstage and see her, she would not let anyone in her dressing room until she had changed back into her street clothes and I had left. I lived quite a ways away and she would not let me stay late just because she had guests.

Now, Colleen wasn't a very neat person. I kept it neat for her though. And she wasn't a saint. I saw her lose her temper a few times. But she never lost it with me. She lost her temper with Jason when he was drinking, but that's because she loved him. She lost her temper with George, too. Same reason. Even after he was gone, his new wife would call Colleen and ask her to talk to George. She always seemed to be the one that could reach him and do the most for him.

Colleen tried so hard to stop smoking. That bothered me a lot, the smoking. She told me once that she thought it was going to cause her death. Well, we all have to die with something, no matter what it is. If it's not smoking, it's something else. That's not what matters. It's how you live and Colleen lived a good life. She did a lot of good for a lot of people. I came into the city and we went out to dinner on Broadway about six months before she passed. We just chatted. She was such a wonderful person and I miss her. I think about her often. You know, I have a poster from *Queen and the Rebels* that Colleen signed for me. She wrote, "Dearest Darthula, As always, I love you. We will do this again and again forever. Love, Colleen."

Knowing Colleen made me a better person, a stronger person. It's the truth. I'm just telling you how I feel about her.

EDWARD ALBEE

I had known Colleen's work for years. As far back as my memory of New York theater goes, Colleen is a part of it. My admiration for her goes back a long way. Colleen was one of two or three actors that I have worked with in any frequency who were invaluable to me. She was one of Albee's women. She understood and had an intuitive response to what I was trying to say. She gave extraordinary performances in *The Ballad of the Sad Café, All Over* and, of course, *Who's Afraid of Virginia Woolf?*

I always insist on cast approval in all my productions. While I'm very happy to work with the producer and director, the final choice must be mine. I've always been able to judge when someone was right or not—and in the case of some of the actresses, Colleen, of course, and Jessica Tandy, who were absolutely on target from their first reading. If you've chosen the right actors, they will give you the enthusiasm that they had in the first cold reading. Of course, in rehearsal they must start all over and dismantle everything. But actresses such as these knew what my lines should sound like, when the attitudes should turn. You didn't really have to give them stage directions; they knew.

When we did *The Ballad of the Sad Café,* she and Alan Schneider, the director, did not get along. There was always one person in every production that Alan did who didn't get along with him, but it was very seldom the star. Alan was a splendid director, but I think there might have just been a chemical thing between them that kept them from liking each other. Alan was enormously methodical, meticulous and detailed. Colleen didn't work that way, she didn't live that way. I do know that Alan occasionally had trouble with strong women. Uta Hagen and Alan did not get along terribly well in *Who's Afraid of Virginia Woolf?*, and memory tells me that Irene Worth and Alan didn't get along well. So maybe the problem is there.

On *Ballad,* they disagreed about interpretation basically. From the start, Colleen looked to Alan for the explanation of what happened on Miss Amelia's wedding night. Alan couldn't answer the question, because I couldn't answer the question, because Carson McCullers left it the unanswerable question. I remember telling Alan that he, Colleen and I were going to have to come up with some subtext as to what happened that night offstage. Well, we didn't and they couldn't.

Colleen and Jessica Tandy worked wonderfully together in *All Over.* I thought Colleen was splendid as the mistress. That was directed by John Gielgud. Colleen was a little concerned about her hips and her ass. She liked those nicely covered. I remember her tugging at her costume. But actors and costumes, it's a cover-up. Literally and figuratively. If they tell you they are unhappy about their costume, they are up to something else, some other insecurity. I liked her performance.

Colleen was smoking an awful lot during *All Over* and it was taking a terrible toll on her vocal cords. I finally had to tell her during rehearsal either to keep smoking onstage and stop offstage or stop smoking onstage, one of the two. I couldn't tell you which she did, which prompts me to believe she did neither. But it was doing serious damage to her performance. She was destroying a glorious voice.

My concern with actors is that they are prone to want to cover over their own identities. The best actors have strong personalities. They are not chameleons. Colleen was like that onstage. I was always aware that Colleen was the character and that was good. I despair for actors who do not let their personalities be consumed into the character they are playing. Colleen was always able to do that, perhaps because she always chose roles where she knew she could do that. Even with me, there was a play I wanted Colleen to do, *The Lady from Dubuque*, that she wouldn't do. We talked about it a lot, but she just didn't think she was right.

What Colleen did beautifully was *Who's Afraid of Virginia Woolf?* No two productions of a play should be identical, unless you are using identical actors and they take place within two months of each other, because the actors aren't the same after a period and no two actors are going to accomplish the same results in exactly the same way. I was very happy to have Colleen play Martha because if there was anything that I thought Alan Schnieder's original production, with Uta Hagen and Arthur Hill in 1963, missed, it was both the sexuality of the relationship between George and Martha and some of the humor. I didn't change a line and I didn't change the nature of the characters. Yet, casting Colleen made things more classical, a bit funnier. Working on *Virginia Woolf* was a very happy time. I know she loved working with Ben Gazzara—when he would show up on time. The production got great reviews. It was very, very good. I was disappointed it didn't run forever.

The only time I saw Colleen do bad acting was on television. Oh, some of those made-for-TV movies she did. I think she was bad because she realized they were shit. She was much too much of a stage actress to accommodate a TV close-up. She was too large of an actress, much too large of a person.

I was not really a part of Colleen's social scene. We did not see that much of each other if we were not working together. But Colleen was one of the most visible people I've known. I find it hard to believe that she wasn't famous all over the world, admired by everybody, as she was by us, always. I think of Colleen all the time. I could have used her in *Three Tall Women* and much more since then. We wanted to work together on *Marriage Play*. Her death was a great shame and a great waste. But her friendship and love were—are—invaluable to me.

BEN GAZZARA

I first met Colleen when I was shooting *Anatomy of a Murder* with Jimmy Stewart and George C. Scott in Michigan in 1958. George and I became pals and hung around together through the shoot. Then one Friday, George and I were in the bar, as George and I often were, and this beautiful woman with long black hair came in. It was Colleen; she was there to visit him for the week. This was in their wooing stage. God, I remember thinking this woman had the most beautiful smile I had ever seen. It just lighted up the room—which being a bar was fairly dark.

It seemed like we were shooting on the other side of the moon. There were no planes. You had to take a train and then a bus. It was a helluva long way to come. I remember thinking, *This must be love.* Certainly no one came to see me or any of the other actors. Just Colleen for George. So she stayed a few days and I got to know her a little bit, not too well; we actually didn't see a lot of her or George while she was there. But when we did, I quickly discovered what a great sense of humor she had. I loved when she laughed. Her face got red and her eyes twinkled and she just really let loose. I loved that.

That was the only time I spent with Colleen until nearly twenty years later, when the phone rings and Edward Albee asked if I would be interested in playing George to her Martha in the revival of *Virginia Woolf.* I was very flattered that Colleen and Edward wanted this son of an Italian to play in this intellectual, highly cerebral and passionate piece. The offer came at just the right time. There was a film of mine, *The Killing of a Chinese Bookie,* that had just opened and did not fare well and my spirits were down. I took its failure very personally. But those feelings were just right to start rehearsing *Virginia Woolf,* this play about feelings. It slid me right into the character. The pain was there. I felt Colleen react to that immediately and I think she was pleased. We got along famously, workwise and otherwise.

It was a very supportive rehearsal process. Edward was a wonderful director, even as author of the piece. He was never a snob about his work at all, never suggested a line reading or looked for what had been done before. We opened out of town and then in New York to great reviews. Colleen never read them, so I read them to her. Great reviews! Some said it was the best production of *Woolf* yet, that we had found its wit, passion and sexuality. But, unfortunately, being a revival perhaps, there were no lines around the block. We didn't pack them in and ran only a few months. I think that hurt Colleen's feelings. I know it hurt mine. But we braved it out and enjoyed each other's company. It was a joy to do this play with Colleen. She brought such sensitivity and sensibility to Martha. She wasn't just a harridan. There was a wounded animal there. Her performance was filled with heartache.

Soon after we closed, somebody got the idea to do *Dance of Death* with Colleen and me and George Hearn at a repertory theater in Boston. It played successfully for a few weeks, and then that was it. I didn't see Colleen again for a few years, not until the "Night of 100 Stars," one of the those huge benefit extravaganzas, this one for The Actors' Fund at Radio City Music Hall. It was insane backstage, there were so many people dashing around. In the middle of it all, Colleen came up to me and said very simply, "Benjamin, you look good because you're happy."

"You guessed right," I said. Since we had last seen each other in Boston,

I'd changed my wife and turned my life around. She saw it, and flashing that great smile, the one I'd fallen in love with in Michigan over twenty-five years before, pulled me in to her for a hug.

MAUREEN ANDERMAN

I met Colleen in the producer's office before rehearsals began for *Who's Afraid of Virginia Woolf?* I had seen Colleen's work before—*A Moon for the Misbegotten* literally stopped my breath—but had never met her. I was very excited and terrified to be meeting this giantess of the theater. I remember walking in and seeing this big mink coat thrown across a chair. There was Colleen, in the dead of winter, in a sweater, jeans and moccasins.

It was a great revival. Colleen and Ben Gazzara were a terrific match. He's so sexy and she really needed that, demanded it even. They liked each other and there was a lot of heat onstage, which for her was good. She craved that, so it really worked. She adored Ben and always called him Benjamin or Benny. Colleen loved Edward so. Even when he would do things to displease or hurt her, she never denied his genius. Edward loved having someone in the role of Martha who was sexy, raunchy and unafraid. Not that Uta Hagen wasn't. She was all of that. But Colleen mixed it up with such a sense of humor. She and Ben had just the comic rapport that Edward wanted. He wanted people to understand that the play was more than a domestic tragedy. It was also funny, heartbreakingly funny. Colleen made that possible for him.

We had a lot of fun, Colleen, Ben, Richard Kelton, Jimmy Karen, Betty Miller, and me, particularly once we opened in New Haven and then traveled to Boston. We were kind of wild, going out after the performances, dancing and carrying on. One night, in New Haven, Ben let it be known that he wanted me to come back with him to the hotel to help him run lines. Colleen overheard this, sidled up beside me and said under her breath, "Listen, baby. I know what Benny's after. You go back to your room." And she was right.

Colleen and I became close friends during this production. I wasn't married at the time and she always wanted to fix me up, although I was perfectly happy on my own. But Colleen loved having a family around her. I was very fortunate to become a part of that family, and if you were part of Colleen's family, that meant she wanted to take care of you. And for me, I guess, that meant fixing me up. "I want you to meet so-and-so," she would say. So I would go out with so-and-so, and the next day she'd want to know, "Well, baby, how was it?" Colleen always thought that everyone should be with someone. So she was always trying to smack people together. She'd invite you up to the Farm or to a party and at some point, she'd pull you aside and say, "How about———?" It wasn't a neurotic thing. It was a mother thing. She wanted you to have a good time. And much of the time, we did.

To this day, people say to me, "I saw *Virginia Woolf* the night Colleen broke up." We were well into the run in New York and had been doing the play for a while. This was during one of the times that Colleen had tried to stop smoking. She had the hypnotist come, she had tried Smoke-Enders with Jimmy Karen, she had the jar of cigarette butts on her table—whatever it took. We were all trying to help her stop, because she was losing her voice. She hadn't had a cigarette for a few weeks which, as anyone will tell you who has tried to stop, is quite stressful but also quite exhilarating.

One night during this time, I was onstage as Honey with Colleen. She asked me a question and, as per the script, I answered. Colleen suddenly got this look on her face, as if she had heard for the first time how stupid Honey's response was, and started laughing. She had to go over to the mantel and compose herself. Then she'd come back, look at me, and begin to laugh again. She literally couldn't go on. Finally Ben just made his entrance and had this "naughty, naughty" look on his face, which somehow sobered us up. I couldn't even tell you what the line was now.

Afterward, Colleen just walked by me backstage and said, "I'm getting too much oxygen, baby." But this was what was so wonderful about working with Colleen. She was so free, so receptive. Whatever was going on she was really taking it in, and that night, that line just really flipped her out.

I often would go out into the house and watch the third act of *Virginia Woolf*. Her acting was so complete. She taught me an enormous amount about just being present, not closing anything off. On- and offstage, Colleen took all of life in. I remember she would hang out of the window of the Music Box Theatre, where we did *Virginia Woolf*, and wave to the policemen on horseback. They would shout up to her, "Hey, Colleen!" She loved those cops, even invited some of them up to the Farm that Memorial Day for a picnic. Those kind of men loved her: the crews, the policemen, construction workers. I still can't see a policeman on horseback in Times Square without thinking of her.

A few years later, we shared a dressing room during the Broadway run of *You Can't Take It with You*. We were like two girls together. I would help her with her makeup, because she really never wanted to do any. She hated all of that, but she'd allow me to help her just to get me talking. You learn everything about a person sharing a dressing room. Colleen hated to buy underwear. But she needed some. Finally I said, "Colleen, I'll go buy them for you." "No pink!" she shouted back to me. She would have been perfectly happy spending her life in a bulky sweater and jeans.

Sharing that dressing room saved me a fortune in psychiatrist bills. I had just married Frank Converse. She loved Frank and was thrilled that I'd married a Gemini, which is what she was. Whenever I would complain about something he did she'd just say, "Well, darling, he's a Gemini." Colleen felt that was the explanation for just about anything. Over time, she became my mentor and advisor; she knew more about me than anybody. I'd call her about people, about roles, about a moment. You could talk to Colleen about anything, from your deepest secrets to Monday-night football or the NBC soaps. She knew more about the soaps than anyone, but she liked that we could discuss sports. If you went to the Farm, the TV was always on.

Colleen was extremely generous in sharing herself with me and looking after me. In the summer of 1986, just after my brother died, I ran into Ken and Colleen at Barrymore's after a show. I had been trying to hold myself together but hadn't been faring very well. Colleen told me over dinner that she was going to be doing a play, *Real Estate,* at the Westport Playhouse. The next thing I knew, Frank and I were both doing *Real Estate* with her. Later, I learned that the following day she had called Clifford Stevens, her agent and mine, and said, "Listen, baby, we have to get Mo involved in this." I played her daughter. We all hated doing the play, but it served its purpose. It took my mind away from some of the sadness I was going through. Bless her heart, she even helped me when I did *Moon* at Hartford Stage. We went through the script and she gave me clues, told me where things were coming from in a way that gave me the confidence to work on this incredible role.

I was a late mother, like Colleen was. And when I first had the girls I would ask her, "How do you do this? How do you be a wife, a mother and an actress?" All she said was, "You can," and then drew parallels between our situations that would guide me. "The babies will be all right," she'd say. "You can still work."

There are so many things every day I would love to talk with her about. Without her, there's just a part of our lives that is so meager now.

19

"Knees high, Colleen, knees high!"

In the winter of 1977, I was standing in the dressing room of a fancy Chicago department store, vaguely uncomfortable but laughing, as I do when I'm embarrassed. Suddenly, the curtain separating me from what seemed like the rest of the world was whipped back and a manicured hand appeared, holding various pieces of lingerie.

"Do you like these, Colleen? Try them all. Do you prefer the one with the lace? How does it make you feel? Put that one up against your body. That kind of silky, satiny feeling, is that good?"

"Well, yes," I said, trying without success to slow down the onslaught of bras and panties, as well as the running commentary that accompanied them.

"Yes, but do you love it, Colleen? Does it give you a certain feeling? It gives me a certain feeling. Which do you really like?"

As it was clear that I was not going to escape from this dressing room without making a very precise and personal decision about lingerie, I chose two pairs of panties, lace trim, two very pretty bras and two slips.

"These," I said, handing my choices through the curtain with as much aplomb as I could muster.

"Good," said Zoe Caldwell, the director of a new play I was to do, *An Almost Perfect Person*. I followed Zoe like a dutiful child as she made her way to the cash register. Who ever heard of trying on lingerie? You see it, buy it and take it home. One size fits most. But no, not good enough for Zoe. Everything had to be tried on to see how it felt, how it made me feel. For weeks, I changed faithfully every night into the aforementioned underwear. Not because I was absolutely sure that I was somehow being motivated by my panties and bra, but because I was certain that if Zoe were in the audience she would know, as soon as I stepped onstage, if I had them on or not. And the idea that I would receive a note from Zoe, the director, via the stage manager to the effect, "Colleen, are you wearing the lacy drawers?" was more than even I could bear.

Before working with her on *An Almost Perfect Person,* I didn't know Zoe Caldwell very well, although as with so many in the theater, our paths had crossed from time to time. I was more acquainted with her husband, the producer Robert Whitehead, whom I had known from my earliest days as an actress and admired greatly. When Zoe had called, months before and quite out of the blue, to ask me to read a new play by Judith Ross, I thought in a split second that she would be a brilliant director. Nevertheless, upon first reading, I didn't really feel that *An Almost Perfect Person* was for me. I tried my best to explain to Zoe why it seemed to be lacking in certain areas that were important to me. "Well," Zoe shot back, always one to lay every card on the table, "it's not O'Neill. I know that." Despite my reticence, Zoe asked if I would be willing to do a reading of the play in order to help the playwright perhaps hear what I thought was missing. How could I refuse? Zoe's direct approach to all of life was eventually going to overwhelm any indirect response that I might have to her question.

The reading went better than I expected. So when quite coincidentally an old and very good friend, Wally Perner, called asking me to come up to his theater in Arlington, Illinois, for three weeks to do any play I liked, I called Zoe and suggested she send him *An Almost Perfect Person.* Wally's invitation seemed like an excellent opportunity to work with Zoe, take a look at this play in front of an audience, and see what we had. Coming off *Moon* and *Virginia Woolf,* I was also very eager to do a comedy. Zoe, in the meantime, seemed intent not only on directing the play with me in it, but in getting me in condition and seeing to it that for the first time, I was going to come onstage dressed up and looking as good as she could possibly make me in this role. I imagine Zoe driving back to Pound Ridge after seeing me in anything before *An Almost Perfect Person* and muttering to herself, "She was wonderful tonight, but God, Colleen always looks like such a wreck up there. If she could just have one role where she could wear something lovely!" And clearly, like the best directors' work with any actor, if I was going to be lovely, Zoe saw to it that she worked on it with me from the "inside" out. Lace, silk and all.

An Almost Perfect Person was great fun to rehearse, and Zoe was just as I suspected—amazing. Zoe Caldwell is one of the finest actors anywhere. She has an appetite for life and embraces living in a way that I adore. Unlike some directors who seem to have a problem with one sex or another, Zoe enjoys women and loves men, so that, as actors, neither gender feels threatened or ill at ease when they work with her. Zoe gave each of us, man and woman alike, an incredible feeling of ourselves as being attractive and amusing and, above all, intelligent. She treated us as people who had something to contribute to the entire production. As your director, Zoe worked with you in a way that asked for that contribution. Zoe gave that gift which is so important to the actor and so rare. She gave us a sense of approval and appreciation that, within an aura of complete freedom, allowed us to feel safe enough to work with great invention and spontaneity, all in service of the play.

After a rocky run-through in New York for an invited audience of family and friends that sat on its hands, our small band arrived in Arlington. The theater was part of an elaborate complex that included a bar, restaurant, and even a racetrack, which, unfortunately, was closed when we arrived. I say *unfortunately* because although we opened to relatively decent notices and were quite near Chicago, audiences were not clamoring to see us. Perhaps they would have come by if the horses had been up and about as well. I felt bad for Wally Perner since he was such a good and generous producer and here I was, his star, not drawing flies. Zoe was wonderful through it all. She was not only director; she became den mother. I have an image of her standing in front of us and tapping her hands together, saying, "Let's get organized here," but with the unspoken implication of "naughty, naughty, naughty." When we weren't rehearsing, Zoe literally ran me through her daily exercise routine. "Knees high, Colleen, knees high, knees high," she would say, watching me trot around the hotel suite with her. I felt like a clumsy thirteen-year-old kid running with her gym teacher. But I was also pleased as punch to have her announce one day, "Who is this slender lady we have here? Very good, very good, Colleen."

Thus *An Almost Perfect Person* began its intermittent and long road to Broadway with stops in Atlanta; Palm Beach; Ogunquit, Maine; and Falmouth, Massachusetts. Audiences along the road were surprisingly responsive, much more so than in Arlington. The medium-size theaters we played in, particularly those in Ogunquit and Falmouth, were perfect for this wonderful summer stock play. We all enjoyed playing it, and George Hearn, Rex Robbins and I left the theater each night feeling good about ourselves. I was particularly fond of our stage manager, a young man named Peter Lawrence, who has since gone on to be one of the best production stage managers in the business. Even at this point early in his career, Peter had the makings of being just the kind of solid, reasonable and responsible "rock" that makes for the kind of stage manager any actor or director would treasure. But there was one small incident that, I fear, may have tested even Peter's mettle.

When we arrived in Palm Beach, our producer informed me that Maureen Stapleton had just finished some play in Fort Lauderdale and wanted me to know that she was in town for just this one night. Could I come over? Arrangements were quickly made for me to join Maureen in her hotel room for, as she put it, "a glass of wine." Not knowing quite where I was headed, I asked Peter to accompany me. Now, I knew that I had rehearsal and an opening night the next day, and I knew that never in my life have I—or anyone—ever had just one glass of wine with Maureen anywhere, but off we went. Hours and many glasses of wine later, I left the "safety" of Maureen's hotel suite and ended up with Peter in a cab in the middle of the night trying to remember how to get back to Palm Beach from Fort Lauderdale. I have very little memory of the rest of the evening, but at some point, Peter and I were not in the cab any longer, though still quite a few miles away from Palm Beach. I have no idea why. Peter tells me that without warning, I jumped from the cab, dragging him along with me intent upon finding someone who could get us back to Palm Beach. Apparently, only through Peter's skills as both a diplomat and drill sergeant that he did manage to push, drag and carry me God knows how many miles back to the apartment complex. All I know is I woke up the next morning fully clothed across my bed with that dreadful and peculiar feeling of *What happened to me?* Here it was, my first night in Palm Beach, the leading lady of a new play about to open, and I'm apparently dead drunk, running through town asking directions. Oops.

As anyone will tell you who has awakened in the same condition, I couldn't believe that I couldn't remember what I'd done—but what could it have been to leave me feeling so rotten? And in an hour, I had rehearsal. With Zoe. I got into the shower, pulled myself together as best I could, and went over to the theater. I dreaded seeing Zoe, knowing that she would sense that I was entering rehearsal in what would not be considered tip-top condition. I felt particularly bad because I have always said that the only place that I have true discipline in my life is in the theater. It is my one source of pride, because there are so many areas where I seem to be lacking discipline. I went directly to my dressing room. On the table was this small box-like contraption. I thought, *What a classy theater. This must be for hot-rollers.* I lifted up the top. It was a portable phonograph. Zoe came into the room.

"Maureen called. She wanted this playing as you came in."

"Well, let's put it on," I said. Zoe took one look at me in the mirror before turning to place a record she had on the turntable. It was Eydie Gormé singing sad love songs very loudly and dramatically in Spanish. Now, Maureen and I love Eydie Gormé. But just then, loud and dramatic was particularly excruciating, as of course my darling Maureen would know.

"Perfect," I said, looking back in the mirror at Zoe, who smiled and nodded before going to check on George and Rex in the other dressing rooms. Who knows what kind of evening *they* might have had. Just before we began, I saw Peter.

"What happened last night?" I asked him. He was gracious enough to laugh, but it was obviously not one of the best nights of his life. Being not only a good friend, but the man in charge of getting the show on, he couldn't just leave his leading lady's limp body on the streets of Palm Beach curled around a bush.

Somehow, I got through the rehearsal and went home to sleep for a few hours before opening. Although we had been warned that the opening-night audience in Palm Beach could be deadly, they were so social, in fact, their response was marvelous. That evening, in spite of the excesses of the night before, we all three were racehorses who came out of the gate like gangbusters. There was a marvelous party afterward, and with Maureen safely a thousand miles away back in New York, I turned my attention to the ocean and didn't touch a glass of red wine for weeks and continued to play Eydie's Spanish hits every night in the dressing room, much to the consternation of my fellows, whose tolerance for loud and dramatic fell somewhat short of mine and Maureen's.

Sometime after we closed in Ogunquit and Falmouth, a producer named Burry Fredrik picked up *An Almost Perfect Person* for a three-week tryout in Philadelphia before opening on Broadway at the Belasco Theatre. This merry band that we had nicknamed "Caldwell's Raiders" once more entered rehearsals. But there was a difference this time, a little more tension, a lot more nervous energy because now we were going for it all. Zoe began to move like a dervish, watching us, walking up and down the aisle of the theater, conferring with the playwright and her husband, Bob Whitehead, who was suddenly much more on the scene, as was Ken. At the end of any performance when Bob and Ken had been there, Zoe would go out with Bob, and I would go with Ken. The next morning, Zoe and I would barely greet each other.

"Well, what does Bob think?" I'd ask.

"What did Ken say?" Zoe responded.

"Nothing, really."

"Well, Bob had a great deal to say," Zoe stated with great frustration. "Did you see their faces afterward, Colleen? Just those stares. What is happening here?" Suddenly, this play that had been so much fun to do seemed slight as the stakes became high. We were all tired and tense for our first few performances in Philadelphia. Nothing seemed to be working, which made us angry—angry at Zoe, who was angry at us, angry with each other, angry at the audience, and especially angry at Bob and Ken, who behaved as if they had expected just this. It's difficult to be funny when you're playing in a rage. It's even more difficult when you've made up your mind that you hate the audience. Worst of all, George, Rex and I were acting like strangers, protecting ourselves with whatever armor we had. My inclination, horribly enough, is to march on as though I'm leading an army over a cliff. I play with great authority, which had no meaning at all. Humor, of course, is out the window. George retreated. He became quieter, more urbane, sitting mentally in the local bar creating space around himself. Rex, who is a terribly funny man, simply went for his schtick.

Thankfully, after a few performances, we were able to find each other again. With a stronger play, all our previous rehearsal and performances would have stood us in better stead; for *An Almost Perfect Person* to work, each of us needed to be at our most alert and vulnerable. Surprisingly, the Philadelphia reviews weren't bad, just not stellar. With our next stop New York City, we really had no idea if we stood a chance of gliding through to a decent run or simply clanking to a quick stop.

We opened *An Almost Perfect Person* on Broadway nearly one year after we had first started rehearsals for Arlington. Whatever the outcome, Caldwell's Raiders had become a small family, knowing and sharing things with one another that only families do. Peter Lawrence had a wonderful sense of discipline, as well as being a great deal of fun. I don't know how he remained supportive and enthusiastic about us all for the full year, but he did. Rex Robbins, who is truly an eccentric, was a delight, as neat as he is funny and always eager to plan something for us all to do. To this day, I cannot hear the song "Danny Boy" without thinking of dear George Hearn, whose numerous love affairs and escapades of finding and losing true love were truly incredible to witness. Wally Perner, without whom we would have never started this year-long trip, stayed with us in spirit the whole way. And finally there was Zoe, who literally danced her way madly to the end of her first directing assignment. There is no one like her, no one who understands the human condition better or loves every twist and turn of what it is to be alive. Zoe could sit in a room of incredibly beautiful women of all ages and, I will tell you, any man would sense that she is the most sensual, passionate and dangerous of any there.

In New York, our reviews were respectable but not enough to keep us running through two snowstorms in January. The first one nearly knocked us out of the box. But our producer kept hanging in there. By the second one, a week later, we knew we had had it. I still think that I may have been a detriment to the play. So many people like to see an actor in the same type of role again and again. One critic made that quite clear when he said that while he enjoyed himself and thought *An Almost Perfect Person* was a pleasant and entertaining play, he wondered when Miss Dewhurst would go back to playing the serious roles she usually did.

What I do is act. That is my profession. If I like the lady as written, I'll play her. Like any instrument, if acting talent is not used, it gets rusty. Sadly, plays like *A Moon for the Misbegotten, Who's Afraid of Virginia Woolf? The Ballad of the Sad Café* and *All the Way Home* come around very rarely. And, I might add, only one of those was a hit. Finally, if you continue to play the same note over and over, you cease to reach and, worst of all, you stop creating, instead simply banging out the same tune again. No one wants to disappoint, but at the same time, I really cannot stand to be bored doing the same thing over and over again. So you come in with less than a winner. But it is not always just about winning. It is not all about being a hit. Even those experiences that are considered failures leave you with memories most lovingly remembered and people whom you will love forever.

ZOE CALDWELL

I had been given the play to read by the playwright, Judith Ross, when it was called *Winning Is Better*. She wanted me to play it, which I didn't want to do. "So why don't you direct it?" she said. No, I couldn't do that. I'd never directed anything before in my life. But then I was always thinking, *Gosh, I wish I could help that actor, but I can't because I'm an actor and I don't believe actors should tell other actors they're working with what to do. So,* I thought, *why not?* We tried to get Ellen Burstyn, who had just done *Same Time Next Year*, but she wasn't interested. So, who else? This character has to be very, very feminine, but strong and bright. She is in politics, so she must be articulate. But the overriding thing, the one thing she must have, is a wonderful femininity; her strength must come from her womanliness. Well, of course, when you lay it out like that, why not Dewhurst? Colleen is all those things. She didn't expose her femininity a great deal, but she surely had it. You see, up to then, I think Colleen had only been directed by men. And she kept playing that "earth mother" thing, you know, with the very deep voice and all the hair. I was a little bit bored with that, so I said to her, "Look, I know this isn't what you normally play, but would you read it? Because if you do it, I'll direct it."

Colleen was in a bit of a down period just then. She was at home, at the Farm a lot and not doing very much. She could sit up in that room and watch TV all day. I have the feeling she had just gone through menopause and was depressed. So she read it, I think just to humor me, but wasn't really interested. But I insisted we talk through her trepidation and finally, I think just to get out of the house—or perhaps to get me out of the house—she said yes.

Once she began, Colleen was game for anything, and I found her so marvelous to direct. She didn't fight me and she wasn't afraid of her femininity at all. She trusted me and she really had no good reason to trust me, which was very sweet of her to do. We explored all kinds of things. Goddess things. I remember one day asking her to stretch out on the couch, not feeling that she had to be in control, not with the cigarettes, but just really like a Goddess. And she did it and was just swell. In fact, she was more than swell. I took her to the hair man, the one with one name—Kenneth—and had her hair beautifully cut. I had her manicured, pedicured; and Jane Greenwood dressed her marvelously, of course, as Jane always does. But then we came to her underclothes. Now this was not so easy because, how can I say this, Colleen didn't wear underclothes, or if she wore them, I mean it was a token pair of briefs or worse. Dreadful! As for petticoats or lace panties, all that swell stuff, no. So finally when we got to Chicago I said, "Colleen, I think this woman would have very pretty underwear."

"Oh, no," she said.

"Oh, yes," I replied. "And that's why we're going to Marshall Field's this afternoon." So we went, and I ensconced her in a mirrored cubicle, which is never pleasant for anyone, let alone Colleen, and I said, "You stay in there and I'll bring you things to try on." A saleswoman and I brought her racks of beautiful lingerie to try on, and she did, even if she got a little impatient at times and, after much picking and choosing, we ended up with a beautiful trousseau of underwear.

"OK, Colleen," I said, "you can get dressed now. I'll go pay." At the checkout counter, the saleslady who had been helping so wonderfully tapped me on the hand.

"Excuse me," she said. "Is that Colleen Dewhurst?"

"Yet it is," I replied.

"Are you her mother?" she asked. Well. What could I say?

"Yes, I am."

"I thought so," she said. "You must be very proud."

And without a moment's hesitation, I replied, "Yes, I am."

And off we went, back to the theater. Colleen wore the silken underwear, she wore the beautiful clothes, she had the wonderful hair and her nails done and her feet done, and she just had one heck of a good time. Now, I never intended this to be a remedial thing. It was just that I thought Colleen needed, at that particular time, to play into her femininity, to be assured that she was beautiful. And she was and it was good for her. It certainly also helped that she greatly liked her leading man, George Hearn. He was terrific for her, strong, in that Spencer Tracy kind of way. He also had great humor, and that's very necessary for Colleen, and necessary to cope *with* Colleen. I just wish the play had been more of a success for her in New York. It would have lifted her up.

GEORGE HEARN

I don't think Colleen would have even remembered the first time we met. It was 1963 and I was cast in a small role in Joe Papp's production of *Antony and Cleopatra* in which she starred with George C. Scott and Michael Higgins. We met a few times socially after that. But it was really in that awful, bitter winter in Chicago doing *An Almost Perfect Person* that we became fast friends. God, I adored both her and Zoe. Seven months with those women, in rehearsal and on the road. It was just wonderful. They certainly knew how to have a good time, which is always fine with me.

The theater in Chicago was part of a hotel complex, which meant, of course, that it had a bar to which we would retire after performance. Zoe and Colleen were just drinking white wine. That's the joke, right? Just white wine; a couple of bottles of white wine, thank you. I was doing shots and beers. I do believe we ended up really wreaking havoc upon the place. The next day, we went in for rehearsal and, of course, we're all dreadfully hungover and I'm thinking, *Oh Christ, what am I going to eat? I've got to eat something that will stay down*. As I walked through the hotel kitchen, I saw the chef preparing a BLT sandwich. "Forgive me," I said, "but I've got to have that BLT," which I then scooped up from the table and put in the pocket of my overcoat. I sat down in rehearsal with Colleen and Zoe, both of whom were not in much better shape, but talking and moaning. Suddenly Colleen says, as if struck by a lightning bolt, "I'd sell my soul right now for a bacon, lettuce, and tomato sandwich." Well, I pulled that sandwich right out of my pocket in a flash and poor Colleen about fainted. I remember her saying to Zoe at some point in rehearsal, "Can I kick off my shoes here? I have to," she said. "It's important for me in every play I'm in, if I possibly can, to at some point walk barefoot on the floor of the stage." As if somehow the strength of the earth was coming up through her feet. God, we had good times doing that play.

Colleen could tell three jokes. I wouldn't even begin to attempt to remember them, but she could only tell these three. Something about a bird that fell in a pile of shit, another about some guy knocking door to door wanting money for the Ashmolean Marching Society, and another about a guy who kept bees in Rutherford, New Jersey. Don't ask. I've tried to tell them and they always fall flat. But when she told them, they were devastating. She couldn't tell any others to save her life. Many a night at Barrymore's, we'd be talking and drinking and she'd stop and say, "George, it's time to sing 'Danny Boy.' Sing 'Danny Boy.' So I'd start, "Oh Danny boy, the pipes the pipes . . ." and she'd start to cry and then we'd laugh and laugh.

One of those "Danny Boy" nights at Barrymore's changed my life. I'd been asked to come in and audition for the part of Zaza in the then-new musical version of *La Cage aux Folles* in a dress, full makeup, wig, and high heels. I guess I was suddenly feeling very macho and announced to the table, "No! I won't, goddamnit. What the fuck, forget it!"

"Oh, come on, George," Colleen said quietly, "go with it. Just do it. You're secure enough in yourself. Don't worry about it, just go in there and have a good time."

"Well, I guess . . ."

"The quality of your fan mail may change a bit," she added. Only *she* could have talked me into it. But I went, got the part, won the Tony Award for that role and, just as she said, had a great time.

What a pair she and Zoe were together. They loved to dish. Colleen loved gossip, not the malicious kind, but she loved to know what kind of mischief people were up to. She loved human behavior. So we're at rehearsal and she and Zoe were going on about some actress and Zoe said something that made Colleen cackle. She threw her head back to laugh and cracked it hard against the back of the rehearsal couch. "Ouch!" she said. "God is so quick with me sometimes."

But I also remember Colleen saying quite seriously, "George, you should keep a little black book and a little white book. If somebody doesn't know how to work with others or is selfish and mean, it's just as important to pass on that information as it is to pass on the good stuff." She always felt a little messy when she said anything unpleasant about anyone; at the same time, there was no one who was more loyal to those she loved. She had tremendous loyalties. I had done a dozen shows for Joe Papp, but it had ended on a sour note and once, over dinner somewhere, I was shooting down Joe in front of her. She just looked at me and said, "Don't! He was terrific to me back when I really needed him. He was always there. So stop." If she loved you, like she did Joe, she would stand with you forever, even if something went wrong at times. Her loyalty was fierce. I surely would not have wanted to be her enemy.

Has anyone talked about when Maureen Stapleton came to visit us in Palm Beach? I will. There we were, all together in this swank hotel restaurant, Zoe, Zoe's husband, Robert Whitehead, Colleen, me, our stage manager, Peter Lawrence, a tableful of people. Well, we got very drunk and at some point Maureen sees this very wealthy old man walk into the place with two women. He makes the mistake of sitting close to Maureen who, upon noticing him, stands to announce, "I live in this goddamn hotel. I pay two hundred and fifty bucks a night for this fucking room and, let me tell you, the walls are so fucking thin that every time this guy"—pointing to the elderly gentleman entertaining his guests—"farts, my closet doors blow open! And, while you all are here," she says, motioning to his female guests, "let's talk about blow jobs!" People were grabbing their coats and running for the door. Zoe was about to die, and she and Bob left in a hurry. I was out, unconscious practically, so Colleen, who'd been trying to tell Maureen to "sit down and shut up," dropped me off before she and Peter hauled Maureen off into a cab as she was still expounding to the man's female companions: "Some people are just average cocksuckers, but now you two . . ." It was a very quiet rehearsal the next morning. And I don't think any of us saw Maureen again until we got back to New York. I can't vouch for the old guy and his dates.

PETER LAWRENCE

I had been working at the Arlington Theatre in Chicago as the stage manager for about seven months. Just as I was to leave, the producer said, "You've got to do one more show for me." I wasn't interested. I wanted to go home. But he was insistent. "It's with Colleen Dewhurst," he said. I still wasn't sure, but I flew to New York with him to meet with Colleen at her home in South Salem. When we arrived at the Farm, we walked into the middle of Jane Broder's eightieth birthday party. Jane had been Colleen's agent for years. There was everyone in show business whom I had ever wanted to meet: Colleen, Zoe, Robert Whitehead, Robert Drivas, Terrence McNally, Maureen Stapleton, Jimmy Coco, everyone. The afternoon was fabulous, and at one point Colleen and Zoe walked me away from everyone and, each taking one of my hands, said, "Peter, you have to do this show." Well, what was I going to do? Has anyone ever said no to those two at the same time? So, of course, I did *An Almost Perfect Person* and it was one of the happiest experiences of my life.

I'll never forget that first afternoon. I was overwhelmed to be there with these incredibly gifted people whom I'd only ever seen onstage or read about. We were all sitting at that huge dining room table of Colleen's, about twenty of us. I remember she had a parrot at the time that had plucked out nearly all its feathers but was still quite talkative. So there was a naked bird sitting on its perch near the table, commenting on the proceedings, and any number of cats and dogs wandering in and out of the room. After dinner, Colleen made sure that we all had fresh wine, then clinked her knife against the edge of her glass to quiet everyone down.

"We are all here to celebrate Jane Broder's eightieth birthday," she said, beaming that incredible smile down the table to Jane. "Jane has been my agent for over twenty-five years," she continued, "since I first got to New York. Very early on, Jane taught me something that I will never forget." And Colleen went on to tell her tableful of guests that years before, she had been offered and agreed to do a play for Joe Papp for twenty-five dollars a week. Before she had signed her contract, however, another offer came to her to do a week's worth of television for five hundred dollars, a huge amount of money for Colleen at the time. But she could not do both.

"So I called Jane," Colleen said, continuing her story. "What should I do? I haven't signed the contract and I really need the money. And Jane simply said," Colleen went on, nodding to her beloved agent at the other end of the table, "'Colleen, you've given your word. Do what's right.' That play was *The Taming of the Shrew,* but more important, I would like to thank Jane Broder today for teaching me about honor in the theater. It's a lesson I've never forgotten. I hope that I can live my whole life with the same integrity as Jane Broder. To you, Jane." And with that, the table raised their glasses to toast this woman whom Colleen clearly loved so very much. I will never forget that moment. I really count that day as the real beginning of my career, because that was the day I recognized what kind of integrity I hoped that I could have in a life working in the theater.

An Almost Perfect Person took a very circuitous route to Broadway. We opened in Chicago and then played a godawful theater in Atlanta, where Zoe got so enraged with the producer over the condition of the theater that she stabbed him in the arm with a fork. From there we went to Palm Beach. The run was uneventful, but one particular evening is still talked about. The evening started in a hotel restaurant with Colleen, Zoe and Maureen Stapleton, and ended, many lost and drunken hours later, with getting thrown out of a cab with Colleen about four miles from the theater and our rooms. It was, shall we simply say, a staggering experience. We then did a summer stock tour before coming into Broadway with a new producer. This producer did not want me to come in with the show as production stage manager, since I had never worked on Broadway before. I figured I was out. But no, Colleen refused to do the show unless I came in with everyone else. That was my first Broadway show and I am convinced that I wouldn't have a career on Broadway today if not for Colleen. Colleen was incredibly loyal, but unlike a lot of people in this business who claim loyalty but don't mean it, Colleen would lie down in front of a car for you. If you were her friend or more, if she considered you part of her family—like she obviously considered Jane Broder and so many others around that table the first day I met her—she understood that to mean something, and you never left her heart. Even if, as was our case much later, we didn't see each other for years at a time.

Even though I hadn't seen Colleen with any regularity or worked with her in a number of years, I miss her. I miss knowing that she's around and part of this business. For me, she set the benchmark for how a star should behave.

Recently I was in Toronto directing one of the touring companies of *Sunset Boulevard,* and in my final remarks to the cast I quoted Colleen:

"It is the job of the actor to unite the audience into a single thought process."

Colleen united much more than just any one audience. Her spirit propels many of us in this business who had the great good fortune to work with her to do our best work—and to have a good time doing it.

20

"Dear Colleen:
They gave it to the right girl."

Some people say that the reason I did not have a film career was because I had the children, and so gave up everything. Nothing could be further from the truth. I continued to work in the theater. I was not out of sight. By working in New York, I was able to leave the house at night after I had put both boys to bed, and go into the Circle in the Square and do *Desire Under the Elms* and return home. The next morning, when the children got up and started plodding around the house, there was Mom. That's their memory of that time and mine. Their dad would have to leave for longer periods of time now and then for a film. And always, through every job, there was Nana.

There was one period when it appeared George and I had fallen through the cracks and did not have much money coming in. We decided to fly out to Los Angeles, took a house on the beach at Malibu, and did anything that was offered to us. We did a lot of television, shows like *Gunsmoke, Ben Casey* and *Dr. Kildare,* but to tell the truth, I can't remember now who did what when and to whom or for how much. The high point of our time in Malibu was that Campbell, who turned one, and had, up until that time, only accepted his dad, Nana and myself—and, of course, Alex—with some kind of joy and welcome, became accustomed to the many friends who dropped by. Alex had been social from the day he was born. Campbell viewed everyone as if they were from another planet.

Sometime later and long after leaving the shores of Malibu and world of forgettable guest TV shots, I received a call from Jane Broder telling me that I had been offered a role in *The Cowboys,* starring John Wayne and to be directed by Mark Rydell, whom I had known in Harold Clurman's class. The role was that of a madam who was taking her girls across the plains to meet with those poor gentlemen who had been isolated for years out there with the cows and whatever other livestock there was.

Alex and Campbell, who were now in grade school and vaguely aware of what their mother did for a living, were very excited. They knew who John Wayne was, and despite all the many wonderful and accomplished actors they'd met, it was only the Duke who gave me—or I think the entire acting profession—any credibility in their eyes. For it was only Mr. Wayne who had made any memorable impression on them on the big screen. As it turned out, by the time I arrived on the set, Mr. Wayne had been killed in the film and returned home. For certain, when I returned home without a photograph or anything that could prove that I had indeed met John Wayne the boys were, I think, quite disappointed in me.

But, to me, this very modest job became a great joy when I was greeted at the motel upon arrival, somewhere in the wilds of Colorado, by my dear Roscoe Lee Browne, with whom, it turned out, I would have my scenes. This appeased the boys somewhat when I called to tell them, as Roscoe was family and known to my sons always as Mr. Apple. I, however, couldn't have been more delighted to see Roscoe, whom I have loved madly from the moment we met. I can't remember why, but it began sometime in Italy, when Roscoe stayed in the guest house of our villa while GC was shooting *The Bible*.

A few years later, I received an offer to do another movie starring Mr. Wayne, *McQ*. Now the boys were really excited because in this film, my scenes were actually with John Wayne. It so happened this was during Watergate. Jane said that she trusted me to be intelligent enough not to get into any political discussions with Mr. Wayne, who did not share many of the more liberal political beliefs. I said of course I was not that stupid. The one interesting thing I noticed at the production office in the hotel was that the television was constantly tuned to the Watergate hearings. It was turned off only when Mr. Wayne was going to be present.

I went to the set the first day an absolute wreck. I had not been conscious at all about how nervous I was about meeting the Duke. I was in my trailer and the director, John Sturges, came in to talk about the first scene we were to shoot. I simply nodded. I was called onto the set which, for the scene, was my house. I entered the living room, which was very small, and Mr. Wayne, who was already there sitting on a couch, stood up and kept standing up and up. I just couldn't believe it. He was so tall in this tiny room and I thought, *Good God, what we have here is a legend*. I was looking at the Duke. Who cared what he thought politically? This was the "Quiet Man." As a woman, I was looking at a girl's dream of what a man would be. The truth is, I felt suddenly like a little girl again, sitting in a movie theater.

Since I was playing a cocktail waitress, I asked Mr. Sturges if I might remove my shoes when I entered, as my feet would probably be sore from work. There was a glance between him and Mr. Wayne, but he said yes. So I came in the door, removed my shoes and, as the character, was surprised to see him in my living room.

I say my first line to Mr. Wayne, who in turn bobbles his first line in response to me. The director cuts the scene. John Wayne apologizes for "blowing my damn line," winks at me, and we begin again. This time I enter, no shoes (God, how this suggestion must have annoyed/amused him—so "New York"), and say my single line. Mr. Wayne replies. Perfectly. And in one simple line, I could feel his entire screen persona fill the set. On camera, he was enormous, and the first time out, could be truly overwhelming.

I believe to this day that, aware of my nervousness, Mr. Wayne deliberately goofed the line. From then on, he never missed a beat. He was always prepared, and in an environment that he so clearly ruled and that would have to accommodate his every whim, he was always professional. John Wayne extended to me an incredible courtesy that day that I will never forget. He relaxed me completely and in a way that made it immediately easy for me to work and improvise with him. I knew the politics would have made me crazy, but I found myself liking him immensely. John Wayne was one of the best actors I ever worked with. And I will not hedge that remark with "believe it or not." He simply was.

I remember asking him if he would mind autographing pictures to my two sons so that I could prove I worked with the Duke. He said, of course. The public adored him and he was good to them. From John Wayne I learned a great deal about my perceptions of actors whom I knew only by their work. Some I adored, but when I met them, there was nobody at home. And others, like Mr. Wayne, I discovered were much more than what they portrayed on-screen.

The loveliest memory I have of John Wayne was the night that I won the Tony for *A Moon for the Misbegotten*. I had stayed overnight in New York City. The next day, when I called home, Alex answered the phone very excited.

"Oh, you have a lot of telegrams here," he said, "but let me read one to you."

"OK," I said, knowing that Alex opened every bit of mail in the house regardless of to whom it was addressed.

" 'Dear Colleen,' " he read, " 'they gave it to the right girl.' Guess who that is from?" he asked.

"From Mr. Wayne," I answered immediately.

"It's signed 'the Duke,' " Alex replied. "How did you know it was from him?"

"John Wayne," I replied, "is the only person I know who would call me *girl*."

Perhaps one of my most strange and brief appearances in a film came about in an equally strange and unusual way. One evening, after a performance of the Broadway production of *A Moon for the Misbegotten*, I was removing my makeup in the dressing room and became aware that someone was standing in the doorway. I looked over and could not believe that it was Woody Allen. He didn't enter the room. He simply mumbled something I didn't understand, and disappeared.

A few weeks later, Mr. Allen appeared again, standing once again at my dressing room door. This time, I nodded. He nodded back and, once again, disappeared. Ed Flanders, who played my father in *Moon* and had the dressing room next to me, came around the corner.

"Tell me if I'm crazy, but wasn't that Woody Allen?" he asked.

"Yes," I replied.

"Wasn't he here before?"

"Yes."

"What did he say?" Ed continued.

"He doesn't say anything."

I have come to the conclusion, after all these years, that Mr. Allen never came to *Moon*.

Three years later, while playing in *Who's Afraid of Virginia Woolf?* on Broadway at the Music Box Theatre with Ben Gazzara, Mr. Allen came to my dressing room between a matinee and an evening performance. He stated very quickly that he was doing a film. There was no script as yet. But he said that he would leave some pages for me in a week or so. Sometime later, I received a few pieces of paper with handwritten dialogue. I didn't quite understand what was happening. I was so bowled over each time Mr. Allen appeared that I was never quite sure of what was going on between us.

An offer came in to play a part in what would later be called *Annie Hall*, but I still wasn't sure what the part was. And, frankly, I didn't care. I was very excited. There appeared to be great secrecy about this script, and I understood that I wouldn't even know who else was cast until I arrived on the set.

By this time, I was represented by Clifford Stevens, as my darling Jane had passed away two years before. Clifford's experience with Mr. Allen was similarly strange. He had given Clifford no script, no character description, no money, no offer—nothing. Clifford took me out to dinner at Sardi's after the show.

"All right," he said, "let's talk about Woody Allen."

"OK."

"I'm going to speak to you now as an agent," Clifford continued, "not as a friend. As I have received nothing, I would advise you not to do whatever it is he's doing."

"Clifford, I have to," I said. "It's Woody Allen. I think he's the greatest. I'd do it for nothing."

Clifford just looked at me. "I knew that was the answer," he said, and promptly ordered a double martini and a glass of white wine for me.

I was scheduled to shoot my scenes in *Annie Hall* a few weeks later. Early one morning, I was picked up in front of the Algonquin Hotel in a private car and I was driven, by myself, to the location in Englewood, New Jersey, which was one of those nice, big, upper-middle-class suburban homes. It had been a lonely drive and, once again, I was extremely nervous. I felt like a secret agent in that I didn't know what my assignment was.

Upon arrival, it was business as usual. Makeup, hair, costume. I met Diane Keaton, who was so wonderful as Annie Hall, and Chris Walken, who was playing my son, her brother, as well as the actor playing my husband, and a wonderful lady playing Grandma—an interesting and somewhat intense group of actors who immediately gave the impression that this was an intense and most interesting family. We were all seated at a Thanksgiving meal. Mr. Allen had the camera set up and facing me. In his role as director, he got behind it for a moment before slipping into the chair at the table opposite me. After we spoke some dialogue at the table, Woody said, "Cut," and got up again to look through the camera. He then indicated we should rehearse it with his stand-in sitting in his place. We did. Woody took his place, we shot again, and that was it.

I worked two days on *Annie Hall*. The second day, I was sitting out on the steps of the house and Mr. Allen came out and sat down beside me. There were four young boys who had ridden onto the lawn on their bicycles, looking, it seemed, for Woody Allen. One of the assistant directors was explaining to them that they had to leave. What they didn't know is that they were only about twenty-five yards from Mr. Allen and didn't recognize him.

"Isn't that sad?" he said, watching the kids leave.

"What?"

"I mean, what kind of a life is that?" Woody continued. "They all look alike. They've got the same bikes. They live literally in an encampment. This is all they know. They don't know what's going on or what's happening anywhere else. And nothing is happening to them to make them think about it."

My jaw must have been down to my knees because anyone else's view would have been of privileged children living a privileged life. We sat in silence for a moment.

"You live in the country," he said.

"Yes."

"How can you stand it?" he asked. "I hate to go to the country. I mean, it's a bore. You go for a weekend and there's nothing. You can't go out in the street and buy a paper. You can't go to a bookstore at midnight. There's nothing to do. You just sit around, right? Meanwhile," he added, "everybody's talking about how great the country is."

I had no response. It's true, you can't walk out and get a paper. But I remember his description and think that in some ways, Mr. Allen's view was very close to Harold Clurman's. One night in class, many years before, Mr. Clurman suddenly began to speak of how much he loved the city.

"The most beautiful things in the world are cars," Harold said. This astounded me because I don't think he ever drove. "And streets and honking horns." The country drove him crazy.

"It's nothing but watching the grass grow and talking about how green it was that year and what they were doing with it."

It's interesting to me that when Edward Albee was directing *Who's Afraid of Virginia Woolf?* in Los Angeles, he picked a small, clean motel in Santa Monica where he could walk the street at night. There were stores open, book-stores, record shops and people on the move at all hours.

Woody Allen, Harold Clurman and Edward Albee love the city because they are consumed by what they observe. It is a constantly changing panorama of life at every level. They are three men whose life's work is stimulated by studying the human condition and re-creating it for us.

What I love about Woody, when I observe the casting of his movies, is that he reaches so often into the theater. He has always expressed, in his films, a great allegiance to New York and the actors who live and work there.

We know that the word *genius* is overworked. But Woody Allen, within our world of entertainment, can safely be acknowledged as just that.

21

"That's what Ned Shelton could do for his friends, Colleen."

Years ago, when I first arrived in New York City and was living in a cold-water flat in "Hell's Kitchen," on West Fiftieth Street, there was a wonderful public library on Tenth Avenue, between Fiftieth and Fifty-first Streets. If I was not in school, at the American Academy, I most often could be found there. I entered that library at least every three or four days, leaving with an armful of books that I would return, only to leave with another armful, bound for my tiny apartment around the corner.

One day, the librarian said she had a book that she thought I should read, and handed me *The Man Who Lived Twice*. I don't remember much about the book, but I never forgot the man I read about, Ned Shelton.

Shelton was one of the most successful writers of the 1920s. Urbane, handsome and wealthy, he was one of the most successful and popular men in the Broadway theater community. This alone would not have made him extraordinary had he also not been struck down in his early thirties by a disease that fused his joints and made him blind. Nevertheless, during his decline, through years of great pain and loss that eventually turned him into an invalid, he never withdrew from his friends and the community in which he had once been a leading light. I immediately loved the story of Ned Shelton and found his courage and commitment to living under tremendous duress inspiring.

Years later, in June of 1980, Ken and I flew up to Toronto, Canada, to see a production of *Richard II* that Zoe Caldwell had directed at Stratford. While there, we went to a matinee of a play that I had never heard of entitled *Ned and Jack* by Sheldon Rosen. Ken was particularly eager to see it and, in fact, said that months before, he had asked me to read the manuscript. He claimed, as we headed for the theater that afternoon, that I never got around to it once he informed me that there was no part for me. As I sat in the darkened auditorium, I had no idea what I was about to see on the stage. But as the play unfolded, I whispered to Ken, "Oh, my God, *Ned Shelton*. This is about Ned Shelton."

Ken smiled. "Yes," he said. "And John Barrymore."

Nearly a year later, Ken surprised me again when he announced that he had optioned the play we had seen that afternoon. For the next few months, we both became very close to the playwright Sheldon Rosen as he continued to work on *Ned and Jack* in anticipation of a production that Ken hoped would be done at a leading regional theater prior to opening in New York City in the spring. But as April approached, Ken had been unsuccessful in booking a production anywhere. Just as we were all ready to admit defeat, until at least the start of the next theatrical season in the fall, David Heefner, the producing director of the Hudson Guild Theatre on West Twenty-sixth Street, called. He told us that the final play he had planned for his season had been withdrawn and, if we were willing and could move quickly, he would like to do *Ned and Jack*. For several months, Ken and I had discussed directors, usually as we drove back and forth from the Farm to the city. We could never agree on anyone. Some I liked, he didn't. A few he suggested, for one reason or another, I loathed. Now we suddenly had a production just weeks away and no director, no one to take the helm.

"Colleen, I think we should do this at Hudson," Ken said, one day in the car.

"Well, why not?" I replied. "Fool around anymore and we'll never get it on. We'll find the right director. Tell David we'll do it." Ken stared straight ahead as we drove.

"What?" I said, thinking that he was reconsidering moving ahead. "What?" Ken looked back at me.

"You're going to direct it," he stated in such a way that I knew he was neither anticipating nor wanting an immediate response. Nevertheless, by the time we arrived home I spoke up.

"Are you crazy?" I said, coming into the kitchen. "No. That's it. Just no." But Ken would not let up.

"Colleen, you know the play better than anyone except Sheldon. You've worked with him on it. You've seen it. You've read it over and over. You love the characters and know exactly the way it should be done. Who better than you?"

I was flabbergasted and had no response. I had never in my life thought of directing. It had been suggested to me now and then as other actresses began to direct. But I had never been interested. I am too impatient, too subjective and, God knows, too unorganized.

"Think about it," Ken said, going upstairs. He was gone for twenty minutes. When he came back downstairs, he pointed to the phone and said that someone wanted to speak to me. I picked it up and before I even put the receiver to my ear I heard Sheldon's voice. "I think it's a great idea to have you direct it. I would love to have you do it." I stared across the room at Ken. Over the next few days, other friends called, also no doubt at Ken's instruction, encouraging me to do it. As I thought about the play and the actors, I couldn't help but get excited. As I also considered the organizational talents a director must have, my excitement became tempered with terror. But somehow, in that mix of emotion, I finally found it within myself to agree. Ken was right. I could—I would direct *Ned and Jack*.

We found Peter Michael Goetz, our John Barrymore—"Jack"—very quickly, and after a series of auditions, cast Dwight Schultz as Ned Shelton. I immediately met with the set, costume and lighting designers, and although my uncertainty in these areas made me terribly nervous, I knew that the only way around my fear was to be straightforward. All three came highly recommended by David Heefner. I would simply discuss points that I wanted onstage and, as the designers had not asked me for my résumé of past directing jobs, we entered into this endeavor with full trust that each one knew his own job.

As Ken, Sheldon and I sat down with the cast for our first read-through, I was consumed by two fears that ran parallel to each other. I had long ago fallen in love with Ned Shelton and, to a lesser degree, John Barrymore. I wanted to be sure that neither of them was done an injustice by this production. At the same time, I would lie awake at night fearful that I would lead these wonderful actors portraying these men down the garden path.

From the first day of rehearsal, the actors were delightful, diligent in their study of their individual characters, completely cooperative and willing to try many various approaches. I would sit and watch them attempting to reach emotionally for what I was asking, each day bringing more and more to the play. One thing I clearly understood as a director is the way an actor works and what he or she needs to do their best work. I was not looking for immediate results, and as we rehearsed, there was in each one a slow merging with each character's psyche, until we reached a point where the actor and character had come together as one.

The designers were terrific. It was amazing to me how each could manage with very little money to give the most professional appearance to set, costumes and lights. Nevertheless, Ken and I stripped parts of the living room at the Farm and loaded a chaise, table, rugs and various small pieces down to the theater to fill the stage that was to become Ned Sheldon's apartment.

Once we moved from the rehearsal hall into the theater, I could not have been surrounded by a more supportive group of allies, led with great diligence by a wonderful young stage manager, Buzz Cohen. Buzz was one of the complete joys of *Ned and Jack*. No matter what you put to her, all things were possible. "Exactly, to be sure," she would say. Buzz stands about five feet tall and is quite petite. I'm five feet eight and would never be described in such a way. Together, we looked like Mutt and Jeff. But in no time, I realized that I could lean on her completely and know that what needed to be done would be done. There is no better definition of a stage manager.

Once we began rehearsals, my first fears dissolved as I threw myself into the play. But at the end of our first dress rehearsal, I was stunned to discover that I—the charming, easygoing, helpful and supportive director—was becoming more and more enraged as each producer, designer and technician quietly told me what each felt had to be done before we opened. Pure and simple, I was not taking criticism, constructive or otherwise, well. In fact, as my mother would have quickly pointed out, I was not taking it *at all,* which was certainly not good for the play, the actors or me. The worst thing I could do was to pass on my anxiety to the company and, thankfully, after a long tirade in the car from Ken on the way home, I settled into paying more attention to what needed to be done and less to my own insecurity.

We began previews. I found that in directing, as in acting, I really trusted the opinions of only a handful of people. I have always felt that if you leave yourself open, you end up in that dreadful state of hanging on to every reaction, comparing notes and comments of friends—friends of mine, friends of Ken's, friends of the cast, friends of the usher's, friends of the dog's. You can get so you don't care who it is. All you want to know is "What do you think?" Then you slip into analyzing which friends came but left, never coming backstage to speak to anybody, as well as the ones who did come back but clearly could not think of anything encouraging to say but felt they could not get away unnoticed. And then, of course, the ones we love, those who dash backstage high in praise. God knows, you know that none of these people—the ones who leave, stay or gush—should be trusted. It takes a great talent—and a great friend—to know and tell you what can and, as important, cannot be dealt with in the space of time you have left. For me, once again, that friend was my agent, Clifford Stevens.

The play was now finding a life of its own. Ken and I could tell the slight ups and downs of each performance. Likewise, the actors were performing beautifully, allowing the playwright's words to carry them so that they could bring to it their full energy and magic. The critics came, as they always do, during our previews. And with the exception of what we came to call "nightmare Sunday," when we played to a house as deadly as a tomb with the critics from both *New York* magazine and *The New Yorker* in attendance, we all eagerly anticipated opening night, knowing the critical die was already cast. For better or worse, we were all free.

The opening of *Ned and Jack* at the Hudson Guild was a great success. After the performance, we all headed to Chelsea Commons, a nearby restaurant, and pretended not to notice that Ken was missing from the table. We ate, drank and laughed until Ken came bursting through the door and threw two newspapers onto the center of the table saying, "They're terrific!" And as we read each one aloud, we were each and all in seventh heaven. At one point, as we continued to drink and now dance, I said prophetically to any within earshot, "Let's enjoy tonight, because there are so damn few nights like this in a lifetime." And enjoy it we did.

From then on, *Ned and Jack* played to full houses at the Hudson Guild. The actors moved with great security and grace onstage, and Sheldon, Ken and I felt that what we had all so carefully and then so hurriedly put together had been worthwhile. Before long, there was very real talk of moving the production to a Broadway house in the fall. And so we closed at the Hudson Guild on a great high, hoping we would continue this success in a few months uptown.

By the end of summer, we were in high gear. Sheldon and I spent a great deal of time together, reworking portions of the script we felt weren't quite right, while Ken had raised the money to book us into what was then called The Little Theatre (and is now the Helen Hayes Theatre) on West Forty-fourth Street, next to Sardi's. I had spoken to Peter Michael Goetz about doing Barrymore again, but felt that another actor would be better suited to play Ned Shelton. Dwight Schultz, though a wonderful actor, was a big, tall, handsome man, and no matter how well he played, he always had a sense of health and indestructibility that was not Ned Shelton at that point in his life. After much discussion as to whether or not we should cast a "name" actor, I decided upon John Vickery, an actor previously unknown to me.

When I was told that an actor named Vickery would be reading for the role, the name obviously stayed in my mind because it was my first husband's last name. As John walked to the stage to read, I prayed that I would not slip up and call him James. John read beautifully, but initially seemed too young for the role. When he came in again, Ken asked him to wear a suit and tie and to pull his long hair back from his face. His reading was even more precise than the first. When he finished, I said, "Mr. Vickery, may I ask you a personal question?" There was a pause as he stared at me from stage.

"All right," he finally said.

"How old are you?" I asked.

"I'm thirty," he said. "But listen," he added rather quickly, "it's all right, because my agents told me that I was probably too young for the part and that you had been married to a man named Vickery. But what the hell, I'm here anyway!" We all laughed and thanked him. That night we called John's agent to say, despite his age and last name, he was our Ned Shelton.

Rehearsals began in October, later than planned because of some difficulty in raising all the money. With the delay, I was now scheduled to report for filming in Arkansas on a television miniseries *The Blue and the Gray*, the very day after our opening night. We kept juggling back and forth trying to work out a slightly more reasonable schedule, but to no avail. There was even discussion that I might have to miss opening night in order to be on set. This I would not hear of and kept praying that filming would fall behind schedule so that I would not have to actually be there until at least a day later.

Once rehearsals began, we very quickly got down to serious work. The new company knit together at once. Even though we had rehearsed and opened before, with the rewrites and new cast, *Ned and Jack* felt like a new show. It was a magical time, discarding what had not worked and discovering all we could that would bring new life to these beloved characters. During previews, what I had most feared began to occur. People who had known the real Ned Shelton and John Barrymore came to see our Ned and Jack. The actress Ruth Gordon was first, arriving with her husband, director-writer Garson Kanin. After the performance, word was sent backstage that Ruth would like to speak to me. I was truly frightened that she would think we had used these two men solely for our own purposes. When I saw Ruth in the lobby, she had tears in her eyes. She reached over and took my hands. "Oh, Colleen," she said. "I came by myself last night and told Garson he must come right back with me tonight to see him." I assumed she meant one or the other of the actors.

"Do you know Peter or John?" I asked.

"No. I knew Ned," she said, "very well," her eyes filling again with tears. "He," she began, "I mean they—the actors and the play are so wonderful. Thank you," she added, pausing for a moment. "It's been such a long time." She turned to leave without saying another word. I was so excited I thought I was going to cry. I hurried back to the dressing rooms to tell the cast of Ruth's reaction.

Opening night came and once more we knew that everything had been decided days before. The reviews were already in and ready to be printed for the following morning's papers. And I could not believe it, but filming for *The Blue and the Gray* was right on schedule and I was due on the set in Arkansas the very next day. But the most frightening thing for me about the whole evening was not the critics or the schedule or even Arkansas but that Helen Hayes and Lillian Gish, two of Ned Shelton's closest friends, were to be in the audience. Indeed, Ned had been godfather to Helen's two children.

After the performance, Miss Hayes and Miss Gish appeared backstage. I will never forget seeing them standing together and then allowing themselves to be brought into each dressing room to be introduced to the actors. Their enthusiasm and kindness were extraordinary. As she was preparing to leave, Helen came over to me.

"He was a saint, Colleen," she said, touching my hand lightly. "Tonight brought it all back. I was always so tense and frightened before an opening, so I would go to his apartment on my way to the theater. There he would be, lying on a chaise which by then had been moved to the living room, just as you have it. He always insisted on ordering the hotel to bring me the same thing: poached chicken. I would eat and he would lie there not able to see me and speak to me." She closed her eyes for a minute, as if she might not continue but did not let go of my hand. "And by the time I left," she whispered, beginning again, "I was calm and serene. That's what Ned Shelton could do for his friends." Miss Hayes squeezed my hand for just an instant. "Thank you," she said, and turning to see Miss Gish joining by her side, left through the stage door.

Ken and I went over to Sardi's to have a drink before going to the opening-night party at the Piccadilly Bar. While we were there, Ken stepped out for a minute and when he came back, gave me an odd look and then a thumbs-down gesture. The most important review, the *New York Times'*, was not good. We joined the company at the Piccadilly, where word got around very quickly that we had not received good reviews. The rest of the party was a blur. The next thing I knew, I was landing in Louisville, Kentucky, at five-thirty in the morning, refueling for the final approach into Fayetteville, Arkansas.

The perfect end to a perfect evening, I thought. *We're not going to get off the ground again. I'm going to be sued for holding up production and have to spend the rest of the day in Louisville.* But we took off and I landed in Fayetteville at seven-thirty. I was picked up and taken to my hotel, where I called Ken back in New York.

"How are you doing, baby?" he said.

"OK," I answered, barely awake. "You?"

"I'm going to have a meeting at ten o'clock. Out of the three main papers, two reviews are bad, one medium-to-good, and even though the outlying reviews are excellent, with no advance, no stars, and a knock from the *Times,* we have to close. I'm so sorry. I'm so terribly sorry."

I went to my trailer on the set in shock. The wardrobe and hair people came in and we laughed and talked. It helped keep me awake. I didn't mention the play. None of them would have heard of *Ned and Jack*. This morning, as luck would have it, we were shooting the scene in which one of my sons was marrying a young lady from the North. The Civil War was over. I walked into a crowded room filled with actors dressed in various nineteenth-century finery for the wedding. The director explained the scene quickly. On "action," we would all come through the door, onto the porch, laughing and talking with the new bride and groom before coming down the steps to tables laden with food.

"Places, please, ladies and gentlemen," the assistant director called. Actors scrambled to various prearranged corners of the room. The actor playing my husband came and took my hand. "And action!" the director barked. I did as I had been told, laughing and celebrating something—a marriage, the end of the Civil War, anything that would get me out the door, down the porch steps, and to the banquet tables without thinking about what I had left behind in New York.

For the rest of the day, I kept thinking of Ned Shelton and somehow, as the hours passed, the deep depression I felt as I hung up the phone from Ken began to lift. Perhaps I was just too exhausted to feel any more tension and disappointment. Or perhaps what Miss Hayes had said was more to the point.

"That's what Ned Shelton could do for his friends, Colleen." I would like to think that Ned might have had something to do with it.

PETER MICHAEL GOETZ

I met Colleen long before *Ned and Jack*—though I'm not sure she'd remember. I have a brother, Tom Wheatley. When I was young, in high school, he was in *All the Way Home* on Broadway with Colleen. This was 1960. I remember coming into town to see it and being introduced to her very quickly backstage. What stays with me about that even today was that she had one of her sons, Alex, I think, sleeping in an open dresser drawer in the dressing room backstage.

Years later, I was doing *Solomon's Child* at the Long Wharf Theatre. Colleen came to a performance and afterward introduced herself to me backstage and said she had a project that I might be right for. I didn't hear anything for a while and just forgot about the whole thing. Then, when I was out in California, I got a call from her. I thought it was someone playing a joke or kidding around. But it was Colleen, and she offered me the role of John Barrymore in *Ned and Jack*.

Anytime you have an actor who directs, you hope that he or she will understand the actors' problems. Colleen was a wonderful director for just that reason, and many more. She instinctively understood how much could be accomplished in a day. If I was a little behind on lines or stumbling, Colleen understood. If I was overboard one day, a little too flamboyant, a little too staggering, she let me work through it. She understood that she could bring me back or perhaps even push it more. There was a total and constant understanding of the actor's process, which is an extraordinary gift. Actors are extremely vulnerable in rehearsals, and you can be very embarrassed when directors take you to task for not finding a character sooner than you can. Colleen had a wonderful understanding and sense of humor that gave us all complete confidence in what we were doing. The way she worked with us, it felt like she was another actor in the play.

So much of what a director does is strictly technical. Colleen struck a brilliant balance between "I don't know too much about that" and "I know exactly what I want." She worked from an acute sense of artistic integrity, knowledge and talent, but she didn't pretend to know more than she did. She didn't ever have to bluff it. Because of her honesty, people around her—particularly the technicians and crew—were always willing and wanting to help. They knew she would make the right decisions from the selection of their suggestions.

It was sad, ultimately. After opening to such great success off-Broadway at the Hudson Guild Theater, we closed in one night on Broadway at the Helen Hayes. The morning after opening, I walked in front of the theater just as the marquee lights were shut off. The box office manager saw me and said to come inside and get my things. We were closing. In spite of that, it was an absolutely fantastic experience for me.

Colleen was devastated about it and particularly upset that she could not be with us. We all talked to her over the phone on that set where she was making some television movie.

We became good friends and had a great simpatico. I greatly enjoyed Ken and her family. She was wonderful to my children. She loved the kids. We would talk late into the night over dinner or drinks about raising children and being in the business. She would share a lot about her life, the times with George, and the struggles of it all. Colleen was also very concerned and interested in other people and other actors. She approached everyone in the same way, from her costars to those in the smallest roles. I think that's why so many people in the theater remember her with such affection.

Later, we did a play for Ted Mann at Circle in the Square called *The Queen and the Rebels*. At the time, Circle had a big hit with *Present Laughter*, starring George C. Scott, no less, which they wanted to extend, knocking Colleen and *The Queen and the Rebels* off the schedule. So we opened instead on Broadway at the Plymouth Theater. *Rebels* was a difficult melodramatic piece. Colleen was wonderful in it and I was probably just fair.

Anyone who knew Colleen will tell you that she was quite a baseball fan. *Rebels* was running during the play-offs for the World Series that year. Before an evening performance of a very big game, Colleen had worked out a series of signals with some of the young actors playing soldiers, including her son, Campbell, so that she would always know the score even if she was onstage. The soldiers would come on and blink to indicate the number of runs for one team and tap their cheek for the other team. It turned out to be a particularly high-scoring game. So here we were in this melodrama—Colleen and I shouting at each other—and each time these soldiers came in, they'd be tapping and blinking like crazy and it began to break us up a bit. We'd start to laugh but then quickly pull ourselves back. But it soon got worse with the anticipation of the soldiers' entrances, so that by the end of the first act, we were both really out of control. We couldn't continue because when Colleen really starts to laugh but can't, she cries. And there I am, this big, tough terrorist-type—giggling. It got so bad, the stage manager brought the curtain down on the first act early. We lost half a page of dialogue and Colleen kind of shouted her last lines as the curtain fell, but we couldn't stop laughing.

Once the curtain was down, we both were very upset with ourselves. But it was like being in church and trying not to laugh. It was catastrophic. I don't know who won the damn game. And for the rest of the run, long after baseball season was over, we would get to those same places and not be able to look at each other for fear of losing it again.

Colleen noticed everything that was going on onstage. That's what made her a real person out there. The things going on around her affected her and that's what made her such a wonderful actress and a delight to work with. Over the years, this story of Colleen "losing it" has practically become myth, and more people than I think ever came to *The Queen and the Rebels* claim to have been in the audience for that one fateful performance.

22

"Remember the mortgage, Colleen."

In 1979, David Eidenberg, my West Coast agent, called to tell me that he had a script for an original television movie, *And Baby Makes Six*, written by Shelley List. I had met her, he said, at a small dinner party at Doris Roberts' about six months previously. David thought the script was good and said that he would forward it to me at the Farm.

I read *And Baby Makes Six* and loved it. It had all the elements that I look for in a play. It was beautifully written, had characters who were true to life, and revolved around a situation that was universal. I accepted the role and asked for Waris Hussein to direct. I had met Waris several years before when I had done an interesting television film with him called *Death Penalty*. Waris is a film director who makes the actors feel that his full attention is always with them. He will take the time to work on a scene as if you were working on a play. Unlike some other film directors I'd worked with, he comes to the set fully prepared. He not only knows the script inside out, but understands what the production should look like, down to the finest detail.

The cast of *And Baby Makes Six* included Warren Oates, Mildred Dunnock, Timothy Hutton and Alex Corey. All were terrific. Shelley knew nothing about my personal life. Yet, in *And Baby Makes Six*, she had written for me two sons who correlated almost exactly with my sons. While shooting the film in Los Angeles, the four of them, my TV sons, Tim and Alex, and my own sons, Campbell and Alex, became very close.

And Baby Makes Six is the story of a husband and wife, the wife's mother, and their children, two boys and a girl. The father, about to retire from business, looks forward, with his wife, to a long vacation traveling around the world. At this point, they discover, to their amazement, that at her age, she is pregnant. The family goes into shock. The film is then about her decision to have the baby.

The amazing thing about making *And Baby Makes Six* was the emotional involvement of everyone associated with it, including the crew. The story had a foundation of truth and humor that touched everyone involved, no matter what age. To this day, when strangers meet me they will often say, "I loved the movie you did about the lady that had the baby late in age." I have also met three or four people with stories similar to my character's. Not long after *And Baby Makes Six* aired, a stewardess, on a flight from San Juan to New Orleans, introduced herself.

"I don't wish to disturb you," she said. "But I have a sister who has three grown children and became pregnant. My family thought she should have an abortion and my sister agreed."

I knew what was coming, but I couldn't believe it.

"My sister watched *And Baby Makes Six*," she concluded, "and the next morning announced to my family that she was going to have the baby."

It was a little girl, she told me, who was named Sarah, as the little girl in the film had been named. I just sat there silent. Although the stewardess seemed very pleased, I didn't know whether to say thank you or to apologize. I still don't.

When I first entered television, I was doing televised plays. Now, thirty years later, I found myself working in this same medium doing original scripts or adaptations of books. An original script requires a very good writer who is able to bring depth to characters and believability to a story line that must be completely told in an hour and thirty-five minutes of viewing time. Like the best play, the emotional life of the characters must all be there on the page, rich yet concise.

Often in an adaptation, the actor will have only the action and its direct result to play without necessarily the thought or emotional process that took the character to that point. When this happens, it is easier for the actor, working in the adaptation of a novel, to study the original material to find the depth of character missing in the condensed adapted script. The danger, of course, is that there just is not enough in the script and that, even by studying the original material, you end up with a scene that is shallow, glib and confusing. It can cause a terrible problem for the director and writer of the adapted version if the actors go home and study the original and enter the set saying, "I think it is much better in the book" or "You've changed my motivation from what it is in the original book."

I have found myself in this position and have been told in no uncertain terms that "the script that you are holding in your hand is the one that is being shot. Go to makeup and we'll start on time." And you do.

Glenn Jordan, whom I knew in New York, asked me to do the television miniseries adaptation of *The Women's Room*, a best-selling novel by Marilyn French. The day I first arrived on the set, at UCLA, I was surprised to see Glenn waiting there to greet me. I found out why when he took me into "hair and makeup" and introduced me to the two gentlemen there.

"This is Colleen Dewhurst," he said, "and I am telling you, in front of her, that she is not to leave either of your chairs until you are finished, even if you have to chain her." The men stood there smiling.

"She will keep saying, 'That's good, that's fine' and try to leave," Glenn continued. "Ignore her." And with that direction very clear, Glenn walked out and left me in their charge. They followed Glenn's instructions to the letter.

It was an extraordinary cast, including Lee Remick, Patty Duke, Lisa Pelikan and Tovah Feldshuh. A strange thing did occur, however, during shooting, when the young actor who had been set to play my lover was released. When his replacement arrived on the set, to my dismay, it was Alex Corey, who had played my son in *And Baby Makes Six*. I couldn't explain to anyone that both of us found this faintly distasteful. I do remember Tim Hutton coming to visit the set and laughing when he found his "mother and brother" now playing lovers.

I was only three days away from finishing my role in *The Women's Room* when, on the Saturday before, Elizabeth Wilson—one of my dearest and oldest friends, whom we have affectionately called Aunt Liz for years—and Lily Tomlin, who both were shooting the movie *Nine to Five*, came to the house in Malibu that Ken and I had rented. Nana was cooking dinner and Ken was making his famous strawberry daiquiris. Before long, we all decided to take a stroll down the beach even though it was dark. Los Angeles had been having very heavy rains, and army vehicles had come onto the beach to remove the debris that had washed up onshore, leaving deep tire tracks in the sand. Lily and I were dashing ahead, leaving Ken and Liz in the middle of some conversation or another.

"That's Flip Wilson's house," Lily said, pointing in the direction of one of the beach houses. "Let's visit him."

We went up the deck stairs and knocked on the glass door. A young lady answered and said that Mr. Wilson was out. We turned around and went back down the steps. Upon reaching the sand and not to be deterred by not being able to visit with Flip, I decided to make a mad dash for the ocean. Aunt Liz and Ken, who were still behind us, saw me run toward the surf and out of the light that shone from the house. I disappeared into the dark.

Unfortunately, in the darkness and with my exuberance, I did not see a large hole looming somewhere before the shoreline. By the time I did, I was full in it. Realizing at the last moment what I'd done, I felt as if I had tried in vain to turn around in midair and go back, like a cartoon character. Instead, very human-like, I fell. Hard. I got right up with that "I didn't fall" attitude that always accompanies stupid accidents, but it was too painful to stand on my right foot. By then, the rest of the group had arrived.

"Can you walk?" Ken asked.

"Maybe, with some help."

"Did you hear anything when you went down?"

"Like what?"

"A break," Ken replied, slightly annoyed.

"Oh, not really—just a little click," I assured him.

With Ken and Liz on each side, and Lily leading the way, I was literally dragged back down the beach, past Flip's (I have a hazy recollection of waving) and up the deck stairs to our house. I lay on the couch while Ken tried to reach Malibu Emergency—which was closed. Never an emergency among the rich and famous, I guess. Undaunted, Lily took the phone and began to call numerous numbers trying to reach a doctor. We could reach no one. I have no idea why. As it became evident that I would not be able to see anyone until morning, Lily and Ken propped up my leg and wrapped my now hideously swollen ankle in ice. I resigned myself to spending the night on the couch, and two guests who had simply come over for dinner stayed the night.

The next morning, we traveled once again, as a group, to Malibu Emergency (open for business), where I was X-rayed and informed that my ankle had been fractured. *No.* I insisted that I had never fractured or broken anything in my life and that this was impossible.

"Well, you have now," said Ken, who was by now truly irritated.

We went back to the house. Nana told us that Ms. Tomlin had received many calls from her numerous messages of the night before. But too late. At this point, poor Ken got on the phone and called my agent, who tried to reach Glenn Jordan. I was due on the set the next morning at seven o'clock. An hour later, Glenn called back.

This had not been an easy shoot for Glenn. The rain and the flood had destroyed sets and made it very difficult for the cast to reach the locations. I told Glenn what had happened. I will never forget his first response.

"Oh, God, honey," he said. "How are you feeling?"

I explained how sorry I was and said that I was sure I could work the next morning. The scene was to be four of us driving out to a camping site, strolling through the woods, and having a picnic. I was sure I could stroll. I *would* stroll. Ken drove me to the set where they had a nurse waiting. I loathed her on sight.

"There's no reason for a nurse," I said. "Please do not touch me."

By now, I had a huge cast going from the middle of my foot to my knee. Refusing the nurse, I picked the strongest-looking gentlemen on the crew to help me to the blanket where the picnic was taking place. It seemed, contrary to my pronouncement, I could not stroll. So rather than walking with the others, I was discovered—prone—already picnicking, sitting on a cloth covering the ground, with another blanket casually thrown over the offending leg and ankle. I found this somewhat amusing since running ahead of the others had gotten me into this mess in the first place. Of course, the script didn't call for Ken's daiquiris.

That same morning, David Eidenberg called Toronto from his office to explain to Garth Drabinsky, the producer of *Tribute*, a film I was scheduled to do with Jack Lemmon and Lee Remick and to which I was due to report in five days, that I would arrive wearing a cast. Garth's response, David reported, was, "We'll take her with two broken legs." This was the best news I'd heard in days. I never did meet Flip Wilson.

DAVID EIDENBERG

I met Colleen in 1971, when I was a production supervisor at the New York Shakespeare Festival. She had been cast to play Gertrude in *Hamlet*, the Festival's first production to be done that summer at the Delacorte Theater, outdoors in Central Park. Colleen didn't want to be in the production, but Joe [Papp]—as he could with people who had once worked for him—had strong-armed her into doing it. Colleen's relationship with Joe was both very intense and ambivalent. They clearly loved each other. But Joe used people when he needed them and then, when he didn't, he was suddenly a very busy man. So he wasn't necessarily very involved as a friend; it was always about work. Perhaps because of this, Colleen wouldn't communicate with Joe directly. She had always liked going through another person to get to Joe, although she could have called him directly at any time. During *Hamlet*, she'd often ask me to ask him things. Despite this odd way of communicating with each other, when they spoke *of* each other, there was clearly a deep attachment and a great deal of respect—but always from a distance. Nevertheless, for whatever reason, Colleen gave in to Joe and reluctantly joined a company that included Kitty Winn, James Earl Jones, Barnard Hughes, Sam Waterson, and Stacy Keach, who played Hamlet. Gerry Freedman was to direct. Before rehearsals, he and I drove up to the Farm in South Salem to discuss the production. When we arrived, Colleen greeted us in the driveway saying, "Well, you're probably wondering whether the old bitch is gonna feed you anything to eat!" We were very fixated on food and, of course, there was nothing prepared. But we all three managed to fix some kind of lunch before sitting down to discuss the play.

Although Colleen and I became friendly during *Hamlet* rehearsals, we nearly got off on the wrong foot. Joe had gotten what he wanted when he talked Colleen into playing Gertrude; what the rest of us got at first was having to contend with how Colleen acted out her frustrations about doing something she really didn't want to do. At one point early on, she walked out of a rehearsal. Then she was late a few times in a row. Someone had to say something to her about it and I, as stage manager, was elected. She was initially quite taken aback that someone like me would reprimand her, and then she was embarrassed that anyone had had to. It was a very difficult rehearsal period for everybody. In the week before we opened, every rehearsal that was called at the

Delacorte was rained out. The set was huge and built on a big turntable, all of which became very slick when wet. James Earl Jones had to do one of his soliloquies way up high on this thing, dead center. You could tell he was scared to death. But Jimmy's reaction to heights was nothing compared to Colleen's rage about her costume. She hated it, particularly the crown, which she felt was too large. When the costume designer wouldn't replace it after numerous requests, one night Colleen simply came offstage, marched to the back of the set, and pitched the damn thing into the lake behind the theater. It was certainly an effective way to ensure that she got a more manageable crown.

Our first performance was very rough. Gerry Freedman was particularly upset that those wonderful opening speeches of Hamlet's father were dying. The actor was having a terrible time with them. I suggested that perhaps George [C. Scott] might do us all a favor and record the speeches, which could then be played over the sound system. It would have required some restaging, but you could have put anyone in that costume and it wouldn't have mattered. Not with George's voice booming above it all. Even though Colleen and George had just separated for the second time a few months before, everyone thought it was a wonderful idea. Surprisingly, George agreed to do it, but he wanted to see the production first. The show was horrible the night George came. The evening was hot, humid, and it was on the verge of raining all night. Worse, the play went on for nearly four hours. By the end of this endless performance George stood, announced that he was having a heart attack, and left. There would be no taping of Hamlet's father. When told of George's sudden departure, Colleen, who had been uncharacteristically quiet about the entire situation, simply replied, "It's not Mummy's problem anymore." End of conversation.

After *Hamlet,* I didn't see much of Colleen again until *A Moon for the Misbegotten* opened in 1974. At the same time that she was doing *Moon* on Broadway, Colleen had gotten herself very involved with an acting troupe called The Family, which had together created and presented Miguel Piñero's play *Short Eyes* way uptown at Riverside Church. *Short Eyes,* a very rough play about a child molester, takes place in prison. The group of actors that worked on it were as rough and angry as the characters they played. They knew firsthand about life "on the inside" (as a prison term is referred to on the street), but they were also a wonderful group of people. Colleen had somehow seen the play early on at Riverside Church and, true to form, practically became its patron. I must have been stage managing something for Joe uptown while Colleen was doing *Moon,* because we began to run into each other after the show and one evening, over late dinner at Barrymore's, she insisted I come to see *Short Eyes.* I did and loved it, although it clearly wasn't a finished piece. At some point, I brought the troupe down to The Public and did a run-through for Joe. Joe clearly liked what he saw but was impatient, and after the first act walked over to me and said, "Can I go now?"

"No," I said. "You have to stay." After the first scene in the second act, I sneaked back over to him in the darkened theater and whispered, "Now, you can go." So since Joe didn't stay to the end, he didn't find out that there really wasn't any ending to the play. But he liked it enough to give us about twenty-five thousand dollars for a workshop production. After a lot of rewriting, Joe opened *Short Eyes* at the Anspacher Theater at The Public, and then moved the production up to Lincoln Center, where it was very successful.

Although she wasn't often physically present for the workshop, rehearsals and performances, Colleen's involvement and support, not only with the production but with this group of men in the play, was key. *Short Eyes* was extraordinary theater and it was quite remarkable the way the whole piece took shape. Once she saw it and also realized how extraordinary the environment was, Colleen very much wanted Joe to do this play and, very uncharacteristically, prevailed upon their friendship in order to turn his attention toward it. The guys adored her, not only for what she had done for them but just for who she was, and they were always up at the Farm, so much so that I think one of Colleen's neighbors got involved with one of them and it got rather crazy. Everybody was drinking themselves silly. It's a wonder everyone survived and anyone got anything done.

I remember Colleen telling me about one of the actors. It seems that his stepfather had gotten out of jail, where he had been serving time for killing the actor's mother in a drunken fight. He stuck a knife in her. So the day he gets out of jail, the big question at the theater was not "How's the house?" but whether the actor would show up to do the show that night or go kill his stepfather. Not your usual backstage banter. Colleen loved that sort of thing and was heartbroken when she heard a few years later that the actor had been shot and killed in Newark. Many of those guys are dead now, including Miguel Piñero. But the whole situation was so typical of Colleen. There she was, starring in one of the most prestigious hits on Broadway in years, with everyone— people like Katharine Hepburn—coming backstage to meet her and compliment her. And then she'd go out the stage door and invite this troupe of ex-cons and street hustlers home for a barbecue. Ah, life at the Farm.

I left the Shakespeare Festival in 1975. Colleen had a big Christmas party up at the Farm that year, during the two weeks she had insisted on having off over the holidays from doing *Moon* in Los Angeles. I hadn't worked since September and was trying to figure out what I was going to do. Colleen suggested I come back with her to California. Before the party was over, I had decided: what the hell, I would. And, at first, it was wonderful. *Moon* was a big hit at the Ahmanson. Colleen had a house on the beach in Malibu. The sun was shining and the Santa Anas were blowing. There were magical nights, one after another, like the evening Colleen, José, his boyfriend and I went to see Ingrid Bergman in the opening of some dreadful play at the Shubert. Even though the play was bad, the evening afterward was unforgettable. Bergman came out to dinner. I couldn't believe it. Ingrid was so beautiful and a totally wonderful person. She clearly loved Colleen and José. They had all worked together in *More Stately Mansions* a few years before.

But eventually *Moon* closed and Colleen went back East. I stayed and immediately went into a depression when I realized what I had done. I had moved out to Los Angeles without a job, without a career, and working for Joe Papp didn't mean anything to anybody out here. But again, through Colleen, I had gotten to know her agent, Clifford Stevens, who worked with another agent, Susan Smith, in Los Angeles. Susan hired me and I soon learned how to be an agent. By the time we all formed STE Representation a year or so later, I was representing Colleen for film and television.

Although Colleen wasn't a big commercial name in the traditional sense in Los Angeles, there were a lot of people in the business who had wonderful memories of her from New York. A number of these people thought they could make Colleen a series star, like Bea Arthur had become with *Maude.* But she would never agree to it or be willing to commit to the amount of time required. The closest she came was doing a television movie, *And Baby Makes Six,* which was also being made as a pilot for a potential series. The script was wonderful, but Colleen made life on the set impossible the entire time. I've always thought that she was so afraid that the movie would go to series, she just kept doing small things that would keep it from happening. And it didn't, although the finished film was terrific. In truth, I think Colleen felt, at that time, that those were her last few years to be able to play a vital, sexual woman, and she didn't want to fritter away this valuable time on television. I never understood it completely. I think she was just frightened of what was happening to her personally, as a woman, and was therefore irrational about the whole situation professionally. She could have done it, made good money, and had a lot of the year to herself. But she had in her head so many clichéd "New York" stereotypes about what living in Los Angeles meant, what doing a series meant, that she wouldn't stay. Her roots just weren't here.

Colleen did come out and do a number of guest appearances and a few good films, particularly a television movie called *Between Two Women* in which she starred with Farrah Fawcett. It was film director Jon Avnet's first big credit. Jon, Farrah and Colleen all became very fond of one another, and Avnet would endlessly try to hire her in the feature films he went on to do, most notably at the end of her life, *Fried Green Tomatoes.* But it didn't happen.

Colleen came in to do an episode of *Moonlighting.* Bruce Willis and Cybill Shepherd were going at each other the entire time, but they had the sense to be nice to her. Colleen didn't care. She thought the whole situation was funny and just needed the money. She always needed the money, so she'd come out, do a week or two and go back to the Farm. Nothing, however, hit the way *Murphy Brown* did. Casting the role of Avery Brown, Murphy's mother, eventually came down to Lauren Bacall and Colleen. I made a lot of calls on this. The network nearly went with Bacall because she was the bigger name. But ultimately, they decided she was also a bigger pain in the ass, and Candice [Bergen] loved Colleen. The episodes she did over the next two years were very successful, both for the show and for Colleen. The producers, the writers and the cast adored her. They would have written her into the show as much as she wanted to do it. And they were devastated when they received the unexpected news of her death. You'll notice that Colleen's picture, as Avery, has never been moved from where it sits on the table behind the couch on the Murphy living room set. Who knows what might have happened for Colleen from playing just that part. Before *Murphy Brown*, Colleen was never really "on the list" with the network types—although she certainly had many fans out here in the business. *Murphy Brown* put her on the list and, you know, she probably couldn't have cared less.

୭୭ ୭୭ ୭୭

I was shooting in Toronto when a script entitled *Between Two Women* arrived. I read it, liked some of it, but was unsure that I wanted to play "the mother." I was interested in the property but had doubts about the character. I let the project more or less drop, and two weeks later I flew to San Diego for one of the first meetings I was to attend as the new president of Actors' Equity.

While in San Diego, a rewrite of the script was delivered to my hotel and I met with Jon Avnet, the producer-director, for dinner the following evening.

Mr. Avnet sent a car and I was driven to a restaurant in the Pacific Palisades. I liked Jon at once because he has what I call "New York energy." This is a combination of being a producer who knows what he wants and is determined to get it, and a director who knows his script inside and out and yet is willing to discuss the problems it may present to an actor.

After about thirty minutes, Farrah Fawcett arrived with her baby son. We ate and talked for an hour and a half about the script. I was quite impressed with Jon and Farrah's discussion of the material and the ideas they wished to implement. I knew then that I wanted to work with both of them.

Between Two Women was one of the most rewarding experiences I have had working in television. I arrived three days early, in order that we might rehearse in Jon's office before the actual start of production. What a luxury. As we rehearsed we improvised, with much of our improvisation appearing in the final script. It didn't take long for me to realize that Farrah and Jon were both hardworking professionals who stayed with a problem until it was solved.

The cast of *Between Two Women* included Michael Nouri and Steven Hill, who played my husband. This was a joy in itself. Following those first three days of rehearsal, I came to the studio knowing that it would not be the usual "set up and shoot." Each day, there were revelations, mainly through improvisation and discussion, which often resulted in a completely different approach to a given scene.

Farrah was tireless and completely immersed in the work, which was difficult and sometimes debilitating. But as I would drive back to the beach, I was tired in a way that an actor wishes to be. These were not days that drained you because of boredom. Instead, we each reached down and pulled out everything we had to give. I could tell, even in the first two days, that I would be able to look on *Between Two Women* with pride.

JON AVNET

Between Two Women was written for Colleen. I knew what a wonderful actress she was and after I saw her in *A Moon for the Misbegotten* with Jason Robards, I just always wanted to work with her. I don't think I could have done *Between Two Women* without Colleen. It was probably a stupid thing to get involved in it not knowing if she would do it, but, thankfully, it worked out because she did. No one could play a witch better than Colleen. She could turn a phrase and blow cigarette smoke in someone's face better than most. With material like this, she could have such an edge. Just as with material like *Moon*, she could break your heart. The role Colleen played was that of an enormously destructive woman who, because she is so unhappy that she had given up her career prematurely, nearly destroys the lives of those around her.

Farrah [Fawcett Majors] was a big fan of Colleen's. She and Colleen first met over dinner to discuss the material. Basically, a dinner like that is just to see what, if any, chemistry there is between two actors and to try to get a sense of how things will work out. It also gives the actors an opportunity to gracefully get out of the project if they want to before things get really too far along. Colleen and Farrah connected with each other right away. I know you wouldn't necessarily expect that, their professional backgrounds being so different. But they seemed to like each other very much as women immediately. Once we began to rehearse, it became very clear that what they sensed about each other over dinner would work very well for them in the film.

Although this was my first directing job, I wasn't intimidated by Colleen. I was really impressed by her, but I've found since then that the more talented the actors are, usually the easier it is to work with them. Jessica Tandy and Robert Redford, whom I've since directed, come immediately to mind, as does Colleen, as examples of that ideal. If I could think of it, Colleen could do it. There was no limit to her talent or to her willingness to explore the role. I was thrilled when Colleen won the Emmy for *Between Two Women*, even though she wasn't there to accept the award. She was doing some play in New York and wouldn't skip a performance for "just" an awards show, although I'm certain she could have requested a night off, if she had really wanted to be there. I know she had long been recognized for her work in the theater, but I could never understand why her work had been so diluted out here in Hollywood until the last few years of her career. It was nice to be part of that feather in her cap. I nearly had the chance to work with Colleen again. She almost did my film *Fried Green Tomatoes*. When it didn't happen, I was very disappointed; later, when I realized why—that she was already sick—I was very sad. *Fried Green Tomatoes* is dedicated to Colleen.

∞ ∞ ∞

I fear it is too easy to become creatively lazy in television, as your good work is too readily accepted as your best. Often, that's all there is time for. There are two extremes that allow this to occur. One is the production in which you appear on time and are put through hair and makeup. You arrive on a set you have never seen. The camera is ready and you quickly shoot someone else's version of the script before repeating it all for the next shot. The other involves the self-indulgent director and actors who waste time and money forever discussing how each one "sees it," with no one in command, each only wishing to show off their depth or, more often, their lack of it.

When you work with two people like Farrah and Jon, who will not settle for anything but their best, it demands that you bring everything you have to your own work. It is difficult sometimes in this profession to feel that what you do has an importance. Working with professionals such as these allows you the opportunity to do the kind of work that makes you proud of the project and of yourself.

Unfortunately, in many cases the best thing about any number of the television movies I did was often not the script but the location. For a few weeks of work, I would have the chance to travel to places I'd never been and might never have reached were it not for the job. And, of course, the checks were always greatly appreciated. So I cannot complain. In most cases, I was very grateful for the work. Case in point: There was yet another television version of the Old Testament in which I was to play Rebecca. Another strong woman of the desert, you might say, all hair, flowing garments and sheep. There are always sheep. Or if it's one of those epics about ancient Rome—and I was also happy to do my share of those—same hair, braided this time, big rings and red wine. There is always red wine.

Nevertheless, I was very excited that this Old Testament film would shoot on location in Israel. Jane Broder had originally planned to surprise me by flying with me to Tel Aviv but had to cancel, at the last minute, when she began not to feel well. Instead, Jane took me to the airport. There she gave me a small piece of paper, asking that I go to the Wailing Wall in Jerusalem and, as is the custom, place this prayer for her in a crack between the ancient stones.

Two days before I was to leave, there was a terrorist attack at the airport in Rome, killing many innocent passengers, some of them children. When Jane and I arrived at the departure gate at Kennedy Airport in New York City, it was jammed with people who had been waiting there for hours. Miss Broder, as usual and like a ship in full sail, pushed her way to the ticket counter while I stood frozen against a wall in the middle of the crowd waiting. I could see Jane arguing with first one and then another El Al official.

Nearly half an hour later, Jane came back and told me that all flights to Tel Aviv but mine had been canceled. She was informed, however, that all first-class passengers would be flying coach. This, Jane said, was unacceptable. I was going to Israel to work in a film and it was a union rule that I fly first class. Despite the situation around us, to Jane, this was a perfectly logical demand. And somehow, she managed to convince them.

I took my seat in first class. It was empty except for me and one very distinguished-looking couple sitting four rows ahead of me (who I can only assume had an agent as persistent as mine). As the plane began to taxi down the runway, a gentleman came up the stairs from coach and sat down beside me. He was very polite, but clearly did not wish to engage in small talk. We were served dinner, after which the lights in the cabin were lowered. I looked up from my book and noticed across from me was a curtained area. As one of the stewards passed through the curtain, I could see a gentleman sitting with a carbine across his legs. I fell into a light sleep. Each time I awoke, a different gentleman was sitting awake and alert beside me, and in the aisles three or four men who had not been there before were lying asleep. I, however, spent the rest of the flight wide awake.

So here I was about to enter the world of the Old Testament carrying, for my dear friend, a prayer to a land that had been holy for thousands of years. How strange, that as I would be reliving the stories of Isaac and Rebecca and their sons, Jacob and Esau, I would be flying back with their descendants, who now were being called to active duty to protect that sacred inheritance.

A few years later, I flew to Israel again to do *Joseph and Mary,* this time a Canadian-American television production of the Bible. I was to play Elizabeth, the mother of John the Baptist. It did occur to me that lately I seemed to be portraying many women who were past the childbearing age and went on to surprise everyone by giving birth. It was better not to dwell on the subject, but I did have to be grateful for never fully embracing "the Method."

Elizabeth was much easier than Rebecca, who seemed to be in a constant state of depression about the situation, poor woman. I remember one line I had, as Rebecca, who, running up and down the hills, exclaims, "Why now, O Lord, why now?" At times, I thought the same thing myself. Not about childbearing, but about the film. I'm sure if God had spoken to me, he would have replied simply, "Remember the mortgage, Colleen."

I loved working in Israel and the chance it gave to visit Jerusalem, Masada, the Dead Sea and Galilee. So much of all of our spiritual history is tenuously held and preserved here. It was extraordinary to me that you could see the whole country in such a short space of time. Yet every area is completely different in feeling and with such a peculiar dual personality of ancient spirituality and current events.

To stand on top of Masada and hear the story of that siege, to look upon the shore of Galilee and know that these are the waters where Jesus calmed the storm and told his disciples to cast their nets is to understand that this land spiritually belongs, in many ways, to all men and women.

When *Joseph and Mary* was screened for critics prior to its television broadcast, I was told that one of the critics, upon exiting the screening room, said to the producer, "It's wonderful. It has something to *offend* everyone."

Why me, O Lord, why me? Indeed, why not.

Clifford Stevens called one day to tell me that PBS would be producing a series about five thousand years of Jewish history. As you can imagine, there were to be many installments. And, as you can imagine, by now I was practically an on-location biblical expert. One installment would include an actor and actress to play many roles. Judd Hirsch had been cast and they had approached me to play the female roles.

"But Clifford, if this is five thousand years of the history of the Jewish people," I said, "how are they casting only two actors to portray them, and please, don't you think they would want somebody else? Please."

Without missing a beat, Clifford replied, "Honey, you are obviously acceptable to my people."

I prayed—a word I do not use lightly in either my personal or professional life—that this series about five thousand years of Jewish history would be the end of my being cast in biblical epics to be shot in Israel, unless—God forbid, and in this case, asking Him would seem appropriate—I was to be cast as Sarah, who gave birth when she was eighty.

Two years later, Clifford's voice came over the phone informing me that indeed there was one woman whom I had missed.

"Our leader," he said, "Golda Meir."

And so I found myself cast as Mrs. Meir in the Canadian production of *A Sword in Gideon*. This part consisted mostly of wigs, noses, and wrapped legs. *Oy.* The only discussion Clifford had with the producers was to inform them that it would be unacceptable for me to fly on a non-Israeli airline to the Holy Land.

"Miss Dewhurst only flies El Al to Israel," he said, "as they are the only pilots she feels secure with."

I knew, from experience, that I would have fighter pilots at the helm—and possibly a few in first class.

23

"... you have somehow survived such bad directors!"

In the early 1980s, I had been doing a great deal of television and wanted more than anything to go back to the stage. Clifford Stevens knew this, so when he called me to say that he had a call from Nikos Psacharopoulos at the Williamstown Theatre in Massachusetts, I was very happy. Nikos was doing Anton Chekhov's *The Cherry Orchard* and wanted me to play Madame Ranevsky, the owner of a once-grand country estate which must be sold. I had never done Chekhov but it had always intrigued me. I told Clifford that I would get the play and read it. I found a copy in the house and on reading it thought, "Well, I'm not the first person who would come to my mind for this role, but I would love to try it."

I was also very interested in going to Williamstown. I had heard a great deal about it and knew many of the people who worked there. It seemed an enviable company, with many returning each summer, year after year. I also had heard Nikos' name in connection with Williamstown for years, but didn't know much about him. I had been told, however, that he was a great expert on Chekhov and, as I was not well versed in the playwright and faced a very short rehearsal period, I felt I should be in the directorial hands of someone who would be able to give me the subtext quickly.

As I thought about the offer, however, I did remember one statement made to me by a very good friend and director who also knew Williamstown very well. I had been speaking to him about my son Campbell, who had been thinking he might like to apprentice as an actor.

"No, Colleen," he replied quite certainly. "Not for Campbell. Certainly not the first time out; as a teacher Nikos can be very destructive." I immediately dropped the idea because when I first came to New York, I had my own run-in very early with the woman at the American Academy who had been exceedingly destructive. It took all my energy to protect myself from her. In the end, there was little energy to create or learn. I didn't want Campbell to fall into a first situation like that.

But I pushed the thought aside, called Clifford back, and said, "Yes, I would very much like to do this." Clifford was not particularly enthusiastic about my working with Nikos, but made the arrangements. In the few weeks that followed, I found myself looking forward to going to Williamstown. I read the play whenever I had an opportunity. I felt it was a challenge for me. I was also somewhat nervous because it had been a while since I had been onstage. I doubt that there is an actor alive who doesn't worry after a long lapse between stage performances that he's forgotten all he knows, with the recurring thoughts: *I'm fooling myself; I can't really act, and if I get back on the stage in this, I will only prove that to myself and to all concerned.*

I drove to Williamstown on a beautiful day. I easily found the theater in the beautiful New England town, parked the car, and went looking around for the powers that be. The staff was very nice, happy to see me, and eager to get me oriented. Rehearsals had begun two days before with members of the resident company. I quickly followed directions sending me to where I was to stay, and returned an hour later to join the stage manager, two actors and two understudies in a small rehearsal room nearby. They put me into some blocking that had supposedly been worked on over the previous two days. I was not very comfortable with this process, but before it could go on too long, Nikos sent word for me to join him in his office upstairs.

"At last!" he cried, jumping to his feet as I entered the room. A charming and attractive man in his sixties, he sat down opposite me and we proceeded to talk.

"I'm so happy to be here, Nikos," I began, making typically mundane chatter. "I've heard many wonderful things about you and look forward to getting to work."

"It's a joy for me to have you here," Nikos responded, very nice, but still just chatter. "I've seen you onstage many times and I know we will have an exciting experience together."

I just kept nodding and smiling as he went on about Chekhov, the theater, and other actors who had worked with him there. "But the truly amazing thing about you, Colleen," he said, "is that you have somehow survived such bad directors." I could feel the smile freeze on my face, although I kept nodding as he went on about the "bad directors," but without ever naming anyone in particular. The conversation wound down. I got up to leave and as I turned at the door to say good-bye, Nikos took my hand and repeated, "You have survived so many bad directors. How do you do it?" I could not respond. But as I drove to my house in town, I kept thinking, *Who does he think I have survived?* I should have thought less about him and more about the inner warning bell that had just gone off.

The next morning, after a tortured night of no sleep, I arrived for my first rehearsal. When I entered, I was thrown to see that all the other actors were already there, sitting in a horseshoe formation with an empty chair at the center. As I entered, Nikos greeted me effusively and led me to just that chair. It was an incredibly good group of actors, including Blythe Danner, Maria Tucci, Austin Pendleton, who is such a delight, Chris Reeve, John Glover and Kate Burton. We sat there while Nikos held forth.

"We have no stars in this company. It is an ensemble. No one at Williamstown is treated like a star."

I felt uncomfortable. It seemed odd that Nikos was compelled to make this announcement to a company that had been—with the exception of me—playing together all summer. But we began, proceeding to read through the play. One of the actors and I got up to begin working on our feet. Nikos asked us to stop. We were just to read; he would put individual scenes on their feet later. After the read-through, we continued to rehearse, with Nikos picking scenes out of sequence to stage.

For the next few days, Nikos would call for certain scenes over and over again, approaching them one way and the next day asking for an interpretation quite the opposite. The next day we would give him that, and then be asked for the scene again, following the approach we had given the first time. It got to be a company joke that when Nikos would ask for certain scenes I would actually scream—in good humor. But that "approach" also changed as I began to realize that he didn't quite know what he wanted.

This began to take its toll on all of us. Maria Tucci was practically perfect from the first reading. As I watched through the early days of that ten-day rehearsal period, I began to see her buckle, becoming confused as she tried to perceive what it was Nikos wanted from her. She could not, however, because Nikos could not make himself clear. Worse, never in all the time I was there did I hear him tell the actors that they were on the right track or that they had done well. I've heard it said again and again that actors are essentially children whose relationship to their directors is essentially parental. This is probably true. But if actors, similar to children, are only criticized for their behavior and never given clear direction or guidance, which in turn isn't acknowledged for being followed, they begin to go crazy. You begin to doubt yourself. You get angry. Children do. Actors, too.

We continued to rehearse the play's individual scenes out of sequence. Now, I've done this many times, but there finally comes a time when you must start at the beginning and work to the end to find out if the scenes fit together in terms of character as "the play." This is essential since the person you play is revealed and develops from scene to scene, as the playwright has written her, up to the final curtain.

"Chekhov is wonderful," Nikos announced one day, as if he knew I was at my wit's end about this process. "Each scene is so extraordinary that you don't have to rehearse in sequence. The play is like a necklace of beads. You simply snap them together and it works."

I was dumbfounded but thought, *I've never done Chekhov before, maybe he's right.* But sadly, I found I was no longer looking to him for guidance, but listening to such statements as this and wondering, as I studied and studied on my own, what must he mean? I also began to be troubled by how Nikos related to me as a person in rehearsal. He always seemed to be talking to the side of my neck, breathing on it, speaking to me in whispers and low tones as if we were in a seduction scene instead of a director speaking to an actress.

All the while Nikos was reminding the company that "there are no stars at Williamstown," my scenes with other members of the cast were staged in a "V," with me at the apex, much as an insecure star would insist upon being directed in a summer stock star vehicle in order to upstage the rest of the company. I began to feel the long-forgotten frustration and dread of going to rehearsals, instead of looking forward to them, knowing that I was going to learn nothing. I was tired of looking for help from a man who had no intention or ability to offer any, who was working only to satisfy his own ego. We were in the hands of an egomaniac who could not make himself understood.

One morning, I woke up in a rage and talking—practically shouting—to myself as I got dressed. I jumped into the car and drove over to where Maria was staying. I burst through her kitchen door and found her making breakfast.

"You're wonderful in this, Maria," I began, scarcely taking time to say hello. "And don't you let anyone interfere with that. Don't let yourself get angry. Don't let yourself get upset. Just keep working the way you are. You are excellent. You must not let him tie you up in such knots that you are unable to get free."

"Who are you talking to, Colleen?" Maria replied when I had to take a moment to breathe.

And we both laughed because obviously she knew—and now, so did I.

Eventually, as I always do in a situation such as this that I cannot remedy, I blocked Nikos out completely. I went as far inside myself as I could. I tried to protect myself by being present but untouchable. I knew what I was doing was not right; it was worse than not right, it was wrong and very close to being bad.

Now Nikos was frustrated and as his frustration built, he began to make even more interesting statements, not about my performance but more about what he had hoped to accomplish by inviting me there.

"There's a mystery about you, Colleen," he said. "No one has ever really seen you onstage because you hold back. There is something you don't reveal."

I stood looking at him but would not respond. This man wants me to break down completely. He was trying to find my Achilles' heel, as I watched him poke for it in other actors. I knew what kind of breaking down he wanted, but without the protection of any real direction, I was not going to give it to him just to be snapped into place with the other actors' psyches punched into place on either side.

"What are you thinking of when you stare at me like that?" he said. "I don't know how to get through to you. I don't know what you're feeling. You make me ill at ease."

You deserve to be ill at ease, I thought, *because with the exception of two or three actors who have been here for years and seem to know how to go about their business with you, you have made us all extremely uncomfortable, with you, the play and your process.* But all my anger couldn't change that I was in desperate need of help and that my performance had been caught in a web of confusion and innuendo from which I could not break out. Clifford was out of town at the time; Ken was unable to come up until the opening; and there was no José to depend on. I am reminded of wonderful lines from Noël Coward's *Hayfever:* "Is this a game? Yes. And one that must be played until the end."

I was at the point where I couldn't wait—despite my fear—to have an audience in order to sever myself from this entire rehearsal process and attempt in performance to find out what was wrong. At one point, just before we opened, Nikos explained that the Library of the Performing Arts at Lincoln Center in New York wished to come and tape the performance for their archives. He seemed so pleased to make the announcement. I stood there thinking, *Just say no, Colleen. It's simple. Speak up. Say no.* But standing there with my fellow actors, I also thought, *I have no right to stop this for everyone just because I feel inadequate.*

At another rehearsal, a day closer to opening, Nikos continued to ask for scenes that had already been overworked. I was still waiting for the run-through that would give us all some idea as to where we were. I could no longer ignore the fact that some of the other actors' biggest scenes were still being played straight upstage to me, a nonmoving, nonspeaking actress whose reaction was not important for the audience to see at that time. Perhaps the most uncomfortable example was in a scene with Kate Burton. Kate, a lovely actress and dear friend of my family's, played my daughter and had a very important scene in which she comforts me after the cherry orchard is sold. She was directed to play it on her knees in front of the chair in which I was sitting. I kept thinking, *Nobody in the audience can see this child's face.* We would try to shift one way or another to turn Kate slightly downstage, but to no avail. With every attempt, Nikos would insist that she speak upstage to me. At that point my control, which I had been hanging on to so desperately, broke. I stopped and, turning to him, asked simply if we were going to be rehearsing the areas that had gone so dreadfully the day before on the new set. Upon receiving one of Nikos' spaced-out answers and realizing his inability to face reality, I lost it and began to scream, doing what I hate most in myself. I was by now so angry and speaking so furiously that I could not control what I said and happily, on the occasions when this has occurred, cannot usually remember it afterward.

Now, however, as I think about it, I'm not even sure that my fury was all about my scene with Kate. What ultimately pulled the trigger for me was coming to rehearsal early and watching Nikos rehearse a scene with Austin Pendleton and another actor. I had sensed through rehearsals that Nikos was not very fond of this actor. On this day, I entered quietly and sat behind Nikos, where several other members of the company were sitting. Austin and the actor were standing in front of Nikos, facing us. It became quickly and painfully apparent that Nikos was methodically and sadistically annihilating this actor, and there was no way for any of us in the room to exit quietly.

Austin Pendleton is one of the most compassionate men I know. As he stood by, I could see him trying to figure a way to breach into what was happening and stop the tirade. I had no idea whether this was a particularly good actor or not, as Nikos had dealt with him in the same way he had dealt with us all. But while some of us were at least holding our own, this poor actor was not. And now Nikos, through some personal frustration, was making him his target, asking him questions, pushing him and embarrassing him. The actor was responding courteously, trying as best he could to hold on to his dignity. I watched as he tried to find out what Nikos wanted. But he consistently failed because Nikos' object was not to help him but to make him appear stupid for not being able to deliver what was required.

I didn't know where to look. I kept staring into my lap, pretending that I could not see or hear what was happening, as were the others still in the room with me. Nothing stopped Nikos. He finally reached the stage where, in front of us all, he began to question this man's talent. This was unforgivable. Nikos had hired this actor, who had a good reputation. It was now his responsibility to find a way to work with him. Simply to criticize his abilities, when he was unwilling to address his own inability to make clear what he wanted, was to me reprehensible behavior.

Thankfully, Austin finally found a legitimate point where he could break in and, speaking quietly to the actor and Nikos, bring this abusive display to an end with some courtesy and understanding. I now understood all I needed to know about Nikos Psacharopoulos and, consequently, when my own walls came tumbling down two days later, I, unlike Austin, was neither courteous nor understanding and could find no good reason to be.

At our first preview, I realized that I was in as much trouble as I had thought. We each continued playing our roles with very little change. By the time we opened, I was giving a performance that I wished were taking place somewhere in the middle of Idaho or anyplace where I could be certain that no one I ever knew would see me.

Nikos, however, seemed pleased with the production. This only served to make me furious and more determined to have nothing whatsoever to do with him. Yet I was shocked to find that he continued to try to make contact with me. During performances, I asked my dresser—a very sweet young girl who had been assigned to me and was more nervous than I on opening night—never to leave my dressing room if Mr. Psacharopoulos entered. Nevertheless, Nikos continued to drop by even though he could never manipulate a moment with me alone. I could see him in my mirror glaring at my dresser, waiting for her to leave. I would look back threateningly in the glass at this poor child in case she might dare think of leaving. She didn't. Nikos would make some statement. I would reply without looking at him or turning around. Nikos would leave. At times, I thought the dresser would cry.

Ken came on opening night with Maureen Stapleton and her escort. After the performance, there was really nothing for them to say, although they came back to my dressing room and tried. By the time I got dressed and was ready to leave, Ken and the other gentleman were still there, but Maureen was missing. We three moved on to the parking lot to find her leaning against the car with her arm cozily around Nikos' neck talking. I dreaded us all having to make some awful small talk before we could get into the car and leave. As we came over and just before they saw us, I heard Mo exclaim, "Nikos, my dear, you must never direct again. You cannot direct shit!" I was more tickled to overhear this remark than I care to admit and it did break us all up. Nikos turned to see us but seemed oblivious to what had just happened.

Our run was short but seemed interminable. And, of course, because Williamstown is as popular as it is, there were many friends and associates who came to see us. There were also the dreaded matinee and evening performances which were taped for the Performing Arts Library. That night, during the curtain call, I wondered if there must not be some way I could waylay the film crew on their way back to the city and burn the tape.

In a perverse way, once I could shake off Nikos in rehearsal and preview, I began to enjoy playing the role, coming onstage and trying, in front of an audience of six or seven hundred people, to do the work that should have been done, with his help, two or three weeks before. I was fortunate to be working with such a wonderful company of actors who were willing to try with me to find the answers onstage.

After the final Saturday night performance, I piled all my things into the car and early Sunday morning, headed home. I thought a great deal about what had happened and the old joke, "Was I there? And if I was, what went on?" I wanted to get back on the stage. I wanted to do something that would challenge me and that was dangerous. In spite of the process and results, I had studied this script more fully and with more commitment than anything I had done on film over the past two years. I had been with a company of actors who are some of the best on the American stage. The theater was beautiful and the New England setting perfect. I had seen two other very different productions while I was there, both guided by directors other than Nikos. One, *The Front Page* with Ed Herrmann, and the other, *Whose Life Is It Anyway?* with Blythe

Danner and Richard Dreyfuss. I enjoyed them both, particularly watching the actors I was rehearsing with and playing with in *The Cherry Orchard* put themselves as fully as possible into these American plays, creating a true repertory company.

Mr. Psacharopoulos had found himself a home in Williamstown and had been able to build an incredibly worthwhile theater ensemble. Perhaps that was his skill, as an administrator and gatherer of talent, not a director of it. On late nights, as a number of us in *Cherry Orchard* would talk about what we were going through with this production, these same actors all agreed that they wanted to return to Williamstown, whether they would be in a play directed by Nikos or not. They simply loved the theater too much not to want to work in this home, of sorts, that had been created. I know that Nikos had many successes at Williamstown, as I must say Alan Schneider had many wonderful successes in spite of my experience with him on *Ballad of the Sad Café*. I can only assume that as far as these two men are concerned, I did not get the message. Or if I did, I found it unbelievable.

Since that time, I've read *The Cherry Orchard* again. And I think that someday, with a José Quintero or someone with whom I speak the same language, I would love to try it again.

CLIFFORD STEVENS

There was a great love and trust that Colleen and I shared. We would fall into talking about her career choices in social situations or over the phone. But I've also always believed that an agent can't force an actor to do something or not do something. You can make suggestions, you can advise, you can cajole, but the actor is ultimately going to do what he or she wants. When Colleen said yes to a project, that was it. Even if she would reconsider and think her decision was a bad idea, she just would never pull out. I would encourage her to remember that it was always her right to change her mind. But she simply could not go back on her word. This was one area where Colleen and I didn't always agree. And she never tried to hide that. We'd talk about it. I'd say, "I don't think you should do this." She'd listen and then go do it. Perhaps the best example of that was when she agreed to do a production of *The Cherry Orchard* for Nikos Psacharopoulos in Williamstown. I told her from the start that I didn't feel that she and Nikos would be a good match. "I just want to suggest that I don't think he is going to direct you in a way that you're going to find acceptable," I said. It was just an educated guess, but knowing them both well, I suspected that there would be no chemistry between them. Well, they got off on the wrong foot from the day Colleen arrived and it just got worse from there. When I called her at one point, having heard how poorly things were going, our conversation was short.

"I forbid you to come and see this!" she said. And I didn't. But it seemed that just about everyone else in the world did, including Bob Whitehead, Zoe Caldwell, Maureen Stapleton and many others from New York. I mean everyone showed up and she was not happy about it. But there was nothing she could do. "What am I doing in this thing?" she cried over the phone.

"You're asking the wrong person," I replied.

Probably the only project she said no to that I thought was a big mistake was the role of Nurse Ratchet in the Oscar-winning film version of *One Flew Over the Cuckoo's Nest*. Colleen turned down offers to play that role three times, the last time from Michael Douglas himself. With each offer, I begged her to reconsider, but she wouldn't. "I hate that woman," was all she said.

"So think Stanislavsky," I told her. "Please, Colleen, find the niceness in her."

"I can't," she replied. And with that, the subject was closed. We spoke the morning after the Oscars, after *Cuckoo's Nest* won for Best Picture and Louise Fletcher had won the Oscar for Best Actress, playing the woman Colleen hated. "Don't worry about it," she said. "I wouldn't have won it. You can't play someone you hate." And that was that. Colleen went about her career with very few regrets. I remember the night we watched the Tony Awards together at my apartment, a year that she was nominated! When she announced that she wouldn't be going, I said, "Colleen! You're nominated. You have to go!"

"Oh, no," she replied. "This is Julie's year," meaning Julie Harris, who was also nominated.

"So what are you going to do if you win?" I asked. "Make a speech in the living room?"

"Don't worry about that, Clifford," she said. And she called it. She didn't win. Julie Harris did.

Colleen always brought such an excitement to her work. She loved being in rehearsal. The process was a joy for her. I remember going back to see the last performance of *Who's Afraid of Virginia Woolf?* It was remarkably different from what I had first seen in tryouts at Boston. Not that she had completely refashioned her performance, but it had grown into something quite wonderful. On the other hand, she knew she wasn't very good after the opening of *Long Day's Journey into Night*, at Yale in 1989. After seeing the performance, I gave Colleen a copy of Huxley's *Between Heaven and Hell*, for her to read how people operate under the influence of drugs. We never discussed whether she read it or not, but by the time she came into New York, she was quite good. Colleen always said to people, "There are only two people I let come near my work. That's my director and Clifford." We would always go out when she was in previews or out of town and I'd like to think that I was a help to her.

I don't think Colleen really had the opportunities in film and television to work on the same kind of excellent material that she did onstage. But some of that work was quite wonderful. I think the television films *And Baby Makes*

Six and *Baby Comes Home* were quite good. If you saw them today, you'd see how she elevated both projects and everyone with her, even though they were done as all television is done—very quickly and without the kind of rehearsal process that allowed Colleen to bring such depth to her work onstage. Of course, *Murphy Brown* was a delight. I loved her in those few episodes, because they gave her the wonderfully rare opportunity to be funny and light. You know, this whole image of Colleen as "earth mother" was ridiculous. She was a needful, caring and complex woman. Playing Avery Brown allowed her to play against all that "O'Neillian" heaviness that people had come to associate with her and, in fact, play someone much closer to herself.

I don't think anyone referred to Colleen as the "earth mother" before *A Moon for the Misbegotten.* But that performance brought everything about her and everything that people wanted to *perceive* about her together. That production, coupled as it was to her cello voice and that laugh which could be about so much more than humor, was breathtaking. Hers was an extraordinary performance. It was a performance that is forever. As someone wrote in *Time* magazine about an actor brilliantly playing Malvolio, in *Romeo and Juliet:* "Retire the Malvolio cup." I think you could safely say the same about Colleen in *Moon*: "Retire the Josie Hogan cup." Without a doubt, *A Moon for the Misbegotten* elevated Colleen's entire body of work, but success like that can also haunt you. *Moon* put Colleen over the top at age fifty. But if you look at it from another perspective, it took her exactly that many years to arrive, although that was really only about the general public's awareness of her work. She had long been "an actor's actor." And the recognition and celebrity that *Moon* brought to Colleen in no way takes into account how much living carried her to that moment, and how much of herself she continued to pour into her professional and personal commitments for the next seventeen years.

24

"Just give the library speech."

In March of 1982, the phone rang. I picked it up.

"I have a collect call for anyone from Alex Scott," the operator said. "Will you accept the call?"

"Yes, I will."

"Hi, Mom," Alex said. "So, you're not in jail?"

"Listen to me, Alex," I said. "I did that because it was important to me and I believed in it. There are many issues at stake, not just the destruction of an old theater in order to build a new one in a new hotel. It's about—"

"Wait, wait, wait, Mom," Alex shot back. "I'm not calling to say you were wrong. I'm only asking why does it have to be your face on the front page of the *New York Times?*"

This is one of the drawbacks of being the son of people who can, at times, be highly visible. Unfortunately, I have nothing to do with what writers put in a newspaper. Of the two boys, Alex, in particular, has fought hard for anonymity. He has been always most vociferous about it if the publicity did not involve my profession, but, as has been often the case in the last few years, is due to causes or issues that I have been drawn to, such as in the aforementioned case, the ill-fated attempted to save the precious Morosco and Helen Hayes theaters from the developer's wrecking ball. For some reason, this he finds particularly annoying.

A few winters ago, Campbell displayed a rather incredible softening of the boys' stance on their mother's extracurricular activities. I had gone to Stevens Point, Wisconsin, to speak at a theater conference. Campbell stunned me by actually coming from Lawrence University in nearby Appleton, Wisconsin, to hear his mother speak. Thankfully, I did not see him in the audience during the presentation. But when I was finished, there he was, waiting for me, unannounced, in the lobby. We got into his Jeep and drove back to my motel and went up to my room. Twenty minutes passed and he still had not mentioned anything or commented on the presentation in any way.

"Did you hear me speak this morning?" I asked, finally unable to stand it any longer.

"I heard you," he said. Silence.

"Campbell," I said, "are you or are you not going to tell me what you thought of your mother's discussion this morning? Or were you so humiliated that you have blocked it out completely?"

Finally he replied, "It was OK. I mean, you have to understand that I've heard a lot of it at the dining room table for years. This time, I had to buy a ticket, of course. It was interesting, I guess. Especially for people who never heard it before."

This I take as high praise.

There have been many battles over the years, many a good fight and a few lost causes, valiant efforts and some things that I became very upset about that, in the end, ultimately were a waste of time and emotional energy. But no matter what the issue at hand, every time you fight for what you believe truly to be right, every time you stand up to someone or some group that thinks they can take advantage of you or ignore your rights, you cannot hope to prevail without what I like to call the "natural fanatic." Yes, you need the foot soldiers. Yes, you need people of reason who can sit down and "take the meeting." But they can't get into the room to have the meeting unless the fanatic has made it in his foe's best interest to listen and hopefully respond to his demands. The fanatic, as I define it, is the person who sees exactly what it is that must be done, and nothing deters him—or her—from that goal, even when facing great criticism from those who stand with him. Others of us fight for things, but it becomes difficult, during the struggle that invariably occurs, not to feel that the opposition you are facing is personal and not to suffer from the embarrassment and humiliation of personal attacks, from within your own ranks, as well as from without.

I have known only a few who have that tremendous energy and the ability to sweep people along and support them to work toward a common cause. But, without doubt, the best was Joe Papp. Joseph did not allow anyone or anything to interfere with a goal he had set for himself. For this, he and others like him are often harshly criticized. The natural fanatic, like Joe, who determined a line of action, could not be deterred from what he set his sights on. These are mental street fighters. And they invariably have people who love them and people who, as long as they are successful, quietly hate them and attempt to undermine them. But they also have an enviable ability to get things done by encouraging and empowering others to do their best work.

I'm not naive, but I do believe it is possible to fight City Hall. I believe in people. I believe that people banded together have a power beyond any of the manufactured power that "we, the people" give into the hands of elected government officials or, worse, unelected corporate executives. That may sound idealistic or uninformed. But I also understand that any such offensive must be carefully planned and acted upon on many levels. For some within our business there is often a great emotional desire, perhaps even a need, to stand up and be counted and to give a voice to people who cannot be heard. There is also for many others an equally understandable lingering fear that makes them avoid anything controversial at all costs. Some still remember the horror of a blacklist and the irresponsible actions of government against performing artists. It may seem long ago, but the painful memories are not erased. Nor should they be. Others want only to remain safe, neither jeopardizing themselves nor their livelihoods in any way. Others want to pretend that nothing is wrong that will affect them, hoping that if something really needs to be done, someone else will do it. Whatever their reasoning, it is dangerous still today to forget that unscrupulous men—and women, sadly—will reach out, and for their own benefit and with malice aforethought, describe any opposition, individual or group, in such a way that it turns that person or group into the "other"—into "them." As soon as that whispering campaign begins, it can build into a tempest from which there seems no recourse and no place to go for justice.

People like Joe—and others from our profession whom I have met in meetings, hearings, rallies, and demonstrations over the years—find it within themselves to do more than simply stand around at interminable cocktail parties, rubber-chicken dinners and ostentatious dances. They speak out, knowing that their voices will be heard for reasons that have nothing to do with the cause. And in speaking out, they create the dialogue that allows those who truly can effect some change to step into the spotlight. This is what we actors can do. In the political arena, we can pull focus, draw the cameras, raise money and, in some cases, force debate. Some of us can even make a damn good speech. Others are best given something else to do. I'm not sure where I fall on that chart. But I do remember my first foray into this arena.

I had been asked to give a speech on Memorial Day, quite a few years ago, for the laying of the cornerstone of a new addition to the local library. Nothing too risky first time out. At the appointed moment, I rose to speak and saw my two young sons, way in the back of the crowd, take off and run down Main Street, so as not to have to watch their mother make an ass of herself. The "library speech" became a point of reference in our house for years. I have no idea what I said that day, but I daresay the cornerstone fell right into place and would have with or without my verbal attention. But whenever I have to speak and find myself at the point where I am striding around the house in a fit of nerves wondering why anyone has been daft enough to ask me to do this again, someone will always call out, "Just give the library speech."

The truth is I hate to speak. It truly frightens me more than I can express. I think the majority of actors feel that way. When asked to do it, I always wish I had other talents and could sing or dance. An ability to speak another's words in no way comes with the gift of speaking extemporaneously with any sense or style. And, sadly, some people, particularly those who plan these kinds of events, always assume it does. On the other hand, do not ask me to write a speech. I refuse to get up with a speech in my hand. This probably goes back to the fact that I have sat in too many places and listened to too many speeches read from a sheaf of papers that were boring, lifeless, or worse—self-serving. I like speakers who get up there with no paper—maybe a few simple notes to remind them of key points—and just say how they feel, talk about why they are there—*briefly*. Unfortunately, if you don't really feel much about what's going on and are there simply for some kind of public-relations reason or are afraid to say how you really feel, a prepared speech is the way to go.

I actually feel sick before getting up to speak. It's an agony ten times that of opening night. People outside the business cannot comprehend this. They think I am being self-effacing or falsely humble. They don't understand the nature of the beast. Many actors are basically shy. It can be excruciating to stand up and be identified only as ourselves, speak what we feel. We become actors because it gives us a chance to be masked. This comes with a freedom to express dreams, fantasies, sorrows and joys with an identity other than our own. You can go to the edge of the cliff, jump, and know that you can come back unscathed. Unlike the stage, there is no invisible personal safety net on any political or social platform.

Then there is the question of credibility. Actors are often questioned about their decision to offer an opinion on the issues. It is felt—particularly by those who disagree with us and can see that we have been able to speak up for people they would rather keep silent—that because we are mere entertainers, we must not be well informed on any subject other than show business. Or, and I find this particularly offensive, that since we are performers, we must simply wish to be in the public eye and crave attention of any kind in any arena. I am a citizen of these United States. I have children and grandchildren. I earn a living here. I pay my taxes. Therefore, as a citizen, I have a right to speak out. Since I also carry a sort of visibility because of the profession I am in, I feel it is my responsibility to speak out when others cannot.

However, I can tell you with great certainty that after a few times, it is far less fun and far more exhausting to allow yourself to stand up for what you believe in than you might imagine. If you're only doing this for the ego gratification or as a way to gain some sort of attention, it's a lousy deal and a waste of breath.

Over the years, I guess I can stand accused of rallying to many causes and around many people. But my two primary loves—organizationally, that is— have been The Actors' Fund of America and Actors' Equity Association. I am a member of the Board of Trustees of The Actors' Fund and serve as Chair of the Human Services Committee. I am currently in the middle of my second term as the president of Actors' Equity, the union representing actors and stage managers working professionally on the American stage. But I'll say it here now: I have no intention of running for a third term. And to quote General Sherman, "I will not accept if nominated and will not serve if elected." In other words, no one should try to talk me into it. Mother is retiring from politics. I love all that I have done and with which I been involved, but it is time to let someone else throw the baton. I have caught it in my teeth often enough.

In 1990, Colleen was invited to speak at the gala opening of the Wexner Arts Center in Columbus, Ohio, built by Leslie Wexner, owner and chief executive officer of The Limited, *a clothing chain. The grand-opening ceremonies took place in the weeks following one of many battles over funding for The National Endowment for the Arts, and just following attacks made by conservatives in the Congress looking to defund the Endowment, so that government should not support art that they considered to be obscene. What follows is a transcript of Colleen's remarks.*

> *Ladies and gentlemen [applause]. Thank you. Thank you. This morning, we have heard gospel singers, seen videos, heard speeches, applauded visionaries and sampled a feast of our nation's most innovative and controversial artists. We have also witnessed the preamble to the Wexner Center's purpose. What an act of faith! What an act of courage!*
>
> *You heard me say earlier that I was grateful. I wish now to explain to you why I am grateful. We realize that the arts in the United States are always in danger because some consider some portion of them controversial. But controversy is good. That is what we are all about: looking at life differently, questioning the status quo, asking through the arts, "Why?"— presenting through the arts all of life. And some consider this to be very dangerous because you are asking people to think, asking them to feel.*
>
> *I served for three years on the theater panel of The National Endowment for the Arts and I was, shall we say, outspoken [laughter]. But I became outspoken because we are threatened. We are threatened by a claim of obscenity that would force the government first to cut funds and withdraw support and then to censor. The playwright Edward Albee wrote a particularly stunning statement about just this in his magnificent play* Who's Afraid of Virginia Woolf? *In it, George is speaking to Nick and he says something like this: "You take the trouble to construct a civilization, to build a society based on principles. You endeavor to make communicable sense out of natural order and the unnatural disorder of man's mind. You make government and art and realize that they are and must be one and the same. Then you bring things to the saddest of all points, to the point where there is something to lose. And all at once, through all the music, through all the sensible sounds of men building,*

what does the trumpet sound? Up yours! There is no justice to it. Simply, up yours!"

I apologize to Edward for my faulty memory. But it is not only his words that are brilliant. It is actually his thoughts and ideas, and those I hope you have understood. We are being told "up yours," and when that is not sufficient, we are being made the "other." I was in Washington, D.C., recently to speak in support of the National Endowment for the Arts. And when I asked one member of our government, "Why would you cut back on the arts when it is actually so little money that we can prove bears so much good?"—do you know what he said? "Because it is so easy." He considered that a legitimate response.

And if it becomes difficult, the rallying cry is always obscenity. They are not concerned about what is obscene. What they are afraid of—what is obscene to them is that people should think and then, God forbid, choose. When it comes to obscenity, I will choose my obscenity. My obscenity may be the poor and homeless lying on the street. My obscenity may be prejudice, my obscenity may be the choices made for women without their vote. My obscenity—[applause]—my obscenity may be that my grandchildren cannot be properly educated. My obscenity may be that the arts, which feed the soul and can bring about real change in the human condition, are considered valueless when held up against the cost of weapons.

Some might question my right to say all of this, some will acknowledge that it is my right, but where, they ask, is my expertise? My right comes because I pay the bloody taxes. My expertise comes from living and yes, living as an artist. I wish it were my right to come down there with my tax money in my hand and tell them exactly where I wish it put. Then we will have a very lively discussion of what is and is not obscene [applause].

I am so grateful that in this dangerous time, an edifice of this size and beauty can be built by a man who has prospered and wants to return some of that prosperity to his city, to his home. And you know as well as I that some of what may be done or presented within these walls will be considered controversial, thank God. Because that means we have the freedom to question ourselves and examine our existence. What Leslie Wexner has really done and said to this country is that we believe in the arts. We believe that they have something to give and that if any of us think something is obscene, we can get up and walk out [applause].

I have, in this moment of being overtaken emotionally, nearly skipped something I've been asked to do. But I've remembered, thank God, because now I speak to the workers who have made all this possible. This morning, we have with us the contractors and architects who made the dream of this center a reality, who made sure that everything would go well in order that we could be here today. We are surrounded by the crafts people and I am delighted to introduce to you the crafts people whose knowledge, skill, strength and muscle raised the Wexner Center up. Ladies and gentlemen, please stand up and be acknowledged [applause].

How exciting that in this time I should be asked to come here and do this and shoot off my mouth [applause]. But before I go, let me say, thank you, on behalf of so many, to Leslie Wexner, who, having prospered, continues to acknowledge his responsibility to his community. Because of him, artists and those who love the arts have a new home today.

BOBBI HANDMAN

Colleen and I were political buddies. Although I had great admiration for her as an actress, we really knew each other strictly in that other arena, politics. I've been at People for the American Way for twelve years, working as an organizer and activist. But I've been working on political campaigns since 1950.

Colleen and I naturally gravitated to each other around progressive issues, women's issues particularly. Colleen had an activist's mentality. Forget about organization or the business of politics, but wherever there was an issue, she salivated. She responded to injustice emotionally; the muscles in her neck would stand out; if she became outraged, every part of her being responded. That is what made her an activist. This meant a great deal to me, because as an operative, it meant that I could ask Colleen to do things that other well-intended people who agreed with us politically wouldn't do. At her best, Colleen would travel to somewhere in the middle of the night, get there with nobody meeting her, having no fancy place to stay, and then get up early in the morning to make the speech or meet with some legislator in his or her office.

Colleen was very much against the war in Vietnam, and in those days you could ask her to go anywhere on that issue—nuclear disarmament as well. Civil rights were enormously important to Colleen, for people of color and for women. I know that she would be in the middle of the gay and lesbian movement if she were with us today. Remember that she was one of the first stars to stand up and speak out for people with AIDS. She also had an instinct for the hierarchy of politics; that you didn't just work for a presidential candidate, that you also have to work and vote for congressional people, city council members and other local officials. Some celebrities aren't as interested in that. Colleen understood it. And when you're sitting in my place, making the arrangements to get people places, getting the issue out there and talked about, creating a dialogue, getting our viewpoint well represented—whatever it is at any particular time—then someone like Colleen is absolutely a pearl and very, very unique. I can't find many of them today. Not like Colleen. Not someone who could speak to an issue from the heart with such passion that even her political opponents would pause to listen. She was a beautiful person and a wonderful resource. I miss her desperately. We desperately need someone like her today.

CLIFFORD STEVENS

Colleen found it difficult to say no to just about anyone asking her for help. And as we all know, she did not pay particular attention to details. But there was one time—and this is a true story—where she nearly walked onto the wrong stage, so to speak.

She told me that she had agreed to go to Dallas to speak at some antinuclear rally, an issue which she was very involved in at that particular time. As it got close to the day she was to arrive, I said, "Should I call these people? What arrangements have been made?" Of course, she didn't know whom she had spoken to but told me they would probably call me. Well, someone did all right, someone representing a group putting together a *pro*nuclear rally. You would think that Dallas might have been a tip-off. But one can just picture Colleen going down there and giving the right speech to the wrong people and never quite understanding how she got there. Needless to say, in this case, I suggested that another speaker be found.

25

"You know, baby, your reputation can be made or ruined in one night."

One night, over dinner, Clifford told me that Jason Robards, Maureen Anderman and Elizabeth Wilson were all going out to do an eight-week run of the Moss Hart and George S. Kaufman classic American comedy *You Can't Take It with You,* for director Ellis Rabb, at the Paper Mill Playhouse in Millburn, New Jersey.

"No kidding," I said. "That sounds like fun. You know," I added after shaking my memory up a bit, "I played what's-her-name . . . the countess."

"Olga Katrina," Clifford answered.

"Exactly. In stock with Charles Coburn. He was very popular because he was a man who pinched any female who turned her back on him. Audiences loved him for it. Members of the cast learned not to draw too close." Clifford looked at me in silence for a moment. Somehow, I knew it wasn't Charles Coburn he was thinking about.

"Colleen—" he began.

"Clifford," I interrupted, "it's too—"

"Small a part," he volleyed.

"Right. And Paper Mill is—"

"So far away," he replied. From anyone other than Clifford, a conversation like this would be infuriating. "It's not," he continued. "In fact, it's probably closer to the Farm than Broadway and West Forty-fifth Street."

"Probably," I answered.

"Why don't I give them a call tomorrow?"

The next day, Clifford called back. "Of course, they'd love you to do this." And as quickly as that I joined some dear friends in a wonderful cast for what became the most fun I've ever had in eight minutes on any stage. We rehearsed for two weeks at Michael Bennett's rehearsal studios at Eighteenth Street and Broadway before opening the show at Paper Mill to great success. Everyone seemed to love it and, sure enough, before long, there was all that talk of "coming in." One producer after another came out to see us, professed to love us and then, upon figuring out the economics of producing a show with such a large cast on Broadway, politely lost interest.

With just three performances before we were to close, our stage manager and an old friend, Mitch Erickson, heard that Roger Stevens at the Kennedy Center in Washington had lost a show and was looking for a replacement. Mitch, who had worked for Roger quite a bit, spoke to him about *You Can't Take It with You.* Roger was unsure, and there was no time for him to come to Millburn before we closed. Clifford suggested that I call him. I got through to Roger's office very quickly, but it took about ten minutes for him to come to the phone. "Hello?" he said at last. "Is this you, Colleen?" Figuring him to be a very busy man, I skipped right to the point.

"Roger, listen. You've got to take this show." And, the next day, based solely on Mitch's professional opinion and a very brief nudge from yours truly, Roger Stevens brought New Jersey's *You Can't Take It with You* to Washington, D.C.

The first night that we arrived there was a gala premiere of the movie of *The Pirates of Penzance,* which we were all invited to attend. At the party afterward, I saw Roger for a moment. "It's all your fault," he whispered to me.

"What?"

"This play," he said with a smile. "I'm holding you responsible."

"They are going to love it," I whispered back. And sure enough, "they" did. We opened to rave reviews and packed houses. Best of all, in the weeks following, Ken and two other producers were able to raise the money for us to come in to Broadway. *You Can't Take It with You* was not as well reviewed in New York by the critics as it had been at the Kennedy Center, where I think we began to have such a good time onstage, giggling and laughing and practically waving at the audience, that we weren't really on the ball as an ensemble anymore. We had gotten so sure of ourselves that, with no one really in charge, some things became overdone and played as much for laughs for us as for the audience. We were all occasionally guilty of this, but certain actors, like Alice Drummond and Rosetta Le Noire, remained exactly on target and unbelievably wonderful from their first performance in New Jersey through opening night at Broadway's Plymouth Theatre. Nevertheless, despite the critical reservations, we settled in and cast and audiences alike continued to have a very good time.

I shared a dressing room with Maureen Anderman, who played Alice, the lovely and sane daughter in this family of crazies. Maureen had just been married the previous fall to a wonderful actor and very handsome man, Frank Converse. By the time we opened in New York in April, she told me she and Frank were very eager to get pregnant. To our great joy, she did, even though she eventually had to leave us, as the ingenue in a play as all-American as this could not possibly be showing "that way" in her simple cotton dress.

Jimmy Coco joined the cast in Washington, replacing George Rose as Boris Kolenkhov. George had been wonderful, but Jimmy Coco was a sheer delight and one of the great joys to work with. He could—and would—make me laugh at almost anything, practically anywhere.

JASON ROBARDS

I loved Colleen's selective memory. When we did *You Can't Take It with You*, Colleen would tell the story for press and the like that she had played her role, Olga Katrina, once before in summer stock somewhere. If that's true, then she had played it twice before. First at the American Academy, and then in stock. I quietly mentioned this to her, figuring if the story was good enough with her playing it once before, why not up the ante with "twice." She swore I was thinking of someone else. I was certain I wasn't, but who the hell can remember half of what they did anyway? Well, sure enough, one night after a performance, a friend of mine who was with us at the Academy but wasn't an actor anymore came backstage to see me. "Look at this," he said. And there it was, the program from the American Academy production—with Colleen as Olga Katrina. He left it for me to give to Colleen, which I'm sure I did and I'm certain she ignored.

ELLIS RABB

To be perfectly frank, Colleen wasn't speaking to me when she died. I tried up to the very end—although I didn't know how near the end it was—to see if there was some way that we could repair our misunderstanding.

I only knew Colleen through working with her on *You Can't Take It with You*. I certainly had seen her work and had met her very casually at a couple of theater parties, but we really only got to know each other during that production. It was love at first sight. I remember distinctly—to contrast what eventually happened—Colleen coming back after lunch after the second or third day of rehearsal in New York. She turned to me, gave me a big hug and said, "I want you to direct me in everything I do." Now I knew she was kidding, but she was also sort of telling me something.

You Can't Take It with You was a very happy production. Clifford Stevens—who at that time was my agent also—called me and said, "Guess what? Colleen Dewhurst wants to play the Grand Duchess Olga Katrina."

"You're kidding!" I said. "That would be wonderful fun."

I had originally directed the first revival of *You Can't Take It with You* with Rosemary Harris playing Alice and Donald Moffatt playing Grandpa in 1965 for APA Repertory Company. Rosemary and I had stuck the play at the end of the season, figuring it would be simple enough to do and would end the season on an up. We were shocked and thrilled when it turned out to be such a big critical and commercial success. It was really the first time that a major American comedy had been revived on Broadway. That wasn't done then. "No one does those kinds of plays," people said. "It's not a great classic. It's summer stock." I didn't care what they thought, I think it's a brilliantly written play. Well, it did work. Audiences did come.

Angelo Del Rossi called. He said that he'd thought of that 1965 production all these years and now what he wanted most of all was to open the Paper Mill Playhouse as the state theater of New Jersey with that production. I said I couldn't, but then he named a figure that caught my attention and just to get out of it I said, "You'll have to double it." And he said, "Done." As I thought about casting, I kept hearing a voice in my head saying, "Well, sir, you should have been there, that's all I say. You should have been there." It's Grandpa's first line. Suddenly, I realized the voice was Jason's [Robards]. *He'll never do this*, I thought. But I called him anyway and I was stunned when he said, "Hey, that sounds like fun. Let's do it!" I never expected an actress of Colleen's stature to play this role of about eleven lines, even though it is a very flashy bit. But I'm sure it didn't hurt that Angelo was also willing to pay her a star salary.

We got along extremely well at first. One day after we'd opened at Paper Mill, she had a party at the Farm for the company. We were talking in the yard and suddenly I saw her eyes look over my head and she interrupted herself midsentence to say, "Oh, my God, I've got to get the peacock off the roof!" I replied the only possible way one might, "Colleen, did you just say you have to get the peacock off the roof?" But by that time she was off, clapping her hands and calling for assistance from anyone expert in such things. Which, I'm certain, turned out to be only herself. She was as casual about it all as if she was just letting the dog out to pee.

In rehearsal, I just asked Colleen to play it straight. Once she came onstage in that hat and fur, there was really very little she actually had to do. She was much more like a Russian peasant than Russian royalty, and that alone made for the comedy. She was marvelous. Audiences loved her. It was so unexpected to see her in a role like that, especially considering the kind of work she was so famous for, O'Neill and all, that she practically got a hand after every line. I also think it manufactured more work for her along those same comedic lines, particularly on television. So it was a smart thing for her to do and a publicist's dream.

Our falling-out came about during the Broadway run when we were running a bit low and I was furious with Clifford Stevens and Ken Marsolais, who was one of the producers as well as Colleen's boyfriend, for assuming that I would cut my director's royalty in order to lower the weekly nut. It makes me just furious when people assume that. So I said no. It got very messy and Colleen got very mad, since it involved Ken and all, and just as suddenly as she thought I should direct her always, she cut me dead. Oh, that sort of thing happens all the time in the theater. You know, we're all such a passionate lot.

SUSAN SAMPLINER

I met Colleen in 1983 on the Broadway revival of *You Can't Take It with You.* I was the assistant to the general manager, Jay Kingwill. I got to know her because Ken Marsolais, Colleen's partner at the time, was also a producer on the show and working out of our office. She would come in and just hang out. When she stopped by, she liked to be the receptionist, answer the phone and take messages. People recognized her voice and asked who they were talking to, and she would say, "Colleen. Do you want to leave a message?" and keep going. It was very funny. One afternoon when she was in the office, Colleen said that she had a very early meeting the next day and needed a place to stay in the city so she wouldn't have to drive to the Farm and back at the crack of dawn. I had an extra bedroom and offered it to her. I really didn't understand who she was then. I was very new to the business. I'd never seen any of her other performances and just didn't have that star-struck thing going on. I knew her as another member of the company of *You Can't Take It with You.* So she spent the night. We stayed up talking until four in the morning. And she did this a few times during the show's run.

We would talk all night. God, there was so much. Some professional things, but mostly personal. Colleen was curious about everything. Those nights she would ask questions about my background, about my family, my parents and brothers—but never did this in an intrusive way. She made it very safe to talk about yourself, to explore yourself. It was all very interesting.

Very early on, we got into this whole conversation about my sexuality. She said, "So what's your story, baby?" I can still hear her asking the question. No one had ever dared to ask so simply. I said, "Well, you know, I think I'm really pretty bisexual. I feel kind of fifty-fifty about things. You know, if the right person is really right, it won't matter—"

"Bullshit!" she said. "Something makes your motor run. If you say it's fifty-fifty or it doesn't matter, you're not thinking about it enough!" I'll never forget the conversation, because it completely blew me out of the water. Over the years we knew each other, we talked about this a lot. It was very important for me. She was incredibly supportive of my choices and encouraged me to come out to my family. "You have to do it, baby," she'd say. And she was right. That Colleen died before I had the chance to introduce her to my partner, Emily, is very sad to me. I think she would have been very happy for us and very proud of me.

As I got to know Colleen, I began to spend time at the Farm, which was about forty-five minutes from my parents' home. I loved being at the Farm, but I think my parents got a little jealous that I would want to go over there for the holidays rather than spend all my time with them. The relationship my parents and Colleen developed was funny. Colleen was totally intimidated by my mother. My mother, on the other hand, was nervous about who this

Colleen Dewhurst was and why was she playing such an important role in her daughter's life. They were very different. My mother was the perfect house-keeper and I think Colleen was afraid that she would come into Colleen's house, look around, and wonder, "What the hell is going on here?" It was a funny reversal of who intimidated whom. But a lot of it had to do with how Colleen felt about her own mother, whom she so adored and thought was the perfect human being. And by that definition, that meant Colleen was somehow less than that. In those late-night talks, Colleen would say how much she admired how her mother handled her father's not being around and the lessons she taught her about independence. She really worshiped her and never really got over her death. I've wondered since whether she ever found a place for that loss in her life. Perhaps that's why this extended family she created around herself was always so important.

The first time I went to the Farm was for Thanksgiving in 1983. I had never been to such a huge dinner. I had never seen a table that could seat more than thirty people. I was instantly struck by how unpretentious and comfort-able it was to be there. The kitchen should have had a revolving door on it, there were so many people in and out. Someone would walk in and nobody would look up. Nobody would introduce anybody to anybody else. Nobody seemed to care, yet people stayed as long as they liked. If you spent any time there with Colleen, you began to realize that sometimes she would see people while they were there and sometimes she wouldn't. She'd often stay upstairs in her room and occasionally just wander through. Until it was dinnertime, and then everything became much more formal, with Colleen overseeing who was going to sit where. Only then would she really get an idea of who was around and find out who was who. Around that large table in the dining room there was always some kind of very fluid structure that was missing from the rest of the Farm. I was fascinated by all of this. I came from a very formal family and a household that was always in order and had very few guests.

There was so much to learn from Colleen just by spending time with her. I often think about one night during the run of *You Can't Take It with You.* There was a party for new cast members at the Wyndham Hotel, during which Colleen and Ken had a big fight. They had both had too much to drink. Colleen asked if she could stay at my apartment. I said sure, but that first a bunch of us were going to Freddy's, a small cabaret, to hear Dixie Carter sing. So we left the party and she came with us. It was a sold-out show, but the maitre d' made room for Colleen and me to sit close to the stage and my three friends to stand nearby at the bar. Dixie started the show and Colleen began talking very loudly back to the stage. Dixie would sing a song about men and Colleen would call out, "Tell it like it is, Dixie!" Colleen had her elbows on the table and every time she would applaud, which she did with great gusto, the whole table shook. It got to where as a number would end, I would pick up our wineglasses while Colleen applauded. Dixie knew how to deal with all this and could not have been more gracious. And of course, the audience, recognizing Colleen, loved it. But I was embarrassed and scared to death that this would make the papers the next day.

After the show, Dixie sent word for Colleen to come backstage, which she did and it was the usual, "Oh, I'm so glad you're here" and "You're so wonderful," but really, Colleen couldn't have cared less. As we finally left, Colleen grabbed a glass of wine from the bar and sat on a stoop across the street from Freddy's. "Where are we going next?" she called to us when my friends and I stepped out of the club.

"Colleen, we're going home," I said. "If you need a place to stay, you're coming with me now." The guys I was with thought this was all very funny, but I was very upset. At that moment, I could see Colleen look at all of us and assess the situation. "Can I get you a cab?" one of the guys said.

"Yes," she said.

As the driver drove from the club on the East Side to my apartment on the West Side, Colleen sat silently looking out her window at the lights in midtown.

"You know, baby," she suddenly said, as if she had completely sobered up, "your reputation can be made or ruined in one night."

I never saw her like that again and we never spoke of it. But I still remember so much of what she said to me: ". . . made or ruined in one night"; "What makes your motor run, baby?"; even, "Tell it like it is."

She was so unsparingly generous with herself and all that she knew about life. I do miss her.

ಲ ಲ ಲ

As much as I think of *You Can't Take It with You* as a time of great fun, I can't help but also associate it with the first days of what would become, for me and so many others, years of anger and sorrow. There was a young man who joined the company in Washington whom I especially came to love, Orrin Reilly. Orrin came on at the end of the play as one of the FBI men, and understudied Nick Surovy, the young leading man playing opposite Maureen Anderman. Orrin went on for Nick a number of times and whenever he did, I would go to the back of the house to watch because he and Maureen were so sweet together. He was lovely in the part.

You Can't Take It with You opened in April of 1983, a time that many people, myself included, were first hearing about AIDS. I didn't think I knew anyone who had come down with this mysteriously fatal illness. Now I know that I did, but my denial fed their fearful silence and that silence created an atmosphere where even people like me could comfortably think of AIDS as something very far away.

I left *You Can't Take It with You* for a few weeks toward the end of its run to shoot a film. While I was away, Eva Gabor played the Countess, opposite her old pal from *Green Acres*, Eddie Albert, who had replaced Jason. The press was delighted to have them together onstage and they were equally delightful in their roles, ensuring the production a few more months of activity at the box office. When I got back, after hearing all the stories about Eva and Eddie, Ken told me that Orrin had been out for a while. I was concerned, particularly since no one seemed to know what was wrong, just that he was tired, as if with mono. With some rest, I was assured, he would be all right. Then Orrin came down with pneumonia. Still, I kept any notion of AIDS far from my mind. With the proper care, people recover. Young men in the prime of life get well. The show went on with all of us expecting Orrin's return. When he was delayed yet again, Ken was the first to bring up the unspeakable. He thought Orrin had AIDS. I was shocked. Still, Ken's statement barely registered. It seemed so foreign to me. What was this? How was this happening to the people I knew? Suddenly, Orrin's absence felt very strange, and I missed him more as I began to fear that he was not coming back. Still no one in the company talked much about it.

Orrin Reilly was a very bright young man, as tall and attractive as he was loving. He and I and Jimmy Coco would regularly go out for Japanese food to laugh and talk about everyone in the cast: who was doing what to whom; who wasn't doing what they were supposed to do; and who was doing anything they supposed they could get away with. The usual backstage chatter that occupies a company of actors in a long-running show. Jimmy would regale Orrin and me with outrageous stories, encouraging the same from us until we all would be laughing uproariously. When Orrin finally came back—in no small part because of Ken's insistence—his vibrant laughter seemed to be missing. He was pale and thin, clearly glad to be with us and working, but often short of breath and tentative. He tired easily. So we didn't go out for Japanese with Jimmy anymore.

I was at home one afternoon when Orrin called unexpectedly. We made some small talk, but I could tell that he wasn't saying something he wanted to say. "Orrin, what is it?" I said.

"Honey, I want to talk to you about something," he replied, stalling. "I've made a decision that I have to tell the people I love . . . that I have AIDS." For a moment, neither of us spoke. My denial about Orrin's ill health, indeed about AIDS at all, was so complete that I could not believe what he had said, any more than he seemed able to continue speaking once he had said it. Finally I found my breath. "I love you, Orrin, and I'm leaving right now to meet you at the theater." When I arrived, he was sitting downstairs in the basement under the stage in a common area usually crowded with people. But as it was a few hours before curtain, it was deserted. I sat next to him. "How do you feel? Do you feel OK?" We talked a little, Orrin telling me how worried and helpful his friends were, particularly his friend Victor Garber and a member of our cast, Carol Androsky, and how grateful he was that Ken had encouraged him to stay with the show. He was very open and very scared. I was confused, heartbroken and also scared. Short of holding his hand, I didn't know what else to do. But that day I woke up. Someone I loved had AIDS. How many more would there be? How long would other well-meaning people be able to remain as numb to this as I had been?

I left the show for good to do some television film in Knoxville, Tennessee, with Jason. While I was there, I received a call from David Eidenberg, a dear friend of Orrin's who was also my agent on the West Coast. "Orrin's gone," he said quite simply. "I thought you should know right away before you hear it from some fool talking about someone and something he knows nothing about." I returned from Knoxville just in time to attend Orrin's memorial service at the Plymouth Theatre, where we had played together in *You Can't Take It with You*. It was my first AIDS memorial. Sadly, nearly seven years later, I am enraged to know that I have not been to my last. When I rose to speak that afternoon, I wasn't quite sure what I wanted to say. "Well, Orrin," I began, "the nails are done. The hair is done. But I have to apologize for the shoes. The dogs must have chewed the heels before I left and I didn't notice until I got out of the car." Everybody broke up knowing how impeccably groomed Orrin had been and how he would have appreciated whatever effort I valiantly made to pull myself together, no matter how fruitless. I don't quite recall what I said next except that Orrin was tremendously loved because he was so loving. And so understanding. And that I missed him.

Consequently, I have had too many similar phone calls as the one from David Eidenberg: Terrence McNally calling to tell me that his dear friend, the actor Bobby Drivas, "is gone"; Joe Papp to tell me of Michael Bennett, after a brilliant career, dying practically alone and ashamed in Arizona; Leonard Frey; Charles Ludlum; Fritz Holt; and so, so many others.

At the same time, I began to hear incredible public suggestions of quarantine and stories of people being removed from their apartments or fired from their jobs if it was even suspected that they might have "it." It was inconceivable to me that this was the response to the loss of so many lives and, for us in this theater, the loss of people with great gifts. People who were geniuses in what they could create. The very people we needed to help us see our way through what was clearly becoming an epidemic. It was obscene to watch the government and much of the media still pay little or no attention to AIDS because it was only about "them," the undesirables—gay men, people of color, drug addicts and the poor.

I became particularly aware of the devastation AIDS was having in my position as a member of the Board of Directors of The Actors' Fund of America and chair of the fund's Human Services Committee. Every Thursday, when this committee met to go over an increasing number of requests for assistance from people with AIDS, I was being educated not only to the horror of this disease but to the venom of bigotry, denial and misinformation that was as deadly as the virus itself.

In November of 1985, a determined group from Actors' Equity joined forces with a number of other organizations and individuals willing to fight this same battle. They produced "The Best of the Best," the first mainstream, gala AIDS benefit that raised over one million dollars for three then-fledgling AIDS research and service organizations, Gay Men's Health Crisis (GMHC), the AIDS Resource Center, and the American Foundation for AIDS Research (AmFAR). I have always felt that the event finally punched a hole in an invisible wall of silence, a wall that is still not completely torn down today. A phenomenal list of entertainers—Bette Midler, Christopher Reeve, Mikhail Baryshnikov, Lily Tomlin, Victor Borge, Carol Burnett, Jerry Herman with the cast of *La Cage aux Folles* and many others—came together onstage at the Metropolitan Opera House at Lincoln Center and before an audience of well-connected and influential New Yorkers said that it was time to speak out. It was time to do something. AIDS was not "them"; AIDS is "us." For many onstage and behind the scenes, the evening was less an entertainment and more a call to arms. For by the end of that gala event, a statement was made loudly and clearly that we would not sit by and do nothing.

As I came to the stage door that evening, I was astonished to see cameras from the networks and reporters eager to talk to people who supposedly were untouchable because of this particular disease. And the statement of the evening was that we were all threatened and would all suffer the loss of people we loved, unless the country moved forward in terms of responsible education, and money was immediately brought forward for research and services. I will always believe that that night was the beginning. Yes, the entertainment industry has been horribly hard hit by AIDS, but AIDS is taking its toll on every industry and moving through every community. We in the "business" are simply more visible. But since we are, it is our responsibility to call attention to the unacknowledged, speak of the unspeakable and, if we can, use whatever this celebrity is that people are attracted to, to raise money and move people to do the right thing.

Since that night, those of us in the theater have come together around three wonderful organizations of which I am so proud: Broadway Cares, Equity Fights AIDS and, of course, The Actors' Fund. We are doing what we can to take care of our own and hopefully, at the same time, be able to offer assistance to those organizations helping our neighbors, our audiences. But it is still not enough and won't be until we understand that we must look after each other. There are times when we are all indeed our brother's keeper, because there have been times, or there will be times, when we all of us have needed to be helped, to be kept. So we keep fighting. And we do what we can, each in his or her own way, some on the street, some from the stage, and some behind the scenes from positions of great wealth and power. We do what we must.

And then there are the days when I long just to be able to have Japanese food with Orrin and Jimmy again and laugh about wondrous and silly things.

RODGER MCFARLANE

I was on the board of Gay Men's Health Crisis when "The Best of the Best" was produced as the first AIDS fund-raiser to draw headline talent into the battle. It was a very early time; we were fighting for funding and political support. There were no AIDS Walks or AIDS Dance-a-thons yet. There were very few prominent individuals willing to speak out against the ignorance of a Ronald Reagan or Ed Koch. "The Best of the Best" put AIDS on the fund-raising map. I was a nervous wreck the night of the performance. The tickets were sold, but no one knew what to expect. I saw Colleen just as she arrived backstage at the Met. "All right, baby," she said, "what are we doing here tonight?" It was more a challenge than a question. I watched the evening from the wings. Colleen had been given the "pitch" and she hit that stage like a bolt of lightning. She was articulate and authentic, speaking to the audience about AIDS without notes, scarcely knowing the agenda of the evening. At first, I don't think anyone could follow what she was saying, then something clicked and she had the house in tears and then on its feet cheering. I couldn't believe how she was ad-libbing. We had been prepping others on what to say for weeks, and not one spoke as well as she did.

That night, Colleen defined the professional obligation show business had to use the resources of the industry to address the challenges of AIDS. She set the standard of willingness to use whatever privileges or prominence she had to draw attention to issues that mattered. She knew how to choke up, almost to tears, exactly three and a half seconds before she made the pitch, making her not only a great actress but a formidable fund-raiser as well.

While most could not go beyond the point of fund-raising and public relations, Colleen would press on as an activist, fearlessly taking on controversial and unpopular issues, challenging government, calling in favors and twisting arms to cajole people into action. Before the advent of AIDS, when we were trying to pass a Gay Rights Bill in New York City, Colleen would testify, often with Joe Papp, before the City Council when we could get few others of her stature to show up. She was quite simple and eloquent. "Gay men," she said, "helped me raise my sons. I trusted them with what was most precious to me. How can they not be protected equally under the law?"

It took twelve years for the bill to pass, but she was with us from the start. The same with AIDS. Colleen was there in the first wave of support, in some of the most difficult days, doing whatever she was physically capable of and often more. On the AIDS fund-raising circuit, Colleen was most politely referred to as the "ubiquitous Ms. Dewhurst." The truth is Colleen Dewhurst was the best friend a person with AIDS ever had.

26

"President . . . of what?"

One afternoon at the Farm, I received a phone call from a gentleman who asked if he might make an appointment to speak with me about putting myself up for president of Actors' Equity Association, the forty-thousand-member union representing professional actors and stage managers in the American theater. "Wait a minute," I said. "What are we talking about? President? Of what?"

"Actors' Equity," he replied. "The union." I did not respond. "The actors' union, Miss Dewhurst. The one *you* belong to."

"I'm not sure I have this straight," I finally replied. "You're asking me to come in and speak to . . . what did you say?—a nominating committee?"

"That's right."

"About becoming president of Actors' Equity Association?"

"Yes," he responded confidently. "Exactly."

"You realize," I asked him, "that you are speaking to a person who can never find a pencil?"

Without missing a beat, he replied, "We have someone who will find your pencil for you, Miss Dewhurst." I thanked him for calling, but said that I just did not have the faintest, the vaguest idea how I qualified to become president of anything. Organization of any kind is simply beyond me. But at that time, in the early 1980s, whenever I would run into Ellen Burstyn, then the current president of Equity, she would say, "I want you to run for Council." Again I was blank. "Council of what?"

"The Council of Actors' Equity," she would explain. I would politely decline. I had no understanding of how the union ran or what I could possibly bring to that kind of volunteer position. I was already on enough boards, most of them groups associated with the theater. Ellen was characteristically persistent, explaining that as working actors in the theater, we both had a responsibility to share our understanding of employment conditions, as well as whatever celebrity we had, with those who could not speak out and draw legitimate attention to a variety of issues. So finally and fatefully, I agreed to go to lunch with Ellen and hear her out.

ELLEN BURSTYN

I had never spent much time with Colleen prior to our discussions about Equity. But I just had a feeling that she would be a good president. Colleen was smart, instinctually smart. Whenever there was a reason to be out on the front lines about anything, Colleen was there. She was strong, and seemed to me to be someone who was a natural leader; more important, she was someone people responded to as a leader. I always thought that the person in the office of the president of Equity should be someone who had accomplished something in the field of acting—on the stage—and had the respect of the membership. On both counts, Colleen fit the bill.

When I first asked her, Colleen's response was immediate and brief. "No," she said. "Go away." I told her I would accept her *no* if she would go to lunch with me. "All right," she said, half smiling at me, "I'll go to lunch with you." At the lunch I told her about some of the things I'd been able to work on as Equity's president: the Mayor's Advisory Council for the Theatre District, Save the Theaters, and a number of other issues. I gave her an overview of how important it was to the union that its president be able to bring public attention to specific problems and areas of concern, and that as a person in the public eye, as well as being a working actress who was respected by other working people in the business, she could draw focus in a way that would get things done. She said nothing while I spoke and I probably went on a while. She just listened very intently, her eyes never leaving my face. When I was finished, she just kept looking at me, still saying nothing. It was a bit unnerving. Finally she spoke. "You really think I can be of some help?"

"Yes, you can," I replied. That simple question was very indicative of her. Without going on at length about any of the specifics I'd been speaking of, she got right to the heart of the matter. She understood exactly what would be expected of her and what she had best to offer. The presidency—of anything, I imagine—is not an easy position to be put in. It's very difficult. You have much less control than anyone thinks, particularly the person going into the job. There are so many different personalities and varying points of view just within the Council itself that it's hard not to be drawn into little things that waste your time. It takes a special skill and talent to chair one of those Council or committee meetings that has nothing to do with how good an actor you are and all to do with how much patience you can muster.

After Colleen was elected in June of 1985, we were both in Seattle shooting separate films when my term expired and hers was to begin. It was arranged that we would meet at my hotel. There, we went out on the terrace and literally posed, me passing this gavel to her, for a photographer. It seemed silly. We were very pressed for time, but it needed to be done, so we had a couple of good laughs about it and posed, gavel in hand: hers.

I came back to a Council meeting only once after Colleen was elected. I arrived late and she saw me as I came into the room and sat to listen to the discussion. It was particularly long and drawn out that day, even for the Council. Afterward, she walked up to me and said in that throaty whisper, "You owe me." I guess I do. The fact is, we all do.

In 1984, Colleen appeared before the Nominating Committee of the Council of Actors' Equity Association in order to be considered on the slate of candidates to be recommended by the committee for election to the Council, the governing board of the union.

Actors' Equity Nominating Committee, 1984

I'm reading into the record the biography of Colleen Dewhurst, who says she joined Equity "sometime in the fifties." We'll find the exact date. She has worked under all our contracts. Has not served as a deputy. Belongs to SAG [Screen Actors Guild] and AFTRA [American Federation of Television and Radio Artists]. The most recent work under Equity's jurisdiction is You Can't Take It with You, *which I believe is current. She has written that her primary interest regarding the union is "the ability to understand the times and what will benefit the industry." We'll ask for a little clarification on that. She is being taped and agrees to it. She does participate in other organizations, but she has not listed them. Her questionnaire is not signed as yet, so we'll get clarification on that as well. Please invite Miss Dewhurst in.*

Colleen Dewhurst to the
Actors' Equity Nominating Committee

First and ultimately, I have always taken pride in belonging to Equity. But I have to admit that I've never been very comfortable with any system of going to meetings and discussions. It never feels as if it has any relevance to me. That is simply how it has always been for me. Alan [Eisenberg] tried to get me to come to one particular meeting dealing with negotiations of some sort, but it always seemed to come at the same time as The Actors' Fund Human Service Committee *meetings, which I never miss. Those feel very relevant to me and are important to individuals. And it all has to do with understanding the actors' true situation out there, which is often not easy. I understand the protection of the union, but I suppose I'm more of an actor who negotiates on her own.*

I'm not very good at sitting through negotiations and discussions about

everything. That can be a lack in myself. I'm not interested in all the com-
plaints that I feel do not really affect what I consider to be some of the
larger issues. So I think that is why I am unsure of my participation on the
Council. Does the Council really change anything? Or do we arrive on the
scene after the blood is gone and then attempt to take more blood? I hope
this isn't a prejudiced viewpoint.

I want the union to be aware of all sides and have the ability to know
what is happening beyond the Council room. I realize that I have been
involved in many things without ever having been actively involved in the
union. And it is always too easy to criticize from the outside and never
enter the arena. So that is why I am here. Do all of us in this room under-
stand that there are many of us in desperate trouble? We can't just talk
about whether a dressing room is big enough or if someone's hotel is on the
right side of the street. I understand that it may be very important to the
person asking in that moment, but sometimes I hear of this sort of thing
and it is bloody nonsense. What we should be talking about is getting out
there and earning a living.

I'm interested in the proper use of power. I mean, we all know in this
room what's happening to the theater because of the unions, all of them. I
don't want to be part of any organization that abuses power. And we know
that happens all around us. It doesn't serve any of us to put the producer
out of business. So you can't blame them for acting up. But, unfortunately,
we know that the softest place for them is always the actor, because we're
hungry. Because they know that we came into this business wanting to do
the job and being willing to do it for nothing because we love it. But, ulti-
mately, they have to hire us and we must make sure that it is done fairly.
I don't know how to change the other situation. But I would surely like to
be part of the discussion.

Colleen won a seat on the Council, serving for the next year. In 1985, she was nominated, again by the nominating committee, for the presidency. She ran unopposed
and was elected. In 1988, she was elected to a second three-year term, which she
completed in June 1991. Recently, Alan Eisenberg, executive secretary of Actors'
Equity since 1981, and senior staff members Guy Pace, executive assistant, admin-
istration, and Judith G. Anderson, executive assistant, policy, joined Council members Scott Barnes, Judy Rice and Patrick Quinn to discuss Colleen's six years as
president.

ALAN EISENBERG

We all know how scattered Colleen could be. We all know how dis-
organized she was, how she couldn't find a pack of cigarettes or matches seconds after she found a pack of cigarettes or matches. So much in her life always

seemed to be in disarray. Yet you would present a problem to her and although she would not have training or background in any of the specific economic, legal or administrative issues that you were talking about, somehow, with a flash of her hand—you know that thing she did—she would get to the nub of the question immediately. You could count on it. Her instincts were that remarkable. She would get through all of the junk, and come up with an answer that hadn't been thought about, or offer an observation from a perspective that was uniquely hers that would be invaluable to the process.

PATRICK QUINN

There was an extraordinary body language attached to that process. As you were talking to her you could almost see her listening to you, as if she were translating what you were saying into whatever internal language it was that she understood. And often, while you were talking, she wouldn't look at you, which could be disconcerting. If she was smoking, she'd be staring off into some distance or she might have her head in her left hand, cigarette in the right, her hair falling over the hand supporting her forehead. Then she'd sweep that hair back down her neck, take a drag off the cigarette, and look right at you. It seemed to be the way she absorbed the information.

ALAN EISENBERG

Another variation on her uncanny instincts would be when we went out together to California on some Equity business. She said she was going to rent a car, that she would drive us around L.A. I couldn't believe that we were going to get through this trip with her at the wheel. She was smoking in the car all the time, driving with one hand, lighting up with the other. She'd veer off the highway and drive down side streets all over L.A., make a wrong turn, then turn around, end up back on the highway, and then take off in some other direction. I never knew where the hell we were. But she invariably got us to where we had to go. And sometimes on time. I couldn't believe it. But she would find her destination in that same instinctual way that she could work her way through a problem or an issue.

PATRICK QUINN

She said very early on, "I have no intention of spending eleven A.M. to six P.M. every other Tuesday in Council meetings talking about rules and regulations. I can be of much more value speaking of other things in other rooms." Colleen understood her strengths and she knew that presiding over those kinds of parliamentary meetings wasn't her gift. And she had no interest in pretending it was or trying to impress people in that forum. But she knew how to summon all that she was to appear on the union's behalf. And she knew when it was important for her to speak.

GUY PACE

Exactly right. I met Colleen in 1984 through her agent in New York, Clifford Stevens. We were working together on negotiating an agreement with the talent representatives. After one of those meetings, Clifford invited me to join him for dinner with Colleen and a couple of their friends. I was a bit intimidated, but Colleen was very nice to me. She was like that with people; if the person who introduced you to her was someone she loved, you were immediately all right because of your association with that person. She trusted her friends' taste in their friends. At one point in this dinner, Colleen leaned over to me. "I suppose you've heard," she said in a conspiratorial whisper, "I'm going to do this Council thing . . . whatever that means." And then she laughed.

I didn't work closely with Colleen until about two years later, in 1986, on the tax project. She was president by then, and Equity was lobbying to have tax deductions for performing artists built into Reagan's new tax code. I saw then what an asset she was to the union and how she could do for us what no one else could. Colleen was all over the place in Washington, D.C. We would schedule a series of meetings for her on the Hill, and she would allow herself to be led around the Congressional offices all day, talking to everyone she met. Now, she truly didn't understand any of the specifics of the tax bill, but it didn't matter. Her presence would command attention. She would walk into a meeting and these "suits" would stop whatever they were doing to speak with her. I remember one unfortunate congressman saying, "Why do you need these deductions? You've all got swimming pools," implying that actors are rich. She stopped, looked directly at this guy, and said, "This is not about actors with swimming pools. This is about the little guy, which is most of us. This, sir, is about the actor who pays rent." And you could see in that simple exchange that she had made the union's point better than any of the rest of us had with all our charts and employment figures. And you know, we got the deductions, in no small part because of Colleen stepping up to bat.

JUDY RICE

Colleen laughed a lot about the perception of all actors being well off. *She* certainly wasn't, not in the way that people would assume. She once received one of those brokerage solicitations that read, "Dear Miss Dewhurst: Because of your stature in show business, you probably need investment counseling." She scrawled across it, "No, what I need is a job," and posted it on her refrigerator.

I remember when we were helping her get her pension set up. Here she was, president of the union, and she didn't know what she was entitled to. But her dear friend Elizabeth Wilson had explained to her that even though she was still working, the addition of the income from her pension would help make her comfortable and take some of the pressure from wondering where the next job might come from. Colleen was very enthused with this idea but said, "You know, baby, I don't really know how much there will be in Equity for me. I didn't have a lot of hits." I was dumbstruck by that remark, but it was true. That kind of observation, however, was also what gave her a very unusual clarity about the entire profession, particularly the whole spectrum of people who just made a modest living working in the business, which as she said, "is most of us."

Colleen was so thrilled when she was able to keep some of the wardrobe that she wore when she appeared on *Moonlighting,* the television series. She wound up with a couple of great suits that she would wear whenever she had to appear somewhere for Equity. She never dressed for the office. She just wore what she always wore, slacks and a sweater or one of those Indian-style shirts. Invariably, if she had to attend some event, there was always the famous mad dash into Colleen's office to try to pull her together at the last minute. Often, she wouldn't remember that she was scheduled to go out in the evening until she came into the office and was reminded by her assistant. It then became all about, "Who has the earrings?" "Where is the eyebrow pencil?" "Could we send somebody out for a new pair of stockings?" I once gave her the sweater I was wearing because she had forgotten that she was being photographed and had come into the office wearing a corduroy work shirt. I think she was probably the only union official who kept hot rollers on the windowsill behind her desk.

SCOTT BARNES

One afternoon, she was going on some cruise up the Hudson to Helen Hayes' home in Nyack. She was fretting about what she was wearing. I was in her office, trying to help her pull something together from the collection of skirts and sweaters she kept hanging in the closet. Invariably, this clothing was there because they'd been worn and discarded for something else in the office. Tom, her assistant, would gather them up, have them dry cleaned, and then put back in the office closet, and every now and then you'd see Colleen leaving Equity with an armful of clothing, as if she'd just come from shopping at a secondhand shop. She'd dress right in front of you, like she was backstage. The hot rollers would be plugged in and she'd sit there at her desk, looking for a lipstick or trying to find her shoes, smoking and saying, "So, bunny, what's up?"

But I do think there was a part of her that despaired at not being able to ever quite get herself together. "Oh, bunny," she'd say, "all those women, like Helen and Zoe and Kitty Carlisle Hart, they see me coming and I know they turn to each other and say, "'Here comes Colleen. Oh, God, look at her. If I could just get her to Mr. Blumphy, he could do something for her. She'd look so good.'" She thought all those women of a certain station were perfect, perfectly put together. She just didn't have it in her to do it. But when someone got it together for her, she was dazzling. She just didn't care to do it for herself.

And she could never remember anybody's name. It was always "bunny" or "blumphy"—"Mr. Blumphy." I'm not sure she ever knew mine, she just knew that somehow I was OK. I remember once standing outside her office and hearing, "Bunny! Bunny, come in here and talk with me." I looked around. I didn't know who she was talking to at first. "Bunny," she repeated, "get in here and talk to me. I don't want blumphy to come in and disturb me, so let's act like we're having a serious conversation." Now, she wasn't certain who "blumphy" was, but she knew she didn't want to talk to him that day. So we sat there huddling over her desk, as if she were attending to some kind of serious business when, in fact, she was asking me for the latest dish: "So what's new, baby?"

JUDITH G. ANDERSON
Colleen's door was usually open and she was always welcoming. To be invited in for a private conversation with her was a treat, an exchange of secrets with lots of laughs and giggles, even if you were discussing the most public of matters. I always felt as if I was being taken into her confidence, and many times I was, but the hushed whispering atmosphere she imposed lent itself to that. She would be sitting at her desk. There were two chairs directly in front of it, where visitors would sit. She would lean forward and speak in soft tones, dropping her voice at the end of sentences that she rarely finished. I would lean into her across the desk, straining for sounds that would provide me with some clue as to what she was saying, knowing all the while that if she chose to, she could make the windows rattle with the power of her voice.

JUDY RICE
It was astounding. Onstage, she was a clarion bell, but in private conversation she mumbled. And whether the cigarette was in or out of her mouth—usually in—the mouth moved the same, never really opening wide unless to laugh. And names? Forget it. She didn't remember them, or she made them up, rushing right along, assuming you knew who she was talking about. "Maureen," she'd say. All right, is that Stapleton, Anderman, or Moore? Who knew? I just listened long enough, hoping to eventually figure it out. Early on, I thought for sure I had always missed something, that something had been said that I didn't hear. Finally, I began to realize it wasn't me and I'd just say, "Colleen, I don't know who you're talking about!" She'd look completely surprised and say, "Oh! Stapleton," and rush right on with whatever unfinished thought had been interrupted.

ALAN EISENBERG

But don't kid yourself, she was very sharp. That incredible disorganization in her personal effects and mumbling in private conversations in no way reflected how she handled her feelings. She could be very clear about that. The first time I met her, she yelled at me. This was well before she was active in the union. There was some dreadful misunderstanding surrounding the videotaping of the Broadway production of *You Can't Take It with You* that she appeared in. After the disaster of the taping of the Broadway musical *Sophisticated Ladies*, Equity would not allow a camera to roll unless everything had been signed, sealed and delivered between the actors and producers. We did not have a signed deal the day before *You Can't Take It with You* was to tape. So I went over to the Plymouth and met with the cast backstage to tell them that there was a good possibility the taping would not be taking place. The meeting left everyone in shock, if for no other reason than this meant they would not be paid. As soon as I got back to the office my phone rang. I answered and immediately heard this deep, familiar voice that ran me up and down about "how dare" I do this, and how I'd "better not" do this and that she was "expecting to do this taping!" That was my first one-on-one conversation with Colleen. Thankfully, we were able to come to an agreement with the producers at the last minute and everything went ahead as planned.

The only other time she got sharp with me was when I once made some passing derogatory remark about The Actors' Fund. The conversation between us stopped abruptly. She looked at me across her desk and said, "Cut that out. I don't ever want to hear anything like that again. If you feel there's a problem, help us correct it." No matter how justified my comment may have been, she simply would not permit anyone to run The Actors' Fund down. She held that organization very, very dear to her heart. And today, I'm a member of the Fund's board of trustees.

PATRICK QUINN

You know, when there was that rare councillor who didn't like Colleen, I hate to admit it, he or she was pretty much cut out of my will. If I could not talk that person into understanding what Colleen was doing for us, that was it. I think most of the time, it was just a case of someone being jealous of what he or she assumed Colleen to be—especially around her status in the business—and not being able to see past that to what she really was.

Colleen had a great dedication to service here. She really understood how important her presence could be, but never in a way that was about ego-tripping, which is exactly what made her so effective. If she was asked, or even just sensed that somebody really wanted her to do something, she would try to do it. It was really a very impressive trait that indicated how moral she was, and it is not usual for someone of her stature in that kind of unpaid position. It could also, however, be her biggest failing. She really needed somebody to say, "Colleen, you don't have to do this." That eagerness to help, which made her so wonderful in many ways, could also get to the point where it would screw up her own life.

JUDITH G. ANDERSON

She was a tremendous presence in the office. There was a kind of stirring in the air even before you knew she was on the premises. You would hear the click of the numbered combination lock to the entrance on the sixteenth floor, and everything moved in a domino effect from that. Next, you'd hear that deep, edgy voice and, invariably, the laugh that seemed almost like a throaty yelp. As she came down the hall from her office, we all knew to hang on to our glasses and cigarettes. She never remembered either of her own and would visit office to office, looking for replacements, always with that ever-present can of Diet Pepsi in her hand. Once, as she rose to speak before a gathering sponsored by the National Coalition Against Censorship, and not finding her glasses at hand, she practically swept Kurt Vonnegut's off his face in order to read her statement. I have no idea whether she was nearsighted or far-sighted—probably, neither did she know—but she clearly had wonderfully adaptive eyes. Anyone's glasses would do.

Colleen was also very generous in her gifts and generous in her praise. Her time and energies were given without restraint to the people she loved and the causes she cared about. But she needed help in packing her own bags, remembering her purse, and locating the instructions that would enable her to fulfill her promises. It was not that she was light-headed, for Colleen had great depth, passion, and understanding. It was that she cared so deeply and had such fun much of the time that she couldn't be burdened with details. She was confident that she would get to the right place at the right time because of the people she chose to entrust with those details. And for those chosen, assisting Colleen in any way was a labor of love.

ALAN EISENBERG

Although I appreciate how beloved she was personally, I keep wanting to get back to how important she was to the very workings of the union. When she first arrived as president in 1985, she saw quite clearly a very cancerous situation that existed between the staff and a few high-powered councillors—the union's elected representatives—that had been going on for years. She made it her business to correct that. She said to me once, "When I sit across a table from someone, I like to look that person in the eyes and have him or her talk to me, so I can then talk to them. And that is not what is going on around here!" She immediately disliked that councillors felt free to bash or second-guess the staff. This would not have been corrected but for her. Colleen simply would not tolerate it and made that clear. By her second term, most of those people were gone, and we can all be very grateful for it. She changed how the union operates and does business, even today.

PATRICK QUINN

Before Colleen came on board, everything was based on technicalities and overlapping rules. Colleen, as a person, just had no time for that. She wasn't interested. She was a bit of a cowboy when she came in. Sometimes she would play dumb around all the procedures and rules of order in meetings. But let me tell you, she was dumb like a fox. She'd say, "Oh, geez, I didn't realize that I should have . . ." and by then, the wheels were moving. Her supposed confusion was very well thought out. And she knew that by dismissing it in that way, even if it came somewhat at her own expense, she could streamline the whole process. This empowered those of us who felt the Council should let go of micromanaging everything. She wanted a producer to come in here on Monday and have an answer on Friday. She had very little patience with endless discussion and committee meetings. I remember her frustration boiling over once to where she finally blurted out, "Oh, for God's sake, stop this nonsense and let's get something done!"

ALAN EISENBERG

But we have to look at one point where Colleen hit a snag: *Miss Saigon.* Colleen and I both recommended to the Council that Jonathan Pryce, the English actor who originated the Asian role of "the Engineer" in London, be allowed to come to Broadway. But for a variety of reasons, technical and emotional, the Council rejected our advice and denied producer Cameron Mackintosh's request. And then the firestorm hit. This was excruciating for Colleen. She didn't support the Council's action but she knew that, as president, she had to speak for the decision made by the union. It was really the one time where her lack of clarity on specific legal arguments and not quite understanding the minutiae of the debate hurt her. All the legal reasoning and knee-jerk emotional posturing that led to this initial decision to reject the request went against all that she believed in and felt the union should espouse. There was no one, no one, who wanted to see minorities—the breadth of Equity's membership—working, more than Colleen. She loved the idea of nontraditional casting. To hear those principles twisted for the sake of legal arguments or, worse, have her stalwart support and love for minority actors questioned broke her heart. And because in her heart she believed Pryce should have been admitted, when she spoke on this issue, all the qualities that made her such a dynamic profile for the union failed her.

Of course, we know that eventually the Council reversed itself and, following the course that Colleen and I had advised in the first place, granted permission for Pryce to open in *Miss Saigon*, for which he went on to win the Tony Award. But by that time, the damage had been done, both in the perception of Equity's decision-making process and, in some ways, to Colleen's prestige. And that is very unfortunate. We got to the right decision but at a very high cost, much of which was paid by Colleen. It should be noted, however, as an important historical footnote, that after Jonathan Pryce, there has never been another Caucasian cast as "the Engineer" in any company, in New York or on the road. It was a very sad time, but the consequences were ultimately positive. This terrible incident made everyone aware of what was a subtle discrimination in casting. It raised everyone's consciousness of that issue. It also forced the Council to become much more grounded in reality. We rightly lost some of our grandiosity and arrogance. Equity had to look at its behavior in terms of the entire theater community and understand how our actions would not only be experienced, but perceived. I know Colleen ultimately understood this and took some pride and comfort in that. I am also certain that she was very moved by how many of us at Equity rallied around to protect her. But she took the personal attacks in the press and from some in the Broadway community very badly. The entire experience took a terrible and unfair toll on her. It still saddens me.

But Colleen's legacy is much more than that. We often went to the theater together during her presidency. And whenever we did, she would insist that we go backstage to say hello to the membership, the actors and stage managers— although she invariably knew just about everyone—crew, management, dressers. When we came through the stage door, there would be just this feeling for her. You could see people being so eager to meet her. Character actors fifty years old and young kids in the chorus barely in their twenties all had great admiration and respect for her. There was something about her face that made her seem so real. You'd look at her or watch her speak to other people and see so much life. There was a lot of pain in that face, a lot of sorrow and tough times, but there was also an enormous beauty that everyone seemed to respond to. I think they loved that she had lived such a full life in the theater, in this neighborhood with all of us. And here, at Equity, you walk around the office even now, five years after her death, and there are pictures of her tacked to people's bulletin boards or framed and taped to their desks. That is really its own very special kind of tribute.

On a late night in February of 1991, the offices of Actors' Equity were swept by fire. No one was hurt, but damage, particularly to offices on the fifteenth floor below Colleen's office on the sixteenth, was severe. For the next seven months, the union's staff worked out of cubicles in the fourteenth-floor Council room as repairs were made upstairs. The president's office was one of twenty or more offices that had to be completely gutted and rebuilt. For the first time in five years, Colleen's "home away from home" at Equity was unavailable to her. Although very few were aware of it at this time, Colleen's health was becoming fragile. Even before the fire, after returning home to the Farm in December 1990 from shooting the film Dying Young, *in California's Napa Valley, her appearances in the office were rare. After a brief visit to inspect the damage from the fire, Colleen never returned to the Equity offices. Most figured it was due to the extreme conditions in the office. The staff and Council had been told that Colleen's back was very bad, and for her to move around amid the rebuilding would be dangerous. When she wasn't working, doing two or three weeks at a time in the national tour of* Love Letters, *Colleen stayed in touch by phone, handling union business long distance. But very few saw her.*

Colleen Dewhurst's second term as president of Actors' Equity Association ended in June of 1991, in the midst of the reconstruction. The president's office would not be completed until sometime after the beginning of the term of her successor, Ron Silver. On May 28, 1991, at the last Council meeting of her presidency, Colleen addressed those assembled by phone hookup.

Minutes of the Council Meeting of May 28, 1991

Miss Dewhurst has served as our president for the past six years and the Chair [Patrick Quinn] advised her that the Council had, in an earlier meeting, unanimously declared her a Life Member of Actors' Equity Association and president emeritus. . . . The Chair expressed the hope of the entire association that President Dewhurst would continue to be an active part of Actors' Equity in her role as president emeritus, that she would continue to lead, assist and guide us. He concluded by expressing his own deep love and that of the association to President Colleen Dewhurst. President Dewhurst thanked the Chair for his loving and gracious words:

I'm so sorry that I can't actually be there with all of you today. It really is the one place I really wish I could be. I have learned a great deal from each of you, mostly because you taught me to really listen to what people are saying. There were many times that I came into a Council meeting with my mind made up about something. Then, after listening to the debate, I realized that there were other equally valid points of view that sometimes would prompt me to change my mind or help confirm for me what I believed to be right. Some people believe that our meetings are all about talking, but finally and ultimately, the answer is in the listening.

I am constantly amazed by the amount of time you give to ensure that problems are solved, large and small, and I don't think the membership really understands this and they most likely never will. But it has been an honor for me to speak on your behalf and to represent an organization that fights so hard, even sometimes among ourselves. We have certainly faced many difficulties together. But we are stronger, individually and as a union, for doing so.

I'm so proud of what we do for each other. And not just in terms of contracts and employment, but also in such unique endeavors as The Actors' Work Program and Equity Fights AIDS. There were many people who thought these things would never go, that they couldn't be done. But they happened because so many of you came forward and in many different ways made it happen. And I love you most for just that. It's also been a particular joy watching Patrick [Quinn] chair these meetings in my stead. He has been a marvelous first-vice [president], all I hoped for, with just the right touch and just the right humor. I am especially grateful to Alan [Eisenberg], whose understanding of the difficulties faced by actors, skills as a negotiator, and willingness to fight for this union has brought dignity and great benefits to our membership.

I told Ron Silver [who had just been elected to follow Colleen as president] that this will not be an easy job and not for just the reason he expects. Just wait until he does his first play as president. You can't imagine what it is like to be waiting to go on with all the usual fear that situation brings up and then think to yourself, I'm now president of Equity, the actors' union, and if I'm lousy, I'll have thirty-nine thousand other members to answer to.

Finally, I want to send my warmest greetings and love to members of the Equity staff whom I have grown to appreciate, love, and respect in so many ways. I never dreamed that I could take such pride in being your president. You have given me great joy. Know that I am thinking of each of you today, even if I cannot be there with all of you.

27

"We are not being paid to enjoy ourselves!"

As a child, I loved the book *Anne of Green Gables*. It was the first book my mother ever read to me. As I grew older and learned to read, I read all of Lucy Maud Montgomery's "Anne" books myself.

Twenty years ago, in February, I flew with Tony and Stuart, two very good friends of mine who were always looking for something to do, to Prince Edward Island to look at a house on Fortune Bay. I bought that house. It was only when I returned in the following June to move in that I discovered from the many tourist signs that Prince Edward Island was the home of Lucy Maud Montgomery and, of course, of Anne.

Years before, I had bought the book *Anne of Green Gables* and read it aloud to my two sons. Little did I know that much later, I would be playing Marilla, who, in the story, with her brother Matthew, takes young Anne into her home.

Clifford Stevens told me that he had received a call from a young man from Toronto, Kevin Sullivan, who said that he wished to do a film adaptation of *Anne of Green Gables* and I was his Marilla. Mr. Sullivan had been very frank. He was having trouble clearing the rights to the story and was having a difficult time raising the money.

Kevin would call every two or three months and report to Clifford on his progress. Clifford is a very tough and discerning agent. He receives many calls about my participation in projects that are in no way near being able to make a definite offer. I am always informed of them even if his concluding line will be, "Believe me, Colleen, this is never going to happen."

This time, however, when telling me about the last call he had received from Kevin, Clifford said that he liked this young man and that he believed that he would succeed. Feeling as he did, Clifford had agreed to inform Kevin anytime I was about to sign for another film, in order that he would know when I would not be available to shoot *Anne*.

In 1984, I was in London, shooting an episode of *Love Boat*—they had made me an offer I couldn't refuse—when Clifford called to say that *Anne of Green Gables* was "a go" and that he was mailing me the script. I couldn't wait for the package to arrive and when it did, two days later, I read it at once. As it turned out, Mr. Sullivan was not only the producer, but the writer and director as well. I couldn't believe how beautifully he had captured the story and the mood of Lucy Maud Montgomery's writing.

I had signed to do the film *The Boy Who Could Fly*, before receiving the definite offer to do *Anne* and, after London, was scheduled to work ten or twelve days on the film in Vancouver. Fortunately, Clifford and Kevin were able to arrange a compatible shooting schedule with the producers of *The Boy Who Could Fly*. My first commitment contractually was to them and they could have made it very difficult, if not impossible, for me to do both films. To this day, I am very grateful to those producers.

When I met Kevin, I was looking at a twenty-eight-year-old man with a nice Irish face who could have been my son. Kevin and his wife, Trudy, who was very much involved in the production and a wonderful friend, were now faced with an awesome task. *Anne of Green Gables* had, over the years, become symbolic of Canada, and Lucy Maud Montgomery was one of Canada's most universally known writers. Every Canadian child, like myself, knew these books inside out. And although they are also well known in the States, there is a national pride attached to them by Canadians. As a producer, Kevin had done only a number of documentaries. There was a fear within the Canadian film industry that he was out of his league, facing a monumental challenge, and could only be setting himself up to fail as producer, writer and director.

Most of the actors working on *Anne* lived in Toronto. Arrangements were made for me to stay in a lovely suite in the Castle Harbour Hotel, which has now become my home away from home, as it is for most actors working in the city. The first few days I was there were set aside for costume fittings and makeup and hair tests. *Anne* is a period piece, set in the country in the nineteenth century. I was given many books with pictures of Canadian farm women in order that I could study not only their clothes and hair but their attitude and how they carried themselves.

Megan Follows played Anne and was incredible from beginning to end. Many times she would be required in the middle of shooting not only to change costume—as we all expect—but to have her makeup changed and her hair redyed and styled, as she would jump back and forth in the shooting schedule from Anne as a young girl to a young woman. One bit of temperament on that set would have finished us all. Megan's unbelievable study and concentration on the role, as well as her willingness to be a team player on *Anne of Green Gables*, was instrumental to the success of the film.

I was amazed by the talent of each and every one of the players in *Anne*. They came prepared, but above all, each one seemed to have that extra little spark that distinguishes actors one from another. Anyone who has seen *Anne of Green Gables* knows that after Richard Farnsworth, no actor could ever again be acceptable as Matthew. From the moment the camera touches Mr. Farnsworth's face you know everything about him and you love him.

Once in a while in film you will see a whole crew begin to move as one. It is as if they develop a sixth sense that tells them that they are working on something special. They are no longer just the crew doing a job; they know now that they are craftsmen, as responsible for the success of the material as anyone standing in front of the camera.

Naturally, the whole atmosphere of a set hinges on your director. Kevin's love of the material and his respect for his company of actors and his crew made you feel that you were in a quality production. Through the years, I have learned, in theater as well as film, to determine my trust in a director by listening closely to how he directs the other actors in the scenes with me. When I can see that a director has hit something exactly right with another actor, I know to pay close attention when he speaks to me. Kevin directed effortlessly and made us always feel that we were somehow accomplishing his objective without laying a heavy hand on our performances, sometimes shooting a scene five or six times until we reached the same conclusion that he had started with. That is a great talent.

I had thought that *Anne of Green Gables* would be a lovely children's film. Shooting it had been a wonderful experience and I hated to leave it behind. I was doing *Seagull* at the Kennedy Center in Washington when *Anne of Green Gables* was first broadcast on television in Canada. David Staines, a friend who was teaching at Ottawa University, called to say that Part I had shown three nights before and Part II would be shown the next evening. David had a friend, who also taught at the university, who had agreed to watch a little just because David knew somebody in it. The next day, he told David that he had watched through to the end and would not miss Part II the next night. When David called me again, a couple of days later, he said the streets were literally empty during the broadcast of Part II. It seemed nearly everyone was watching. Later I was told that the only show that had ever received a better rating in Canada was the championship hockey play-offs. In Canada, you don't do better than that.

Playing Marilla in *Anne* found a whole new audience for me. Children will now stand and stare at me as their mothers say, "Darling, this is Marilla" as I sign my autograph, "Colleen Dewhurst, aka Marilla." Even today, I continue to receive mail from people across the world telling me how much they love the film, many assuming I am truly Marilla, asking me to come and visit their farm or ranch, as they have plenty of room. But most amazing is to walk on the streets of New York, with its great cross section of age, color and ethnic backgrounds, and hear someone shout, "Hey, Colleen, I loved you in that thing where you were the mother of that orphan kid." Many people who saw the show insist on identifying me as Anne's mother. It is interesting that not only children, but grown men on the streets of New York will remember the relationship between Marilla and Anne as mother and daughter.

The only time that I found myself completely at a loss was when I was doing Eugene O'Neill's *Ah, Wilderness!* and *Long Day's Journey into Night* in repertory at the Yale Repertory Theatre in New Haven, Connecticut. A group of mothers had brought their children to *Ah, Wilderness!* as this is the only one of O'Neill's plays that is truly acceptable for all ages. No one had warned me in advance that they had been in the audience, and as I opened my dressing room door, I was greeted by five or six mothers and about eight young children who had come backstage to meet . . . Marilla. There I stood in the doorway, in jeans and a shirt, hair flying every which way and, of course, smoking the last half of a cigarette. When I saw them, I was horrified and wanted to turn around, slam the door, put my hair up on my head, jump into the full skirt from *Ah, Wilderness!*—put out the damn cigarette!—and reappear as a 1988 version of Marilla. But no, there I stood, the 1988 version of Colleen. The children just stared at me. To this day, I will never know what the shock of seeing me as I truly am may have done to them. I know what it's done to others.

KEVIN SULLIVAN

Working with Colleen, as I did on *Anne of Green Gables* and a number of other projects, was like entering a privileged world of honesty and humor. I'd been a great admirer of her work in film and theater. When I was putting together the film of *Anne of Green Gables*, I always pictured Colleen in the role of Marilla. So when the shooting script was complete, I called her agent Clifford Stevens to offer her the role. Clifford and I had a very general conversation about salary and such, and he encouraged me to send him the script. Before I could even get it in the mail, Clifford called back. "Colleen wants to make sure that the part you are offering her is Marilla," he said.

"Yes," I replied. "Absolutely."

"I'll call you back." Sure enough, Clifford called the next day. "She really, really wants to do this," he said. "Why, I have no idea."

Anne of Green Gables was one of the books Colleen's mother had read to her as a child. It always held a very special place in her heart. While I knew of Colleen's Canadian roots, I didn't know, when I offered her the role, that she also had spent a great deal of time on Prince Edward Island, where the author Lucy Maud Montgomery lived and the books are set. I was simply looking for an actress of stature who would be able to carry such a pivotal role. Of course, as Colleen's personal history with the story was much deeper than I expected, what she brought to the project professionally was profoundly more than I ever could have wanted.

I was terrified of meeting Colleen initially. I had heard that she could be strong-willed and demanding. I was certain she came to the role thinking, *Who is this kid who thinks he can produce, write and direct this project?* Fortunately for both of us, humor gave us great and immediate common ground. We would both laugh uproariously at anything ridiculous that happened on the set. Although she is usually first thought of as a great dramatic actress, Colleen was also a first-rate clown whose laughter was intoxicating. It was not long before I discovered an outrageous, almost giddy schoolgirl underneath that woman of years. Colleen bumbled around rehearsal, often keeping the cast and crew laughing to tears as she tried to remember where she was or what day it was. In rehearsal, her lines would often escape her. But as soon as the camera would roll, suddenly her presence was riveting. The crew would become speechless at her ability to concentrate, let alone energize the character she was playing.

Colleen had an immediate connection with her character, Marilla, and seemed to understand innately what I was trying to do with the material. It's very dangerous to do a film from a classic. You can lose your way trying to second-guess what will please everybody. Like Colleen, I also remembered the book from my childhood, but when I sat down to read it as an adult, I was surprised to find myself thinking, *This is a girl's book, a piece of Victorian sentimental nonsense.* I couldn't remember what I had felt so drawn to as a kid. Nevertheless, I still wanted to tell this sentimental story in as unsentimental and realistic a way as possible in order that it work for an audience of boys and girls, children and adults. I was delighted to find that Colleen was immediately plugged into that level in a way that not all the other actors were initially. Her unique personal combination of humor and pathos played against the material's sweetness. Marilla is a sixty-five-year-old spinster who has never opened herself up emotionally, living with her brother in this remote community. When Anne arrives to live with her, she doesn't know what's hit her. Colleen understood what that kind of bonding is about, as well as what living in that kind of insular community is like. It was amazing, and because of this we developed an innate friendship.

"This is really quite wonderful," she said to me on the second day of shooting. "This is not the way Hollywood or an American television network would tell this story." I was thrilled. Colleen's goals with her character, Marilla, were the same as what I wanted to accomplish with the entire piece. As shooting progressed, she remembered a scene from the book that I had left out of the original script and that she insisted on retrieving for the film. In this scene, her brother, Matthew, has just been buried and Marilla awakens in the rain to hear Anne crying in the adjacent room. Without any dialogue, Marilla simply gets up and goes to the child's side. I will never forget the power that Colleen brought to it in the most subtle ways. She brought more to it with each take, each being a bit better than the one before. After the third take, the crew had to break, they were so devastated by this moment of overwhelming compassion and hope that I know came out of Colleen's own passion for life. They literally didn't want her to do it again, as if they knew what they'd just seen was perfect for the film and would remain indelible in their memories. This wasn't melodramatic acting. This is one of the great actresses of her generation being able to make a moment so powerful and still that it rips your heart out. I'll never forget it. Colleen had captured the feel and the texture of the material in a way that I had never seen done before.

Soon after, I overheard her being interviewed on the set. She was asked how she prepared for her roles. You could sense the writer expected a very serious and complex answer.

"Oh, my," Colleen replied, practically laughing off the question. "I don't know, really . . . you know, some people say that I just go along with the script and with whatever happens to be going on with me at the moment, I step in front of a camera and, somehow by the grace of God, something happens. Well, let me tell you, they're not wrong," she continued, "and sometimes it does and sometimes it doesn't." I never experienced working with Colleen when it didn't. She was like a woman without a skin.

"I like Marilla," she said to me. "It never bothers me what a woman supposedly is as long as I can find something to like about her. Playing Marilla is simply putting parts of myself to sleep and bringing out a very specific part of me."

Over the years, as we worked together on a number of projects, I began to understand what Colleen meant. As an actress, she could emit such passion because she seemed truly thrilled with the soul of whatever character she was playing. It was as though she was blessed with a second sight. Yet, she didn't take herself entirely seriously. Her sense of humor kept her passions in balance.

One of my favorite memories of Colleen occurred when we were on location shooting a film called *Lantern Hill*, in which she played a mystic who appears in the dreams of the story's hero. We were in the midst of a special-effects scene that really should have been done in the controlled environment of a studio. Instead, we were working outdoors at four in the morning in order to try to keep to the production schedule. Everything went wrong. Colleen kept getting tangled in the cheesecloth curtains that were being blown around her by a wind machine that was firing like a cannon. All of us were trying to hold it together in the vain hope that Colleen would untangle herself long enough to get the shot. Just as it seemed she might, her wig blew off her head. Of course, we cut. As the hairdresser fixed her wig, Colleen saw me doubled up with laughter near the camera.

"Kevin!" she called out. "Stop it. Stop it right now! This is about money. We are not being paid to enjoy ourselves!" And with that she started laughing, nearly shaking the wig off her head again. But when she put herself into this very bizarre effects shot again, she appeared transfixed, sensing when all the elements around her—the lighting, the wind machine, the blowing cheese-cloth—finally came together around her and in that instant, she made the character happen.

I think Colleen loved the freedom and the dangers that her great talent brought her. She was also modest enough to respect that talent as a gift. But what made her truly a delight was her irreverent take on life itself, particularly all that life dealt to her. She said once in all seriousness that she never was completely secure in her abilities as an actress or who she was as a celebrity because, she noted, "just as you have achieved something, God will always get you." As proof, she recalled how she was to receive an honorary degree from a prestigious university at which she had also been asked to speak. As usual, Colleen was late for the pregraduation ceremonies, having insisted on driving herself to the campus. She hadn't prepared anything specific to say and wasn't even sure why she had been asked to speak. Was this a drama school? But she eventually found her way and hurried up to the podium with just minutes to spare. As she walked past the other speakers on the dais she thought she heard someone whisper behind her, "The higher you get, the harder you fall." This was sobering enough for Colleen that she pulled out all of the stops, as she could invariably do in such situations, and from the whirlwind of thoughts going through her mind, delivered an address off the top of her head which truly moved the audience.

"I stepped away from the podium feeling quite good about myself," she said, "and that perhaps I had really achieved something in my career." Just then, one of the university staff came up behind her and whispered, "Miss Dewhurst, do you realize that you left a hot roller in your hair?" I can still hear Colleen laughing to tears as she told that story.

Professionally, *Anne of Green Gables* became quite a unique experience for both of us and, without being sentimental or manipulative, a highly commercial film. But it was Colleen's strong heart and soul that most affected me and I know is still reflected in how I continue to see life. Still today, when I see her smile light up the screen, I am enchanted.

◌◌ ◌◌ ◌◌

I had been approached several times to do the pilot for a number of hour-long television series. Each time I refused, simply because the work would have taken me away from the theater for what could be, with a hit series, five years. It is a nine-month commitment to shoot a complete season of hourlong television, usually twenty-six episodes. I understood from friends who were working in the medium that such a schedule left you neither the time nor energy to do a play.

For over ten years, at the beginning of my career, I did nearly a hundred plays in summer stock. Easily three-quarters of those (usually rehearsed and opened in a week) were comedies. But as I established a place for myself in the theater, I became known—in the eyes of many producers, directors and, therefore, the public—as a "dramatic" actress. Audiences came to expect my journey onstage to be one of great travail. After the performance of one of these many tragedies, I was often heard to say, "Oh, if only I could do a farce, with slamming doors, smart-mouthed maids and mistaken identities." This was always received with a verbal pat on the head, as if I had just said something very amusing.

You can imagine my surprise when I received an offer to appear in the CBS situation comedy *Murphy Brown*. My Los Angeles agent, David Eidenberg, told me there was no script but that the producers, Diane English and Joel Shukovsky, wished to send me the show's reviews. I said that was not necessary, as everyone at the Farm, including my sons, who are not easy, had already reviewed the show and had been watching it regularly for weeks and it was thumbs-up all around.

I accepted the offer on a Thursday and, within an hour, Diane English called to tell me that I would be playing Avery Brown, Murphy's mother, and that they were just now beginning to work on the script. I suppose it was crazy to agree to work on anything where I hadn't seen a script first and had no idea what kind of character I would play, but, from what I had seen, I felt secure that it would be fun to do and that I was in the hands of possibly one of the best writing teams currently on the air. I thought *Murphy Brown* had shown great wit, always with an undercurrent of truth.

Arrangements were made very quickly. I flew out to Los Angeles two days later, where there was a script waiting for me at the Chateau Marmont—and a rented car in its garage. That evening over the phone I was given the time of my call and directions to the Warner's studio in Burbank.

It always makes me very uneasy first meeting people, particularly in a work situation in which I know no one. Yet I am always amazed to discover later that people assume me to be confident and relaxed, the picture of one who has great composure and immediately understands what is happening in any given situation. I suppose that having been so painfully shy all through my childhood, always the new kid on the block, I developed, in self-defense, what appeared to be a very calm and controlled exterior.

That first morning of rehearsal I woke up early, showered and dressed in what I thought would be the most appropriately nondescript way. I went to the garage and got into my car, clutching last night's directions in my hand, and drove over to Burbank. I found the studio with no problem but, as I was twenty-five minutes early, I passed the entrance, went a few blocks, turned left onto a small street, and parked. I sat there for fifteen minutes watching the clock, waiting for it to read eight minutes before the hour, at which point I drove back to the entrance, hoping it looked like I'd just arrived, perfectly on time.

I was immediately anxiety-stricken again over where I was to park my car. The guard at the gate was very courteous and gave me directions to the sound-stage where *Murphy Brown* shoots. Having found it, I was moving close to hysteria as I realized that every parking space was taken or empty, with the words RESERVED FOR——— painted impressively on the wall. After sort of skittering around in that tiny area from one unavailable space to another, I finally addressed the first friendly face that came by and was told to leave the car: "Someone will park it." A wave of relief came over me. Someone had recognized that I belonged there. The day's first problem had been resolved.

I entered the soundstage, and the producers and a few members of the cast casually came over to me and introduced themselves. Across the stage, I saw the table of coffee and rolls and headed for it at once. This was a familiar oasis that gave me something to hang on to. The cast was soon seated at a large, U-shaped table and proceeded with the first read-through of that week's script. Once we began to read, I could feel myself relax. I was in safe territory.

Three or four days later, Candice Bergen and I had begun to know each other and were standing around talking between setups.

"We were all so nervous that first day when you came in," she said.

"What?" I said, now with a laugh. "*You?* I was a wreck."

From the start, rehearsals were relaxed but very efficient. This atmosphere was created by the director, Barnett Kellman, who, at that time, had directed every episode of *Murphy Brown* from its inception. Usually on sitcoms there are several directors coming and going each week. I had never thought it to be important one way or the other. In fact, it is. Working with the same excellent director each week ensured that *Murphy Brown* had continuity of story and, for the actors, someone who was completely familiar with ongoing truth of character and each one's reality of behavior. Barnett knows his actors and their characters. He instinctually understands the individual strengths and easy comic mannerisms of each actor. He recognizes when one of us gets into trouble and, to get out, falls into schtick, just going for the laugh. Successful comedy must be played absolutely straight and with great truth. The actors must always be aware that they are in comedy, but that what is happening in the script is, for them at that moment, a completely sincere and believable situation.

During one rehearsal, I was thrown by the presence of half a dozen people who came on the set and sat there, saying nothing, just observing.

"Who are they?" I said to Candice.

"Those are the writers," she said.

This group, whom I might mistake for some of my sons' friends from college just dropping by for an evening of beer and poker, would sit in those ever-present directors' folding chairs, facing the set and watching the run-through. They were very courteous and attentive. They would laugh and occasionally even applaud. Then they would leave. Before long, sheets of paper would begin to arrive on the set with changes. What hadn't been working the moment before, they removed and rewrote, with no suggestion that the dialogue had been cut because the actor was unable to make it work. What amazed me most was how the line that stopped you dead each time had been neatly excised and a new, truly brilliant bit of dialogue appeared in its place. These revisions were incorporated into the week's script right through the final run-through, some just before our performance on camera before the live audience.

For example, in the original scene in which Murphy and I return from having had dinner together, Candice was to turn to me and say, "It was bad enough you making the waiter take the steak back, but did you have to follow him into the kitchen and make the chef eat it?" My original response had been, "If you continue to let people get away with shoddy work, you will always get overdone meat." From our first rehearsal this exchange had received a laugh, even though my response seemed a bit weak. During Friday's run-through, I was handed a piece of paper with a single rewrite of that one line: "If you keep letting people get away with shoddy work, you end up with President Quayle." Suddenly, what had been a good laugh became a brilliant exchange. It was not only funny, but perceptive, catching the audience off guard. They now laughed not only at the joke, but also with recognition at the jab that had been taken at a situation we all would rather not address. This is what makes ordinary comic writing extraordinary.

I love *Murphy Brown* for its class, innovation and particularly its recognition of where many women are today. Here is a sitcom in which the title character is a beautiful woman who has just come out of the Betty Ford Clinic. She is capable, intelligent and in a position of leadership. She is a woman of strength. Professionally, she has the best credentials. She is aware, as is everyone around her, that she can do this job better than anyone else . . . and she is insecure.

Murphy Brown makes a statement to women across the country that is not often made anywhere else, including the stage. Much has happened since the women's movement first began. In the seventies, women with whom I had gone to college would come backstage to say how proud they were to watch my career, to know a woman who had done so much with her life. Several times following this statement was the remark, "I haven't done much with mine." I would then discover that they had been married for twenty-five years, raised three children, were very well read, active in their communities—sometimes politically, sometimes as volunteers. How was I to explain to them that their lives might be enviable to someone like me? As women, they, too, have many accomplishments of which they can be proud. Instead, they somehow feel that these more traditional efforts don't count, that they should be out working and making more publicly recognizable contributions. We had truly believed, and still do, that women should have equal standing with men. That they should be recognized for the unique qualities that they, as women, bring to the community. We have found that we were right. Women *do* belong in government, in management, and as the creators and owners of their own businesses. We bring to these positions a feminine strength, compassion, a brilliance of intellect and, yes, that truly frightening word to some: *intuition*.

But then we women created another monster when we began to emulate the behavior of the very men to whom we had long objected. After thousands of years of submission being ingrained into our genes, in too many cases we turned around and embraced their patronization of others, particularly other women in subordinate positions. Sadly, the executive woman sitting behind her desk has too often become an almost perfect replica of the dispassionate, disconnected male executive, interested only in power.

Is it not true that we all cringed when Geraldine Ferraro, who has a brilliant mind, was shot down politically? And did we not hate ourselves for cringing when Patricia Schroeder broke down and cried as she withdrew from the presidential race? Why? Pat was right to cry. She was tired. She was disappointed. She had the credentials for her job. But we, the public, were embarrassed because she reacted like a woman. Our great fear is that this vulnerability, or better, this ability to feel, takes away from our ability to do and diminishes us in some way. It does not. The ability to display emotion appropriately does not diminish a situation or anyone's ability to perform a job. Stultifying rigidity will bring you down long before being able to express your feelings will. But somehow, we have come to consider one kind of behavior male and the other female, one business-like and the other not. One strong and one weak. When we restrict what it is to be masculine or feminine, we lose out on the fullness of what it is to be just human.

The insecurity written into Murphy Brown and so brilliantly played by Candice Bergen is the inheritance of women everywhere. Murphy Brown is successful and vulnerable, sending a message to all women that even those who seem to "have it all" are frightened, and that being frightened does not have to stop you. Having it all—particularly having to have a man in order to be complete—is not the important thing; having a sense of your own self-worth is. I love what the writers wrote for me, as Avery, to say to Murphy when she states that she's not sure that "great love" happens to everybody.

"Murphy," she says, "you know I never read you fairy tales as a child. The knight in shining armor isn't always going to ride up on his white horse and rescue us. We have to make our own way. And if he does show up on our doorstep one day, how wonderful. But you know that he's still going to use your eyebrow pencil to write down phone numbers."

There was a sense of great camaraderie on the set of *Murphy Brown*. This, I believe, starts with Candice, a woman who in her own life has truly been there and back. Here is a woman of very good background who has known every luxury, who in many ways had a career handed to her, and then had to re-create herself totally, and in doing so, earned the admiration and respect of her peers. Candice created an atmosphere that was easy to work in because you felt that she truly cared not only about the entire piece, but had learned to take care of herself. This caring then extended to everyone, cast and crew. It created an interdependent company, much like live theater, where each is highly aware of the importance of the work being done by every member to ensure the project's total success.

The Friday night of taping that I had been dreading since I first drove onto the lot, finally arrived. That morning, wardrobe and makeup moved in quickly. I loved their imagination and, in their own attention to detail, the understanding they showed of the characters we actors were trying to create. It had been directed that elevator doors would open on the newsroom set, and I would make my first entrance saying, "May I have everyone's attention, please." God knows, it rarely gets better than that, even onstage. I felt nervous and numb as I stood behind the closed door of the elevator, and can scarcely remember listening to the actors on the set, waiting for the line that would cue the elevator doors. Suddenly, they slid open and I stepped forward into the newsroom, speaking my first lines as Avery Brown. The audience laughed, as if right on cue, and immediately I relaxed, loving it all; the camaraderie of rehearsal, the excitement of rewriting and reworking the script and, finally, the tension of a live audience. It was like an opening night.

Several months passed before this episode was televised. The day after the show aired, I went into the city to do some work at my office at Equity. I parked the car in a lot I've used for over twenty years on West Forty-fifth Street and as I got out the attendant said, with what I thought sounded like a slight hint of surprise, "You were terrific last night on that *Murphy Brown* show." When I arrived at Equity, coworkers and friends kept stopping me on my way to my office to say that the show was wonderful last night. "You were so funny," they said. "I couldn't believe how funny you were. I mean, you were really *funny*."

I thought, *Wait a minute, thank you, but what's the big surprise here? I can play comedy, that's one of the things that actors do. We can make you laugh as well as cry.* Obviously, the producers of *Murphy Brown* had taken a great chance. It seemed suddenly clear that not only the general public but my peers, upon seeing my name in the credits, thought, *Oh, my God, it's Dewhurst. We'll have no laughs tonight.*

I won an Emmy for my portrayal of Avery Brown, mother of Murphy.

28

A Eugene O'Neill Centennial Celebration

I n February of 1988, during the second term of her presidency at Actors' Equity, Colleen went to Yale Repertory Theatre, in New Haven, Connecticut, to participate in the Eugene O'Neill Centennial Celebration. There she joined a company of actors, including Jason Robards, George Hearn, Elizabeth Wilson, Jamey Sheridan, Campbell Scott, Raphael Sbarge and Kyra Sedgwick in the repertory productions of Long Day's Journey into Night *and* Ah, Wilderness! *which played from March 22 through May 21 before opening on Broadway on June 14* (Long Day's Journey into Night) *and June 23* (Ah, Wilderness!) *at the Neil Simon Theatre as part of the Second International Festival of the Arts.*

ELIZABETH WILSON

The O'Neill plays were really a very happy time. It was the late winter of 1988 when we all assembled to do *Ah, Wilderness!* and *Long Day's Journey into Night* at Yale Repertory Theatre as part of the Eugene O'Neill Centennial Celebration. This was going to be some big adventure because we were to do these two very different plays with two different directors. José Quintero was to direct Colleen, Jason, Campbell and, originally, John Heard in *Long Day's Journey into Night.* Then George Hearn, Raphael Sbarge, Kyra Sedgwick and I and a number of other actors, would join them to be directed by Arvin Brown in *Ah, Wilderness!* José began rehearsing *Long Day's Journey* about a month before the rest of us arrived. It was going to be quite a mouthful for Colleen and Jason, who would be in both. But no matter how daunting the task, we were all looking forward to coming to New Haven because many of us knew each other well and had worked together many times before. It was really the ideal repertory company. It was also very exciting because *Long Day's Journey* would be the first time José had worked since his throat operation, and the thought of him, Colleen and Jason coming together to do O'Neill once again created quite a stir beyond Yale.

Well, as these things go, it all started off very well, but before long, there was a problem with John, and José had to let him go. It was uncomfortable for the entire company but it was particularly devastating for Colleen, who had grown quite fond of John and had become his only protector. She tried to talk John out of whatever trouble he was having, which I guess is kind of typical of Colleen. But, as happens at times to all of us, he was just in a bad place and had to go. José recast the role of Jamie Tyrone with Jamey Sheridan, who was all sunshine and light and also very gifted, and the company of *Long Day's Journey into Night* trudged on along its way as the rest of us came up to begin rehearsals for *Ah, Wilderness!*

Both plays opened at Yale to a big advance and full houses. It was such a swell time. Jane Greenwood did the clothes and we all had worked with her many times before. So we were even comfortable about what we wore. I know Colleen was very happy during those days. I remember she stayed at another college nearby. The faculty had asked her to come up and speak to the student body just before she arrived at Yale and, of course, they were all—faculty and students—so completely enamored of her that they said, "Come stay with us!" And in true Colleen fashion, she did, forgoing a hotel suite and living instead in one big room in the faculty building and eating many of her meals in the main kitchen. For a while there, it seemed as if everything just fell into place.

We were rolling and for three very wonderful months, March, April and May of 1988, played both *Ah, Wilderness!* and *Long Day's Journey into Night* to very full and appreciative houses. Of course, there was soon talk about bringing the plays into New York as part of the upcoming International Arts Festival that summer. Here it gets a little bit hard to talk about how difficult things became around raising the money necessary to successfully bring the productions to Broadway. Some money that was promised fell through or we discovered was never really committed in the first place. It was all heartbreaking, particularly when viewed from the great success we had all experienced at Yale. Because Colleen was involved with a number of the investors and producers of the New York production, she took it all very personally, felt responsible for what was going wrong, but at the same time was completely unable to do anything about it. We shared a dressing room on the second floor of the Alvin Theatre and I don't think I have ever seen her so shattered. It was a very bad time. Although we opened to good reviews and managed to keep it going for a few weeks, ultimately, we couldn't overcome the managerial and financial mess behind the production and we closed. Colleen's sense of responsibility about it all brought her such pain. I have often felt in my bones that this was when she may have started to get sick. What could be worse for our friend than to feel she was somehow responsible for the death, if you will, of these beautiful pieces of work, so superbly cast with people she loved—and now, everybody was out of work. No one blamed her. We all tried to reassure her and cheer her up. But what started as such a high ended on a very sad and low note.

I loved Colleen dearly. We had the sort of friendship that we would just pick up again and again, depending on the circumstances. Sometimes we would be working together. More often, our personal lives would intertwine. We were like family and like any family, had such fun together and survived some very tough times. But I love to think back about being in a play with Colleen—and there were a few of them: *Taken in Marriage* at The Public; *The Good Woman of Setzuan* at Lincoln Center; *You Can't Take It with You* and *Ah, Wilderness!* on Broadway—and those many nights we would go out together afterward to Delsomma's or someplace like that. We'd have our clams casino and our pasta. I'd order my martini, Colleen would have her wine. People would join us as their shows came down, and it was just great.

We first met in Harold Clurman's class in 1953. I was in *Picnic* with Kim Stanley. Harold came to see it, and the next day Kim told me that he had liked her and me and that he was inviting us to be in his late-evening class. I was thrilled. Colleen was in the class. The first thing I ever saw her do was Lady Macbeth. I remember thinking, *God almighty! Here is this huge girl who is so talented but will never work because of her weird deep voice.* Colleen's voice was so odd, it was disturbingly riveting. But what do I know? I have no idea now how it happened that we became friends, but we did. Even then, there was such an unusual radiance about her.

When the classes finished, I didn't see Colleen again until I went into the old SAG [Screen Actors' Guild] offices to get my union card before I went out to do the movie of *Picnic*. There was Colleen, working at the reception desk. This was before she had really started getting work as an actress regularly. She was then married to Jim Vickery and I guess they needed the money. So we caught up with each other as she helped put my SAG application through. I went out to California and didn't cross paths with Colleen again until I came back and saw her and George [C. Scott] in *Children of Darkness* at the Circle in the Square on Bleecker Street. I still have a very vivid memory of them in that, particularly George. But I still can remember how sensuous Colleen was, and it was apparent right away that there was something volatile between them. I'd never seen George before that night, but our lives crossed many, many times for years to come.

The first time Colleen and I worked together, however, was much later, in 1978, I think, on a disastrous production of *The Good Woman of Setzuan* at Lincoln Center. What a mess! Colleen was the good woman and, of course, I was the bad. Jules Irving was the artistic director. Bob Simon was directing for a while and neither of them had a clue about directing Brecht, at least not then. Stephen Elliott and David Birney were in it, David playing opposite Colleen, and she hated them both. We were all so hysterical and unhappy that on the night of the first dress rehearsal, Colleen was so fed up with them all that she came in drunk. I couldn't believe it! She was pie-eyed. Everyone was horrified. "Miss Dewhurst, indeed!" We tried to plow through it, but by the time we were singing these ridiculous songs with Colleen—that the elephants were coming—"Here they are, the elephants!"—you could see that she was getting herself into more and more of a rage with each verse. I'm certain we didn't finish the rehearsal. It was during this same evening that the director gave me a note that has remained my favorite for over twenty-five years. There we all are, fighting for our lives on that stage and Jules Irving comes into my dressing room after this disastrous dress rehearsal and says, "I think it would be better if you put a little more dirt on your face." I thought, *Christ, here I am at Lincoln Center in a mob scene and all he wants is more dirt on my face!* We all should have been drunk!

Working with Colleen often meant that your lives together would extend beyond the walls of the theater. Of course, there were the inevitable visits to the Farm on days off. We all really needed to hold on to each other during that production. Later, I would stay at the Farm whenever she and the boys would go to Block Island or Prince Edward Island in Nova Scotia. I don't know how this got started, but there were even two years in a row when Maureen Stapleton and I rented the Farm for the summer, which was a scream because even though we rented and paid for it, still all of Colleen's friends came, as if she were there. I'm not sure, but maybe they thought she was upstairs. Nana was, but not Colleen. Those were quite crazy summers. The driveway was always filled with cars that Maureen and I didn't recognize and people, some of whom we'd barely know. Like many others, I stayed there whenever I was in any kind of trouble. The Farm really was a place where people could recuperate from all sorts of ills. Colleen got a lot of people through many rough patches.

Colleen also loved playing matchmaker and plotting to get people together. During *Setzuan,* I had a big crush on some guy in the cast who was married, or something that kept us from ever getting together alone outside the theater. So I would just go to his dressing room and sit there. Colleen got wind of this and said, "I've got to figure out a way to get you two together!" So after some thought, she decided that I should have a small party one night after a performance, at my apartment on West Sixty-seventh Street, near the theater. She then invited some of the cast we liked—there were a few. Colleen plotted this party for days, making sure that everyone we invited, except this poor man, knew that they were quietly to leave by a certain time. And, sure enough, it worked. We all arrived, had a few drinks, and one by one everyone, including Colleen, left until it was just me and him. Mission accomplished. Colleen adored pulling this sort of thing off. She loved all that kind of craziness and in many ways, the crazier you were, the more Colleen was drawn to you.

The next time we worked together Colleen came in, as a great favor to Joe Papp, to replace an actress who had been let go in a new play, Tom Babe's *Taken in Marriage* at the New York Shakespeare Festival. Frankly, this production wasn't in much better shape than *Setzuan* by the time Colleen entered, but I think we finally pulled it off. Colleen loved a challenge, and learning that role as quickly as she did was certainly that. "I like to live on the edge," she used to tell me. I've always believed that she liked living like that because her mind was so quick that it took that sort of imbalance to keep her attention. I'm such a sissy about things, even learning my lines. I have to study and study until I think I know every word that's coming out of everyone's mouth. Colleen, on the other hand, often learned her scripts in the car, while driving herself down to rehearsals from the Farm. If you ever tried to cue Colleen before she really learned a role, while she was still on book, you'd think, *Oh, that's a very interesting way to say that . . . but never mind.* But once she had it, she was dead on.

I adored playing in *Ah, Wilderness!* with Colleen. It was the last time we worked together. There was such a marvelous give-and-take because we had been cast as sisters-in-law. Jason played my brother, Colleen's husband. Don't ask me to remember what the names were. But because of the very sweet nature of the play, there was one scene, where we were all setting the table, that was such a lovely expression of the culmination of thirty years of friendship. It was not a major scene in the play by any means, but we were so confident and relaxed in the playing of it that it felt symphonic. We could tell when the other was perhaps a bit down and not really clipping along and there would be a give-and-take that could incorporate into life onstage whatever was going on in our own lives at that moment. It was really quite beautiful the way it would fall into place each performance. But we never talked about it. Ever. Colleen hated to talk about acting and so do I, but today it is heaven to remember.

I'll never forget one of Colleen's wonderful August parties. The house and the yard were filled with people—neighbors, friends, friends of friends, people she had worked with and people she barely knew—plus Colleen's animals and other people's animals. It was a delightful party with so much food, fortune tellers, and a band. It probably went on for days. That's how Colleen loved to spend her money. She loved to have fun and to give people a good time. I never knew anyone like her. It was almost as if she were planted here to take care of people, to love her family, to love her friends, and just to try to do a little good with what she had and to enjoy herself doing it. I know that there was also sadness and pain in Colleen's life; she lived through some very hard times. But she really tried with all her being to enjoy life. I felt so protected whenever I was with her. I knew that anything could happen, but whatever did, I was sure, if I was with Colleen, we'd be OK.

ARVIN BROWN

Having many friends in common, Colleen and I had been acquaintances over the years. She had done a couple of workshops here at the Long Wharf Theatre in New Haven, Connecticut, where I was the artistic director.

Although I wasn't involved in any of them, I was, God knows, one of many admirers she had from afar. We didn't actually meet until she came up to the Long Wharf in the early 1980s to do a new play, *Artichoke*, by Joanna Glass. I don't remember how the play actually got to Long Wharf, but it came with Colleen already attached. Ken Marsolais was producing it, and the thought was that I would direct. So before beginning rehearsals, it was arranged for me to go to the Farm to meet with Colleen. I'd never had anything more than a passing conversation with her, but in a period of about five minutes during which she found out that I was a Gemini, as she was, it was as if we had known each other all of our lives.

It was fascinating to work with Colleen on a play that had a very broad, comic undercurrent, not your usual O'Neill-type drama that everyone expected of her, particularly then, so close to her triumph in *A Moon for the Misbegotten*. Although a comedy, *Artichoke* is a very substantial play. Colleen was cast, in one sense, according to type, as the "earth mother," but in welcoming to her bed a young cuss who is sexually inexperienced, she was able to play much of the humor as well as the complexities of that sort of woman.

Colleen was very directable. She was open to suggestion, which many actors are not. They do what *they* do. Colleen was willing to interpret a role through the whole instrument of herself. As her director, for me it was never a question of saying, "This is the immediate result that I want." Colleen wanted to understand the complexities of the entire scene. She wanted to know what the "back story" of the relationship was. Then, best of all, she didn't take all this information and overintellectualize it. She had wonderful emotional shorthand that allowed her to connect with all that you had helped her to discover about the character she was playing.

Likewise, I found that Colleen had a similar personal shorthand that would allow you to connect emotionally with her, as a friend. Colleen had great wit. You could connect with her immediately if you could make her laugh or if she knew you understood instinctually why she found something ridiculous and therefore funny. She also had an extraordinary love of gossip. You could depend on her for all the information you needed about whomever you were working with. The great thing, however, about Colleen's gossip was that it came from such a benevolent place that you were inevitably delighted to hear anything from her. It never had an edge of that horrible hostility or rage that makes gossip so poisonous and unpleasant. It wasn't shared to belittle another in order to puff up herself. With Colleen, it seemed to come from an almost child-like delight in the foibles of human behavior. She was a total democrat about it all. She was just as interested in the private life of the assistant stage manager or someone sewing in the wardrobe room as she was about her costar.

There was no such thing as hierarchy when Colleen was around. I think that was one of her most wonderful qualities. She had a hunger for life that made her interested in everything that went on around her. But if you crossed her, she could hold a grudge like few others I've known. This was the scary part of her. When she decided for whatever reason that you weren't part of her crowd, it was pretty hard to come back from that. It's difficult to say what it was about a person that would turn her off. Certainly dishonesty would do it immediately. Anyone who tried to bullshit Colleen was in for a big surprise. In many ways, she was a pushover and you found her always wanting to help people out of some rather amazing jams. But she could smell a con and could cut you dead for it. She also felt uncomfortable with a certain kind of self-serving ambition, particularly if she thought you were exploiting a weakness in others to gain some advantage for yourself. She could not stand to witness that kind of behavior. As generous as she was, she had little patience with bullies and a very sharp eye for users.

What truly cemented our relationship, however, was our trip to Russia a few years later in the mid-eighties. This was in the days before Gorbachev and *glasnost,* when the Soviet Union and the States would arrange for these occasional cross-cultural exchanges, in the hopes that it would take everyone's mind off of the fact that we were really poised to destroy each other. A lovely woman, Edith Markson, who has since died, worked with the Russian cultural attaché and the American ambassador to the Soviet Union to coordinate these trips. Edith was not all that organized and tended to just wing these things much more than you might have thought possible. On this particular trip, she had a wild bunch of people: Colleen and myself, the director Des McAnuff, Ellen Stewart, founder of the La Mama Theatre in New York, and a number of other theater types, directors, producers and such from a few other regional theaters across the country. Colleen was there in her position as president of Actors' Equity. I represented institutional theater. We all wore different hats supposedly representing various aspects of the American theater. I don't think there was any more specific agenda than for us simply to become acquainted with Russian theater, see some Russian productions and meet the Russian artists.

We all came from very different walks of life, and there were varied expectations about what traveling would be like on what was assumed to be a V.I.P. tour through Russia. Suffice it to say that accommodations were rough and travel difficult. In no time, Colleen assumed much of the responsibility of shepherding this group of reasonably spoiled Americans across the Russian steppes. Our trip from Moscow to Leningrad seemed like an endless journey. We had been promised first-class accommodations but when the train pulled in, we discovered that instead we were to be four to a compartment, during a nonstop seventeen-hour trip. Colleen, God bless her, tended to be very practical about these things and had a "let's get on with it" attitude. But there was practically a mutiny among a few of the others. They simply were not going to get on this train. I don't know what they thought our options were—call a limousine service? So there we were at midnight, in Moscow, standing on a deserted train platform, behaving as if stamping our feet would get us the first-class accommodations we expected. Our American tour guides fell apart and literally started to cry when they could not get everyone to board this sad-looking train. Finally, Colleen jumped in and basically shamed the rest to get on board, using a combination of rather choice rebukes wrapped in a good deal of laughter. But until she did, they were not going to budge. Now, don't get me wrong, Colleen liked her comforts as much as the next person, but she also had a great capacity to make do and just have a good time, no matter what. Colleen's ability to laugh gave her a great resilience. And it's a good thing, or a few of that crowd might still be waiting for a train in Moscow.

Ellen Stewart, who has been in every cranny of the world eighty-five times, was most often recognized as we traveled, but Colleen was sought out much more than anyone expected. It was not necessarily that people were always aware of her work on the stage or in film and television. But her position as Equity's president carried a great deal of weight. The actors and artists we met were deeply interested in the workings of the American theater unions. I remember on one of the first nights in Moscow we went to dinner at a restaurant that catered to actors. It turned out to be the most decent meal we had during the whole trip. You could feel the Russians observing us, although most were very respectful and careful not to intrude. As we were leaving, a couple of drunken Russian actors came up to Colleen. They told her in very stilted English what an honor it was for them to have the president of the American actors' union with them. Colleen engaged them in a sort of broken conversation about the union and asked questions about the conditions they worked under in Moscow. I doubt that they really understood much of anything that she said. I'm not so sure I did, but her warmth and smile dazzled them beyond any national boundaries or barriers of language.

In 1988, I worked with Colleen again, directing her in a production of Eugene O'Neill's *Ah, Wilderness!* that was presented with *Long Day's Journey into Night* at Yale Repertory Theatre, and then as part of the Second International Festival of the Arts in New York City. Initially, both productions were going to be directed by José Quintero. Then José's health became a bit fragile and it was thought best that he do only one. That's when I became involved. It was a delightful production and a wonderful cast. We were a huge hit at Yale. But it was a big disappointment to all of us when there wasn't enough money behind the production to give us the chance to run in New York long enough for the plays to find a major audience. With a little more time, I still believe, we would have.

Once again, I found myself working with Colleen on a comedy and a comedy by Eugene O'Neill, no less. As when we did *Artichoke,* we were able to work together on material that was very much the opposite of what she was most famous for doing. But even more than on *Artichoke*, I discovered that as Essie Miller, Colleen was capable of a giddiness, a girlishness almost, that she very seldom tapped into in performance terms. During the course of *Ah, Wilderness!*, since she was alternately playing Mary Tyrone in José's production of *Long Day's Journey into Night*, Colleen seemed to enjoy not having to be the sharpest woman, the shrewdest woman, the strongest or earthiest woman when playing Essie. She could really afford just to enjoy the wackiness of the life going on around her onstage.

It was wonderful to be a part of and observe Colleen and Campbell's working relationship as mother and son, playing mother and son. It had a kind of magic about it, even though I'm sure that, over the years, it wasn't always that easy. Working with members of the same family can be even more competitive than what often occurs between unrelated actors in a production. Colleen and Campbell worked together without a moment of competitiveness or conflicted feelings about it. There was a tremendous freedom between the two of them. They would kid each other openly. Keep in mind that in *Ah, Wilderness!* Campbell was playing a relatively small role, compared to the challenges he must have faced playing Edmund Tyrone opposite his mother, as the doomed Mary Tyrone, in *Long Day's Journey into Night*. It was a much more difficult production. There were some difficulties in the *Long Day's Journey's* rehearsals that I know Colleen found very upsetting. An actor had to be replaced. Colleen always comes across at those times as the rock. But I'm sure there was also a part of her that could strike out against always being the peacemaker, always being the one who has to hold it together. This was, in fact, the most interesting and touching side of Colleen. She was not just this pillar of stability, no matter how easily she seemed to get a bunch of whining artists onto a train in Moscow or helped steady a company reeling from the discomfort of someone being fired. She suffered and often felt much more vulnerable and fragile than she let on. She was afraid and not always so sure of her work. What I still wonder is whether all of us who so looked up to her and idolized her for her strengths also understood that it was these frailties of character just underneath her earth-mother persona that made her so appealing and so easy to love.

JAMEY SHERIDAN

I never expected to work with Colleen. I saw her do two things, *Moon for the Misbegotten*, when I was a student, and then *You Can't Take It with You*, when I was first starting out as an actor. I thought of her as sort of this grande dame. When I came into *Long Day's Journey into Night*, I was astounded by her power. Now, some people might think that that power is some external force because of her physical presence. It's not. She had literally a charged field of intention. It felt like she could burn you down. I can still get really heated up that we didn't get to see more of Colleen in the movies, where more of the American public could experience her as I did. I guess she did some, but it sure wasn't enough for my taste. The New York stage is relatively insular. The American public watches TV and goes to the movies. Colleen's was a rare gift that really only a relatively small audience got to appreciate fully. I'm so glad I had the chance to work with her onstage. I got the full force of what she had. Being onstage with Colleen Dewhurst in silence, as I was a number of times as Jamie Tyrone to her Mary Tyrone, has, to this day, been my greatest experience as an actor.

GEORGE HEARN

Colleen was just so fucking good! Zoe Caldwell once talked about working with an actor who was so powerful that "I know the whole male side of the stage is occupied and that frees me to do anything I want as a woman." Working with Colleen did the same thing for a man. *An Almost Perfect Person* went down in a hurry. It wasn't a great play. But I was honored to be onstage with her. *Ah, Wilderness!* was just great fun. We'd all get in our places for the beginning of the second act and one night Campbell [Scott] said, "Now, Ma, don't suck focus, OK? This is my scene." And as the curtain went up, Colleen just laughed. It was perfect.

MITCHELL ERICKSON

Colleen was very anxious about playing Mary Tyrone in O'Neill's *Long Day's Journey into Night.* We started rehearsals for it about two weeks before the rest of the company that would be doing *Ah, Wilderness!* were to arrive. Colleen knew that her "earth mother" persona went ahead of her before she could step out onstage, and I think she was concerned about playing this drugged-out woman who is ruled by the men in her life. Fortunately, she was working once again with José Quintero, whom she trusted implicitly, and he persuaded her that she would be wonderful in the role. But even with his support and encouragement, for quite a while into rehearsals she was very nervous. Playing Essie Miller in *Ah, Wilderness!* on the other hand was right up her alley. Here she was, mother to this large, eccentric family, with lots of people onstage. It wasn't near the memory job that *Long Day's Journey* was, although it was still a major role. At one point we were playing *Long Day's Journey* at night and rehearsing *Ah, Wilderness!* for a few hours each day. We were in previews, but still a lot of celebrities came up from New York to see us. There were no reviews yet, but the response was wonderfully enthusiastic. Nevertheless, Colleen was still fretful about her performance.

One night after a performance of *Long Day's Journey,* I came through the pass door from backstage and walked right into this weeping woman whom I did not recognize but who, with tears streaming down her face, asked, "May I see Miss Dewhurst?"

"Is she expecting you?" I asked.

"No, she doesn't know I'm here. Tell her it's Piper Laurie." Well, I ran backstage thinking, *Piper Laurie, an angel sent you! This is exactly what Colleen needs to see—that she just knocked somebody's socks off.* So I took her backstage, indicated that she should wait just a minute, and ran to Colleen's dressing room. I knocked at the door. "Colleen! It's Mitch."

"Come on in," she called. I opened the door and there she sat in her undies at her dressing table, getting her wig removed. "Colleen," I said. "Piper Laurie's here. She wants to see you."

"Oh, my God," Colleen said, jumping up and throwing on a robe. "Give me a minute." By the time I brought Piper back, Colleen was completely pulled together and as Piper entered, the wig girl stepped aside and Colleen got up from her dressing table to meet her at the door. Piper did not disappoint me. The tears squirted and she said how moved she was and how wonderful Colleen was. "I've seen you do all those mother-courage type of parts," Piper continued, "and this was just so fragile and delicate. I couldn't believe I was seeing this vulnerable woman. And when you played the piano, you were a child. You became that child in the convent. It was so overwhelming, you can see I haven't recovered."

Colleen stood, holding Piper's hand, speechless.

"How on earth do you do it, Colleen?" Piper asked. "I suppose you have an hour or so while the men have the stage," she continued, answering her own question, "to take yourself back to childhood."

"Yes, yes," Colleen replied rather vaguely, and they finished the conversation gracefully.

"Oh, my God, I've got to see Jason," Piper said, changing the subject. "Where is he?"

"Just down the hall," I replied. "A couple of doors. I'll take you." After dropping Piper off with Jason, I went back to Colleen's dressing room just as she was leaving. She grabbed my arm in this vise-like grip and as we walked out of the theater she said, "Oh, God, if she only knew how I regress. I get up here and while I'm trying to change into the nightgown and let these braids down I'm shouting to the dresser, 'Cue me! Cue me! I've got to be off book tomorrow for *Ah, Wilderness!* and I don't know my lines!' That's how I prepare! 'Childhood'! God, I scarcely have time even to think about my next entrance in this play. I don't know my fucking lines for tomorrow!"

So much for the Method.

29

"Colleen Dewhurst: Actress"

What is amazing to me is that you enter a certain profession known as acting, and you declare that this profession is yours. So you move to New York City with thousands of others who feel that they, too, will become rich and famous. If you are serious, you study, you go to classes, but ultimately, you must look for work. Then your life changes. It becomes about auditions, producers' offices, buying the trades and, of course, trying to find that agent. You are neither rich nor famous. And this can go on for years.

I was not an "overnight success." In order to survive, I did the usual things, all the things that young actors still do today: working as a receptionist, waiting tables, running an elevator, working for the phone company . . . for what, at that time, seemed like forever. There were so many jobs because when an acting job came up, even if it paid only ten dollars a week in some dingy loft downtown somewhere, I would quit whatever "civilian" job I had in order to work as an actress. Still, for me it was a very long time from my arrival on the scene until I found what would be steady work in my chosen field: acting.

After he was out of college and had hit the streets of New York himself looking for work as an actor, my son Campbell once said, "Mom, is it true that it took thirteen years before you could earn a living acting?" I replied, "Now you remember all your mother's old stories?"

But what he asked comes from a fear that must be faced by most young actors. How long? When is the struggle over? The fact is, no matter what degree of success you have, the struggle is never over; only the nature of it changes. What must be remembered, throughout a career, is that you are an actor and that you cannot limit or define yourself by your success or lack of it. I hear so many young people do just that. "I'll give this five years," they say, "and if I don't make it, I'll go to something else." With those limitations, most will do just that. Those who stay act simply because they have to. You do not act to become a star or to make a million dollars. God knows, you'll be grateful if that happens. But the bottom line is this: You act because it is the only thing that means life to you. For some, it is the only thing you *can* do. Good or bad, up or down, you are in a profession that is the roll of the dice. You throw the dice because you must. So when I began to work, I was not tabulating anything or keeping time. I made no deals with myself. I had no grand scheme or over-all plan. I did not think, for better or worse, where I was going or in what direction. As in my life up until that time, I just waited for each wave and rode it in whatever direction it seemed to take me.

Today, after what I see as forty-five, close to fifty, years of declaring that my profession is acting, I find that in *Who's Who of American Women* it says, "Colleen Dewhurst: Actress." So now, after all the reviews, good and bad, all the wonderful opening nights and tearful closings, my life has been defined in that one word: *Actress.* This is what I leave my children and my children's children.

I began to see, during the Broadway run of *A Moon for the Misbegotten*, that when I was written about, I was faced with statements such as, "O'Neill inter-preter" or "Dewhurst, who has made O'Neill a career." When interviewed, the reporter invariably would ask, "What do you feel about Eugene O'Neill, Ms. Dewhurst?" "Why do you think that you have a such an affinity for the O'Neill women, Ms. Dewhurst?"

After this happens to you five or six times, you begin to fight back. I've done *many* women in *many* plays. I have done films in which I played women who had nothing to do with O'Neill or the O'Neill-type character. Finally one day I said, "All right, this is it. I'm going to accept the fact that my obituary is going to read: O'NEILL ACTRESS DIES SOMEWHERE. I can only hope that it is either near the ocean or at the Farm, one of the two. And, as Ken says, if the tide is in, it could be both."

WILLIAM H. LANG

I worked with Colleen as a stage manager periodically during the last three years of her life. She would join the national tour of A.R. Gurney's two-character play *Love Letters,* play a few cities, then take some time off. Each time we worked together, she seemed a bit thinner. But it wasn't until we were playing the Morris Mechanic Theatre in Baltimore that I realized she was sick.

Colleen arrived, looking terribly thin and weak, for what was to have been a four-week engagement, playing opposite her old pal George Hearn. She said, to those of us who inquired about how she felt, that she was suffering from chronic back trouble, then stomach trouble. During the first three weeks of the run, her condition continued to deteriorate. Her fight and fire were missing. But though she seemed tired, her sense of humor and sparkling eyes were not diminished. She performed with brilliance, but it was obvious to those around her that she was suffering. When I suggested that she see a doctor at Johns Hopkins Hospital, she declined.

On Tuesday of what was to have been her final week of performance,

Colleen wore a deep grimace as she arrived to the theater at half-hour. I had never seen her that way before. It was the first show of the week and she was already exhausted. Sensing trouble, I quietly approached Ken Marsolais, who had recently joined Colleen on the tour, to see if he might be able to persuade her to see a physician. Ken told me very frankly of her dislike of doctors due to her Christian Science upbringing. Enough said. She and Ken kept the dressing room door shut. At showtime, I tapped lightly and she emerged smiling. The performance was fine but it seemed, probably only to me, that she was rushing to get through it. Our company manager, Alan Martinson, and I made plans for a company dinner the following evening. Colleen declined to attend.

I had taken to meeting Colleen's car each evening to assist her and to politely discourage autograph seekers from detaining her as she slipped through the stage door. The dressing rooms at the Mechanic are two flights up from street level. She took my arm as we ascended, pausing at each landing. I escorted her to her dressing room and, upon seeing her in such pain, once more encouraged her to see a doctor. She buried her face in her hands and cried, "I can't believe there's something wrong with me!" But she again refused to see a doctor, and I never brought it up again. The play was quite good that night and she received a standing ovation, after which she returned directly to her hotel.

Our small company, minus Colleen, reassembled at the Polo Grill after the show. Ken had escorted Colleen back to the hotel but later appeared at the restaurant and seemed anxious to talk privately. Over a drink, I cautiously broached the subject of Colleen's health. Ken's reply was simple. "There's nothing we can do," he said. "But we have to get her out of here." He told me that she was in great pain. "Tell only those you need to tell," Ken concluded, "but we must leave." I excused myself from the table. Alan followed me into the lobby, where I related Ken's disclosure. I immediately called our producer, Richard Frankel, in order that immediate plans could be made to replace her.

The following morning Ken called. "Colleen wants to finish the weekend," he said. "It's very important for her to do this." I readily agreed and decided that we would cancel performances if necessary in order to allow Colleen to continue through Sunday. In the meantime, Elaine Stritch, another *Love Letters* veteran, was prepared to step into the role beginning the following week. Colleen seemed better for the Thursday-evening performance. At half-hour she called me into her dressing room and asked if I had any "ciggies." Whenever I worked with Colleen I always kept a few packs of Carlton 100's in my office. I retrieved a pack for her now, and was oddly relieved that she felt well enough to light up. She and George Hearn gave another terrific performance.

Ken had to be back in New York on Friday and Colleen was in bad shape when she arrived at the theater. Once again, she clutched my arm as I helped her up the two flights to her dressing room, where she fell on the sofa, exhausted. She was obviously too weak to perform. Again I echoed our willingness to cancel the performance. I could see that Colleen was contemplating what to do.

"This has never happened to me before," she said, her voice muffled with fear. It was about a quarter to eight. George waited patiently in his dressing room. We could hear the sound of the audience filling the theater. Suddenly, without a word, Colleen pulled herself off the couch and sat down at her dressing table. "Now it's time to get ready," she said in a way that suggested we should leave her. I closed the dressing room door and waited in the hallway to see if she would emerge and alerted the crew to stand by in case we needed to stop the show. I called, "Places." There was a long delay. Still no Colleen. At last she opened the door in her simple costume and chuckled, saying, "Mommy forgot her rouge, and without that, she looks like the ghost of Christmas past." We walked arm in arm to the wings. She seemed so weak that she could barely say hello to the crew, which she always did. She took her place with George onstage. None of us knew what to expect, but as the lights rose, Colleen found her strength and sparkled to life. Ken arrived midway through the show and watched with Alan and me from the wings. It was a good performance, but it seemed to all of us that Colleen was pushing herself now beyond all endurance. As Ken and Colleen departed after the performance, Ken whispered, "Get a replacement as soon as possible."

It turned out not to be necessary. Once again, Colleen somehow found the strength to play both the Saturday matinee and evening performances to wonderful audiences without incident. Sadly, I notified the crew that there was to be a cast change for the following week and scheduled a Tuesday rehearsal. Nothing else was said.

Sunday afternoon arrived. Colleen was in good spirits when she came to the theater and, wanting to know the latest gossip, seemed almost like her old self as we chatted at half-hour. She was relaxed and did not seem to be in any pain. As she made her way to the stage for the last time, she and George paused briefly for Alan to take a few snapshots. During the performance, Ken packed her dressing room before joining me offstage. As the play progressed, the wings of the stage began to fill with people, many of whom I did not recognize. All were very still. Each was there to wish Colleen well. She was quite strident in this last performance and the audience loved her. The play concluded. She and George took their curtain calls. There was not a dry eye backstage, yet no public announcement about the cast change had yet been made.

Alan had arranged for a car to drive Ken and Colleen from Baltimore to the Farm back in South Salem. Ken had packed the car during the second act. Colleen walked directly from the stage to the waiting car on Ken's arm. We followed her downstairs and waved as the car quickly disappeared. There were no long hugs or good-byes. They had already been said onstage.

HELEN GORDON

Colleen and I met in the late 1940s when we were students; Colleen was at the American Academy and I was studying at the Art Students League. At the time, we also were both ushers at Carnegie Hall, where we often worked the same shift and spent time together at the top of the aisle. As we got to know each other, I began to think, from some of what Colleen said about herself, that she was a Christian Scientist.

Like Colleen, I had also been very ill as a child. Because of my ill health, my grandmother suggested that my parents send me to the Christian Science Sunday School. I loved it, and my mother took me there for years because she saw that it helped me, although she never did understand or follow its teachings. I had always liked what Science taught about God and man's relationship to him. So, years later at Carnegie Hall, I was intrigued when Colleen told me that she had been brought up in Christian Science. I was especially interested when she revealed that her mother, Frances Dewhurst, had been what is in Christian Science called a "practitioner."

A practitioner is someone who devotes his or her full time to the practices of Christian Science. A practitioner is not a minister in the sense of giving sermons in a church, but he—or she—makes him- or herself available to take calls, praying for people who are having problems—health problems, spiritual or emotional problems, whatever. The Christian Science Church does not elect practitioners. Someone chooses to become a practitioner through the study of our textbooks and the Bible. Then a love of Science and a desire to help others might move someone to become a practitioner, as another might choose to become a doctor or a minister. As time goes on, if you decide you want to do this professionally and be listed as a Christian Science practitioner in the *Journal of Christian Science*, there is formal period of study and class instruction. Gradually, as healings are documented, your prayerful work becomes more widely known. Once you are listed in the *Journal*, you are not allowed to have any other occupation, in order to be available to people twenty-four hours a day. Colleen's mother was a listed practitioner, and over the years Frances Dewhurst became quite well known for her extraordinary work.

After we first met, Colleen and her husband at the time, Jim Vickery, and I and my first husband, Neale, shared an apartment. I first spoke to her mother during that time over the phone. Colleen had twisted her ankle pretty badly and had called her mother about it. I could hear her answering what seemed like casual questions from her mother at the other end of the phone. The next day, Colleen was walking on her ankle as if nothing had happened. I didn't get a full understanding of what an important role her mother played in Colleen's life until the first time she came to New York City from Milwaukee to visit. Frances Dewhurst was a very attractive woman, neat and well dressed. And although she wasn't tall like Colleen, she had the same powerfully strong presence. What was most striking about her, however, was not her appearance but her intelligence. She was gracious, but also very discerning. This was not a women who suffered fools gladly. Colleen loved her mother very much. To see them together was quite a study in contrasts. Mrs. Dewhurst was so very pulled-together and neat. Colleen, then and throughout her life, was comfortable just slopping around in whatever she could throw together.

Mrs. Dewhurst clearly was concerned with the kind of life she imagined Colleen to be leading away from home as an actress. I don't recall her mother ever telling her what to do, but I recall her saying again and again, "Think about what you're doing, Colleen. Think about what you're doing." Like so many parents of children who go into the arts, Mrs. Dewhurst felt that life as an actress would take Colleen completely off track. It's interesting because although they did not get along in this area, Colleen's devotion to her work as an actress very much mirrored her mother's commitment to Science. But although Colleen was in awe of everything her mother did, she also felt, like most children, that her mother's viewpoint was limited. It troubled her that her mother objected to some of the roles she was studying and the life she saw her becoming involved in. Colleen was enthralled by it all. Nevertheless, her mother influenced her tremendously.

After about a year, Neale and I left New York to move to Independence, Kansas. We all stayed in touch periodically. I was aware that she had divorced Jim and married George [C. Scott]. We both had children. I would occasionally read in the paper about something or other that she was doing. But it was not unusual for two or three years to go by between phone conversations. When Neale passed away, Colleen called me and insisted that the kids and I come out to the Farm. We went. When Colleen made up your mind for you, it was very hard to say no, and what was to have been a five-day stay stretched into three weeks. While we were there, George was doing *Plaza Suite* on Broadway. During the day, he spent hours watching old newsreels of General George Patton in preparation for going to Europe to shoot the film. It was a wonderful visit. Colleen kept insisting we stay longer and couldn't have been nicer. This was the first time I had seen Colleen since she left Jim Vickery. It was startling to see the change in her that came from being with George. Jim was not a very happy man. He was very much a loner. There never seemed to be much of a relationship between him and Colleen, especially as her career began to take off. It was immediately obvious, upon arriving at the Farm, that there was great passion between Colleen and George. They were very well matched mentally and had great intelligence. They were both very well thought of in the theatrical community, which I know was not the case and had been very troublesome to Colleen when she was with Jim. There is no doubt that Colleen had a very strong connection to George all her life in spite of what became intense disagreements, particularly around the issue of George's drinking. But when he was sober, they were an extraordinary couple. George was not drinking during our three-week stay. Consequently, I think it was a very good time for them both.

After leaving New York, we had our first child. I also lost touch with Mrs. Dewhurst. Then my daughter was born with a herniated navel. When the initial treatments brought no results, the doctors said that she should be operated on immediately. I really didn't want the baby to begin life with the trauma of surgery, so I called Mrs. Dewhurst, quite out of the blue, and told her what was wrong. She said she'd take the case. Mrs. Dewhurst prayed for our spiritual understanding to reveal my daughter's perfection and wholeness as God's clear idea. The next day, when I was bathing her, the bandages came off in the water. Her navel had returned to normal and stayed that way. Children and babies are often healed right away because they have absolutely no fear in their thinking. I had other experiences with Mrs. Dewhurst over the years, some of them quite extraordinary. These reawakened my own interest in the study of Christian Science, and I eventually became a practitioner myself.

Frances Dewhurst passed on in 1956. The medical explanation was that she had a heart condition, but Colleen felt that her mother's death was the result of much unresolved anger. This had a huge effect on Colleen. She so wanted her mother to understand her. After her mother's death, Colleen would occasionally call me. She thought my becoming a practitioner was great. She told me that she sometimes went to practitioners, but she also went to doctors.

Years later, in 1989, when Colleen was diagnosed with cervical cancer, she called. The doctors, she said, had suggested a surgical procedure, but she wanted nothing to do with it. She felt very strongly that it would be invasive. So, at her request, we began to work together over the phone through prayer, studying the Bible and other Science-related literature each day. The study of Christian Science is all basically a process of learning about God and man's relationship to him.

At the same time, Colleen and I had long conversations about what else she could do for herself. Colleen was not a member of the church, and I asked her if she didn't want to go to a doctor. But she was always emphatic about staying with Science. There is nothing in our religion that prevents a person from going to the doctor. But if you go, you should not mix medical treatment with Christian Science treatment, which is treatment by spiritual means alone. As Christian Scientists we believe that if you do not address the root of a problem through prayer, even if you are healed medically, the body will simply produce ailment in some other form. Physical healings through Science come about by correcting our thinking, such as releasing a bitter grudge or long-held hatred or misunderstanding. Any long-held negative thought will eventually affect your health. You can get help from a doctor, but without the healing spiritual insight, you are open to manifesting disease again. Even doctors are looking more and more into this phenomenon themselves.

Such study is not easy work. It is very hard, particularly for an adult, to address and change years of critical thinking and socialization. But it can be done, and the practitioner is engaged to help. Colleen's struggle was that she kept herself on the fence. For the study of Christian Science to be effective, it is essential to quiet the mind. It was nearly impossible for Colleen to become still. She was very strong, but her strength came with a price. Colleen had never before had to do her own work metaphysically. Her mother's ability had been so thorough that she never had to learn to understand how to do the work herself. She went to her mother for help when she needed it, and received it. As a young woman she became accustomed to her mother's being able to fix anything, like the time with the severely twisted ankle. The ankle was better, so Colleen didn't continue to learn what she needed to do in order to understand how the healing took place. Ultimately, Colleen's decision to work in Science was, I think, made less in response to a negative feeling about standard medical practice and more from a very old desire to measure up to her mother's understanding.

However, the fact that she wasn't healed does not in any way mean that she somehow failed in her *own* understanding. As difficult and painful as this process was for her, I know that she found a great deal of peace. I think those closest to her came to understand that as well. Like we all do, Colleen put herself into the situation she wanted to be in. She knew the doctor was not the answer to her spiritual needs.

This was not a stupid or naive decision on Colleen's part. Colleen spoke of having done so much in her life that she felt it was now time for her to do some soul searching. She wanted to learn more about and clarify her relationship with God. She wanted to reexperience what she had long felt was the truth. Colleen had witnessed many healings as a young girl. Sadly, it was very entangled in her complicated relationship with her mother. These were two very strong women who loved each other deeply and, as adults, also held each other to intense critical standards, standards that Colleen felt she could never meet. I believe that Colleen would have wanted her mother to know that she had made the decision at this point in her life to do what she did. She may have even been motivated by a great longing for her mother. As we studied, she would often wonder about how her mother would react or ask if I knew what her mother might say about a particular situation. I'm certain that Colleen very much wanted a healing for her family's sake. I know that she was very concerned with how her dearest friends were experiencing her actions. She also hoped that those who loved her most would understand her decision to attend to her own spiritual, as well as physical, needs. This work is done by us all, sooner or later. Colleen had spent so much of her life taking care of everyone but herself, that it was very hard for her to become quiet enough to experience herself. Finally, to do this work, she had to shut down and remove much of everything else that had filled her life for so long. Colleen's life was such an awesome combination of being highly disciplined and totally scattered, of great love for others coupled with feelings of loss and disappointment.

I think of Colleen nearly every day. I loved her dearly. I remember saying to her, "You don't have to do this, you know."

"I choose this," she said.

ROBERT WHITEHEAD

I loved Colleen and find it hard to talk about how she died because it infuriated me so. I was devastated by what she allowed to happen to her. That last summer, she was not seeing anybody. Finally, she agreed to see Zoe [Caldwell] and me. *Jesus Christ*, I thought. *Here she is, dying five miles away and there is absolutely nothing I can do about it except let it happen.* Which, of course, it did. I was so angry. It was too painful. So I'd go over with Zoe and then we couldn't bring up what was clearly foremost on our minds. I still never think of her today without some of the anger coming up. Why wouldn't she take care of herself? It's selfish almost, how much I miss her. Ken [Marsolais] was marvelous about it all and took quite wonderful care of her, understanding that all this was a choice of hers that he should not interfere with. I still don't understand it and don't expect I ever will.

ZOE CALDWELL

I saw her with Robert and we all pretended that everything was fine because that's clearly what she wanted. But this was all about her mother, much more than just Christian Science. You know, in spite of Colleen's very earthy image, she never wanted to talk about women's gynecological problems. She was immensely modest about anything below the waist. Intensely shy. And that came from her mother. I've always felt it was so ironic then that the very thing about Colleen that her mother never really wanted to acknowledge—sex, her sexuality—that's where the cancer attacked her. I think that if the cancer had been in her throat, she would have dealt with it. There was an underlying sadness to Colleen, in spite of that incredible smile and quickness to laugh, that I think she chose to work out privately in the last months of her life. How can any of us know why others choose to do what they do? So you just love them. Ultimately, that's all there is to do.

ELIZABETH WILSON

The last time I saw Colleen in public was at the benefit for the New York Shakespeare Festival, where they honored Colleen. It was a very strange evening. Joe [Papp] wasn't there. He was so sick himself by then, and now to think that Colleen must have known she was dying as well. I was sitting quite far back in the room and I remember hearing Colleen speak and thinking that she didn't quite sound like herself. The substance was missing. I don't know, it wasn't what she said but what she didn't say. Later, I would hear things about her—that she wasn't well—but I didn't believe them. Then, when I was invited to Campbell's wedding in July and she wasn't there, I began to get really worried. I remember seeing Maureen Anderman in tears, and Kenneth coming over and whispering something to Clifford and then seeing them both disappear from the reception for a while. From that point, I knew something was really, really wrong.

I would call Ken. Our conversations were very brief, but Colleen wouldn't come to the phone. "I'll give her your love," Ken would say. He said it once and I started to cry. Two days later he called back. "Colleen is very worried about you," he said. "She really wants to see you." So arrangements were made for me to drive in. Colleen was standing in the kitchen when I arrived. Ken left us alone in the living room but had warned me over the phone that I mustn't talk about her appearance or the circumstances. You had to be a crazy person to be able to handle this. It was so unreal. There we both were, two actresses doing this funny dance around what is and what isn't happening right in front of us. So we talked about everything and anything and nothing. People we liked. People we hated. "Remember the time you liked him and I hated him? Now, why was that?" Finally, Ken came back into the room. It was time to go. I had just filmed *The Addams Family* and had been telling Colleen about it. I had to go back out to Los Angeles for a retake. "Call me when you get back," Colleen said. It was so strange, both very unsatisfying and absolutely right. We talked for two hours and everything that was most important went unspoken and was somehow understood. What a sad, sad time, but there we sat laughing. I was gone about a week, and a few days after I returned, Alex called to say that she had died.

JASON ROBARDS

I knew that something was wrong with Colleen but no one wanted to talk about it. We did *Love Letters* together for a week to open the Edison Theatre after they threw that nudie show out of there [*Oh, Calcutta!*]. It took more time to wash the shit off the walls than it did to put up the set. We laughed a lot about that. "Don't touch the floor!" she'd say. But she was tired and seemed run-down. She said it was her back. Who knew? So you forget about it. Then I did hear that something was going on with Science. I grew up with it, too, just as Colleen had. My grandmother and father were Christian Scientists. I still say prayers I learned then, and before I go onstage every night, I bless the stage. That's a good thing. But it's nothing I'm not going to have an operation over. I've been through a lot of them, put back together many times. But once Colleen made up her mind, no one was going to get her to change it. So you didn't try. I think that's why she didn't want to see people. She didn't want her energy wasted with people trying to convince her to do something she didn't want to do.

To this day, I still don't feel that she's gone. She has a real sticking power with me. Shit, we're all gonna have to go down to the lobby and check out eventually. But there's something about Colleen's presence that always makes me feel like I just saw her not too long ago. Colleen's still very much a part of me. There is a way you love some people that is much stronger than having to have them present. They become part of your family, family in the largest, yet most intimate, sense.

30

An Irish Wake

Colleen Dewhurst died on August 22, 1991, of cancer of the cervix at the age of sixty-seven. Her obituary, which appeared in the August 24 edition of the *New York Times*, opened almost as Colleen had predicted: "Ms. Dewhurst was closely identified with the works of Eugene O'Neill," and continued for two paragraphs about her roles in and awards for *Mourning Becomes Electra, Moon for the Misbegotten, My Gene, Long Day's Journey into Night* and *Ah, Wilderness!* It closed five columns later with: "Ms. Dewhurst lived on a farm in South Salem in upstate New York, with her companion of 16 years, the Broadway producer Ken Marsolais. The farm's population also includes eight cats, two dogs, one goat and a parrot," marking perhaps the first time that pets had been included in the *New York Times* as next of kin.

ALEX SCOTT and his wife, Irene, Campbell Scott and his wife, Annie, joined Ken Marsolais in opening the Farm to Colleen's friends, neighbors, and colleagues for one last party the first weekend of September 1991. It was a beautiful autumn day. Guests filled the house and yard, eating, drinking, and talking in much the same way they had when Colleen had been there herself as hostess. While it was a terribly sad occasion that brought everyone together, any quiet tears and private thoughts of regret were punctuated with eruptions of laughter, as memories were shared, one with the other.

ELSA RAVEN

Years ago, I think before Colleen and George were even married, Colleen had done a small part in a movie with Ernest Borgnine that, I promise, no one will remember the name of. Colleen was invited to a screening of it. She couldn't go, so she asked George if he would attend and watch for her. When he came back later that evening, Colleen asked, "Did you go?"

"Yeah," George replied.

"How was I?" she asked.

"Tall," he said.

JANE NEUFELD

I was the production stage manager on *A Moon for the Misbegotten* at Lake Forest, Illinois, before moving with the show to Washington and New York. It was amazing to watch Colleen and José [Quintero] work. Colleen would be moving about the stage and José would get her attention and just say, "Colleen . . . you know . . . there." Colleen would listen and reply, "Yeah, right—absolutely," and in the next few minutes you could see something about her performance change. All I can remember thinking is, *What did they just talk about?*

After one of the first performances in Lake Forest, José came backstage. "Colleen, I was just listening to two ladies in the last row of the audience," he said, "and they don't believe that you're a virgin." Colleen looked a bit perplexed. Was this something they were reading into her performance of Josie, whom O'Neill identifies as a virgin? "They debated the issue quite a while, Colleen," José continued, "until one looked to the other and said, 'How can she be? She's married to George C. Scott!'"

"At which point, Colleen," José said, "I tapped one on the shoulder and added, 'Twice!'"

BETTY MILLER

I first worked with Colleen in the television play of *Medea*. With Jackie Brooks, we were the "Greek Chorus" behind Judith Anderson. I went on to understudy Colleen in *A Moon for the Misbegotten*. I remember she said to me very early on, "You're never going to play this, you know." All I could think to say was, "I certainly hope that's true!" And it was. I understudied her again in *Virginia Woolf* and then did *You Can't Take It with You* and *Queen and the Rebels* with her. I came into *You Can't Take It with You* after it opened in New York. When I arrived at the theater for the first time to rehearse, Colleen was there. She gave me this keen look and said, "You're going to share a dressing room with me, aren't you?" It's always difficult coming into a company that's been together for a while and, with this statement, Colleen made me feel at home and let the rest of the company know that I was all right. It was a great compliment. Colleen kept the dressing room door open and people were always in and out. We never talked business but we played a lot of charades, mostly in an effort to help Colleen remember the names of the people who visited her after the show backstage, or she'd do the *Times* crossword puzzle, shouting for help to Alice Drummond—"What's ten down, four across?"—who had the dressing room next door and knew everything. Our stage managers, Mitch Erickson and John Handy, filled the dressing room with balloons for her birthday that year. She just sat right down into the middle of those balloons, she loved it so.

BARBARA MAE PHILLIPS

I met Colleen in the summer of 1971 when she was about to do *The Good Woman of Setzuan* at Lincoln Center. I was one of three assistant stage managers. We hadn't met before but I knew who she was by reputation as an actress. I also had seen her at the opening-night party of Mike Nichols' production of *The Little Foxes* at Lincoln Center that starred George [C. Scott]. That was my first show as an assistant stage manager. It was quite a production and a very heady experience to go to such a star-studded opening-night party. I remember being fascinated by this woman who didn't stop talking, laughing, drinking or smoking the entire evening. I remember thinking, "Whoever this is, she's amazing." Later, someone told me it was George's wife, Colleen Dewhurst.

Colleen hated doing *The Good Woman of Setzuan* from the start. She loathed the director, loathed her male costars, particularly David Birney, who played her love interest. I have no idea why she agreed to do it in the first place and probably neither did she. But there she was in the middle of what was truly a disaster, culminating in what turned out to be a classic disaster of a dress rehearsal. By this time, Colleen was furious at everyone. When we broke for dinner, she asked that a bottle of Chianti be delivered to her dressing room. By the time we started again, she was not about to listen to anybody. Soon she's ranting and raving about this one she hates who can't direct and that one she hates who can't act and this one she just hates and she doesn't know why before storming off to her dressing room, where she continued to scream at the top of her lungs. The director, the production stage manager and various others, including myself, tried to get in there to calm her down, but she was having none of it. Her good friend, the actress Elizabeth Wilson, was also in the cast and I can still see her standing calmly backstage repeating to no one in particular, "Oh, Colleen. Oh, Colleen," as this mayhem broke all around us.

The next day, Colleen had no memory of the afternoon and none of us felt it necessary to fill her in. "Bad, huh?" We never saw her that angry again and somehow we got through the next few rehearsals and opened the show. It was as if she determined for herself from that day on that everything that had so enraged her was now funny. It was a bad production but it was so bad, it was fun. The set fell down around her one evening and from the deck backstage I could hear Elizabeth Wilson hissing to Colleen onstage under her breath between clenched teeth, "Don't you dare laugh!" And no one did, until Colleen said her next line which unfortunately was "the store is gone." No, the store had *fallen over*, and Colleen's composure was *gone*. In some archive at Lincoln Center is a tape of that show, and if Colleen didn't manage to see that it was burned, somebody should. Or present it as a one-night-only benefit screening for the seriously deranged. You'd sell out.

I turned out to be one of the people whom Colleen seemed to adopt and bring home to the Farm. I don't know why. But over the years, there were a number of us, often a stage manager or production assistant type, who would be swept up into her life for a while like this, almost as if she were looking for a daughter to re-create some aspect of the relationship she had with her mother. It didn't matter to me. I couldn't believe that this woman even had the time of day for me. And within weeks, I was introduced to this amazing group of people in residence up there: Stuart and Tony; the boys, of course, who were about nine or ten then; Nana and her son Bobby; and George, who was still living there at the time, not to mention the parade of visitors and horde of animals that made up the household. It was the fall of 1971 and I spent the first Thanksgiving of what would become many holidays there. It was the beginning of an incredible period of my life during which I essentially grew up and gradually, like an adult child, began to pull away. But for those few years, it was an amazing friendship, one that took a lot of work but one that never left any doubt when you were with her and that extended family and crazed cast of characters that you were in the middle of something sort of marvelous.

JILL SAWYER

Colleen and I coached the girls' softball teams together. She had the Fireflies and I had the Bobcats. It was quite a rivalry. Colleen was a wonderful coach. She practically directed the girls, making them feel good about themselves and not caring at all about stupid mistakes. I can still hear her shouting to the outfield, "No handstands, girls! No handstands! Keep your eye on the batter!" We played each other in the play-offs once. It was a very close game, but the Bobcats won. I never had to face victory over Colleen before, and to tell you the truth, I was a little nervous as we looked across the field toward each other, particularly as you spend so much time trying to teach these little girls all that crap about it not being "if you win or lose." *Sure.* Not with Colleen. Next thing I know, she's coming straight across the field at me, swinging her fist in this big roundhouse, and fakes connecting to my jaw in front of everyone. It was great, better than a handshake. Everyone burst out laughing, and those girls probably learned more about what life's really like that day than any other.

I went over there for a lot of barbecues, especially once our sons became friends. Some of the people in town didn't know what to make of that whole scene. On one hand they were very pleased that Colleen took such an interest in the community and then on the other hand they'd say, "You let your kids go over there? And stay overnight!?" The neighborhood boys especially adored Colleen. How could they not? A lot of love, not a helluva lot of supervision. It was a kid's adolescent dream!

JILL SAWYER, HENRY GRIFFIN, CLARE GRUNDMAN AND PEGGY JETT (NEIGHBORS)

No one in the neighborhood will ever forget the day Colleen and George remarried. It was quite the party. George woke up a few of us in the neighborhood at six-thirty in the morning the day before, shouting into the phone, "We're getting married again. I don't care what time it is! Just get your asses over here." So, like lemmings, we threw on T-shirts and sneakers and went over to have a drink with the groom-again-to-be. "Wahoo! You're getting married again!" All of that sort of thing. Colleen was still upstairs. She didn't join us. It was very early. After a round or two, we all left, figuring we'd see her later in the afternoon as preparations were being made for the ceremony and party the next day. But before we could get back, Colleen called. "Do you think I can send José and a few others down to your place for a little while?" It seems that once they had put up a party tent in the yard, George decided the place "looks like a fucking circus!" and "I'm not having anything to do with this bullshit!" Colleen thought she could calm him down if the house cleared out a bit. Soon about a dozen houseguests arrive from Colleen's, carrying all the food, turkeys and hams, vegetables, breads, none of which had yet been prepared. Colleen called again. "Don't start the food. I don't know what's going to happen up here. George is stalking around the place. He just threw part of the front fence in the pool." More time goes by. Is there or is there not a wedding? Has George thrown Colleen in the pool? Finally, the phone rings. It's Colleen. "Start cooking! Everything's all right. We're doing this! As planned. Tomorrow afternoon!"

The next day, everyone arrives and the place is just beautiful. George is dressed in a white suit. Colleen is radiant. The boys were adorable. The fence has been fished out of the pool and everyone's kissing and hugging. The party went on for hours before George and Colleen drove off in the convertible with Nana in the backseat. As the dust cleared, we all settled down to finish off the food and the booze. Fifteen minutes later, they're back. They didn't have any cash. So we all threw whatever we had together and they took off again—who knows where. I can tell you, however, that the party they left behind went on probably as long as the honeymoon and with more than just the fence ending up in the pool.

JOHN O'LEARY

I knew Colleen for a while before we did *A Moon for the Misbegotten* together. I remember coming up to the Farm once during that time and as we sat around, she would ask me questions about people we knew in common or just people she knew I knew. Now, I'm not much of a gossip, but Colleen could sit and dish with friends for hours. I could never think of much to say. "Oh, Christ, John," she finally said in frustration, "you're no good to me!"

But what I'll always remember was the final bow for *Moon*'s opening night. There was no curtain. The lights went out and then came up on us all standing together for a company bow. The force of the applause came up with the lights and was so strong, we all automatically took a step back. It was like being hit by the wind. I've never experienced anything quite like that since.

JILL SAWYER

I sure spent a lot of time over there for barbecues. I remember Colleen, Maureen Stapleton and me sitting around the pool. Maureen had one of those rubber bathing caps on her head, a bottle of wine in her hands and her feet in the pool. Colleen had been chattering away. "Jesus Christ, Colleen," Maureen interrupted, "if you could ever complete a goddamn sentence, someday we might all know what you're talking about." When Colleen started to laugh, Maureen threw herself into the pool.

MAUREEN STAPLETON

Colleen looked like a warrior, so people assumed she was the earth mother. But in real life Colleen was not to be let out without a keeper. She was a marshmallow. A pussycat, a goddamn pushover. Half the time I felt like I had to watch her like a hawk or she'd give someone she'd just met the shirt off her back. She was the madonna of the birds with broken wings, the softest touch in show business. She couldn't stop herself from taking care of people, which she then did with more care than she took care of herself. Her generosity of spirit was overwhelming and her smile so dazzling that you couldn't pull the fucking reins in on her even if you desperately wanted to and knew damn well that somebody should. I asked her once, and still wonder, what the hell would she have done if she hadn't found acting? She had no fucking idea, just as I can't imagine what we would have done if she hadn't found us. Oh, God, how I loved Colleen Dewhurst and miss her this very minute.

ZOE CALDWELL

I met Colleen a long time ago through Maureen [Stapleton]. She used to go over up there and clean Colleen's house. She couldn't help herself. Maureen is a closet cleaner. Maureen looks like someone who would never clean anything, but she's actually incredibly neat. Maureen likes pretty. Colleen couldn't have cared less. On the other hand, Colleen would go to bat for a mouse if it had one leg shorter than the other. It used to drive Maureen crazy. She'd say, "For Christ's sake, Colleen, just because someone tells you a sad story doesn't mean you owe them the best bedroom!"

ROSCOE LEE BROWNE

Like so many others, the thing I remember most fondly about Colleen is the sound of her laughter. She and I were guests, quite a long time ago, at a dinner honoring Eleanor Roosevelt. While most of the dinner guests were moving into the dining room, Colleen and I remained on the veranda with someone who was telling us a particularly funny story. Of course, Colleen laughed. Now I know most of us are city-bound, but have you ever been in the country after a fresh spring rain? Suddenly, when the rain stops, there is a lovely, pervasive silence. That evening, there was a similar moment after Colleen's laugh.

Mrs. Roosevelt, who was walking into the dining room ahead of us, turned and said, "That is laughter from heaven." We were slightly taken aback. Mrs. Roosevelt noticed this and walked back to us, still on the veranda. "My dear," she said to Colleen, "when I said that yours was laughter from heaven, I didn't mean anything ecumenical and I certainly did not mean anything parochial. Your laughter is from a higher region. It's Olympian!"

None of us spoke. Colleen simply looked back into this extraordinary woman's eyes. "I haven't been feeling very well today," Mrs. Roosevelt continued. "But I think that laughter was also therapeutic because it has cleared my head completely." Colleen then did in a most marvelous way what only she could do. Extending her hand to Mrs. Roosevelt, she said, "I thank you for your life." Mrs. Roosevelt smiled her own equally brilliant smile and, tucking Colleen's hand over her arm, walked us all into the dining room.

There was a memorial service for Colleen Dewhurst in late September at the Martin Beck Theatre, a twelve-hundred-seat theater that overflowed with friends, fans, colleagues and admirers.

"It's a sorrowful task to bid farewell to Colleen Dewhurst," New York City Mayor David N. Dinkins read from his prepared text as Edward Albee, Arvin Brown, Zoe Caldwell, Ted Mann, Jason Robards, Maureen Stapleton, Roscoe Lee Browne, José Quintero and executives representing The Actors' Fund, Actors' Equity, The League of American Theatres, and Broadway Cares/Equity Fights AIDS and others settled in chairs that had been set on either side of a spray of five-dozen red roses the size of a small tree. For the next hour, their words about Colleen—prepared, ad-libbed, solemn and outrageous—filled the theater, where nearly thirty years before in The Ballad of the Sad Café *Colleen had made her first entrance laughing.*

"We feel her absence as a truly awesome silence."

"I'm sorry to those that I have my back to. We learn very quickly in the theater never to turn your back on anybody. Edward! It's all right to be in the theater. It's all right . . . it is all right, isn't it?"

"We are all going to have to listen everywhere and for a long time, before we hear the sound of that laugh again."

"Colleen's approach to acting was the same as her approach to life: Look the other person in the eye and tell them the truth."

"Colleen was a lovely daughter. She made that journey from baby girl to sixty-seven-year-old woman with a blaze of light that enabled us all to see a little clearer. Mrs. Dewhurst, wherever you are, you must be proud!"

"We had a lasting friendship that served through triumphs and many, many hard times. She supplied the good humor that led us through dark times. Our families grew up together and she shared the secrets parents need to know to raise young men."

"Miss Dewhurst, did you realize that you have left a hot roller in your hair?"

"What we tried to do under her leadership, we will continue to do in her memory."

"Other actors love the theater, but few loved it as Colleen did. Colleen felt that actors served civilization and that they should be encouraged and protected. She believed that actors were gallant. She was a lovely woman and not a bad actor herself. You can't say that about too many."

"Colleen brought us to the edge of whatever she did."

"This is a letter from . . . oh, shut up. I can't read this fucking thing. We're all here because we love and worship Colleen. But I'll tell you right now, goddamnit, I'm never going to another funeral. Except my own. No more, it's over. I have a million Colleen stories. It took me twenty years, but the thrill was that I finally found somebody dumber than I was! I'll make this as brief as I can. . . ."

Alex Scott spoke last.

My mother loved the country of her birth, Canada, and the one she adopted, the United States. She loved her state and her town. My mother was an actress. My father is an actor. My brother is an actor. As a child, I had great difficulties with the fact that I was a child of this profession. But as I stand here today—a young man—I want you to know that I am honored, and I thank God that I am from, and of, a family of actors."

In 1977, Colleen Dewhurst was invited to speak to the graduating seniors at Sarah Lawrence College. What follows are bits of that speech, thoughts with which she might have closed this book, had she seen it through to its completion.

First of all, I feel like I am on a nostalgia trip today. . . .

Now, I cannot give a speech or tell you what you should think, and I am unguarded because I do not have a script or character to play. So, therefore, I can only speak to you about the time that I have spent trying to get wherever it was that I was trying to get. My mother made one statement to me when I told her that I wished to act. She said that I would have to act at some time in the school for her to see me because there was no room for mediocrity in the arts. . . .

Now that, my dears, began the first line of a lot of reviews. I should have been warned. When I came to New York, it was a long, long road and I went to many classes and met many talented, wonderful, exciting people. As I think back, the danger that entered for those creative talents was that they permitted themselves at some point to begin to give power to "they" and "them." We would sit and we would rap for hours, and over the years, I began to hear more and more about "they" and "them." "*They* won't give me a break. I can't get going. Nobody wants me. I have something to give but *they* won't take it."

I watched that bitterness and hatred corrode them until, when the moment came that they had the break, they had nothing left to give because they had permitted themselves to give power to something outside of themselves. I have been hit many times and I remember every hit, much better than I remember the strokes.

Listen, my darlings, it's terrific out there, it's really terrific. What it's about is joy. It's about joy and it's about agony and it's about pain and, believe me, you can't go around it, over it, or under it. Forget it. You've got to go through it. And when you're going through it, you *say*, "I'm going through it. I'm dying. I am humiliated. I have been hurt." Sometimes there is legitimate pain. The pain of loss. The pain of loss of love. The pain of loss of something that you felt belonged to you. You've got to go through it. But you must not, must not make that the be-all, end-all. You must not let that eat at you.

We talk now about freedom and liberation all the time. I've tried to understand for the last twenty years what freedom and liberation are. I know what it is for me. It is freedom of choice. But it is not freedom with lack of responsibility. We are being threatened with a bondage of hate, irresponsibility, lack of compassion and lack of understanding. Oh no, my babies. Don't waste your time.

Give is the word. You have something to give. You're not out there to take. You have at least two things to give: your talent and compassion with no judgment. My mother once said to me, "If you have a great talent for banging nails into a board, my darling, and it gives you joy, you do *that*." All I have to say to you is that the greatest talent is for living. It is a great talent, whatever way and however—with responsibility—you live it. Every day is important. Every minute is important. And every commitment should be fulfilled. Don't let anyone take that joy, don't let "them" take it out of you.

All right, my darlings, all I can say is that life is a joy. This is what it's about.

Don't waste your time. For there will never be enough or all that you would need.

And now, I would just like to quote from a play called *The Shadow Box* that won the Pulitzer Prize. It's by a young man named Michael Cristofer.

> *Your whole life goes by and it feels like only a minute. You try to remember what it was you believed in. What was so important? What was it? You wanted to make a difference. And then you think, someone should have said it sooner. Someone should have said it a long time ago. When we were young, someone should have said, "This living. This life. This lifetime doesn't last forever. A few days. A few minutes, that's all."*
>
> *This face. These hands. This world. It doesn't last forever.*
>
> *This air. This light. This earth. These things you love. These children. This smile. This pain. It doesn't last forever.*
>
> *It was never supposed to last forever. These things you have. This moment. They will not last forever.*

I thank you again for the honor, and I wish you joy.

Colleen Dewhurst

ACKNOWLEDGMENTS

As detailed in the introduction, Colleen's autobiography could not have been completed without a great deal of help from her friends. In addition to those whose voices within these pages have been added to Colleen's own, thanks must be given to those who generously agreed to be interviewed but whose anecdotes and observations have not been directly quoted herein.

In this way, I am especially indebted to Joseph Benincasa, Candice Bergen, Kate Burton, Alexander H. Cohen, Buzz Cohen, Andre Ernotte, Barbara Gelb, John Glover, Gerry Hall (whose heart is especially sweet), John Handy, Bernard B. Jacobs, Jimmy Karen, Larry Kramer, Alan Markinson, Anne Meara, Thomas Morrisey, Gail Merrifield Papp, Martin Segal, Jerry Stiller, and Rosemary Tichler. While their contributions do not directly appear in this book, their thoughtful remembrances of Colleen also have helped shape and complete it.

Although it took me nearly three years to start, once I had begun, I would not have been able to finish this manuscript without the expert and selfless research and transcription assistance of Stefan Fitterman, Forrest Mallard, Darren Doutt, Michael Ashley and especially Michael Graziano. Their efficiency made manageable what might have been a very tedious and insurmountable process. Special thanks to Blaine Campbell, Bob Fabiszak and SweetPea, whose affection, encouragement and companionship in the early days of this project makes their absence at its completion particularly bittersweet. I miss you.

Colleen and I would be remiss in not thanking Roger Anderson and Chuck Blasius who, nearly seven years ago, gave, delivered and set up the extra computer from their garage at the Farm. We never returned it. Thanks also to Roger for not asking about that.

Thanks in more recent years to Larry Cook for his expert computer assistance and his insistence that I back up the manuscript *regularly.* In one case, Larry's careful watch narrowly avoided disaster.

Thanks to Lisa Drew for her incredible patience and encouragement and to her assistant, Marysue Rucci, for not rolling her eyes.

Finally, I am deeply grateful to Alex Scott and Campbell Scott, first for making me feel so welcome at the Farm and then for being willing to share their mother with me in the very tender years immediately following her death.

And, of course, *thank you, Colleen*. Like so many others, I love you and I miss you. What you left behind for me to complete seemed initially to be a huge burden. It has become instead a unique and wonderful gift.

Why are you laughing?

T.V., 1997

INDEX